New Developments in Financial Modelling

New Developments in Financial Modelling

Edited by

João O. Soares, Joaquim P. Pina
and Margarida Catalão-Lopes

Cambridge Scholars Publishing

New Developments in Financial Modelling,
Edited by João O. Soares, Joaquim P. Pina and Margarida Catalão-Lopes

This book first published 2008 by

Cambridge Scholars Publishing

12 Back Chapman Street, Newcastle upon Tyne, NE6 2XX, UK

British Library Cataloguing in Publication Data
A catalogue record for this book is available from the British Library

ISBN (10): 1-84718-674-2, ISBN (13): 9781847186744

TABLE OF CONTENTS

Section 3 – Portfolio Selection

Section 4 – Market Microstructure and Liquidity

Section 5 – Risk and Volatility in Financial Markets

NEW DEVELOPMENTS IN FINANCIAL MODELLING: AN INTRODUCTION

JOÃO O. SOARES, JOAQUIM P. PINA AND MARGARIDA CATALÃO-LOPES

This book gathers a selection of refereed papers from the 41st Meeting of the Euro Working Group on Financial Modelling, held at Lisbon, Portugal, on November 8-9, 2007. Thirty authors, from different countries and with diverse experiences, contribute with new insights on some of the most relevant topics of corporate finance, bearing in mind the great concern of the Euro Working Group with the practical consequences of the research undertaken by its members. These contributions have been grouped in five different thematic areas, corresponding to the five sections of the book: banking; corporate governance; portfolio selection; market microstructure and liquidity; risk and volatility in financial markets.

The first section – Banking – integrates three papers. The first paper, by Diana Bonfim, Qinglei Dai and Francesco Franco, studies the impact of the number of banks a firm borrows from on the price of credit. The paper uses information for Portuguese firms, for the period 1996-2004. The interest rate on bank loans is found to vary negatively with the number of bank relationships, a result which is robust across firm size. The second paper, by Filipa Lima, investigates the impact of product differentiation on banks' cost efficiency. In an empirical contribution applied to the Portuguese banking system, the author uses a parametric approach for a multi-output production function that also includes off-balance sheet outputs, and takes into account different loans and deposits' segments. Banks' dimension, the quality of the loans' portfolio and mergers are found to be relevant for the explanation of differences in efficiency across institutions and over time. The banking section ends with a paper by Maria Blangiewicz and Paweł Miłobędzki. This paper tests for a nonlinear mean reversion in the term structure of interest rates at the Polish interbank market, due to transaction costs. Transaction costs may be a more serious problem in transition economies, such as the Polish, than in mature ones. The results obtained for the period January 2003-December 2006, however, are ambiguous. Co-integration tests show that the term spread is mean-reverting, but, despite the strong evidence of nonlinearity in mean-reversion, the use of a three-regime threshold vector error correction model to capture the transaction costs is of little success.

The second section – Corporate Finance – has two contributions. The first paper, by Lars Nordén and Therése Strand, investigates the behaviour of Swedish portfolio managers at firm's annual general meetings. From their research, the authors sustain that the behaviour of portfolio managers in these meetings is mainly determined by their goal of achieving notoriety, an attribute usually associated with large firms benefiting from wide media coverage and important stockholders. Another possible and more useful motivation – to intervene preferentially in cases of bad performance – seems to be neglected by the desire of 15 minutes of fame, according to this research. The second paper, by Jasper Blom and Marc Schauten, focuses another issue: the existence of a relation between the quality of corporate governance and the cost of debt. The authors collected data for the 300 largest European firms (FTSE Eurotop 300), concerning corporate governance performance (Denominor Rating for the period 2000-2004) and the cost of debt (yield of bonds issued during 2001-2205). Their analysis concludes that there is a negative relation between these two variables, which supports the idea that debt holders use the attribute 'quality of corporate governance' in their assessment of risk profile of each particular firm.

The third section – Portfolio Selection – integrates three contributions. The first paper, by Panagiotis Xidonas, Dimitrios Askounis and John Psarras, presents a multiple criteria approach for the selection of stock portfolios. This approach is based on a multi-stage procedure: first, the use of outranking methods for selecting an initial set of assets according to the preferences of the decision-makers in terms of several financial and market criteria; secondly, an usual Markowitz mean-variance optimization model, comprising some additional constraints; at a final stage, an outranking MCDA (Multiple Criteria Decision Analysis) model is still used in order to rank and restrict the efficient portfolios selected in the previous stage. This integrated methodology is applied to a sample of stocks from the Athens Stock Exchange. The second paper, by Jaap Spronk and Ghassan Chammas, focuses an interesting and rather new topic: the principles that guide Islamic equity investment. As pointed by the authors, Sharia compliant investors seek additional objectives beyond those pursued by the traditional or conventional investors. They seek to incorporate their doctrine and ethics into asset choice. So, this paper details the multiple filters that have to be applied before an asset can be included in a Sharia compliant portfolio. Finally, the last paper of this section, by Andrzej Skulimowski, deals with the theoretical background for employing dynamic programming models in portfolio selection. This is an approach that entails an increased flexibility, since assets can be evaluated based on multiple criteria, and this evaluation can change and be adapted in response to external events or as a result of achieving certain goals.

Section four – Market Microstructure and Liquidity –integrates three papers. The first paper of this section, by Emmanuel Kopp, Michael Huetl, Otto Loistl and Johannes Prix, examines cross sectional liquidity in Xetra trading system of Frankfurt Stock Exchange. Systematic liquidity components are estimated by Projection-Pursuit principle and a multi-stage Principal Components Analysis (PCA) is proposed in order to overcome the lack of interpretation in standard PCA. Further, alternative trading related measures are taken into account, allowing to capture different information pieces from the entire limit order book. Intraday data has been selected, tick-by-tick from 6th to 13th of December of 2006, for all stocks in DAX-30. The findings point out that market wide liquidity factors are relevant for explaining individual stock liquidity. The paper by Theodoros Stamatiou focuses on volatility and price limits, drawing lessons from Athens Stock Exchange experience. Volatility and overreaction implications are analysed using daily data from June 2008 to May 2001. The range under scrutiny covers a "bubble" period and during the whole sample period there was a band of 8 per cent daily variation limit. The results show that price limits actually implied an increase in volatility and a decrease in liquidity in the days after hitting a limit. Market overreaction was also found, but only after hitting the Up limit. The paper closing this section, by Serkan Aran, studies the relation between liquidity and returns of small-cap stocks in Istanbul Stock Exchange. The findings are conclusive for an asymmetric relation between volume and return.

The fifth section – Risk and Volatility in Financial Markets – gathers three papers. The first one, by Dorra Hmaied, analyses the relationship between trading volume and volatility around takeover announcements in the Paris Bourse. The issue is analysed for the market for corporate control and also takes into account the different means of payment. The findings, from mixture distributions methodology, are that both for *pre* and *post* bid periods a significant effect of volume in conditional volatility exists and differs according to the mean of payment, being weaker for cash offers, namely, in *post* bid period. The second paper, by António Afonso, Pedro Gomes and Philipp Rother, investigates the determinants in sovereign debt rating. This issue is crucial for pricing public debt, which besides being a reference for other assets and portfolio choice, may be central when countries have binding rules for deficit and debt limits, e.g. as in the European Union. Using data from Fitch Ratings, Moody's, and Standard & Poor's, covering 1995 to 2005, the authors apply a panel data approach, considering alternatively a linear model and an ordered probit. The findings indicate that the most relevant variables that emerge are: GDP per capita, GDP growth, government debt, government effectiveness indicators, external debt, external reserves and default history. The final paper, by Young Shin Kim, Svetlozar T. Rachev, Dong M. Chung, and Michele L. Bianchi, introduces a variant of the tempered stable distribution, which the authors call "modified tempered stable" (MTS) distribution, and develops a GARCH option pricing model with MTS innovations. The Modified Tempered Stable distribution is sufficiently flexible in describing the skewness and kurtosis of asset returns and has all moments finite. The authors argue that the MTS-GARCH model can be more realistic than the normal-GARCH model, and they use it to describe some stylized phenomena of financial markets, such as volatility clustering, leverage effect, skewness, and heavy tails of the return distribution.

This is a brief overview of all the matters that can be found within the chapters of this book. We believe that they constitute a rich and interesting set of new topics. So, we would like to reserve our last words to express our gratitude to all the authors and reviewers, including our colleagues Alain Chevalier and Wolfgang Kursten. The list of all the authors that contributed to this volume, as well as their contacts, can be found at the end of the book.

Good and pleasant readings!

CHAPTER ONE

THE NUMBER OF BANK RELATIONSHIPS AND THE COST OF BORROWING: AN EMPIRICAL STUDY

DIANA BONFIM, QINGLEI DAI AND FRANCESCO FRANCO

Abstract

We construct a unique dataset containing 17,516 Portuguese small, medium and large firms and spanning from 1996 to 2004. Using this dataset we study the impact of the number of banks a firm borrows from on the cost of bank loans. We find that the average Portuguese firm borrows from three banks. The firm's interest rate on bank loans lowers as the firm borrows from more banks, controlling for relevant firm characteristics. When a firm borrows from one more bank, the interest rate on bank loans for this firm becomes 12 to 34 basis points lower, on average. This pattern holds across firm size categories. Our results are consistent with bank competition and bank risk diversification.

Keywords: banks, relationship banking, borrowing costs

1. Introduction

A frequently visited question by banking researchers is: what is the optimal number of banks for a firm to borrow from? This question is also important to firm managers because the answer to it is related to how to obtain the lowest cost of loans and how to cnsure easy access to bank loans. In this study, we focus on the relationship between the interest rate charged by banks and the number of banks that the firm borrows from.

The classical delegated monitoring argument introduced by Diamond (1984) and tested by Petersen and Rajan (1994) says that in the presence of asymmetric information between firms and investors, a firm is best off borrowing from only one bank where the cost of borrowing is minimized. However, many other empirical works find that firms rarely keep exclusive bank relationships. For example, Ongena and Smith (2000) in a survey including 1079 firms across 20 European countries find that the majority of firms (85%) use more than one bank. They find that firms in countries with the French legal system, such as France, Italy, Spain and Portugal, have on average, more than 10 different bank relations. This observation has also been found in D'Auria, Foglia and Reedtz (1999). In our dataset we also find that the majority of Portuguese firms, including micro firms, borrow from several banks.

What makes monogamy with a bank undesirable? There are many theories attempting to provide an explanation, some of them with implications for borrowing costs.

First, in an exclusive bank relationship, the informationally privileged bank might exploit its bargaining power over the firm and extract rents from loan contracts (Sharpe 1990, Rajan 1992). This implies that micro and small firms with a unique lender pay a higher cost of borrowing.

Second, the refusal of a credit from the firm's only lender may provide a negative signal to the market which makes the exclusive bank relationship undesirable (Berger and Udell, 1998). Detragiache, Garella, and Guiso (2000) show that this is especially true in economies with high bankruptcy costs and low fragility of the banking sector .

Third, some predict that multiple bank relationships will occur when banks face financial constraints or monitoring costs (Dewatripont and Maskin 1995, Holmstrom and Tirole 1997, Carletti, Cerasi and Daltung 2007).

Fourth, multiple bank relationships might prevent the firm manager from strategic default by holding up the renegotiation process (Bolton and Scharfstein 1996).

Fifth, in the face of fierce competition, multiple arms-length lending might substitute relationship lending as analyzed by Boot and Thakor (2000). The authors predict that bank competition will lead to lower interest rates and that firms will not commit to exclusive bank relationships. On the other hand relationship lending might protect banks from price competition.

Sixth, multiple bank relationships allow banks to diversify their lending risk (Carletti et al. 2007). The authors predict that the banks are more attracted to multiple-bank lending when the bank has lower equity, when the cost of monitoring is high, and when the profitability of the firm is low.

To answer the aforementioned question we use a unique dataset that spans from 1996 to 2004 and includes 42,263 Portuguese firm-year observations, referring to 17,516 different firms. We find that an average Portuguese firm borrows from three banks. The firm's interest rate on bank loans lowers as the firm borrows from more banks, controlling for relevant firm characteristics. When a firm borrows from one more bank, the interest rate on bank loans for this firm becomes 12 to 34 basis points lower, on average. This pattern holds regardless of the firm size. Moreover, we take seriously the idea that the number of bank relationships and the cost of borrowing may be simultaneously determined, introducing an endogeneity problem in our empirical analysis. For instance, the managerial ability may jointly influence the choice of the number of banks and the interest rate that banks charge. We address this issue by using an instrumental variable approach and find that our previous findings are robust.

Our finding is consistent with Carletti et al. (2007) that banks benefit from risk diversification brought by multiple-bank lending. The decreasing interest rate reflects that the reduction in risk level overcomes free-riding and duplication of monitoring costs. However, to the contrary of the prediction of Carletti et al. (2007) that the benefit of diversification is stronger with small opaque less profitable firms, we find that the negative correlation between the number of banks and the interest rate holds robust across all firm sizes. Specifically, even large mature profitable firms benefit from multiple lending.

The finding that the interest rate decreases in the number of banks can also be consistent with the competition argument by Boot and Thakor (2000) that when banks compete to gain clients, firms are able to borrow from multiple banks at lower costs. During the past two decades, the banking sector in Portugal has experienced a high degree of liberalization.

Most of the state-owned banks have become privatized. Many small banks coexist with large regional banks. Credit granted to the private sector has recorded a remarkable growth and interest rates decreased steadily (Ribeiro 2007). These developments should have contributed to increased competition in the Portuguese banking system, thus allowing firms to borrow from multiple banks at a lower cost.

Our results are comparable to findings from similar studies using European datasets. Degryse and Ongena (2007) literature review shows that in several European countries the cost of bank loans is either unaffected or reduced by 1 to 10 basis points per additional relationship, while in the US the cost of bank loans typically increases with the number of bank relationships.

Finally, this study is related to Farinha and Santos (2002) who also investigated the number of bank relationships in Portugal. They focus on one special event during a firm's borrowing history, i.e. when the firm switches from single to multiple bank relationships. The authors examine some of the determinants and implications of this corporate event and report that almost all firms start borrowing only from a single bank, but soon afterwards they diversify their creditor structure, most notably when growth opportunities are stronger. Our study is different in several ways. First, we look at the number of bank relationship rather than the event of switch from one to multiple banks. Second, we focus on the implication of bank relations on the firm's cost of borrowing which was not examined previously for Portugal. Third, our dataset covers a more recent sample period of 1996-2004, while Farinha and Santos (2002) use a dataset from 1980 to 1996.

Our paper proceeds as follows. In section 2 we describe the datasets used and present some relevant summary statistics. In section 3 we discuss the results obtained under a regression analysis framework, evaluating how does the number of bank relationships influences borrowing costs. In section 4 we discuss possible endogeneity problems in the regressions, given that the number of relationships and interest rates may be simultaneously determined, and we try to overcome this issue using an instrumental variable approach. Finally, in section 5 we present some concluding remarks.

2. Data and summary statistics

Two large datasets were used in this work. All information concerning the number of bank relationships comes from the Central Credit Register of Banco de Portugal. This extensive database includes information on all credit exposures above 50 euros, reported by all Portuguese credit institutions monthly. The reporting is mandatory. The main objective of this database is to disseminate information among participating institutions, in order to improve their credit risk assessment on current and potential borrowers. Participating banks can observe, for each borrower, the number of bank relationships this borrower has, the total outstanding debt, as well as the status of the loans (e.g. whether there is debt overdue). This information sharing mechanism may have important implications in reducing the asymmetric information problem in a borrower-lender relationship[1]. Unfortunately, this database does not include any information regarding loan maturity, collateral or interest rates. Given that our main objective is to evaluate the role of the number of bank relationships in firms' borrowing costs, we obtain information on the cost of borrowing from another large dataset: the Central Balance Sheet Database of Banco de Portugal. This database provides detailed yearly accounting information, including firm age, economic sector, profitability, leverage, etc., for a large sample of Portuguese firms. Reporting to the Central Balance Sheet Database is not compulsory and, as a consequence, this database covers only a limited (but large) sample of Portuguese firms. Nevertheless, the sample is considered to be representative, though its representativeness may be somewhat poorer for smaller firms.

Using end of year data for the period comprised between 1996 and 2004, the Central Credit Register includes 3,990,802 records[2]. Taking into account data for the same period of time, the Central Balance Sheet Database includes 202,364 records. Merging the two databases, we obtain 154,682 common observations, comprising 38,342 firms. Even though both databases were created before 1996, several important fields of the

[1] It is possible to know whether credit has become overdue, if it was renegotiated or if it is an off-balance sheet risk, such as the unused part of a credit line or a bank guarantee.

[2] Banks do not report information on a strict loan by loan basis, given that it is possible to aggregate loans granted to the same firm with similar status. We aggregated loans by firm, in order to count the number of bank relationships. Hence, each record is defined as a firm-year pair.

Central Balance Sheet Database are available only from 1996 onwards, thus imposing this year as a starting point for our analysis.

In our study, we only analyse lending relationships between firms and banks, excluding all lending relationships with non-monetary credit institutions, such as leasing companies[3].

To measure the cost of borrowing, we construct different implicit interest rates using the firms' balance sheet information. We perform several checks to evaluate the reliability of our interest rate measures. Our preferred measure of the interest rate is the interest paid on bank loans as a percentage of total debt to credit institutions. We provide a detailed description of our filters in the data appendix. Our final dataset is an unbalanced panel data containing 42,263 observations, 17,516 firms, between 1996 and 2004.

Figure 1 shows the average, median and weighted mean of our measure of interest rate against the aggregate interest rate on all outstanding debts to non-financial corporations in Portugal disclosed by Banco de Portugal. The weighted average of the implicit interest rate appears to track remarkably well the aggregate interest rate statistics. The correlation between the two series is 0.96.

---

[3] Non-monetary credit institutions are usually small and specialized credit institutions (sometimes included in large universal banking groups), which do not offer checking accounts. Hence, even though these non-bank credit institutions can hold long term relationships with the firms they grant credit to, they will hardly be able to establish exclusive relationships with firms, given that they can offer them only a limited set of financial services. Moreover, the pricing of debt granted by these institutions may be supported by standards very different from those applied by banking institutions, which can benefit from the monitoring of firms' deposits.

Figure 1
Implicit interest rate measures

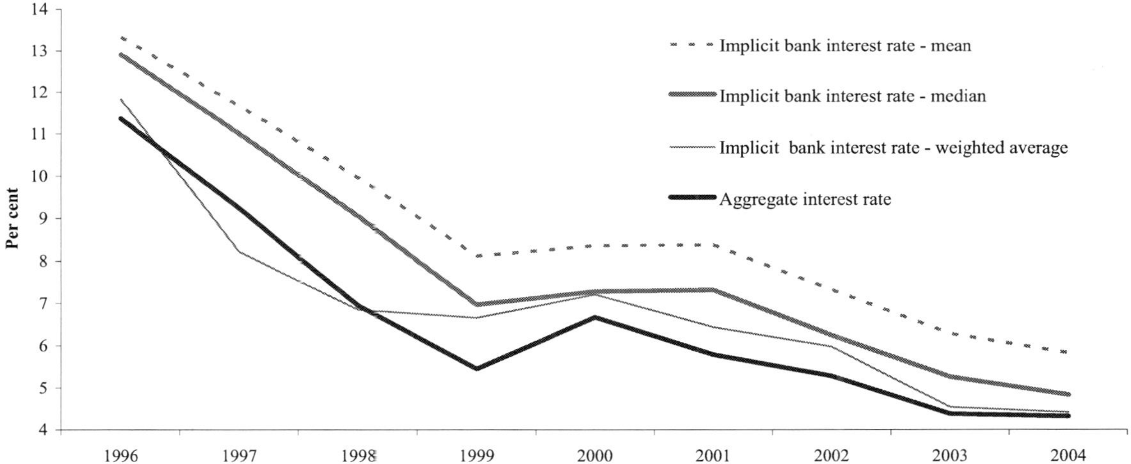

Notes: The aggregate interest rate is the interest rate on outstanding amounts of loans to non-financial corporations disclosed by Banco de Portugal in its Monetary and Financial Statistics. This interest rate is a weighted average of interest rates reported by banks. Implicit interest rates were computed using data from the Central Balance Sheet Database held by Banco de Portugal, which includes detailed accounting information for a large sample of Portuguese companies. This interest rate was computed as the amount of interest paid on bank loans as a percentage of total debt to credit institutions at the end of the year.

The upper panel of Figure 2 (*a* and *b*) shows histograms of both the implicit bank interest rate and the implied spread over the entire sample. The implied spread on banks loans is defined as the difference between the implicit interest rate and a money market interest rate (3-month Euribor). In the lower panel of Figure 2 we present the histograms of both the implicit interest rate and the spread for each year in our sample[4]. Overall the relatively high correlation between our measure and the aggregate interest rate on loans makes us confident about our measure of interest rate on bank loans.

[4] The results reveal that the distribution of interest rates and spreads across firms changed significantly between 1996 and 2004. Whereas in the earlier years of the sample period interest rates and spreads showed an almost uniform distribution, exhibiting a large dispersion in borrowing costs across firms; in the latter years of the sample period the distribution became closer to a log-normal. In these latter years, there was not only a decrease in average interest rates paid by firms, but also a substantial decline in their dispersion.

Figure 2a

Implicit bank interest rate

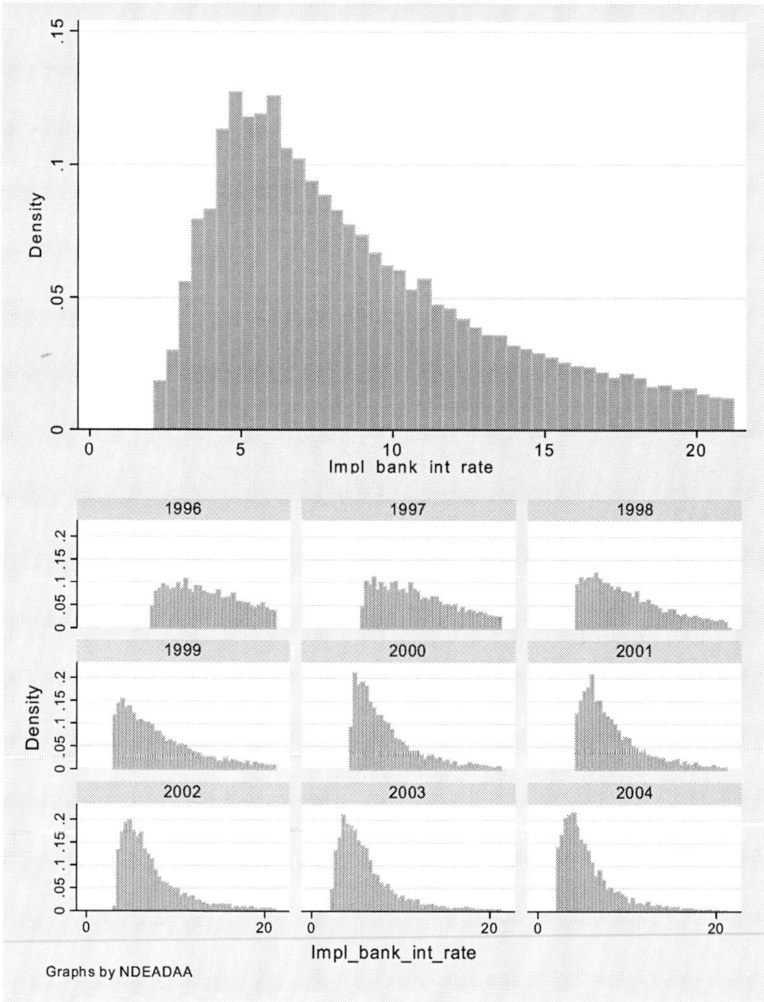

Note: Empirical distribution of the implicit interest rate on bank loans, computed as interest paid to banks as a percentage of total debt to credit institutions for each firm. As interest rates show a steady downward trend during our sample period, we also present the empirical distribution of the implied spread on banks loans, defined as the difference between the implicit interest rate and a money market interest rate (3-month Euribor).

Figure 2b

Implicit spread on bank loans

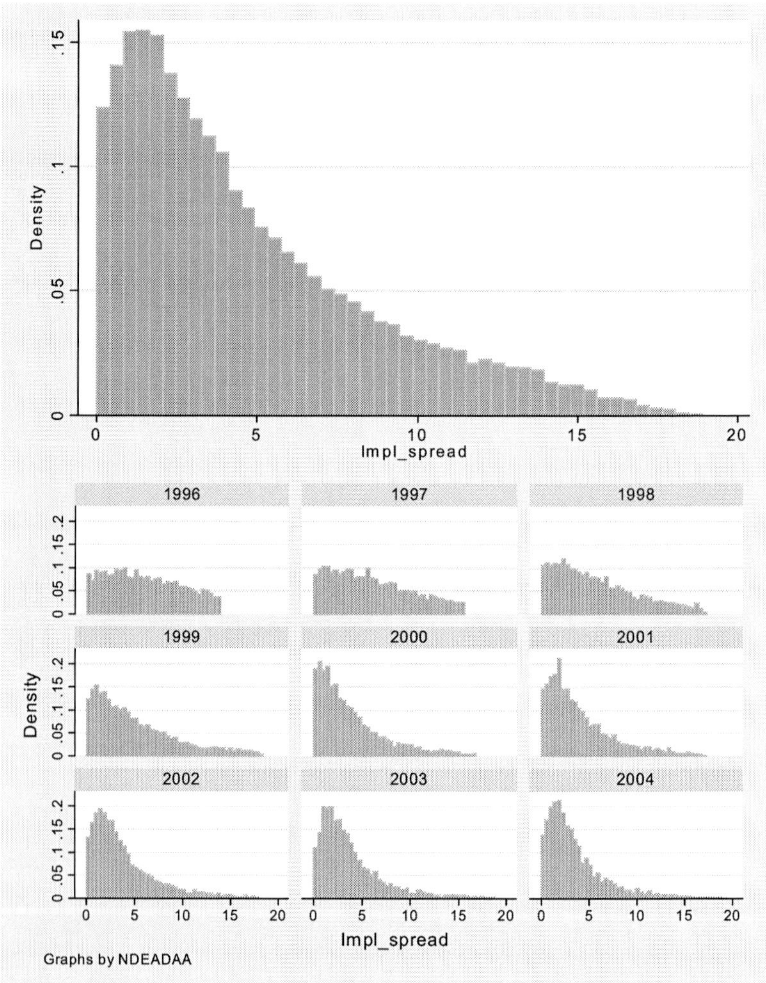

Note: Empirical distribution of the implicit interest rate on bank loans, computed as interest paid to banks as a percentage of total debt to credit institutions for each firm. As interest rates show a steady downward trend during our sample period, we also present the empirical distribution of the implied spread on banks loans, defined as the difference between the implicit interest rate and a money market interest rate (3-month Euribor).

We now turn to some preliminary analysis on the linkage between the cost of debt and the number of bank relationships. Approximately one quarter (26 per cent) of the firms hold one exclusive lending relationship. Across time there was a significant drop in the percentage of firms with unique relationships: from almost 30 per cent in 1996 to nearly 20 per cent in 2004. Figure 3 shows that the average number of bank relationships did not vary significantly over time, ranging between 2.8 and 3.3 across the sample period[5].

[5] The figure shows that the average number of bank relationships exhibits an increasing trend starting in 1998. The observed decrease in 2001 is probably due to the strong merger and acquisition activities during this period in the Portuguese banking system.

Figure 3
Number of relationships and implicit bank interest rates

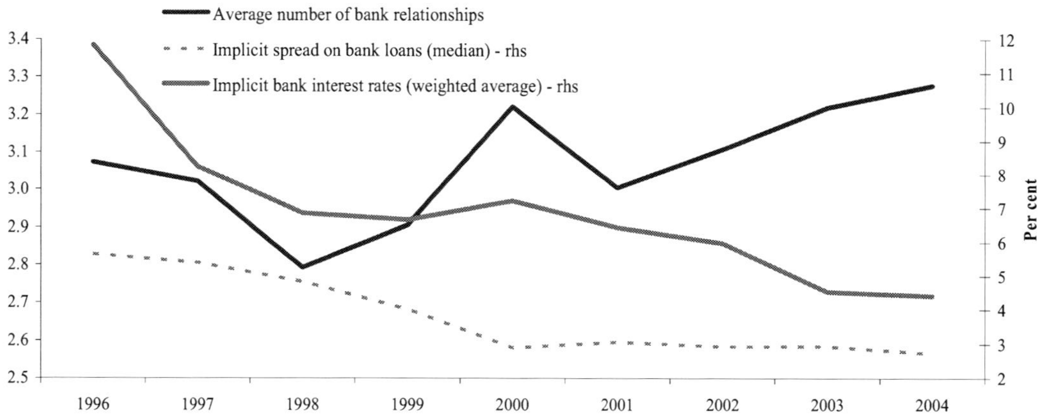

Notes: The implicit interest rate was computed using data from the Central Balance Sheet Database held by Banco de Portugal, which includes detailed accounting information for a large sample of Portuguese companies. This interest rate was computed as the amount of interest paid on bank loans as a percentage of total debt to credit institutions at the end of the year. The implicit spread on banks loans was defined as the difference between the implicit interest rate and a money market interest rate (3-month Euribor). The number of relationships was computed using information from the Central Register of Banco de Portugal, which includes data on all loans granted in Portugal above 50 euros. The number of bank relationships was computed as the number of different banks which were lending to a given firm at the end of each year. These two databases were matched, which means that these two indicators refer to the same sample of firms.

Figure 4 shows that the number of lending relationships increases steadily with the firm age. Start-up firms have, on average, 2 or 3 lending relationships, whereas older firms hold a more diversified credit structure. Furthermore, younger firms pay higher interest rates than older firms, as expected.

Table 1 reports the distribution of the number of bank relationships together with the implicit interest rate and proxies for firm size and maturity such as the number of employees and firm age[6]. Columns two and three show that firms with a single banking relationship pay a higher interest rate than firms with 2 or 3 relations. Columns four to seven show that the number of bank relationships is positively related to size proxied by firm age and the number of employees.

[6] To ease the reading of the table we exclude the firms with more than 15 relationships.

Figure 4
Number of relationships by age

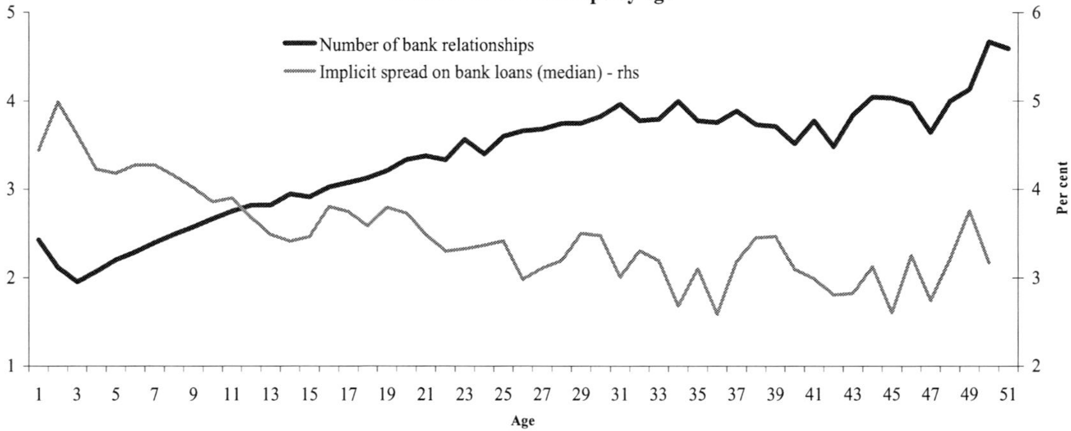

Notes: The implicit interest rate was computed using data from the Central Balance Sheet Database held by Banco de Portugal, which includes detailed accounting information for a large sample of Portuguese companies. This interest rate was computed as the amount of interest paid on bank loans as a percentage of total debt to credit institutions at the end of the year. The implicit spread on banks loans was defined as the difference between the implicit interest rate and a money market interest rate (3-month Euribor). The number of relationships was computed using information from the Central Register of Banco de Portugal, which includes data on all loans granted in Portugal above 50 euros. The number of bank relationships was computed as the number of different banks which were lending to a given firm at the end of each year. These two databases were matched, which means that these two indicators refer to the same sample of firms.

We further construct a measure of firm size following a definition suggested by the European Commission that uses the number of employees and sales volumes and the results in four different size categories: micro, small, medium and large[7]. We end up with 12,417 micro, 18,703 small, 8,918 medium and 2,225 large firms. Table 2 displays the number of bank relationships and the implicit interest rate for these four categories. Micro and small firms hold respectively, on average, 2 and 3 bank relationships, medium-sized firms borrow from more than 4 banks, while larger firms have 6 different bank relationships. Table 2 also shows that the implicit interest rate decreases with the firm size.

Table 1

Number of bank relationships	Obs. (1)	**Implicit bank interest rates** Mean (2)	Median (3)	**Age** Mean (4)	Median (5)	**Employees** Mean (6)	Median (7)
1	10,880	9.4	8.4	14.3	10	20	8
2	10,497	9.0	7.9	16.4	12	33	13
3	7,361	8.6	7.5	18.8	15	49	21
4	4,938	8.4	7.1	21.4	17	72	31
5	3,172	8.2	7.0	22.4	18	100	41
6	1,999	7.9	6.7	24.2	19	134	60
7	1,318	7.8	6.6	25.2	20.5	168	75
8	739	8.2	7.0	26.9	22.5	209	97
9	466	7.9	6.9	29.0	23	244	120
10	284	8.5	7.2	32.6	27	302	151
11	164	9.1	7.5	33.8	29	329	194
12	76	7.7	6.8	30.4	25	873	215
13	66	8.7	7.4	36.3	28.5	788	290
14	29	9.3	8.3	34.4	27	676	470
15	25	9.1	9.9	49.2	47	1143	828
Total	42263	8.8		18.6		66	

Notes: Interest rate were computed as the amount of interest paid on bank loans as a percentage of total debt to credit institutions at the end of the year. The number of relationships was computed as the number of different banks which were lending to a given firm at the end of each year. To ease the reading of the table we exclude firms with more than 15 relationships.

[7] Micro firms are defined as those than less 10 employees and less than 2 millions euros of sales volumes. Small firms are those with less than 50 employees and less than 10 millions euros of sales volumes. Median firms are those with less than 250 employees and less than 50 millions euros of sales volumes. All remaining firms are considered to be large firms.

Table 3 shows that the average and median number of bank relationships and the implicit interest rate for different economic sectors. The lowest number of relationships is seen in agriculture, fishing and tourism. In turn, mining, manufacturing and public services firms show a higher average number of relationships. The differences in estimated interest rates across sectors seem to be more significant. Agriculture and transport firms apparently have to pay interest rates slightly above those of other firms, whereas utilities, real estate firms or public services firms face lower debt servicing costs.

Table 2

Number of relationships and interest rates by firm size

	Number of observations	Number of bank relationships		Implicit bank interest rate	
		Mean	Median	Mean	Median
Micro	12417	1.8	2.0	9.6	8.7
Small	18703	2.8	2.0	8.9	7.8
Medium	8918	4.4	2.0	7.8	6.6
Large	2225	6.2	6.0	7.3	6.2
Total	42263	3.1	2.0	8.8	7.7

Notes: The implicit interest rate was computed using data from the Central Balance Sheet Database held by Banco de Portugal, which includes detailed accounting information for a large sample of Portuguese companies. This interest rate was computed as the amount of interest paid on bank loans as a percentage of total debt to credit institutions at the end of the year. The number of relationships was computed using information from the Central Register of Banco de Portugal. The number of bank relationships was computed as the number of different banks which were lending to a given firm at the end of each year. The definition of firm size was based on the European Commission Recommendation of 6 May 2003 (2003/361/EC), by taking into account the number of employees and sales volume. More precisely, micro firms were defined as those with less than 10 employees and less than 2 million euro of business volume; small firms were those with less than 50 employees and less than 10 million euro of business volume; medium firms were those with less than 250 employees and a business volume below 50 million euro. All remaining firms were considered to be large firms.

Table 3
Number of relationships and interest rates by firm size

	Number of observations	Number of bank relationships		Implicit bank interest rate	
		Mean	Median	Mean	Median
Agriculture	1627	2.5	2.0	9.2	8.2
Commerce	12721	3.9	3.0	8.9	7.8
Construction	5526	4.2	3.0	8.9	7.8
Education	156	3.4	3.0	7.1	5.7
Fishing	155	2.8	2.0	8.7	7.5
Healthcare	156	4.0	3.0	7.3	6.4
Manufacturing	17145	4.4	4.0	8.9	7.8
Mining	505	4.6	4.0	8.4	7.1
Other public services	226	4.4	4.0	6.8	5.6
Real estate	1311	3.9	3.0	6.4	5.4
Tourism	638	3.0	2.0	7.8	6.6
Transports and communications	1900	4.3	3.0	9.2	8.1
Utilities	197	3.8	3.0	5.9	4.8
Total	42263	3.1	2.0	8.8	7.7

Notes: The implicit interest rate was computed using data from the Central Balance Sheet Database held by Banco de Portugal, which includes detailed accounting information for a large sample of Portuguese companies. This interest rate was computed as the amount of interest paid on bank loans as a percentage of total debt to credit institutions at the end of the year. The number of relationships was computed using information from the Central Register of Banco de Portugal. The number of bank relationships was computed as the number of different banks which were lending to a given firm at the end of each year.

To conclude our descriptive analysis we perform mean comparison tests to evaluate if interest rates are statistically different for firms with many relationships (above the 4th quartile of the distribution of the number of relationships) and for firms with few relationships (below the 1st quartile of the same distribution). Table 4 reports that in the full sample interest rates paid by these two groups of firms are indeed different. Firms with fewer relationships pay, on average, higher interest rates. We also performed these tests for the four size categories. Both for micro and for small firms, interest rates are statistically higher for firms with fewer relationships. For medium-sized firms, the mean comparison tests performed suggest that there are no significant differences in interest rates for firms in the 1st and in the 4th quartile of the distribution of the number of relationships. Finally, for large firms interest rates are significantly higher with many bank relations.

Table 4

Mean comparison tests

	Average interest rate for firms with few relations	Average interest rate for firms with many relations	Mean comparison test Ho: diff=0		
			diff	t-ratio	Pr(|T| > |t|)
All firms	9.5	8.2	1.27	22.44	0.00
Micro	9.9	9.4	0.44	5.44	0.00
Small	9.0	8.7	0.29	3.92	0.00
Medium	7.9	7.8	0.04	0.43	0.67
Large	6.9	8.1	-1.17	-5.54	0.00

Note: Firms with few relations were defined as those included in the first quartile of the distribution of the number of relationships. In turn, firms with many relations were considered to be those in the fourth quartile of the same distribution.

3. Regressions

The descriptive analysis performed above suggests that firms that have one or few lending relationships pay, on average, higher interest rates, most notably if they are smaller firms. In this section, we perform regression analysis and control for several firm characteristics which may influence interest paid on bank loans and have been extensively used in similar studies. For instance, it is reasonable to consider that profitability, collateral, leverage or the firm's credit risk are taken into account by banks when pricing loans. We define *Turnover* as sales and services as a percentage of the firm's assets and use it as a proxy for the firm profitability. More profitable firms are able to generate larger cash-flows with their activity, and may face lower funding costs. Next we define *Tangible assets as % of debt* to proxy for collateral. *Leverage* is defined as debt to credit institutions over assets to control for the influence of the outstanding debt on the interest rate. *Credit risk* is a dummy variable which takes the value one whenever the firm is in default at the end of the year. *Debt coverage*, calculated as net profits over debt to credit institutions, is another measure of the firm's financial health. All firm-specific variables are lagged by one year. This choice is motivated by the fact that the banks can only observe the previous year balance sheet. Table 5 reports summary statistics for the dependent and independent variables. Table 6 contains the correlation matrix of the regressors.

Table 5

Summary statistics for explanatory variables

	N	Mean	Std dev	min	p5	p25	p50	p75	p95	max	skewness	kurtosis
Implicit bank interest rate	42263	8.8	4.4	2.1	3.4	5.4	7.7	11.4	17.9	21.2	0.9	2.9
Number of bank relationships	42263	3.1	2.2	0.0	1.0	1.0	2.0	4.0	7.0	26.0	1.8	8.9
Turnover	42234	138.0	130.8	0.0	18.8	71.7	114.2	167.7	319.2	3343	6.2	80.6
Tangible assets as a % of debt	42241	53.0	122.2	0.0	1.5	13.4	36.1	69.4	143.5	14923	65.4	6867.2
Leverage	42234	78.4	133.5	1.1	39.6	62.5	75.3	87.5	112.9	21565	134.5	19953.7
Credit risk	42053	0.04	0.194	0.000	0.000	0.000	0.000	0.000	0.000	1.000	4.8	23.6
Debt coverage	42263	49.6	5727.3	-670093	-70.1	-0.2	4.1	18.6	119.5	818021	41.0	14880.4
Firm age	42160	18.6	16.4	0.0	3.0	8.0	14.0	23.0	52.0	248.0	2.4	11.4

Notes: The implicit interest rate was computed using data from the Central Balance Sheet Database held by Banco de Portugal, which includes detailed accounting information for a large sample of Portuguese companies. This interest rate was computed as the amount of interest paid on bank loans as a percentage of total debt to credit institutions at the end of the year. The number of bank relationships was computed as the number of different banks which were lending to a given firm at the end of each year. Turnover represents sales and services over assets. Leverage is defined as debt over assets; credit risk is a dummy variable which takes the value one when the firm is in default; and debt coverage is defined as net profits over debt to credit institutions.

The sample period corresponds to a time of structural change in the Portuguese banking sector as well as the convergence and the access to the EMU. These developments contributed to the steady downward trend seen in interest rates during this period, thus emphasizing the importance of controlling for time effects in the regressions.

Table 6 - Correlation matrix

	Implicit bank interest rate	Number of bank relations	Turnover	Tangible assets as % debt	Leverage	Credit risk	Debt coverage	Age	Log assets
Implicit bank interest rate	1								
Number of bank relations	-0.0907*	1							
Turnover	0.0949*	-0.1055*	1						
Tangible assets as % debt	-0.0516*	-0.0029	-0.1898*	1					
Leverage	0.0702*	-0.1011*	0.0636*	-0.4312*	1				
Credit risk	0.0363*	0.0908*	-0.0955*	-0.0163*	0.0944*	1			
Debt coverage	0.0306*	-0.0416*	0.1465*	0.0584*	-0.2816*	-0.0850*	1		
Age	-0.1073*	0.2603*	-0.0849*	0.0843*	-0.1702*	0.0164*	-0.0156	1	
Log assets	-0.2894*	0.6268*	-0.2309*	0.1399*	-0.2340*	0.0532*	0.0273*	0.3197*	1

Notes: An asterisk means that the pairwise correlation is significant at a 5 per cent level. Turnover represents sales and services over assets. Leverage is defined as debt over assets; credit risk is a dummy variable which takes the value one when the firm is in default; and debt coverage is defined as net profits over debt to credit institutions.

Our panel data contains information for 17,516 firms over 9 years (from 1996 until 2004). This is an unbalanced panel and each firm has on average 2.4 years of data. In order to avoid that the results are driven by outliers, we exclude from the regression all observations below the 1st percentile and above the 99th percentile of the distribution of each firm-specific variable.

In Table 7 we present our first estimates of how the number of bank relationships influences firms' borrowing costs, measured by our implicit bank interest rate. We begin by regressing the implicit bank interest rate on the number of bank relationships and time effects with firm fixed-effect. The results, shown in the first column of Table 7, give support to the hypothesis that the number of bank relationships does influence firm's borrowing costs. The coefficient on *Number of bank relationships* is -0.142 with a t-statistic of -6.36. Quantitatively we find that one additional bank relationship decreases the interest rate by 14 basis points, on average.

Columns two to five of Table 7 repeat the same regression for each size category. We find that *Number of relationships* decreases the cost of debt for all firm sizes, the coefficients all significant at 1% level. The largest slope coefficient is for micro firms: an additional bank relationship reduces the interest rate on average by 21 basis points for micro firms and between 12 and 14 basis points for the other three categories.

Table 7 - Regression results

Dependent variable: Implicit bank interest rate

	Fixed-effect regressions					Fixed-effect regressions - controlling for firm characteristics				
	All firms	**Micro firms**	**Small firms**	**Medium firms**	**Large firms**	**All firms**	**Micro firms**	**Small firms**	**Medium firms**	**Large firms**
Number of bank relationships $_t$	-0.142	-0.212	-0.139	-0.121	-0.131	-0.120	-0.254	-0.176	-0.126	-0.191
	-6.36	*-2.45*	*-3.47*	*-3.43*	*-2.55*	*-3.62*	*-1.85*	*-2.97*	*-2.43*	*-2.39*
Turnover $_{t-1}$						-0.005	-0.008	-0.004	0.002	-0.004
						-5.23	*-3.40*	*-2.65*	*0.98*	*-0.89*
Tangible assets as % of debt $_{t-1}$						-0.005	0.006	-0.011	-0.008	0.000
						-2.64	*0.99*	*-3.57*	*-2.27*	*0.07*
Leverage $_{t-1}$						0.032	0.054	0.030	0.021	0.012
						8.32	*5.85*	*5.04*	*2.70*	*0.69*
Credit risk $_{t-1}$						0.451	0.401	0.905	0.043	0.114
						2.42	*0.74*	*2.83*	*0.14*	*0.22*
Debt coverage $_{t-1}$						-0.002	0.000	-0.002	-0.006	-0.003
						-1.59	*0.08*	*-1.20*	*-2.95*	*-0.97*
Firm age $_{t-1}$						-0.667	-0.724	-0.802	-0.723	-0.604
						-31.79	*-12.31*	*-26.51*	*-21.21*	*-8.14*
Assets $_t$						-1.746				
						-11.76				
1997	-1.844	-1.459	-1.775	-2.119	-2.556	-	-	-	-	-
	-21.15	*-6.90*	*-13.69*	*-12.86*	*-6.99*	-	-	-	-	-
1998	-3.642	-2.945	-3.708	-4.041	-4.459	-1.121	-0.854	-1.103	-1.400	-0.944
	-41.13	*-13.65*	*-27.81*	*-24.18*	*-12.05*	*-10.56*	*-2.84*	*-7.00*	*-7.42*	*-2.21*
1999	-5.622	-4.836	-5.684	-6.027	-6.403	-2.280	-2.093	-2.290	-2.709	-2.536
	-65.08	*-22.65*	*-43.41*	*-37.24*	*-17.65*	*-22.31*	*-7.35*	*-14.84*	*-14.93*	*-6.19*
2000	-5.189	-4.564	-5.327	-5.410	-5.139	-1.362	-1.815	-1.401	-1.288	-1.175
	-56.16	*-19.49*	*-37.85*	*-31.96*	*-14.21*	*-13.82*	*-6.62*	*-9.47*	*-7.44*	*-2.97*
2001	-4.937	-4.253	-5.140	-5.057	-4.873	-0.186	-0.546	-0.358	-0.118	0.071
	-53.24	*-17.91*	*-36.29*	*-29.63*	*-13.50*	*-1.89*	*-2.04*	*-2.40*	*-0.69*	*0.19*
2002	-5.859	-5.349	-6.010	-5.975	-5.746	-0.407	-0.667	-0.551	-0.347	-0.298
	-62.95	*-22.14*	*-41.79*	*-35.22*	*-15.97*	*-4.20*	*-2.53*	*-3.70*	*-2.05*	*-0.88*
2003	-6.628	-5.753	-6.795	-6.951	-6.152	-0.399	-0.230	-0.451	-0.622	-0.221
	-69.70	*-23.11*	*-46.00*	*-40.29*	*-16.98*	*-4.28*	*-0.92*	*-3.11*	*-3.86*	*-0.71*
2004	-6.926	-6.167	-7.156	-7.062	-6.687	-	-	-	-	-
	-70.25	*-23.96*	*-46.68*	*-38.95*	*-18.13*	-	-	-	-	-
Constant	13.764	13.895	13.855	13.281	13.079	47.531	19.318	24.454	26.756	26.868
	139.78	*61.03*	*90.37*	*63.70*	*27.86*	*23.52*	*19.12*	*35.03*	*24.93*	*9.70*
Number of observ:	38764	10764	17589	8436	1975	16790	3778	7826	4202	984
Number of firms	16014	5963	7743	3234	739	7694	2173	3818	1874	435
R^2 within	0.268	0.175	0.271	0.328	0.276	0.203	0.138	0.198	0.233	0.169

Notes: t-statistics in italics. The implicit interest rate was computed using data from the Central Balance Sheet Database held by Banco de Portugal, which includes detailed accounting information for a large sample of Portuguese companies. This interest rate was computed as the amount of interest paid on bank loans as a percentage of total debt to credit institutions at the end of the year. The number of bank relationships was computed using information from the Central Register of Banco de Portugal, by counting the number of different banks which were lending to a given firm at the end of each year. Turnover represents sales and services over assets. Leverage is defined as debt to credit institutions over assets; credit risk is a dummy variable which takes the value one when the firm is in default; and debt coverage is defined as net profits over debt to credit institutions. The definition of firm size was based on the European Commission Recommendation of 6 May 2003 (2003/361/EC), by taking into account the number of employees and sales volume. The excluded year dummy variables were 1996 and 1997. R^2 refers to R-squared within.

Next we control for the firm characteristics, including *Turnover*, *Tangible assets as % of debt*, *Leverage*, *Credit risk*, *Debt coverage* and *Firm age*. Columns six to ten in Table 7 report the results of our fixed effects estimates for the full sample and the four size categories. The number of observations is reduced by approximately half because of the inclusion of the lagged variables. All coefficients show up with the expected sign when statistically significant. For the full sample, one additional bank relationship decreases the interest rate by 12 basis points. *Turnover*, *Tangible assets as % of debt*, *Debt coverage* and *Firm age* reduce interest rates, while *Leverage* and *Credit risk* have the opposite effect. The results are very similar to the previous set of regressions without the firm controls. The ranking of the importance of *Number of relationships* across the size categories is preserved. However, the coefficient of *Number of relationships* for the micro firms is significant only at 10% significance level. This is probably due to the relatively small number of micro firms that report continuously to the Central Balance Sheet Database. When we add the lagged firm controls, the number of micro firms goes from 5,963 to only 2,173. The time dummies are highly significant, suggesting that it is important to control for macroeconomic and financial developments.

As a robustness test, we construct a different measure of the number of bank relationships. Specifically, we define *Concentration in Lending (HHI)* and construct it as a Herfindahl Index of the amount of loans from different banks at the firm level, which is a feature not directly captured by *Number of Bank Relationships*. Table 8 shows regression results with this alternative measure. Our previous results are confirmed by these regressions. When *Concentration in Lending (HHI)* increases, the cost of borrowing significantly increases, except for medium firms. The results are broadly consistent with those obtained before: firms which concentrate their loans in fewer banks pay higher interest rates[8].

[8] Another potentially interesting way of measuring the importance of relationship lending would be to consider the length of the relationship. However, given that there were several mergers and acquisitions in the Portuguese banking system during the sample period, the use of this variable could entail some caveats.

Table 8 - Regression results

Dependent variable: Implicit bank interest rate

	Fixed-effect regressions					**Fixed-effect regressions - controlling for firm characteristics**				
	All firms	**Micro firms**	**Small firms**	**Medium firms**	**Large firms**	**All firms**	**Micro firms**	**Small firms**	**Medium firms**	**Large firms**
Concentration in lending (HHI)$_t$	0.537	0.798	0.349	0.259	1.925	0.476	1.177	0.629	0.263	4.310
	3.67	*2.34*	*1.59*	*0.85*	*2.95*	*2.05*	*2.07*	*1.82*	*0.55*	*4.06*
Turnover$_{t-1}$						-0.005	-0.008	-0.004	0.002	-0.004
						-5.15	*-3.35*	*-2.56*	*1.06*	*-0.81*
Tangible assets as % of debt$_{t-1}$						-0.005	0.007	-0.011	-0.008	-0.001
						-2.64	*1.03*	*-3.55*	*-2.26*	*-0.15*
Leverage$_{t-1}$						0.032	0.054	0.029	0.020	0.005
						8.18	*5.90*	*4.87*	*2.49*	*0.28*
Credit risk$_{t-1}$						0.445	0.342	0.909	0.053	0.015
						2.38	*0.63*	*2.84*	*0.17*	*0.03*
Debt coverage$_{t-1}$						-0.002	0.000	-0.002	-0.006	-0.004
						-1.54	*0.11*	*-1.14*	*-2.93*	*-1.24*
Firm age$_{t-1}$						-0.659	-0.726	-0.801	-0.717	-0.579
						-31.62	*-12.35*	*-26.42*	*-21.06*	*-8.27*
Assets$_t$						-1.809				
						-12.30				
1997	-1.849	-1.456	-1.777	-2.135	-2.555	-	-	-	-	-
	-21.20	*-6.89*	*-13.69*	*-12.95*	*-7.00*	-	-	-	-	-
1998	-3.629	-2.938	-3.703	-4.020	-4.388	-1.100	-0.844	-1.085	-1.358	-0.785
	-40.97	*-13.61*	*-27.76*	*-24.03*	*-11.91*	*-10.37*	*-2.81*	*-6.88*	*-7.21*	*-1.88*
1999	-5.624	-4.841	-5.695	-6.037	-6.329	-2.274	-2.101	-2.286	-2.704	-2.454
	-65.03	*-22.69*	*-43.47*	*-37.26*	*-17.44*	*-22.24*	*-7.39*	*-14.80*	*-14.89*	*-6.04*
2000	-5.185	-4.567	-5.336	-5.406	-5.038	-1.348	-1.811	-1.391	-1.272	-1.064
	-56.02	*-19.50*	*-37.87*	*-31.90*	*-13.97*	*-13.68*	*-6.60*	*-9.40*	*-7.35*	*-2.71*
2001	-4.913	-4.262	-5.139	-5.011	-4.702	-0.158	-0.553	-0.336	-0.059	0.215
	-52.95	*-17.96*	*-36.24*	*-29.42*	*-13.28*	*-1.61*	*-2.06*	*-2.26*	*-0.34*	*0.58*
2002	-5.836	-5.356	-6.015	-5.936	-5.573	-0.383	-0.662	-0.532	-0.301	-0.215
	-62.60	*-22.18*	*-41.73*	*-35.04*	*-15.89*	*-3.97*	*-2.51*	*-3.58*	*-1.79*	*-0.65*
2003	-6.614	-5.760	-6.809	-6.928	-5.993	-0.387	-0.230	-0.438	-0.600	-0.170
	-69.41	*-23.15*	*-46.03*	*-40.14*	*-16.87*	*-4.15*	*-0.93*	*-3.02*	*-3.72*	*-0.56*
2004	-6.919	-6.173	-7.178	-7.054	-6.529	-	-	-	-	-
	-70.02	*-24.00*	*-46.78*	*-38.86*	*-18.00*	-	-	-	-	-
Constant	12.978	12.878	13.245	12.604	11.379	47.595	17.916	23.519	25.883	23.448
	111.85	*39.03*	*75.31*	*66.32*	*29.73*	*23.28*	*16.45*	*33.16*	*24.97*	*9.79*
Number of observations	38764	10764	17589	8436	1975	16790	3778	7826	4202	984
Number of firms	16014	5963	7743	3234	739	7694	2173	3818	1874	435
R^2	0.267	0.175	0.271	0.327	0.277	0.202	0.138	0.197	0.231	0.185

Notes: t-statistics in italics. The implicit interest rate was computed using data from the Central Balance Sheet Database held by Banco de Portugal, which includes detailed accounting information for a large sample of Portuguese companies. This interest rate was computed as the amount of interest paid on bank loans as a percentage of total debt to credit institutions at the end of the year. Concentration in lending is as Herfindhal index using bank shares at the firm level. Turnover represents sales and services over assets. Leverage is defined as debt to credit institutions over assets; credit risk is a dummy variable which takes the value one when the firm is in default; and debt coverage is defined as net profits over debt to credit institutions. The definition of firm size was based on the European Commission Recommendation of 6 May 2003 (2003/361/EC), by taking into account the number of employees and sales volume. The excluded year dummy variables were 1996 and 1997. R^2 refers to R-squared within.

To summarize, we find strong evidence that the number of bank relationships is significantly negatively related to the interest rate that banks charge. Thus in Portugal the benefit of keeping an exclusive bank relationship does not seem to reduce the cost of borrowing, at least in the last decade.

4. Endogeneity

We are seriously concerned with the idea that the number of bank relationships and the cost of borrowing may be simultaneously determined, which introduces an endogeneity problem in our empirical analysis. For instance, an unobservable change in managerial ability may jointly influence the choice of the number of banks and the interest rate that banks charge. A manager with good negotiation skills may be able to maintain strong relationships with multiple banks and at the same time be able to bargain a lower cost of debt.

We address this issue by using an instrumental variable approach. We instrument the number of bank relationships by the change in the number of bank relationship from the previous year, i.e. *Number of Bank Relationships(t)- Number of Bank Relationships(t-1)*. We consider this to be a good instrument because a change in the number of banks can influence the cost of debt that the firm can obtain only through the number of bank relationships, other firm characteristics controlled for.

In Table 9, we run the same set of regressions using the above-mentioned instrument for *Number of Bank Relationships* and find that our previous findings are robust. The slope coefficient for *Number of Bank Relationships* is larger: an additional bank relationship reduces the cost of debt by 34 basis points on average, more than doubling the previously obtained coefficient. Moreover, this finding holds significant across all firm size categories.

Table 9 - Regression results

Instrumental variables regressions

Instrument: change in the number of bank relations

	All firms	Micro firms	Small firms	Medium firms	Large firms
Number of bank relationships $_t$	-0.335	-0.456	-0.386	-0.314	-0.450
	-5.55	*-2.11*	*-3.75*	*-3.25*	*-3.07*
Turnover $_{t-1}$	-0.005	-0.008	-0.004	0.002	-0.005
	-5.31	*-3.47*	*-2.76*	*0.83*	*-1.02*
Tangible assets as % of debt $_{t-1}$	-0.005	0.006	-0.011	-0.008	-0.001
	-2.74	*0.99*	*-3.60*	*-2.32*	*-0.14*
Leverage $_{t-1}$	0.033	0.054	0.032	0.024	0.009
	8.56	*5.88*	*5.28*	*2.96*	*0.54*
Credit risk $_{t-1}$	0.453	0.423	0.908	0.022	0.191
	2.42	*0.77*	*2.83*	*0.07*	*0.36*
Debt coverage $_{t-1}$	-0.002	0.000	-0.002	-0.006	-0.004
	-1.74	*0.07*	*-1.20*	*-3.00*	*-1.12*
Firm age $_{t-1}$	-0.683	-0.719	-0.801	-0.734	-0.682
	-31.97	*-12.19*	*-26.44*	*-21.27*	*-8.17*
Assets $_t$	-1.566				
	-10.13				
1998	-1.181	-0.852	-1.148	-1.476	-1.135
	-11.00	*-2.83*	*-7.22*	*-7.68*	*-2.58*
1999	-2.294	-2.069	-2.301	-2.714	-2.492
	-22.38	*-7.25*	*-14.88*	*-14.92*	*-6.02*
2000	-1.389	-1.796	-1.414	-1.315	-1.183
	-14.03	*-6.53*	*-9.54*	*-7.56*	*-2.96*
2001	-0.257	-0.530	-0.399	-0.221	-0.181
	-2.57	*-1.97*	*-2.66*	*-1.24*	*-0.45*
2002	-0.460	-0.648	-0.576	-0.429	-0.493
	-4.70	*-2.45*	*-3.85*	*-2.48*	*-1.39*
2003	-0.427	-0.220	-0.467	-0.662	-0.299
	-4.56	*-0.88*	*-3.22*	*-4.07*	*-0.95*
2004	-	-	-	-	-
	-	-	-	-	-
Constant	46.020	19.661	25.094	27.934	31.237
	22.38	*18.72*	*33.69*	*23.45*	*9.00*
Number of observations	16790	3778	7826	4202	984
Number of firms	7694	2173	3818	1874	435
R^2	0.199	0.137	0.196	0.229	0.153

Notes: t-statistics in italics. The implicit interest rate was computed using data from the Central Balance Sheet Database held by Banco de Portugal, which includes detailed accounting information for a large sample of Portuguese companies. This interest rate was computed as the amount of interest paid on bank loans as a percentage of total debt to credit institutions at the end of the year. The number of relationships was computed using information from the Central Register of Banco de Portugal, by counting the number of different banks which were lending to a given firm at the end of each year. Turnover represents sales and services over assets. Leverage is defined as debt to credit institutions over assets; credit risk is a dummy variable which takes the value one when the firm is in default; and debt coverage is defined as net profits over debt to credit institutions. The definition of firm size was based on the European Commision Recommendation of 6 May 2003 (2003/361/EC), by taking into account the number of employees and sales volume. The excluded year dummy variables were 1996 and 1997. R^2 refers to R-squared within.

5. Concluding remarks

We construct a unique dataset containing 17,516 Portuguese small, medium and large firms and spanning from 1996 to 2004. Using this dataset we study the impact of the number of banks a firm borrows from on the cost of bank loans. The results obtained suggest that the number of relationships significantly decreases borrowing costs. We find that the average Portuguese firm borrows from three different banks, which is a relatively high number of relationships by international standards, but typical among countries with the French law system. Firms pay lower interest rates if they diversify their pool of lenders. One additional bank relationship reduces the interest rate by 12 to 34 basis points.

Our findings are clearly against the predictions of the delegated monitoring theory, even for the smallest firms in our sample, which are expected to face the most severe information problem in the economy. This might have to do with the fact that the Central Credit Register allows Portuguese financial institutions to share crucial information on their clients, e.g. the amount of debt overdue and the repayment record of the firm, regardless of the firm size. The results seem to suggest that information sharing mechanisms such as the Central Credit Register can partially substitute the benefit of relationship banking in overcoming the information asymmetry problem and reduce the need to maintain exclusive relationships with banks.

Our finding is consistent with Carletti et al. (2007), who find that banks benefit from risk diversification brought by multiple-bank lending. The decreasing interest rate reflects that the reduction in risk level overcomes free-riding and duplication of monitoring costs. However, to the contrary of the prediction of Carletti et al. (2007) that the benefit of diversification is stronger with small opaque less profitable firms, we find that the negative correlation between the number of banks and the interest rate holds robust across all firm sizes. Specifically, even large mature profitable firms benefit from multiple lending.

In addition, firms with many relationships should have more bargaining power in their relations with banks, given that they may easily obtain funding from other banks if they are not offered competitive conditions. The stronger is bank competition, the more should a firm profit from having many relationships, as banks may be more willing to beat their rivals bids to lock in a customer. In fact, the finding that the interest rate decreases in the number of banks is consistent with the competition argument by Boot and Thakor (2000) that when banks compete to gain clients, firms are able to borrow from multiple banks at lower costs.

References

Berger, A. N., and G. F. Udell (1998), The economics of small business finance: The roles of private equity and debt markets in the financial growth cycle, *Journal of Banking and Finance*, 22, 613-73.

Bolton, P. and D. Scharfstein (1996), Optimal debt structure and the number of creditors, *The Journal of Political Economy*, 104, 1-25.

Boot, A. and A. Thakor (2000), Can relationship banking survive competition?, *The Journal of Finance*, 55, 679-713.

Carletti, E., V. Cerasi, and S. Daltung (2007), Multiple-bank lending: Diversification and free-riding in monitoring, *Journal of Financial Intermediation*,16, 425-451.

D'Auria, C, A. Foglia and P. M. Reedtz (1999), Bank interest rates and credit relationships in Italy, *Journal of Banking and Finance*, 23, 1067-1093.

Degryse, H. and S. Ongena (2007), Competition and Regulation in the Banking Sector: A Review of the Empirical Evidence on the Sources of Bank Rents, in Thakor, A. and A. Boot (eds), Handbook of Financial Intermediation and Banking (Elsevier), *forthcoming*.

Detagriache, E., P. Garella and L. Guiso (2000), Multiple versus single banking relationships: theory and evidence, *The Journal of Finance*, 55, 1133-1161.

Dewatripont, M., and E. Maskin (1995), Credit and efficiency in centralized and decentralized economies, *Review of Economic Studies*, 62, 541-555.

Diamond, D. (1984), Financial intermediation and delegated monitoring, *Review of Economic Studies*, 51, 393-414.

Farinha, L. and J. A. C. Santos (2002), Switching from single to multiple bank lending relationships: Determinants and implications, *Journal of Financial Intermediation*, 11, 124-151.

Holmstrom, B., and J. Tirole (1997), Financial intermediation, loanable funds, and the real sector, *Quarterly Journal of Economics*, 112, 663-691.

Ongena , S. and D. Smith (2000), What determines the number of bank relationships? Cross-country evidence, *Journal of Financial Intermediation*, 9, 26-56.

Petersen, M. and R. Rajan (1994), The benefits of lending relationships: Evidence from small business data, *The Journal of Finance*, 49, 3-37.

Rajan, R. (1992), Insiders and outsiders: The choice between informed and arm's-length debt, *The Journal of Finance*, 47, 1367-1400.

Ribeiro, N. (2007), "Debt growth: factors, institutional issues and implications - the Portuguese case" in C. Enoch and I. Otker-Robe, eds: *Rapid Credit Growth in Central and Eastern Europe: Endless Boom or Early Warning?*, Palgrave

Sharpe, S. (1990), Asymmetric information, bank lending and implicit contracts: A stylized model of customer relationships, *The Journal of Finance*, 45, 1069-1087.

Data Appendix

Filters were applied, in order to guarantee a reasonable quality of the data used, even if at the cost of a lower number of observations. The first step was to exclude all observations for which debt or interest paid was negative or equalled zero, given that it would not make sense to compute implicit interest rates in such cases. We also excluded all firms which had zero employees. Such firms should be mainly holding companies or firms in liquidation, though this may also reflect isolated reporting problems in the database. Additionally, we dropped all observations below the 5th percentile and above the 95th percentile of the implicit interest rates distributions. Moreover, we dropped all observations for which the estimated implicit interest rate was below the interbank money market interest rate. Finally, we excluded all firms for which we did not have any information on the Credit Register, given that it would be impossible to compute the number of bank relationships for those firms. After applying all these filters to the implicit bank interest rate, we were left with a database with 12,263 observations between 1996 and 2004.

Acknowledgments

We are thankful to Pedro Portugal and participants at the XLI EWGFM meeting for useful comments. The analyses, opinions and findings of this paper represent the views of the authors, which are not necessarily those of Banco de Portugal. The authors gratefully acknowledge funding from Fundação para a Ciência e Tecnologia.

CHAPTER TWO

PRODUCT DIFFERENTIATION AND THE MEASUREMENT OF COST EFFICIENCY IN BANKING: THE CASE OF PORTUGUESE BANKS

FILIPA LIMA

Abstract

Using a parametric approach for a multi-output production function that includes off-balance sheet outputs, in this study we aim at providing an analysis of the impacts of product differentiation on the cost efficiency of the Portuguese banking industry. We show that the consideration of different segments, both in the loans' market – non-financial corporations, mortgage and consumption – and in the deposits' market – non-financial corporations and households – impacts on the analysis of banks' performance. Banks have compensated with productivity gains the increase in operating costs due to changes in the business conditions. In particular, technological progress has contributed to a shift of the efficient frontier allowing for relevant cost savings; nevertheless, the efficiency levels have evolved irregularly over time. Securitisation operations and managed funds are particularly relevant in explaining the changes that occurred in the banks involved in mergers, for which we extend a decomposition technique between scale, business conditions and productivity changes. Regarding the determinants of cost efficiency, variables related to banks' dimension, quality of the loans' portfolio and M&A play a significant role in explaining differences in banks' cost efficiency levels and over time.

Keywords: Banks; Cost efficiency; Productivity; Mergers

1. Introduction

The liberalisation of financial markets in Europe, the adoption of the single currency and the convergence to historically low interest rates acted as a catalyst for a range of structural changes in the financial intermediation services provided in the European context. The banking industry has witnessed an increase in the strategic importance of prices practised in banking operations and therefore an increase in price competition in most banking segments, with banks developing differentiation strategies by type of client. Most studies on bank efficiency do not account for product idiosyncrasies that will likely bias performance measures if evaluated for aggregated outputs only. Pastor and Serrano (2006) provide also additional support for taking bank specialisation into account, decomposing cost inefficiencies into inefficiencies associated with specialisation within the banking system and inefficiencies within bank specialisation.

To the best of our knowledge, the cost efficiency of the Portuguese banking industry incorporating different loans and deposits' market segments has never been covered in the literature.

The progressive elimination of barriers to capital movements and the intensification of the globalisation in the financial markets has fostered a continuous innovation process with banks offering new and more sophisticated products whilst finding highly innovative opportunities to reengineer their activity. In particular, banks have been able to move from being pure financial intermediaries to highly sophisticated financial firms that are able to disintermediate their loans and funds gathered from customers, while keeping the associated benefits. In this context, banks bear costs and obtain profits from activities not recorded on their balance sheets. An important portion of banks' profits and costs are associated with commission-related products as well as with disintermediated (off-balance sheet) assets and liabilities, thus making balance sheet measures of output inappropriate to measure the true dimension of banking activity.

The vast majority of studies on banking efficiency have mainly concentrated on cost and profit measures using (on) balance sheet output variables. It is therefore reasonable to argue that, given the increasing magnitude of financial disintermediation, efficiency measures that do not take them into account will most likely underestimate the efficiency levels of the most disintermediated banks.

Some authors have touched upon this issue. Clark and Siems (2002) provide a valuable contribution to the rationale of considering off-balance sheet outputs, deriving US bank specific measures of cost and profit efficiency, with and without the inclusion of aggregate measures of off-balance sheet activities. They found that cost efficiency estimates increase with the inclusion of such activities, while profit estimates are unaffected. The authors conclude also that the structure of off-balance sheet outputs is also relevant in explaining inter-bank differences. Moreover, in a study on the impact of technical change on the costs of European banks, Altunbas *et al.* (1999) had also included as an output the pool of off-balance sheet business although without isolating the impact of its inclusion in the cost function. More recently, Casu and Girardone (2005), in a study on the relevance of off-balance sheet items in the definition of banks' output, when estimating total productivity change indexes, employed the nominal value of some off-balance sheet banking items as an output measure.

Although these papers represent an important contribution to the impact of off-balance sheet items, these authors' off-balance sheet data were limited to credit commitments and guarantees, and/or off-balance sheet items were aggregated as a single output. However, amongst the banks' off-balance sheet activities securitised loans deserve a special attention and, to the best of our knowledge, have not yet been treated in bank efficiency studies.

We aim with this article to provide an analysis of the efficiency of the Portuguese banking industry from a cost perspective. In the production function we include not only different categories of loans and deposits but also off-balance sheet outputs; on this regard, securitised loans are of particular interest.

The deep transformations the Portuguese banking system underwent since the mid-1970s make this an interesting case study. Following the politic events in 1974, banks were nationalized. For more than a decade, the banking sector comprised a set of State-owned banks and a few foreign banks with an inexpressive share of the business; there were restrictions to the structure of assets and to banks' activity, limits to credit granting, administrative regulation of interest rates and restrictions to the creation of new banks or the expansion of the branching network. The changes to the institutional and regulatory framework started in the mid-1980s, consisting of the lift of most legal constraints on banking, and grew during the 1990s, allowing a more competitive environment. In 1984 the sector was open to private sector. The reprivatisation process started in 1989 gradually transferring most business to private administration. All these events that occurred since the mid-1970s originated important structural changes, affecting inevitably banks' efficiency. The gradual deconstruction of the regime of administrative banking interest rates led to an increase in the strategic importance of prices practised in banking operations and therefore to an increase in price competition in most banking segments. In parallel, with the free fixing of interest rates and the wider range of possibilities for the public to invest savings, which competed with banking deposits, banks developed differentiation strategies by type of client. Moreover, securitisation in Portugal corresponds to a recent phenomenon that has been growing fast and therefore has to be taken into account in a complete profile of the activity in the sector; according to ECB (2008) the weight of securitised loans with respect to GDP ranks third in the Euro Area.

Our results show that the measures of marginal costs are affected by the specification of the production function. Moreover, banks have compensated with productivity gains the increase in operating costs due to changes in the business conditions; in particular, technological progress has contributed to a shift of the efficient frontier allowing for relevant cost savings. In a study on parametric and non-parametric estimates of productivity change in European banking during the 1990s, Casu *et al.* (2004) found evidence that (where found) productivity growth has mainly been brought about by technical change and there does not appear to have been catching up on the part of non-best practice institutions.

We also analyse for the first time the effects on cost efficiency derived from the mergers that occurred in the 1990s. Banking groups in many European countries have been involved in domestic mergers and acquisitions trying to consolidate their market position within national borders, rather than pursuing a cross border expansionary strategy. The number of banks operating in the European Union (EU) reduced 25% from 1997 to 2004, according to ECB (2004; 2005). In Portugal the C5 ratio increased by 21 percentage points (from 46% to 67%) and the Herfindahl-Hirschman index rose from 1091 to 1475, revealing how much the domestic banking market has concentrated in the recent years. We propose an extension of the technique developed by Berger and Mester (1997, 2003), distinguishing not only between changes in business conditions, in best practice and in efficiency levels but also between changes related to the mere aggregation of the banks prior to the merger, the *proforma* bank, and the "pure" merger effects.

The remainder of this article is organized as follows. In Section II we provide a review of the literature. In Section III we present the methodology followed and the cost function to be estimated. Section IV contains a description of the data. The results obtained are analysed in Section V, distinguishing between the three model specifications selected. In Section VI we introduce a technique for decomposing total changes in costs after the occurrence of mergers. Finally, we present some concluding remarks in Section VII.

2. Literature review

Most of the pioneering works on bank efficiency focused on the US market. The past decade witnessed a growing interest in the study of bank efficiency in Europe. Goddard *et al.* (2007) provide an excellent review of the recent academic literature on developments in European banking. Portugal is seldom included in European-wide studies and, if it is, only a small number of institutions are included. As a positive example, in a study of European banks between 1989 and 1997, Altunbas *et al.* (2001) found evidence that Portuguese banks operate at nearly constant returns to scale, with X-inefficiency ranging from 33% to 29% and that technical progress reduces total costs by around 4% per annum.

Bikker (2004) assesses cost efficiency of the European banking industry, examining efficiency and cost levels differences across European countries and providing a sensitivity analysis with respect to bank size, bank type category and time, over the years 1990-1997. Using the stochastic cost frontier approach, it was observed that X-inefficiency in Europe is rather high at on average 30%, in general higher than the 20% often found in the literature. On average, German banks appear to be among the most efficient ones, but this observation is biased, as most banks belong to the very efficient categories of cooperative and savings banks. Banks in Denmark, the Netherlands, Portugal and the UK take an intermediate position, whereas those from Belgium, France, Greece and Italy are less efficient. On average, Spanish banks appear to be among the least efficient ones. Inefficiencies in 1997 are nearly 45% lower than in 1990 suggesting that, over time, deregulation, liberalisation and ongoing financial and monetary integration in the EU have increased competitive pressures and enforced European banks to operate more economically.

This is consistent with Casu and Molyneux (2003), who investigate whether there has been an improvement in and convergence of productive efficiency across European banking markets since the creation of the Single Internal Market, between 1993 and 1997. Overall, the results suggest that there has been a small improvement in bank efficiency levels, although there is little evidence to suggest that these have converged. Their results lead to the conclusion that country-specific factors are still important determinants in explaining differences in bank efficiency levels across Europe.

Weill (2004) provides a review of the main research on banking efficiency in five European countries (France, Germany, Italy, Spain and Switzerland) making some interesting observations: i) mean efficiency scores are relatively dispersed, with an average efficiency score between 80% and 90% in many cases; ii) there is not any general rule for the hierarchy of scores obtained with parametric or non-parametric approaches; and, iii) there is ambiguous evidence across the literature concerning the relationship between efficiency and size.

More recently, Holló and Nagy (2006) estimate bank efficiency differences across member states of the EU, from 1999 to 2003. They show on an empirical basis that the level and spread of bank efficiency in the EU and their changes are significantly determined by characteristics of operational environment and the "conscious" behaviour of management. Their findings suggest that there is a cost efficiency gap and convergence between the old and new member states, irrespective of the specifications of the model. With respect to profit efficiency, however, differences in efficiency between the two regions are only established after controlling for some major characteristics of the varying operational environments. Furthermore, their results suggest that controls for selected distorting factors (inflation, depth of financial intermediation, market concentration, regulatory regime) originating from the operational environment or the absence of such controls may modify the results.

On the measurement and determinants of productivity growth, Orea (2002) provides a parametric decomposition of a generalized Malmquist productivity index that takes into account scale economies; the results for Spanish savings banks show an increase of total factor productivity, which can be mainly attributed to technical progress and the positive effect of returns to scale. Rezitis (2006) uses also the Malmquist productivity index to investigate productivity growth and technical efficiency in the Greek banking industry for the period 1982-1997, concluding that productivity growth is higher after 1992: recent growth is mainly attributed to technical progress, while until 1992 growth is mainly attributed to improvements in efficiency. In particular, the effects of investment in information technologies (IT) in the financial sector are analysed in Casolaro and Gobbi (2007), using micro-data from a panel of 600 Italian banks over the period 1989–2000. The results show that both cost and profit frontier shifts are strongly correlated with IT capital accumulation. Banks adopting IT capital-intensive techniques are also more efficient.

Casu *et al.* (2004) provide a valuable comparison between parametric and non-parametric estimates of productivity change in European banking between 1994 and 2000. The findings of both sets of estimations suggest clear productivity growth in the Italian and Spanish banking sectors, whereas results are mixed for French and German banking. Both approaches however consistently identify those systems that have benefited most (and least) from productivity change during the 1990s. The results also suggest that (where found) productivity growth has mainly been brought about by technical change and there does not appear to have been catching up on the part of non-bestpractice institutions.

Finally it is worth mentioning the work of Pastor and Serrano (2006) on the analyses of the effects of specialisation on the cost efficiency of a set of banking systems of the European Union over the period 1992–1998. Unlike in the established literature in which specialisation differences are not considered, the authors decompose cost inefficiencies into two different components: one associated with the composition of specialisations in each banking system and the other related to specific inefficiencies of banks within their specialisation. The results for the intra-specialisation inefficiencies indicate that the inefficiencies of the European banking systems are much smaller (although high) when the effect of productive composition (specialisation) is discounted. Retail banks exhibit higher composition inefficiencies.

Studies on Portuguese banks' efficiency include Mendes and Rebelo (1999), Pinho (2001) and Canhoto and Dermine (2003). The first authors estimated a translog cost frontier, for the period 1990–95 and found some evidence of technological recess. Pinho (2001) also estimated a stochastic frontier. In this study economies of scale were found for the smaller banks only, whilst economies of scope between loans and deposits were found for all but the largest banks. Canhoto and Dermine (2003) examined the effect of deregulation and analysed the relative efficiency of new domestic banks as compared to that of older existing banks, following the data envelop analysis technique. The paper shows that the rapid deregulation in Portugal was accompanied by a major increase in the efficiency of banks from 1990-1995.

Our study adds value to these prior works in the sense that i) it broadens the output bundles offered by the Portuguese banks, providing a more complete and accurate production function; ii) it simultaneously incorporates explanatory variables for the banks' inefficiencies; iii) it explores the main driving forces of banks' costs, with a specific decomposition technique; and, finally, iv) it captures the main developments in more recent years, namely with a particular focus on mergers.

In a seminal work, Akhavein *et al.* (1997) present three major motivations behind M&A. First, M&A could improve cost efficiency, reducing costs per unit of output for a given set of output quantities and input prices, by increasing scale efficiency, scope (product mix) efficiency, and/or X-efficiency. Merging banks supposedly are capable of improving their operating costs by rationalizing the branch network of the merging banks, reducing back-office operations and common services and achieving higher economies of scale in information technology, brand recognition and other fixed assets. Second, mergers may increase profits through improvements in profit efficiency that involves superior combinations of inputs and outputs. Third, mergers may improve profits through the exercise of additional market power in setting prices. An increase in market share may allow the consolidated firm to charge higher rates for the goods or services it produces, raising profits by extracting more surplus from consumers, without any improvement in efficiency. The empirical literature has mainly assessed these three aspects, with some attention also to stock market performance.

Amel *et al.* (2004) provide a review of established literature on M&A and efficiency in the financial sector along industry and country lines, shedding light on common features. Studies that analyse the direct effect of M&A on banks' efficiency have used both balance sheet ratios and multivariate cost and profit functions. The results vary by country: for the US, there is little evidence of any improvement in cost efficiency following a merger; for the European banks, domestic mergers among banks of equal size improve cost efficiency but this result does not hold for all countries. The evidence from studies that use more recent data is mixed. In any case, the benefits of M&A seem to accrue only after a few years: probably some time is needed in order to restructure a target and integrate it with the acquirer's operations. In terms of profit efficiency assessment, the evidence for Europe suggests that more efficient banks tend to acquire institutions in worse shape. The authors conclude that the empirical evidence suggests that commercial bank M&A do not significantly improve cost and profit efficiency and, on average, do not generate significant shareholder value. There is evidence in favour of exploiting scale economies, but only up to a size well below that of the most recent large deals. Economies of scope are harder to pin down; there is no clear-cut evidence of their existence. These results seem to contradict the motivations given by practitioners for consolidation. According to the authors, to a certain extent this puzzle might be only apparent. The lack of clear-cut results on the effects of M&A could reflect difficulties in measuring efficiency improvements. Further, studies restricted to short post-merger periods might fail to detect value gains that only emerge slowly, after some years. Moreover, deals done in the past might have suffered from stricter regulation that prevented firms involved in M&A from reaping all the benefits of their deals. Finally, the fact that mergers often happen in waves makes it hard to separate the effect of single deals from transformations undergone by the industry as a whole.

To the best of our knowledge the mergers that occurred in the last decade in the Portuguese banking market have not yet been covered by the literature. Furthermore, we propose a new technique to assess the impact of mergers from a cost perspective, isolating the "pure" merger effects from other factors not related to the merging process.

3. Methodology

According to Farrel (1957) we can distinguish between technical efficiency, the ability to maximize the output given a certain set of inputs, and allocative efficiency, the skill to use the inputs in optimal proportions, given their prices and the available production technology. The combination of these two gives us a measure of total economic efficiency. The X-inefficiency comprises the deviations from the best practice banks that shape the frontier.

Regarding the X-inefficiency estimation methods, there are generally four types commonly used depending on the different assumptions made:

stochastic frontier approach (SFA), thick frontier approach (TFA), distribution-free approach (DFA) and data envelopment analysis (DEA). They differ on the basis of the arbitrary assumptions to disentangle efficiency differences from random error using a single observation for each firm. They are further separated into parametric (SFA, TFA, DFA) and non-parametric (DEA) approaches. All approaches have their advantages and disadvantages. In the vast literature on banking efficiency, only a few studies have applied two or more techniques for the estimation of efficiency scores on the same data set. Berger and Mester (1997) have found that the efficiency estimates are fairly robust to differences in methodology. Bauer *et al.* (1998) provide vast research on the consistency of frontier approaches. Their main conclusion is that all parametric approaches provide efficiency measures that are consistent with one another, while DEA does not provide results consistent with parametric approaches. In a summary provided by Weill (2004) several general conclusions emerge from the literature: i) there is a consensus regarding the robustness of scores provided by parametric approaches; ii) studies disagree on the differences between mean efficiency scores provided by parametric and non-parametric approaches; iii) unlike US studies, European evidence tends to show the high rank correlation between SFA and DEA rankings of scores. However, this evidence remains scarce and limited. Casu *et al.* (2004) provide a useful comparison between parametric and non-parametric estimates of productivity change in European banking between 1994 and 2000, noting that both approaches consistently identify those systems that have benefited most (and least) from productivity change during the 1990s. They also conclude that, despite sometimes identifying conflicting findings for the sources of productivity for individual years, the two approaches generally do not yield markedly different results in terms of identifying the components of productivity growth. In our study, we use the stochastic frontier approach with a translog specification.

Battese and Coelli (1992) propose a stochastic frontier production function for (unbalanced) panel data, which has firm effects assumed to be distributed as truncated normal random variables, permitted also to vary systematically with time. A cost function identical to the one proposed in Schmidt and Lovell (1979) can be obtained from a production specification with few simple sign changes.

The cost version of the model may be expressed as:

$$Y_{it} = x_{it}\beta + (v_{it} + u_{it}) \qquad ,i=1,...,N, t=1,...,T, \qquad (1)$$

Where

> Y_{it} is (the logarithm of) the cost of the i-th firm in the t-th time period;
> x_{it} is a k×1 vector of (transformations of the) output quantities of the i-th firm in the t-th time period;
> β is a vector of unknown parameters;
> the v_{it} are random variables which are assumed to be iid $N(0,\sigma_V^2)$, and independent of the
> $u_{it} = (u_i \exp(-\eta(t-T)))$, where (2)
> u_i are non-negative random variables which are assumed to account for technical inefficiency in costs and are assumed to be iid as truncations at zero of the $N(\mu,\sigma_U^2)$ distribution;
> η is a parameter to be estimated;

and the panel of data need not be complete (i.e. unbalanced panel data).

The error term has therefore two components, one to account for random effects and another to account for technical inefficiency.

The parameterisation of Battese and Corra (1977) is used, replacing σ_V^2 and σ_U^2 with $\sigma^2=\sigma_V^2+\sigma_U^2$ and $\gamma=\sigma_U^2/(\sigma_V^2+\sigma_U^2)$. This is done in view of the calculation of the maximum likelihood estimates. The parameter γ must lie between 0 and 1.

Once the predicted firm-level efficiencies using these estimated functions are obtained, it is then possible to regress the predicted efficiencies upon firm-specific variables in an attempt to identify some of the reasons for differences in predicted efficiencies between firms in an industry. This is known in the literature as the two-stage estimation procedure.

However, this procedure has also been long recognised as inconsistent in its assumptions regarding the independence of the inefficiency effects in the two estimation stages. The two-stage estimation procedure is unlikely to provide estimates as efficient as those that could be obtained using a single-stage estimation procedure. The Battese and Coelli (1995) model specification addresses this issue and may be expressed as:

$$Y_{it} = x_{it}\beta + (v_{it} + u_{it}) \quad ,i=1,...,N,\ t=1,...,T, \qquad (3)$$

where

> Y_{it}, x_{it}, and β are as defined earlier;

the v_{it} are random variables which are assumed to be iid. $N(0,\sigma_V^2)$, and independent of the

u_{it} which are non-negative random variables which are assumed to account for technical inefficiency in costs and are assumed to be independently distributed as truncations at zero of the $N(m_{it},\sigma_U^2)$ distribution;

where

$$m_{it} = z_{it}\delta, \quad (4)$$

where

z_{it} is a p×1 vector of variables which may influence the efficiency of a firm; and

δ is an 1×p vector of parameters to be estimated.

It should be noted that these two model specifications are non-nested and hence no set of restrictions can be defined to permit a test of one specification versus the other.

The measure of the technical (in)efficiency score relative to the cost frontier is defined as:

$$INEFF_{it} = E(Y_{it}^*|u_{it}, X_{it})/ E(Y_{it}^*|u_{it}=0, X_{it}), \quad (5)$$

where Y_{it}^* is the cost of the i-th firm at time t, which will be equal to Y_{it} when the dependent variable is in original units and will be equal to $\exp(Y_{it})$ when the dependent variable is in logs. In the case of a cost frontier, $INEFF_i$ will take a value between one and infinity. The inefficiency measures can be shown to be defined as $\exp(u_{it})$ if the dependent variable is logged or as $(x_{it}\beta+u_{it})/(x_{it}\beta)$ if it is not. These expressions rely upon the value of the unobservable u_{it} being predicted. This is achieved by deriving expressions for the conditional expectation of these functions of the u_{it}, conditional upon the observed value of $(v_{it} + u_{it})$. The resulting expressions are generalizations of the results in Jondrow *et al.* (1982) and Battese and Coelli (1988).

In our study, the banks' production function was defined according to the "two phases" approach to banking production, as in Humphrey (1992); that is to say, first banks originate loans and deposits and in the second phase, treasury is used to cover for any mismatch between sources and uses of funds. Following Pinho (2001), the objective function was modeled as the maximization of long-run profits, subject to the balance sheet constraint.

The bank's (static) long-run objective is to maximize economic profits defined as:

$$\underset{\{L,S,SL,D,F,K,N\}}{\text{Max}}\ \Pi = R_L L + R_M M + R_{SL} SL - r_K K - w_N N - R_D D - R_F F - R_E E \quad (6)$$

$$\text{s.t.: } F(L,SL,D,F,K,N) = 0 \quad (7)$$

$$\rho D + M + L + K = D + E \quad (8)$$

where L stands for loans, M stands for securities, D stands for deposits, E stands for financial equity, SL and F represent the off-balance sheet outputs, securitised loans and managed funds, respectively. R_L, R_M, R_{SL}, R_D, R_F and R_E are the respective required rates of return. The equation (8) represents the real resources transformation function of the bank.

We consider both on-balance sheet outputs and off-balance sheet outputs. Regarding on-balance sheet outputs we take the most representative outputs for banks operating in Portugal[1]–loans and deposits; in addition, making use of data reported by the banks for statistical purposes, we are able to identify different market segments within these categories: we have thus, in the loans' market, loans granted to non-financial corporations, mortgage loans and other loans granted to households[2], and, in the deposits' market, deposits from non-financial corporations and deposits from households. Additionally, we consider also off-balance sheet outputs: securitised loans and managed funds. Clark and Siems (2002) and Casu and Girardone (2005) provide valuable contributions to the rationale of considering off-balance sheet outputs. Securitisation in Portugal ranks at the top among European countries, in per cent of GDP, and is a recent phenomenon in the Portuguese banking industry that needs to be taken into account in order to have a complete profile of the activity in the sector; moreover, given that this variable is directly linked to on-balance sheet loans, the interaction between these two variables will only be correctly captured if securitised loans are included in the production function as a different output. Funds placed with banks and managed by the banks, even though without representing a direct liability consume a part of bank resources and should therefore be

[1] Accounting for approximately 60% of total assets, on average.

[2] It includes mainly loans for consumption purposes although other purposes are also covered, namely loans for health care and education.

considered when designing the production function; they may also act as substitutes for deposits, constituting thus an alternative to clients' savings.

Input factors are labour (N) and capital (K). ρ is the nonearning cash-reserves coefficient, r_K is the operating cost of capital and w_N is the wage rate.

With the introduction of the balance sheet constraint and solving (8) with respect to S, the problem becomes:

$$\underset{\{L,SL,D,F,K,N\}}{\text{Max}}\ \Pi = (R_L - R_M)L + (R_M(1-\rho) - R_D)D + R_{SL}SL - R_F F - (r_K + R_M)K - w_N N - (R_E - R_S)E \quad (9)$$
$$\text{s.t.: } F(L,SL,D,F,K,N) = 0$$

Concentrating on the operating cost side of the profit function, the problem is:

$$\underset{\{K,N\}}{\text{Min}}\ C = (r_K + R_M)K + w_N N \quad (10)$$
$$\text{s.t.: } F(L^*,SL^*,D^*,F^*,K,N) = 0$$

where C denotes the sum of real resources costs ($r_K K + w_N N$) with the opportunity cost of financial physical capital ($R_M K$).

Regarding the cost function specification, we used the multi-output translog where branches interact with the other variables, as proposed by Berger *et al.* (1987).

$$\ln (C_{It}) = \ln (C(Y_{It}, w_{It}, B_{It})) + u_{it} + v_{it} \quad (11)$$

where *C* are the operational costs; *Y* and *w,* the vectors of outputs and input prices, respectively, and *B,* the number of branches; *i* stands for the bank's number and *t* for time.

The standard restrictions of symmetry and input price homogeneity apply.

Additionally, in the "efficient" part of the equation, a time trend was included to capture any shift of the frontier over time, according to the so-called Hicksian-neutral technological progress. A negative coefficient associated to this variable indicates a positive effect of the technical progress on operating costs, i.e., costs fall holding all else equal.

Regarding the "inefficient" part of the equation, in the second-step we simultaneously incorporated in the Z determinants of the u_{it}, twelve firm-specific variables and four macro-environmental variables.

The function to be estimated is therefore:

$$\ln(C) = \alpha_0 + \Sigma\beta_i \ln(Y_i) + \Sigma\alpha_j \ln(W_j) + 1/2\Sigma\Sigma\delta_{ii}\ln(Y_i)\ln(Y_i) + 1/2\Sigma\Sigma\gamma_{jj}\ln(W_j)\ln(W_j) + \Sigma\Sigma\rho_{ij}\ln(Y_i)\ln(W_j) + \psi_b \ln(B) + 1/2\psi_{bb}\ln^2(B) + \Sigma\psi_{bi}\ln(B)\ln(Y_i) + \Sigma\psi_{bj}\ln(B)\ln(W_j) + \tau T + u + v \tag{12}$$

where:

$$u = \delta_0 + \delta Z + e, \tag{13}$$

with:
$i = L, SL, D, F$[3]
$j = N, K.$

4. Data

The data used in this study comprise a unique database that combines both accounting and statistical data for each single bank operating in Portugal[4]. Three main sources were used: accounting data reported by the banks to the *Banco de Portugal* under the Charts of Accounts for the Banking System, data reported by the banks to the *Banco de Portugal* for statistical purposes and data published on the annual bulletin of the *Associação Portuguesa de Bancos*. For the purpose of this research we combined these different data sources, crossing individual data for each bank operating in Portugal, in order to have a complete and accurate characterization of the institutions and their activities, both in terms of traditional and off-balance sheet business.

The sample covers nearly all banks operating in Portugal between 1997–2004, the total market coverage being 97% on average. We have an unbalanced panel of 758 observations, with the number of institutions ranging from 30 in 1997Q3 to 22 in 2004Q4. Balance sheet items, number of workers and branches were computed from averages of end of quarterly

---

[3] Depending on the model considered we will have different sub-categories for loans and deposits.

[4] Individual and confidential data are not disclosed and are used for research purposes only.

data. Data for profit and loss accounts has been annualised. Nominal data was deflated to 1996 prices using the GDP deflator. The price of labour was calculated as the ratio of total labour expenses per employee. Depreciation rate was obtained dividing depreciation costs by physical capital; in order to account for the opportunity cost of the banks' investments in fixed assets we used the yearly average money market rate (3 month EURIBOR).

The variables *Loans* and *Deposits* correspond to the values registered by banks on their accounts. The corresponding loans and deposits' segments were derived from statistical data reported by the banks; we distinguish loans according to the type of borrower–non-financial corporations and households–, loans to households according to the purpose–housing and other purposes, namely consumption–, and deposits according to the type of depositor–non-financial corporations and households. *Securitised Loans* correspond to the loans originated by the bank and sold to a third party, although the bank remains responsible for their management. The variable *Managed Funds* was calculated by aggregating the off-balance sheet items that represent a third party asset managed by the bank.

On the determinants of cost and profit efficiency, we have included a set of variables widely used in the literature. We tried to account for firm characteristics such as size (deposits market share), business composition (relative weight of different segments), loan quality (ratio of non-performing loans), solvency (ratio of equity to assets), ownership (national vs. foreign), and involvement in M&A, and also a set of macroeconomic (GDP growth, money market rate and stock index volatility) and bank market structure indicators (Herfindahl-Hirschman index for deposits).

5. Cost estimates

The estimations were computed using the FRONTIER Version 4.1[5].

Both model specifications considered in the programme were computed: an error components specification with time-varying efficiencies (Battese and Coelli, 1992), and a total effects specification in which the firm effects are directly influenced by a number of variables (Battese and

[5] Kindly made available to the public by Tim Coelli at: (http://www.une.edu.au/econometrics/cepa.htm).

Coelli, 1995). However, the estimates obtained under the first model did not reveal frontier properties and significance levels as good as the second one and are therefore not presented here.

In this study we consider three different model specifications depending on which outputs define the production function. We begin with **Model I** where we exclude off-balance sheet outputs and take loans and deposits as two global outputs, without any sector or purpose breakdowns. This is the model specification most used in the empirical studies, covering thus only these two categories. In **Model II** we keep off-balance sheet outputs excluded and disaggregate loans and deposits into the different markets' segments, having thus five different (on-balance sheet) outputs. Finally, in M**odel III**, we analyse the most complete product specification with seven outputs in total, adding two main off-balance sheet outputs–securitised loans and managed funds–to the sub-categories of loans and deposits.

The results of the estimation for Model I are presented in Table A.I in the Appendix.

a. Marginal costs and input prices sensitivity estimates

Prior to a discussion on banking costs (in)efficiency we evaluated the sensitivity of operating costs to outputs, input prices and the expansion of the branching network.

The banks in the sample were grouped into five classes according to their market share in terms of total deposits. Table 1 below shows the results for **Model I**.

Both at firm and at plant level, for all classes except the one with the largest banks, deposits present higher marginal costs than loans. It is interesting to observe that the smallest banks exhibit the lowest marginal costs for loans and the highest for deposits whereas the opposite occurs in the case of the largest banks; in fact, we can observe loans have increasing marginal costs, until class V, while deposits reveal decreasing marginal costs. In what concerns the impact of changes in the input prices on total operating costs, the largest banks are by far the more capital intensive with banks making a more intensive use of capital as they increase in size. This could indicate the existence of large fixed labour costs, for example related to the size of necessary administrative personnel that does not change in proportion to production. Regarding the branching network, in this model specification there is evidence of operating costs being more sensitive to the network expansion as banks become larger.

Table 1

Model I - Outputs: Loans and deposits (aggregated) excluding off-balance sheet
Marginal costs and input price sensitivity estimates

	Plant measures		
Market share[1]	L		D
I - [0%;1%]	0.7%		3.1%
II -]1% - 2.5%]	0.9%		2.0%
III -]2.5% - 5%]	1.1%		1.7%
IV -]5% - 10%]	1.2%		1.8%
V -]10%;100%]	1.0%		0.8%
Average	1.0%		1.6%
	Firm measures		
	L		D
I - [0%;1%]	0.8%		3.5%
II -]1% - 2.5%]	0.9%		2.4%
III -]2.5% - 5%]	1.2%		2.1%
IV -]5% - 10%]	1.3%		2.4%
V -]10%;100%]	1.1%		1.3%
Average	1.1%		2.0%
	Input shares		Branches
	dlnC/dlnN	dlnC/dlnK	dlnC/dlnB
I - [0%;1%]	0.95	0.05	0.28
II -]1% - 2.5%]	0.86	0.14	0.48
III -]2.5% - 5%]	0.69	0.31	0.52
IV -]5% - 10%]	0.71	0.29	0.61
V -]10%;100%]	0.52	0.48	0.73
Average	0.81	0.19	0.46

[1] In terms of deposits.

We introduce now **Model II** to analyse the results obtained by considering the different sub-categories of loans and deposits (Table A.II in the Appendix).

In this model we can see from Table 2 below how the sub-categories for both loans and deposits exhibit different marginal costs supporting thus the view that each sub-category should be assessed separately and included as an independent output in the production function[6].

[6] Nonetheless, in the translog function we account for interactions among all the categories.

We will concentrate on the analysis at firm level where the branching network effects are incorporated.

Again, as in Model I, deposits present higher marginal costs than loans. Starting with loans, for the non-financial corporations (L_NFC) marginal costs are quite similar in all classes. However, when we turn to households (HH) the picture substantially changes. Regarding loans for other purposes granted to households (L_OTH), class I shows, by far, the highest marginal costs; this is related to the high level of specialisation of banks included in this class targeting mainly the non-financial corporations sector[7], thus rendering the households' segment meaningless in this class. On the other hand, in this model, most banks show negative marginal costs for housing loans, which, at first glance, is a striking result.

However, we should bear in mind that in this model specification securitised loans are excluded and that most of the securitisation operations refer to housing loans; these marginal costs will be reflecting thus the decrease in the outstanding amount of on-balance sheet loans not accompanied by a corresponding decrease in operating costs. On the deposits side, except for class I[8], deposits from non-financial corporations have higher marginal costs than those from households.

Concerning input shares, all classes continue to be more labour intensive; nevertheless, comparing with Model I, in this model specification banks in class V are relatively more sensitive to changes in labour prices while the remaining banks became relatively more sensitive to changes in capital prices. This could be related to different output structures, reflecting different weights for each output category, which, in term, will have different requirements in terms of combinations of labour and capital.

Regarding branching network expansion the results are only slightly smaller than the ones in the previous model, which could be an indication that banks do not follow a branching expansion strategy targeting specific market segments.

---

[7] This specialisation is accounted for in the production function by including a dummy variable equal to one in the case more than 95% of loans and/or deposits are vis-à-vis the non-financial corporations sector. By doing this we can analyse these banks together with more universal ones and compare their marginal costs in the markets where they all compete.

[8] Also in the deposits' market the households sector is not relevant for this class.

Table 2

Model II - Outputs: Loans and deposits (by sector) excluding off-balance sheet
Marginal costs and input price sensitivity estimates

	Plant measures				
Market share[1]	L_NFC	L_MTG	L_OTH	D_NFC	D_HH
I - [0%;1%]	1.6%	-0.5%	10.2%	3.9%	1.5%
II -]1% - 2.5%]	1.8%	0.1%	2.2%	3.3%	2.7%
III -]2.5% - 5%]	1.7%	-2.5%	2.0%	9.2%	1.4%
IV -]5% - 10%]	1.4%	-0.8%	1.4%	7.0%	1.9%
V -]10%;100%]	1.2%	-0.1%	1.9%	6.2%	1.2%
Average	1.5%	-0.8%	1.9%	6.4%	1.8%
	Firm measures				
	L_NFC	L_MTG	L_OTH	D_NFC	D_HH
I - [0%;1%]	1.8%	0.5%	10.4%	4.1%	6.0%
II -]1% - 2.5%]	1.8%	-0.1%	2.2%	3.3%	2.8%
III -]2.5% - 5%]	1.8%	-0.7%	2.0%	9.8%	1.5%
IV -]5% - 10%]	1.5%	-1.4%	1.3%	7.8%	2.0%
V -]10%;100%]	1.3%	-0.2%	1.8%	7.5%	1.3%
Average	1.6%	-0.6%	1.8%	7.1%	1.9%
	Input shares			Branches	
	dlnC/dlnN	dlnC/dlnK		dlnC/dlnB	
I - [0%;1%]	0.90	0.10		0.24	
II -]1% - 2.5%]	0.72	0.28		0.41	
III -]2.5% - 5%]	0.64	0.36		0.49	
IV -]5% - 10%]	0.68	0.32		0.60	
V -]10%;100%]	0.58	0.42		0.71	
Average	0.75	0.25		0.42	

[1] In terms of deposits.

Finally we built **Model III**, adding off-balance sheet items–securitised loans (SL) and managed funds (F)–to Model II (Table A.III in the Appendix).

First of all, one should note that in this model specification the estimate for γ is closer to 1 than in the two previous models, which means better frontier properties of the production function.

We will concentrate on the differences with respect to Model II. The first result from Table 3 that it is worth noting refers to marginal costs of housing loans, which are now always positive; this is explained by the interactions with securitised loans, which on their own account for negative marginal costs. Loans for other purposes have the highest marginal costs and deposits from non-financial corporations carry higher operating costs than from households. The outcome for managed funds shows that, except for class IV where various specific operations occurred in the period under analysis, positive marginal costs and below the ones for deposits, which in this model exhibit in general smaller marginal costs than previously.

The inclusion of off-balance sheet outputs impacts the input shares differently among the classes: while in the two lowest classes the response of operating costs to capital price changes increased, the other intermediate classes increased the response to labour price changes. Given that the first two classes have a relatively higher share of off-balance sheet items[9], it could be the case that off-balance sheet outputs are relatively more demanding in terms of capital resources.

The results obtained for the three models provide us some guidance on the need to correctly specify the production function, not only separating the different market segments of the on-balance sheet main outputs–loans and deposits–but also including certain specific off-balance sheet outputs in the production function. Non-financial corporations and households are distinct customers, with different interests and needs from the banking industry; moreover, housing loans represent a totally separate market from other purposes involving different customers, administrative framework, risk assessment and customer relationship. Regarding off-balance sheet outputs, they also have specific originating and maintaining costs that are accounted as operating costs. Ignoring such activities gives rise to inaccurate marginal costs for the remaining outputs, which, in reality, are due to misspecification errors. Moreover, increasing financial disintermediation and financial innovation over time gave a more prominent role to off-balance sheet activities in recent years thus calling for a change in the specification of the production function.

[9] In fact, it is interesting to observe that the amounts involved in off-balance sheet transactions are not directly related to the banks' size measured in terms of deposits; this is particular true in the case of managed funds that refer to specific arrangements between the bank and the customer where the terms of the contract are negotiated on a bilateral basis rather determined by the general market conditions.

Table 3

Model III - Outputs: Loans and deposits (by sector) including off-balance sheet
Marginal costs and input price sensitivity estimates

	Plant measures						
Market share[1]	L_NFC	L_MTG	L_OTH	D_NFC	D_HH	SL	F
I - [0%;1%]	-0.2%	10.0%	14.0%	2,5%	12,6%	0,1%	1,2%
II -]1% - 2.5%]	0.9%	1.9%	4.6%	2,0%	1,6%	-0,3%	0,3%
III -]2.5% - 5%]	0.5%	0.6%	5.8%	4,7%	1,0%	-0,1%	0,4%
IV -]5% - 10%]	0.6%	0.7%	3.2%	3,5%	0,8%	-0,8%	12,6%
V -]10%;100%]	0.2%	0.5%	1.4%	1,9%	-0,1%	-3,0%	0,2%
Average	0.6%	0.9%	3.7%	3,0%	0,8%	-1,0%	3,4%
	Firm measures						
	L_NFC	L_MTG	L_OTH	D_NFC	D_HH	SL	F
I - [0%;1%]	-0.1%	9.2%	16.4%	4,0%	6,1%	0,6%	1,2%
II -]1% - 2.5%]	1.1%	2.5%	4.6%	4,0%	2,1%	-0,1%	0,3%
III -]2.5% - 5%]	0.9%	0.8%	5.9%	8,0%	1,4%	-0,1%	0,4%
IV -]5% - 10%]	1.0%	2.7%	3.3%	7,1%	1,6%	0,2%	10,9%
V -]10%;100%]	0.9%	1.4%	1.7%	9,4%	0,8%	-1,9%	0,2%
Average	1.0%	1.8%	3.9%	7,1%	1,5%	-0,5%	2,9%

	Input shares		Branches
	dlnC/dlnN	dlnC/dlnK	dlnC/dlnB
I - [0%;1%]	0.86	0.14	0.28
II -]1% - 2.5%]	0.67	0.33	0.57
III -]2.5% - 5%]	0.74	0.26	0.55
IV -]5% - 10%]	0.74	0.26	0.79
V -]10%;100%]	0.67	0.33	1.13
Average	0.76	0.24	0.55

[1] In terms of deposits.

b. Cost efficiency estimates

We now turn our analysis to the cost efficiency levels of the banks operating in Portugal, the evolution over time and the differences between the classes according to the deposits' market shares. The results are shown in Table 4.

From Table 4 we conclude that between 1997 and 2004 efficiency levels increased, on average, from 72%-75% to 79%-83% which is equivalent to saying that during this period banks reduced their waste of resources by 6–8 percentage points, from 25%-29% to 17%-21%. These findings are consistent with Pinho (2001) and Bikker (2004), where an average of 20% waste was found. Evaluating at the average operating conditions, the efficiency levels do not differ significantly among the three model specifications, which may be an indication that inefficiencies are intrinsic to infrastructure and management rather than to specific characteristics of the outputs; nevertheless, Model II exhibits slightly lower efficiency levels than the other two.

At a micro level, turning to a by class analysis, in all models we observe that banks at the lowest percentile are the least efficient; in general, the efficiency levels increase with bank size irrespectively of the model specification (this is also illustrated in Section V.4 where the determinants of the inefficiency scores are analysed). The largest banks reveal a very efficient use of the resources available to ensure their output production levels, deviating only by 5% from a no waste scenario.

The differences in terms of efficiency levels among the classes vary according to the model specification: while in Model I banks in class I differ by nearly 20 percentage points from the remaining banks, which in this model have quite similar results, in the other two models the difference is much smaller. Moreover, in Models II and III, the largest difference in adjacent classes is registered in classes III and IV.

Over time, banks have changed their efficiency levels rather smoothly but without exhibiting a regular pattern. In general, for all models considered, efficiency levels increased from 1997 to 2001, declining afterwards.

Table 4

Evolution of average cost efficiency over time

Model	Market share[1]	1997	1998	1999	2000	2001	2002	2003	2004
I	I - [0%;1%]	62	66	65	64	71	69	70	66
	II -]1% - 2.5%]	82	86	92	90	90	90	89	87
	III -]2.5% - 5%]	83	84	86	91	93	94	90	82
	IV -]5% - 10%]	90	91	93	95	95	95	96	96
	V -]10%;100%]	96	96	97	97	97	96	96	96
	Total average	75	78	79	79	84	84	83	81
II	I - [0%;1%]	66	68	69	72	74	70	70	68
	II -]1% - 2.5%]	69	73	79	80	82	82	77	78
	III -]2.5% - 5%]	72	74	79	82	83	79	91	89
	IV -]5% - 10%]	86	88	91	95	95	94	96	95
	V -]10%;100%]	96	97	98	98	98	98	98	98
	Total average	72	75	78	80	83	81	80	79
III	I - [0%;1%]	72	72	73	77	81	77	74	70
	II -]1% - 2.5%]	71	75	85	86	91	91	88	88
	III -]2.5% - 5%]	72	73	81	84	88	88	90	91
	IV -]5% - 10%]	85	86	91	91	93	93	95	94
	V -]10%;100%]	88	88	93	95	96	96	95	93
	Total average	75	76	81	83	88	87	85	83

[1] In terms of deposits.

c. Decomposition of cost changes

Many factors contribute to the evolution of costs in the banking industry over time. We present in this section a technique introduced by Berger and Mester (2003) for decomposing such changes.

We focus on the mean operating conditions faced by Portuguese banks between 1997 and 2004; for period *t*, operating costs of producing average output levels with average input prices, given an average number of branches, would be defined by $C^*(Y_t, w_t, B_t, t)$ times a factor of average inefficiency $\exp(u_t)$. The ratio of the estimated costs between period *t* and period *t+k* gives us the total gross change in costs between the two periods:

$$\Delta \text{ TOTAL } C_{t,\, t+k} = [C^*(Y_{t+k}, w_{t+k}, B_{t+k}, t+k) \times \exp(u_{t+k})] \,/\, [C^*(Y_t, w_t, B_t, t) \times \exp(u_t)] \quad (14)$$

A ratio over (below) one indicates an increase (decrease) in costs between *t* and *t+k*.

This total change is further decomposed into three elements:

$$\Delta\ \text{TOTAL}\ C_{t,t+k} =$$
$$C^*(Y_{t+k}, w_{t+k}, B_{t+k}, t+k) / C^*(Y_t, w_t, B_t, t+k) \quad \textbf{(change in business conditions)} \quad (15)$$
$$\times\ C^*(Y_t, w_t, B_t, t+k) / C^*(Y_t, w_t, B_t, t) \quad \textbf{(change in best practice)} \quad (16)$$
$$\times\ \exp(u_{t+k}) / \exp(u_t) \quad \textbf{(change in inefficiency)} \quad (17)$$
$$= \Delta\ \text{BUSCOND}\ C_{t,t+k} \times \Delta\ \text{BESTPR}\ C_{t,t+k} \times \Delta\ \text{INEFF}\ C_{t,t+k} \quad (18)$$
$$= \Delta\ \text{BUSCOND}\ C_{t,t+k} \times \Delta\ \text{PROD}\ C_{t,t+k}, \quad (19)$$
$$\text{with}\ \Delta\ \text{PROD}\ C_{t,t+k} = \Delta\ \text{BESTPR}\ C_{t,t+k} \times \Delta\ \text{INEFF}\ C_{t,t+k} \quad \textbf{(change in productivity)} \quad (20)$$

Tables 5–7 summarise the results found in our three models for the yearly changes and over the entire period covered in the sample.

The first column in Tables 5–7 measures the gross change in operating costs on a yearly basis and for the entire period between 1997 and 2004[10]. Total estimated costs increased by roughly 20%, between 1997 and 2004, considering only on-balance sheet outputs (Models I and II) while accounting also for off-balance sheet outputs in Model III the total increase is only of 10%. This is related to the relatively smaller marginal costs we found in section V.1 both for securitised loans and managed funds. In 2000 banks registered the largest increase in total costs, continuing to grow in 2001 to start decreasing / stabilising from then onwards.

Business conditions were the main driving force of total operating costs between 1997 and 2004. Business conditions reflect both the evolution of output levels offered by the banks and of input prices; given that, on average, all products registered positive annual (real) growth rates, it is the input price effect component the one responsible for Δ BUSCOND below one in 1998 and between 2001 and 2003. That is to say, in these years the decrease of both labour costs and price of capital outweighed the expansion of output levels. The increase in total costs due to business conditions was partially compensated by productivity gains

[10] Differences from observed costs are are explained by the random error v_{it}.

coming both from better practices over time and efficiency gains in some years.

Table 5

Model I - Outputs: Loans and deposits (aggregated) excluding off-balance sheet
Decomposition of total changes in average costs over time

	Δ TOTAL	Δ BUSCOND	Δ PROD	Δ BESTPR	Δ INEFF
1997 - 98	0.94	1.01	0.93	0.96	0.96
1998 - 99	1.10	1.16	0.95	0.96	0.99
1999 - 00	1.22	1.26	0.96	0.96	1.00
2000 - 01	1.10	1.21	0.91	0.96	0.94
2001 - 02	0.93	0.97	0.97	0.96	1.00
2002 - 03	0.91	0.94	0.97	0.96	1.00
2003 - 04	1.03	1.03	0.99	0.96	1.03
1997 - 2004	1.20	1.67	0.71	0.77	0.93

Table 6

Model II - Outputs: Loans and deposits (by sector) excluding off-balance sheet
Decomposition of total changes in average costs over time

	Δ TOTAL	Δ BUSCOND	Δ PROD	Δ BESTPR	Δ INEFF
1997 - 98	0.94	1.01	0.93	0.97	0.96
1998 - 99	1.06	1.15	0.93	0.97	0.96
1999 - 00	1.23	1.31	0.94	0.97	0.97
2000 - 01	1.12	1.19	0.94	0.97	0.97
2001 - 02	0.95	0.97	0.99	0.97	1.02
2002 - 03	0.90	0.92	0.98	0.97	1.01
2003 - 04	1.01	1.04	0.97	0.97	1.00
1997 - 2004	1.19	1.68	0.71	0.78	0.91

Table 7

Model III - Outputs: Loans and deposits (by sector) including off-balance sheet
Decomposition of total changes in average costs over time

	Δ TOTAL	Δ BUSCOND	Δ PROD	Δ BESTPR	Δ INEFF
1997 - 98	1.04	1.10	0.94	0.96	0.98
1998 - 99	1.00	1.11	0.91	0.96	0.94
1999 - 00	1.16	1.24	0.94	0.96	0.98
2000 - 01	1.05	1.14	0.91	0.96	0.95
2001 - 02	0.94	0.96	0.98	0.96	1.01
2002 - 03	0.89	0.91	0.98	0.96	1.02
2003 - 04	1.04	1.05	0.99	0.96	1.03
1997 - 2004	1.10	1.57	0.70	0.77	0.91

Column on Δ PROD reveals the contribution of banks' productivity to gross change in operating costs; this can in turn be further decomposed into two parts. Δ BESTPR reflects the frontier shift as a consequence of technical progress, which in our model occurs at a constant annual rate. This is a direct result from the coefficient estimate associated to dummy variable T in Tables A.I–III in the Appendix, where the negative signs reveal a positive shift of the production frontier over time. This means that, holding all else equal, operating costs would have decreased 3% to 4% per year, more than 20% between 1997 and 2004. Canhoto and Dermine (2003) also found a positive frontier shift for period 1990–1995, using a non-parametric programming technique, DEA, and a Malmquist productivity index. The fact that similar results are found in all three models is an indication that technical progress is not intrinsically related to any specific outputs but to overall operating conditions such as IT developments, human resources training and management skills.

Finally we have the effect of "pure" inefficiency in column Δ INEFF. As we can see from the Tables, there is no evidence of a steady evolution over time; in turn, we can distinguish between two periods. In the first half of the sampling period, banks registered consecutive efficiency gains, of 6% at the most, in all three models considered but particularly in Model III; in 2001 however there was a stabilisation and, in the case of Model III a deterioration was registered. Overall, during this period, banks benefited from efficiency gains between 7% and 9%.

The combined effect of change in best practice and inefficiency allowed for productivity gains of nearly 30% between 1997 and 2004. Casu *et al.* (2004) provide interesting results for the European banking between 1994 and 2000. Over the entire 1994–2000 interval the cost of the average bank (ΔTOTAL) increased for France at an annual rate of 3.2%; cost productivity declined by the same amount (3.2%) while business conditions did not change significantly. The results for Germany show that cost of the average bank increased at an annual rate of 2.4% and cost productivity declined by 2.2% over 1994–2000, with ΔBUSCOND > 1 over all years. In Italy and Spain the total cost of the average bank fell at annual rates of 4.3% and 2.1% respectively. For both countries this has resulted in a significant improvement in productivity over 1994–2000 (+3.8% in Italy and +2.3% in Spain). However, in Italy business conditions as a whole reduced costs over all years. Furthermore, in France, results for the whole 1994–2000 interval suggest an unfavourable shift in best practice has occurred (–2.7%) and inefficiency has increased only slightly (+0.5%). In Germany results indicate that inefficiency has decreased slightly, while the change in best practice was similar to that experienced by the French banking sector (–2.7%). In Italy, best-practice banks display a significant improvement (5.8%), whereas efficiency worsened by 2.1%. Finally, in the Spanish banking sector both efficiency levels and best practice improved by approximately 0.5% and 1.9% respectively over the period.

d. Determinants of Inefficiency Scores

Irrespectively of the inclusion of a time trend in the objective function, the total effects model allows us to estimate simultaneously the cost inefficiencies of banks over time and the impact of associated variables. The results of this part of the equation are reflected in parameters estimates δ_0 to δ_{16} in Tables A.I–III in the Appendix. It is important to keep in mind that the dependent variable is the u_{it} in the model, the inefficiency score; a positive sign of the coefficient estimate indicates therefore a negative contribution of the corresponding independent variable to the cost efficiency level achieved by the bank because it increases its inefficiency score.

The first explanatory variable considered was **DEP mkt share**, to capture the scale effect measured by the market share in the deposits' market; we included also the squared term to allow for nonlinearities but, although statistically significant, the estimate is close to zero. The estimate for deposits' market share shows that, all else equal, an increase in the deposit market share is always associated with a decrease in cost inefficiency, irrespectively of the model specification.

For a better insight in terms of the influence of the *loan structure*, we used breakdowns by *sector* and *purpose*. In Model II and III, where the different sub-categories of loans and deposits are explicitly accounted for in the production function, the results are not statistically relevant for all variables. On the other hand, in Model I the results for the relative weight of loans granted to non-financial corporations (out of total loans) and for the relative weight of housing loans (out of total loans to households) reveal to have a positive contribution for a better performance in terms of cost efficiency. The positive effect of loans granted to non-financial corporations has to be read *ceteris paribus*, in the sense that, as we have seen previously, banks specialised in this sector are also the smallest ones, with lower efficiency levels. Housing loans (as opposed to loans for other purposes) have revealed to contribute positively to banks cost efficiency. Despite the fact that, *exante*, a housing loan is more time-consuming and demanding than a loan for other purposes, it seems to be the case that overall banks benefit from efficiency gains with this type of loan via, for example, small monitoring costs; eventually, with higher rates of non-performing loans and the almost inexistence of a collateral, loans for other purposes turn out to hinder banks' cost efficiency.

Table 8

Determinants of inefficiency scores

	Model I - Outputs: Loans and deposits (aggregated) excluding off-balance sheet		Model II - Outputs: Loans and deposits (by sector) excluding off-balance sheet		Model III - Outputs: Loans and deposits (by sector) including off-balance sheet	
	Value	t-statistic signif	Value	t-statistic signif	Value	t-statistic signif
δ0	1.09	4.09***	0.87	3.65***	0.02	0.05
Size						
DEP_mkt_share	-0.22	-10.68***	-0.14	-9.06***	-0.08	-3.19***
DEP_mkt_share^2	0.01	8.51***	0.00	5.01***	0.00	2.83***
Structure						
%_L_NFC	-0.02	-7.9***	-0.01	-2.45**	0.00	0.72
%_L_MTG	-0.02	-7.56***	0.00	-1.45	0.00	0.4
%_D_NFC	0.00	2.33**	0.00	-2.13**	0.00	0
Loans' quality						
NPL_NFC	0.06	5.64***	0.03	4.28***	0.03	4.32***
NPL_MTG	-0.26	-7.29***	-0.04	-2.43**	-0.11	-2.59***
NPL_OTH	0.01	1.32	0.01	2.13**	0.01	2.45**
Solvency	0.00	0.37	0.00	1.19	0.00	-0.77
%_OFF_BS	0.00	-10.62***	0.00	-0.97	0.00	-10.98***
dmy_MA	-0.14	-1.21	-0.13	-1.74*	-0.46	-1.77*
dmy_PRT	0.07	1.05	-0.14	-4.14***	-0.06	-1.35
GDP_growth	0.00	-0.15	-0.01	-0.7	-0.01	-0.48
HH	3.44	3.15***	0.52	0.56	-0.86	-0.59
coef_var_MM_ir	-0.01	-1.33	-0.01	-1.41	-0.01	-1.58
coef_var_stock_idx	0.00	-0.13	0.00	0.26	0.00	0.88

***, **, * - Significant at 1%, 5%, 10%, respectively.

The *quality of the banks' loan portfolio* is also often referred in the literature to be highly associated with the levels of cost efficiency achieved by the banks; in our case, only the results for the non-financial corporations sector and for other purposes are in line with the common findings (see Berger and DeYoung (1997), for example), with cost efficiency deteriorating with increases of the non-performing loans ratio. Given that the result is a statistical association rather than a causality relation we can think of interpretations on both directions. On the one hand, this result may be a consequence of the fact that when customers do not meet their regular payments, the bank is forced to engage in a costly and time-consuming process in order to renegotiate the terms of the contract or to execute the collateral, worsening therefore its efficiency levels. On the other hand, a bank relatively more inefficient may try to compensate for its inefficiency granting loans with higher risk, and therefore higher margins, but which are also more likely to default. Housing loans, on the contrary, have an unexpected positive contribution to cost efficiency and this result is common to all model specifications. First of all, we should note that the average for the ratio of non-performing housing loans is 0.6% with a maximum of 4.7%[11]. Nonetheless, it could be the case that, due to the *ex ante* relatively higher risk of such loans which eventually default, banks charge such higher spreads that, on average, allows them to benefit from efficiency gains.

Regarding the relative importance of *off-balance sheet outputs* the results do not seem to have a relevant impact on efficiency scores, even when these outputs are not included in the cost function. Although we would have expected *a priori* a different result, it could be the case that either banks are similarly efficient irrespectively of the specific output they produce, indicating that efficiency is more related to general operating conditions such as IT environment, human resources' training or management skills, or that the differences between banks regarding these activities is not (yet) sufficient to differentiate them regarding their cost efficiency levels.

In order to anticipate the effect of *M&A* on the cost efficiency levels we have included also a dummy variable to signal all banks involved in such processes. Except in Model I, the involvement in a merger process has a positive effect on cost efficiency. This can also be interpreted as an indication that banks involved in merger processes have cost performances better than average. These results will be dealt with in more detail in the next section.

As for the influence of the *bank market structure* we found a significant result in Model I for the concentration Herfindahl-Hirschman index: an increase in the market concentration leads to a strong deterioration of the industry's average cost efficiency which may be associated with some sluggishness effects derived from more market power in some banks.

---

[11] Contrasting with 3.2%-16.5% and 5.5%-30.1% for loans to non-financial corporations and other purposes, respectively.

Finally we tested also for the effects of *macroeconomic variables* which turned out to be not statistically relevant.

6. Effects of mergers

During the period covered in this study six mergers occurred, involving twelve banks. In this section we decompose the changes in total costs that were registered after the merger, distinguishing between scale, business conditions and productivity changes.

In order to assess the effects of a merger, we transpose the decomposition technique of the change in operating costs presented in the previous section to the banks involved in the merger. Let F be the final institution resulting from the merger that occurred in period *t* between bank A and bank B, and let AB be a fictional bank, a *proforma* institution, equal to A+B in period *t-1*. The idea is to break the gross change between bank F and banks A and B in two parts: the first part compares the change in costs that occurs when we move from bank A plus bank B to a fictional bank that produces a joint output equal to the sum of A with B, under conditions that replicate the weighted average of bank A and bank B in terms of input prices; this is observed in the same period, therefore no time effects occur. The second part analyses the change in operating costs between the final institution F that results from the merger, in period *t*, and the *proforma* bank AB in *t-1*. Additionally, each of these parts can be further decomposed into an efficient and an inefficient component.

$$\Delta \text{ TOTAL } C_{F,t;\, A,t-1 + B,t-1} = [C^*(Y_{F,t}, w_{F,t}, B_{F,t}, t) \text{ x } \exp(u_{F,t})] / \{[C^*(Y_{A,t-1}, w_{A,t-1}, B_{A,t-1}, t-1)\text{x}\exp(u_{A,t-1})]+[C^*(Y_{B,t-1}, w_{B,t-1}, B_{B,t-1}, t-1)\text{x}\exp(u_{B,t-1})]\} \quad (21)$$

The decomposition of this gross change is as follows:

$$\Delta \text{ TOTAL } C_{F,t;\, A,t-1 + B,t-1} =$$

$$C^*(Y_{AB,t-1}, w_{AB,t-1}, B_{AB,t-1}, t-1) /$$

$$[C^*(Y_{A,t-1}, w_{A,t-1}, B_{A,t-1}, t-1)+ C^*(Y_{B,t-1}, w_{B,t-1}, B_{B,t-1}, t-1)] \quad (22)$$

$$\text{x } \exp(u_{AB,t-1}) / [p_{A,t-1}\exp(u_{A,t-1}) \text{ x } p_{B,t-1}\exp(u_{B,t-1})] \quad (23)$$

$$\text{x } C^*(Y_{F,t}, w_{F,t}, B_{F,t}, t) / C^*(Y_{AB,t-1}, w_{AB,t-1}, B_{AB,t-1}, t-1) \quad (24)$$

$$\text{x } \exp(u_{F,t}) / \exp(u_{AB,t-1}) \quad (25)$$

where

$$p_{A,t-1} = C^*(Y_{A,t-1}, w_{A,t-1}, B_{A,t-1}, t-1) /$$

$$[C^*(Y_{A,t-1}, w_{A,t-1}, B_{A,t-1}, t-1) + C^*(Y_{B,t-1}, w_{B,t-1}, B_{B,t-1}, t-1)]; \quad (26)$$

$$p_{A,t-1} + p_{B,t-1} = 1. \quad (27)$$

Moreover, component (24) can be further broken in order to separate the effects of change in business conditions from change in best practice, just as it was shown in the previous section. We have for (24):

$C^*(Y_{F,t}, w_{F,t}, B_{F,t}, t) / C^*(Y_{AB,t-1}, w_{AB,t-1}, B_{AB,t-1}, t)$
(change in business conditions) - (24.a)
$\times C^*(Y_{AB,t-1}, w_{AB,t-1}, B_{AB,t-1}, t) / C^*(Y_{AB,t-1}, w_{AB,t-1}, B_{AB,t-1}, t-1)$
(change in best practice) - (24.b)

In component (22) we have the change that results directly from a dimension effect, a higher scale of production; we compare the estimated efficient cost of bank AB jointly producing output A+B against the sum of estimated cost of bank A producing output A with the estimated cost of bank B producing output B. Cost estimate for bank AB is obtained by applying the coefficient estimates of the parameters in our function to the corresponding sum of output levels and number of branches and weighted averages of input prices.

The second component accounts for the different inefficiency scores presented by banks A, B and AB. For banks A and B we use the relative shares in aggregated cost as the respective weights for $\exp(u_{A,t-1})$ and $\exp(u_{B,t-1})$. For bank AB we derive $\exp(u_{AB,t-1})$ as a weighted average of the inefficiency scores of banks with similar dimension to AB in period t. From what was presented in the previous section, component (23) is most likely to be influenced by differences in deposits market share, in the structure of loans and deposits and the quality of the loans' portfolio.

The third component (24) reflects, on the one hand, the changes in business conditions (24.a) between the institution that results after the merger and the proforma bank of similar dimensions in the previous year; it reflects, among other, a change in the output structure, changes in the input prices, a redesign of the branching network. On the other hand, it accounts also for a change in the technology (24.b), a shift of the cost frontier between *t* and *t-1*; some authors argue that it takes several years for the effects derived from the merger to be fully absorbed therefore a period *t+k*, k > 1, can also be used as the reference.

Finally we have component (25) accounting for the different cost inefficiency scores achieved by bank F and AB. Factors that contribute to this difference include all the explanatory variables we considered in section VI.4, although these variables are not expected to change dramatically between *t-1* and *t*. This fact opens the door to look for specific factors associated with the merger.

Table 9

Decomposition of total changes in estimated costs following M&A

	(1)	(2)	(3) = (4) x (5)	(4)	(5)	(6)	(7) = (1) x (2) x (3) x (6)	(8) = (4) x (6)
	C*A +B/ (C*A + C*B)	INEFF A+B / (wA*INEFF A + wB * INEFF B)	C*F / C* A+B	Δ BUS COND	Δ BEST PR	INEFF F /INEFF A+B	Δ TOTAL	Δ "pure" MA
One year after the merger								
Model I	1.07	0.99	0.97	1.01	0.96	0.98	1.01	0.99
Model II	1.15	0.99	0.97	1.00	0.96	0.95	1.05	0.95
Model III	1.13	0.98	0.97	1.00	0.96	0.95	1.01	0.95
At the last observation period								
Model I	1.07	0.99	0.89	1.01	0.87	0.99	0.93	0.99
Model II	1.15	0.99	0.87	0.97	0.88	0.96	0.94	0.92
Model III	1.13	0.98	0.84	0.95	0.87	0.97	0.88	0.91

In Table 9 above, we present the mean results for the six mergers that occurred in the period under study. We consider first the immediate effects one year after the merger and then the longer term effects evaluated at the last observation period. Starting with the scale effects, measured for the year before the merger occurs, we register an increase in costs estimates from 7% in Model I to 13% and 15% in Models III and II, respectively; this cost increase for a higher scale of production is very much explained by the increase in the number of branches; as we saw in the previous section, operating costs are increasingly sensitive to the expansion of the branching network.

The weighted average of the efficiency levels of the banks involved in the merger is nearly the same as the mean efficiency level of banks with an output volume close to that of the *proforma* bank. These two indicators taken together would *a priori* lead to no cost gains from merging. Nevertheless, when we move the analysis to the bank that actually resulted from the merger we see that already in the first year after the merger we register some cost savings, even though quite modest, around 3% in all model specifications. However, looking to the results at the last observation period, we observe much more significant cost gains, particularly in Model III, where off-balance sheet items were included. Columns (4) to (6) reveal the sources from these gains. In the first year, as one would reasonably accept, the business conditions barely change; the "new" merged bank is still at its inception, no structural modifications are likely to be introduced and become effective in the first year. It might even been the case that the bank experiences an increase in total costs due to extra operating costs related to the merger process itself, such as layoffs, new *logo* (advertising and refurbishing the branches) and personnel training, among other things. In the following years, the changes in costs differ according to the model specification. While in Model I nearly no changes occur, in Models II and III banks seem to select a better combination of inputs/outputs allowing for cost savings of 3% to 5%. As expected from the results presented in section VI.4, technological progress–column (5)–also plays a determinant role and is a major contributor to relevant cost savings. However, this effect would have occurred irrespectively of the merger. Finally, in terms of cost efficiency levels, there are some modest gains in the first year with a very slight deterioration considering a larger time lag after the merger. Isolating the "pure" merger effects–columns (4) and (6)–we conclude that, on average, total gains are larger for Models II and III, with cost reductions of 8% and 9% respectively. Total effects are more evident in Model III, with cost savings amounting to 12%. Orea (2002), using data from Spanish savings banks for the period 1985–1998, found that non-merged banks are on average more efficient than merged banks; on the change in technical efficiency over time, the results indicate that technical efficiency is time-invariant for non-merged banks but not for merged banks, which show an initial decrease in technical efficiency, followed by efficiency gains as the new entities reorganise their activity.

7. Concluding remarks

In this article we studied the cost efficiency in the Portuguese banking industry, between 1997 and 2004, using a parametric approach for a multi-output production function that better reflects the output mix chosen by banks. On the one hand, we have treated separately loans (deposits) by type of borrower (investor)–non-financial corporations and households–, and households' loans by purpose–housing and other purposes, namely consumption; on the other hand we have also included off-balance sheet outputs–bank managed funds and securitised loans. Securitisation in Portugal is a recent phenomenon but has grown impressively throughout the last decade justifying the need to be accounted for, in order to have a complete profile of the banking activity. Our results show that the measures of marginal costs are affected by the specification of the production function. Pastor and Serrano (2006) provide also additional support for taking bank specialisation into account, decomposing cost inefficiencies into inefficiencies associated with specialisation within the banking system and inefficiencies within bank specialisation.

We found that banks have compensated with productivity gains the increase in operating costs due to changes in the business conditions. In particular, technological progress (best practice) has contributed to a shift of the efficient frontier allowing for relevant cost savings; nevertheless, the efficiency levels have evolved irregularly over time. Total estimated costs increased by roughly 20%, between 1997 and 2004, considering only on-balance sheet outputs (Models I and II) while accounting also for off-balance sheet outputs in Model III the total increase is only 10%; this results from increases of around 70% (Models I and II) and 60% (Model III) due to business conditions, partially outweighed by productivity gains of nearly 30% between 1997 and 2004 derived from the combined effect of change in best practice (technological progress) and some efficiency gains. Casu *et al.* (2004) in a study on parametric and non-parametric estimates of productivity change in European banking during the 1990s found clear productivity growth in the Italian and Spanish banking sectors, whereas results are mixed for French and German banking; their findings suggest also that (where found) productivity growth has mainly been brought about by technical change and there does not appear to have been catching up on the part of non-best practice institutions.

On the determinants of cost efficiency, variables related to banks' dimension, structure and quality of the loans' portfolio consistently play a significant role in explaining differences in banks' cost efficiency levels and over time. Finally, on the measurement of "pure" merger effects we observe that they are more evident when the different markets' segments are taken separately and when off-balance sheet items are included.

We would like to put forward some caveats in our study that may limit the interpretation of the results. First of all, the conclusions apply to a single country only, which means that the frontier is being shaped ignoring foreign best-practice banks; however, harmonised bank level data for the different segments of loans and deposits and for specific off-balance sheet items are not available in international databases. Another limitation is related to the reduced number of merger events that does not allow for a more robust assessment of merger effects and their determinants.

Nevertheless, these results provide a valuable input for further research. We will conduct a similar study from a profit perspective and, combining the estimates of marginal costs with detailed data on interest rates for each (on-balance sheet) output category, we will assess both the pattern of competition in the Portuguese banking industry and the degree of market power of banks operating in Portugal.

References

Akhavein, J. D., Berger, A. N., Humphrey, D. B. (1997), The effects of megamergers on efficiency and prices: evidence from a bank profit function, *Review of Industrial Organization*, 12, 95–139.

Altunbas, Y., Gardener, E. P. M., Molyneux, P., Moore, B. (2001), Efficiency in European banking, *European Economic Review*, 45, 1931–1955.

Altunbas, Y., Goddard, J., Molyneux, P. (1999), Technical change in banking, *Economic Letters*, 64, 215–221.

Amel, D., Barnes, C., Panetta, F., Salleo, C. (2004), Consolidation and efficiency in the financial sector: a review of the international evidence, *Journal of Banking and Finance*, 28, 2493–2519.

Battese, G. E., Coelli, T. J. (1988), Prediction of Firm-Level Technical Efficiencies With a Generalised Frontier Production Function and Panel Data, *Journal of Econometrics*, 38, 387-399.

Battese, G. E., Coelli, T. J. (1992), Frontier Production Functions, Technical Efficiency and Panel Data: With Application to Paddy Farmers in India, *Journal of Productivity Analysis*, 3, 153–169.

Battese, G. E., Coelli, T. J. (1995), A Model for Technical Inefficiency Effects in a Stochastic Frontier Production Function for Panel Data, *Empirical Economics*, 20, 325–332.

Battese, G. E., Corra, G. S. (1977), Estimation of a Production Frontier Model: With Application to the Pastoral Zone of Eastern Australia, *Australian Journal of Agricultural Economics*, 21, 169-179.

Bauer, P., A. Berger, G. Ferrier, D. Humphrey (1998), Consistency Conditions for Regulatory Analysis of Financial Institutions: A Comparison of Frontier Efficiency Methods, *Journal of Economics and Business,* 50, 85–114.

Berger, A. N., DeYoung, R. (1997), Problem loans and cost efficiency in commercial banks, *Journal of Banking and Finance*, 21, 849–870.

Berger, A. N., Hanweck, G., Humphrey, D. B. (1987), Competitive viability and banking: scale, scope and product mix economies, *Journal of Monetary Economics*, 20, 501–20.

Berger, A. N., Mester, L. J. (1997), Inside the black-box: what explains differences in the efficiencies of financial institutions, *Journal of Banking and Finance*, 21, 895–947.

Berger, A. N., Mester, L. J. (2003), Explaining the dramatic changes in performance of US banks: technological change, deregulation and dynamic changes in competition, *Journal of Financial Intermediation*, 12, 57–95.

Bikker, J. A. (2004), *Competition and efficiency in a unified European banking market*, Edward Elgar Publishing Limited, Cheltenham, UK.

Canhoto, A., Dermine, J. (2003), A note on banking efficiency in Portugal, New vs. Old banks, *Journal of Banking and Finance*, 27, 2087–2098.

Casolaro, L., Gobbi, G. (2007), Information technology and productivity changes in the banking industry, *Economic Notes by Banca Monte dei Paschi di Siena SpA*, 36, 43–76.

Casu, B., Girardone, C. (2005), An analysis of the relevance of off-balance sheet items in explaining productivity change in European banking, *Applied Financial Economics*, 15, 1053–1061.

Casu, B., Girardone, C., Molyneux, P. (2004), Productivity change in European banking: A comparison of parametric and non-parametric approaches, *Journal of Banking and Finance*, 28, 2521–2540.

Casu, B., Molyneux, P. (2003), A comparative study of efficiency in European banking, *Applied Economics*, 35, 1865–1876.

Clark, J. A., Siems, T. F. (2002), X-efficiency in banking: looking beyond the balance sheet, *Journal of Money, Credit, and Banking*, 34, 987–1013.

Coelli, T. (1996), A Guide to FRONTIER Version 4.1: A Computer Program for Stochastic Frontier Production and Cost Function Estimation, *Centre for Efficiency and Productivity Analysis, Working paper 96/07.*

European Central Bank, 2004, *Report on EU banking structure,* European Central Bank, Frankfurt, October.

—. 2005, *EU banking structures*, European Central Bank, Frankfurt, November.

—. 2008, *Monthly Bulletin*, European Central Bank, Frankfurt, February.

Farrel, M. J. (1957), The measurement of productive efficiency, Journal of Royal Statistical Society, 120, sec A, 253–281.

Goddard, J., Molyneux, P., Wilson, J. O. S., Tavakoli, M. (2007), European banking: An overview, *Journal of Banking and Finance*, 31, 1911–1935.

Holló, D., Nagy, M. (2006), *Bank Efficiency in the Enlarged European Union*, Magyar Nemzeti Bank Working Papers, 2006/3.

Humphrey, D. (1992), Flow versus stock measures of banking output: effects on productivity and scale economy measurement, *Journal of Financial Services Research*, 6, 115–35.

Jondrow, J., Lovell, C. A. K Materov, I. S., Schmidt, P. (1982), On estimation of Technical Inefficiency in the Stochastic Frontier Production Function Model, *Journal of Econometrics*, 19, 233-238.

Mendes, V., and Rebelo, J. (1999), Productive efficiency, technological change and productivity in Portuguese banking, *Applied Financial Economics*, 9, 513–521.

Orea, L. (2002), Parametric decomposition of a generalized Malmquist productivity index, *Journal of Productivity Analysis*, 18, 5–22.

Pastor, J. M., Serrano, L. (2006), The effect of specialisation on banks' efficiency: an international comparison, *International Review of Applied Economics*, 20, 125–149.

Pinho, P. S. (2001), Using accounting data to measure efficiency in banking: an application to Portugal, *Applied Financial Economics*, 11, 527–538.

Rezitis, A. N. (2006), Productivity growth in the Greek banking industry: a non-parametric approach, *Journal of Applied Economics*, 9, 119–138.

Schmidt, P., Lovell, C. A. K. (1979), Estimating Technical and Allocative Inefficiency Relative to Stochastic Production and Cost Frontiers, *Journal of Econometrics*, 9, 343-366.

Weill, L. (2004), Measuring cost efficiency in European banking: a comparison of frontier techniques, *Journal of Productivity Analysis*, 21, 133–152.

Appendix

Table A.I

Model I - Outputs: Loans and deposits (aggregated) excluding off-balance sheet

Frontier estimates

Parameter	Value	Std error	t-statistic signif
Constant	-49.67	2.15	-23.15***
β L_NFC	-1.30	0.71	-1.82*
β D_NFC	5.06	0.71	7.11***
α N	3.47	0.72	4.78***
δ L_NFC_2	0.08	0.04	2**
δ D_NFC_2	-0.10	0.05	-1.88*
δ L_NFC, D_NFC	-0.01	0.04	-0.35
γ N,N	0.09	0.09	1.02
ρ L_NFC,N	0.03	0.07	0.45
ρ D_NFC,N	-0.22	0.06	-3.93***
ψ B	-1.22	0.31	-3.89***
ψ B,B	0.08	0.02	4.67***
ψ L_NFC,B	-0.06	0.02	-2.85***
ψ D_NFC,B	0.07	0.02	4.46***
ψ B,K	-0.08	0.02	-3.61***
τ	-0.04	0.01	-6.68***
δ0	1.09	0.27	4.09***
DEP_mkt_share	-0.22	0.02	-10.68***
DEP_mkt_share^2	0.01	0.00	8.51***
%_L_NFC	-0.02	0.00	-7.9***
%_L_MTG	-0.02	0.00	-7.56***
%_D_NFC	0.00	0.00	2.33**
NPL_NFC	0.06	0.01	5.64***
NPL_MTG	-0.26	0.04	-7.29***
NPL_OTH	0.01	0.00	1.32
Solvency	0.00	0.01	0.37
%_OFF_BS	0.00	0.00	-10.62***
dmy_MA	-0.14	0.12	-1.21
dmy_PRT	0.07	0.07	1.05
GDP_growth	0.00	0.03	-0.15
HH	3.44	1.09	3.15***
coef_var_MM_ir	-0.01	0.01	-1.33
coef_var_stock_idx	0.00	0.01	-0.13
σ2	0.08	0.01	11.27***
γ	0.67	0.04	18.52***

***, **, * - Significant at 1%, 5%, 10%, respectively.

Table A.II

Model II - Outputs: Loans and deposits (by sector) excluding off-balance sheet

Frontier estimates

Parameter	Value	Std error	t-statistic signif
Constant	-47.92	5.94	-8.07***
β L_NFC	0.09	0.53	0.17
β L_MTG	-0.53	0.19	-2.8***
β L_OTH	-0.28	0.26	-1.09
β D_NFC	2.22	0.53	4.22***
β D_HH	2.28	0.36	6.26***
α N	3.47	0.85	4.06***
δ L_NFC_2	0.11	0.03	3.11***
δ L_MTG_2	0.01	0.00	2.74***
δ L_OTH_2	0.01	0.00	4.31***
δ D_NFC_2	0.03	0.04	0.77
δ D_HH_2	-0.03	0.01	-3.48***
δ L_NFC, L_MTG	0.03	0.01	3.46***
δ L_NFC, L_OTH	0.01	0.01	0.87
δ L_NFC, D_NFC	-0.07	0.03	-2.22**
δ L_NFC, D_HH	-0.11	0.02	-4.75***
δ L_MTG, L_OTH	0.00	0.00	-0.68
δ L_MTG, D_NFC	-0.02	0.01	-2.37**
δ L_MTG, D_HH	0.02	0.01	3.71***
δ L_OTH, D_NFC	0.01	0.01	0.93
δ L_OTH, D_HH	0.01	0.00	1.9*
δ D_NFC, D_HH	0.03	0.02	2.03**
γ N,N	0.02	0.08	0.22
ρ L_NFC,N	0.06	0.05	1.13
ρ L_MTG,N	0.00	0.01	0.03
ρ L_OTH,N	-0.01	0.01	-1.01
ρ D_NFC,N	-0.14	0.04	-3.09***
ρ D_HH,N	-0.08	0.02	-3.19***
ψ B	-1.70	0.39	-4.31***
ψ B,B	0.09	0.03	3.44***
ψ L_NFC,B	0.00	0.02	-0.17
ψ L_MTG,B	-0.05	0.01	-7.29***
ψ L_OTH,B	-0.03	0.01	-3.14***
ψ D_NFC,B	0.02	0.02	1.21
ψ D_HH,B	0.09	0.01	6.09***
ψ B,K	-0.10	0.03	-2.95***
τ	-0.04	0.01	-6.49***
δ0	0.87	0.24	3.65***
DEP_mkt_share	-0.14	0.02	-9.06***
DEP_mkt_share^2	0.00	0.00	5.01***
%_L_NFC	-0.01	0.00	-2.45**
%_L_MTG	0.00	0.00	-1.45
%_D_NFC	0.00	0.00	-2.13**

Model II - Outputs: Loans and deposits (by sector) excluding off-balance sheet			
Frontier estimates			
Parameter	Value	Std error	t-statistic signif
NPL_NFC	0.03	0.01	4.28***
NPL_MTG	-0.04	0.02	-2.43**
NPL_OTH	0.01	0.00	2.13**
Solvency	0.00	0.00	1.19
%_OFF_BS	0.00	0.00	-0.97
dmy_MA	-0.13	0.08	-1.74*
dmy_PRT	-0.14	0.03	-4.14***
GDP_growth	-0.01	0.02	-0.7
HH	0.52	0.93	0.56
coef_var_MM_ir	-0.01	0.01	-1.41
coef_var_stock_idx	0.00	0.01	0.26
σ2	0.04	0.00	18.07***
γ	0.55	0.06	9.49***
***, **, * - Significant at 1%, 5%, 10%, respectively.			

Table A.III

Model III - Outputs: Loans and deposits (by sector) including off-balance sheet

Frontier estimates

Parameter	Value	Std error	t-statistic signif
Constant	-30.49	6.43	-4.74***
β L_NFC	-1.48	0.44	-3.33***
β L_MTG	-0.39	0.19	-2.08**
β L_OTH	0.51	0.27	1.87*
β D_NFC	2.19	0.43	5.09***
β D_HH	2.42	0.33	7.44***
β SL	0.56	0.10	5.73***
β F	0.36	0.19	1.95*
α N	1.27	0.89	1.44
δ L_NFC_2	0.14	0.03	4.48***
δ L_MTG_2	0.01	0.00	4.82***
δ L_OTH_2	0.02	0.00	6.08***
δ D_NFC_2	0.02	0.03	0.5
δ D_HH_2	-0.02	0.01	-3.12***
δ SL	0.00	0.00	-0.7
δ F	0.00	0.00	0.98
δ L_NFC, L_MTG	0.02	0.01	2.37**
δ L_NFC, L_OTH	-0.01	0.01	-1.38
δ L_NFC, D_NFC	-0.03	0.03	-0.91
δ L_NFC, D_HH	-0.12	0.02	-5.23***
δ L_NFC, SL	-0.01	0.00	-2.94***
δ L_NFC, F	-0.02	0.01	-2**
δ L_MTG, L_OTH	0.00	0.00	0.55
δ L_MTG, D_NFC	-0.01	0.01	-0.67
δ L_MTG, D_HH	0.01	0.01	2.29**
δ L_MTG, SL	0.00	0.00	0.91
δ L_MTG, F	0.00	0.00	-1.21
δ L_OTH, D_NFC	0.01	0.01	1.1
δ L_OTH, D_HH	0.00	0.00	0,09
δ L_OTH, SL	-0.01	0.00	-3.34***
δ L_OTH, F	-0.01	0.00	-2.45**
δ D_NFC, D_HH	0.02	0.02	1.3
δ D_NFC, SL	0.00	0.00	1.14
δ D_NFC, F	-0.01	0.01	-1.13
δ D_HH, SL	-0.01	0.00	-2.59***
δ D_HH, F	0.00	0.01	0.26
δ SL, F	0.00	0.00	1.96**
γ N,N	0.12	0.08	1.5
ρ L_NFC,N	0.14	0.04	3.07***
ρ L_MTG,N	-0.01	0.01	-1
ρ L_OTH,N	-0.04	0.01	-2.85***
ρ D_NFC,N	-0.17	0.04	-4.91***
ρ D_HH,N	-0.04	0.02	-1.97**

Model III - Outputs: Loans and deposits (by sector) including off-balance sheet			
Frontier estimates			
Parameter	Value	Std error	t-statistic signif
ρ SL,N	-0.02	0.00	-4.54***
ρ F,N	0.02	0.01	1.95*
ψ B	-2.21	0.40	-5.58***
ψ B,B	0.07	0.03	2.51**
ψ L_NFC,B	0.03	0.02	1.41
ψ L_MTG,B	-0.05	0.01	-7.13***
ψ L_OTH,B	-0.01	0.01	-1.16
ψ D_NFC,B	-0.02	0.02	-1.03
ψ D_HH,B	0.09	0.01	6.38***
ψ SL,B	0.03	0.01	4.08***
ψ F,B	0.03	0.01	4.42***
ψ B,K	-0.08	0.03	-2.85***
τ	-0.04	0.01	-5.6***
δ0	0.02	0.48	0.05
DEP_mkt_share	-0.08	0.03	-3.19***
DEP_mkt_share^2	0.00	0.00	2.83***
%_L_NFC	0.00	0.00	0.72
%_L_MTG	0.00	0.00	0.4
%_D_NFC	0.00	0.00	0
NPL_NFC	0.03	0.01	4.32***
NPL_MTG	-0.11	0.04	-2.59***
NPL_OTH	0.01	0.00	2.45**
Solvency	0.00	0.01	-0.77
%_OFF_BS	0.00	0.00	-10.98***
dmy_MA	-0.46	0.26	-1.77*
dmy_PRT	-0.06	0.05	-1.35
GDP_growth	-0.01	0.02	-0.48
HH	-0.86	1.45	-0.59
coef_var_MM_ir	-0.01	0.01	-1.58
coef_var_stock_idx	0.00	0.01	0.88
σ2	0.05	0.01	4.84***
γ	0.86	0.04	21.07***
***, **, * - Significant at 1%, 5%, 10%, respectively.			

Acknowledgments

The author is grateful for the support and suggestions from Paulo Soares de Pinho. Any errors or shortcomings remain her responsibility. She also thanks *Banco de Portugal*, and the Directors of the Statistics Department in particular – Mr. João Cadete de Matos and Mr. António Garcia, for providing support for this research. The analyses, opinions and findings of this paper represent the views of the author; they are not necessarily those of the *Banco de Portugal*.

CHAPTER THREE

IS THERE A NONLINEAR MEAN REVERSION IN THE TERM STRUCTURE OF INTEREST RATES AT THE POLISH INTERBANK MARKET?

MARIA BLANGIEWICZ
AND PAWEŁ MIŁOBĘDZKI

Abstract

The paper reports the results of testing for a mean reversion in the term structure of interest rates at the Polish interbank market and its possible nonlinearity due to transaction costs. In doing so the conventional linear vector error correction model (VECM) and its three-regime threshold alternative of Seo (2003) are applied. The analysis is performed on the sample of 208 weekly observations on the Warsaw Interbank Offer Rates (WIBORs) for deposits of maturities ranging from 1 week to 6 months from the period January 2003-December 2006. The significance of adjustment coefficients in the corresponding linear VECMs supports predictability of both the short and the long rates. Despite the strong evidence of nonlinearity in mean reversion, the Seo's model performs relatively worse. The estimated thresholds separate the regions of different adjustment speed of the short and the long interest rates to their long-run equilibrium relation and can hardly be attributed to the transaction costs.

Keywords: expectations hypothesis, transaction costs, threshold co-integration

1. Introduction

In this paper we test for a nonlinear mean reversion in the term structure of interest rates at the Polish interbank market. When doing so we follow Seo (2003), who used a three-regime threshold vector error correction model (threshold VECM) to predict the term structure of the U.S. bond market. He constructed his model presuming that nonlinearity was due to the existence of transaction costs in financial markets which at times could hardly be covered by investors exercising arbitrage opportunities. Building on Mankiw and Summers (1984), he modified the expectations hypothesis (EH) assuming that future changes in the short-term rate were explained by the time-varying liquidity premium, which followed a threshold autoregressive process of Tong (1978). This led him to the long and the short-term interest rates threshold co-integration (Balke and Fomby, 1997). The model allows for an asymmetric mean reversion in the outer regimes in which the term spread exceeds certain levels of transaction costs, and for the persistence of the term spread in the inner regime, otherwise.

We believe that transaction costs in financial markets are a problem of greater importance in transition economies than in mature economies. In the case of the Polish interbank market it is mainly due to constraints stemming from its regulations (bid-ask spreads for deposits of all maturities, limits set on their obligatory acceptance within the daily trade) and from monetary policies held by the National Bank of Poland aimed towards achieving its direct inflationary goal (interest rate targeting, banking sector overliquidity management) (NBP 1998, 2005). We suppose that Seo's model may better capture some of their consequences regarding interest rates behaviour than the linear VECM widely used in the term structure modelling (Hall et al. 1992, Cuthbertson 1996, Tzavalis and Wickens 1997, Jondeau and Ricart 1999, Konstantinou 2005). We estimate this model using the sample of 208 weekly observations on the Warsaw Interbank Offer Rates (WIBORs) for deposits of maturities ranging from 1 week (WIBOR_1W) to 6 months (WIBOR_6M), from the period January 2003-December 2006, and compare its performance with that of the linear VECM. The reason we discarded from the sample pré 2003 observations is that in the beginning and the middle of transition the central bank held the tough interest rates stabilization policy, which is thought to undermine the predictive power of the term spreads (Mankiw and Miron 1986, Kugler 1988). The other reason stems from Konstantinou (2005) who, while working on the set of daily WIBORs from June 1995 through January 2003, found the co-integrating properties of the term spreads on the boundary of acceptance region and a marginal acceptance of parameter restrictions imposed by the EH for the short-end of maturity spectrum.

The rest of the paper is organized as follows. In Section 2 we briefly demonstrate how to model the term structure of interest rates in the presence of transaction costs using a threshold vector error correction model built under the EH, and discuss econometric issues relating to its estimation. In Section 3 we report empirical results of testing for a nonlinear mean reversion in the term structure at the Polish interbank market and assess the levels of transaction costs. The last section concludes.

2. Modelling the term structure in the presence of transaction costs

The EH implies that the term spread between long-term interest rate $R_t^{(n)}$ and its short-term counterpart $R_t^{(m)}$ is equal to (Campbell and Shiller 1991)

$$S_t^{(n,m)} = E_t \sum_{i=1}^{k-1} \left(1 - \frac{i}{k}\right) \Delta^m R_{t+im}^{(m)} + \theta(n,m) \tag{1-1}$$

for any $n > m$ and $k = n/m$ an integer, where $\Delta^m R_t^{(m)} = R_{t+m}^{(m)} - R_t^{(m)}$, E_t and $\theta(n,m)$ stand for the expectations operator at time t and a liquidity premium. If additionally $R_t^{(m)}$ is integrated of order one and the liquidity premium is stationary but not necessarily constant with varying n and m, both rates are co-integrated with co-integrating vector $\beta = [1 \quad -1]'$, so that upon the Granger representation theorem the long and the short-term interest rate behaviour is to be described using a bivariate linear VECM of order p (Engle and Granger 1987)

$$\Delta y_t = \mu + \alpha z_{t-1} + \sum_{i=1}^{p} B_i \Delta y_{t-i} + u_t \tag{1-2}$$

where: $y_t = \left[R_t^{(n)} \; R_t^{(m)}\right]$, $z_t = \beta' y_t$, $\mu - [2 \times 1]$ vector of constants, $\alpha - [2 \times 1]$ vector of adjustment coefficients, $B_i - [2 \times 2]$ matrix of coefficients, $u_t - [2 \times 1]$ vector of error terms. Thus if adjustment coefficients in vector α are close to zero, the interest rates do not respond to the past term spread. If they are different from zero to stationarity, the interest rates react to the term spread, so the latter is said to be mean-reverting.

Alternatively, if s interest rates are integrated of order one, equation (1-1) implies that a set of s yield spreads should span a co-integration space of rank $s-1$ so that any yield series is co-integrated with one period yield, and an s-dimensional linear VECM instead of model (1-2) is to be employed in modeling the term structure. Its estimation is usually performed using Johansen's (1988) method. Restrictions imposed on μ 's ($\mu = \mu_0 = \psi d_0$) allow to test for an appropriate version of the EH, i.e. the pure, the constant premium and the liquidity preference EH[1].

Now following Seo (2003, 2250) suppose that liquidity premium $\theta(n,m)$ in equation (1-1) is time-varying and obeys a threshold autoregressive (TAR) process

$$\theta_t = \begin{cases} \phi_1\theta_{t-1} + \eta_t & S_{t-1}^{(n,m)} \le c_1 \\ \phi_2\theta_{t-1} + \eta_t \quad for & c_1 < S_{t-1}^{(n,m)} \le c_2 \\ \phi_3\theta_{t-1} + \eta_t & S_{t-1}^{(n,m)} > c_2 \end{cases}, \tag{1-3}$$

where: $E_{t-1}(\eta_t) = 0$, ϕ_w–regime specific autoregressive parameters ($w = 1,2,3$), c_1, c_2 –constants. This implies that also a term spread is the TAR process and its mean-reverting behaviour can be described by the following threshold VECM model:

$$\Delta y_t = (\mu_1 + \alpha_1 z_{t-1} + \sum_1^p B_{1i}\Delta y_{t-i}) \times I_{1t} + (\mu_2 + \alpha_2 z_{t-1} + \sum_1^p B_{2i}\Delta y_{t-i}) \times I_{2t} + \\ + (\mu_3 + \alpha_3 z_{t-1} + \sum_1^p B_{3i}\Delta y_{t-i}) \times I_{3t} + u_t \tag{1-4}$$

where: $I_{1t} = 1$ if $z_{t-1} \le c_1$ and $I_{1t} = 0$, otherwise, $I_{2t} = 1$ if $c_1 < z_{t-1} \le c_2$ and $I_{2t} = 0$, otherwise, and $I_{3t} = 1$ if $z_{t-1} > c_2$ and $I_{3t} = 0$, otherwise. The specification implies that all model parameters are regime specific and depend upon the size of term spread in relation to thresholds c_1 and c_2. The latter exhibit the shadow costs of mean reversion. Thus it is expected that in the inner regime, in which the term spread does not exceed the transaction costs, the adjustment parameters in vector α_2 are close to zero, both interest rates do not respond to the term spread, and the term spread is persistent. In the outer regimes, however, in which the term spread

---

[1] In this case a linear VECM reads $\Delta y_t = \psi(\beta' z_{t-1} + d_0) + \sum_{i=1}^p B_i \Delta y_{t-i} + u_t$, where $\alpha = \psi\beta'$, ψ and β are matrices of rank $s-1$, and d_0 is an $[(s-1)\times 1]$ vector of constants representing liquidity premia, see (Tsay 2005, 381-383).

exceeds the transaction costs, the adjustment parameters in vectors α_1 and α_3 are different from zero to stationarity, so that the long and the short-term interest rates react to the term spread with the regime specific speed, and the term spread is nonlinearly mean-reverting.

Testing for nonlinearity in mean-reversion is based on the following respecification of the threshold VECM

$$\Delta y_t = (\mu + \alpha z_{t-1} + \sum_1^p B_i \Delta y_{t-i}) + [(\mu_1 - \mu) + (\alpha_1 - \alpha) z_{t-1} + \sum_1^p (B_{1i} - B_i) \Delta y_{t-i}] \times I_{1t} +$$

$$+[(\mu_3 - \mu) + (\alpha_3 - \alpha) z_{t-1} + \sum_1^p (B_{3i} - B) \Delta y_{t-i}] \times I_{3t} + u_t \qquad (1\text{-}5)$$

The null and the alternative (linear versus nonlinear mean-reversion) are $H_0 : \delta = 0$ and $H_A : \delta \neq 0$, where: $\delta = [\delta_1' \ \ \delta_3']$, $\delta_w = \left[\mu_w' - \mu \ \ \alpha_w' - \alpha' \ \ B_{w1}' - B_1' \ldots, \ \ B_{wp}' - B_p'\right]$, $w = 1,3$, and μ, α, $B_1, \ldots, B_p$ –elements from the corresponding linear VECM model. For fixed thresholds c_1 and c_2 the relevant test statistics is[2]

$$LM_n(c_1, c_2) = [vec(\hat{\delta}(c_1, c_2))]'(\hat{\Sigma}_{\hat{\delta}})^{-1}[vec(\hat{\delta}(c_1, c_2))], \qquad (1\text{-}6)$$

where $\hat{\Sigma}_{\hat{\delta}}$ stands for the estimate of covariance matrix of the $\hat{\delta}(c_1, c_2)$ estimator. In order to account for heteroscedasticity of error term u_t the White or the Eicker-White heteroscedasticity-consistent covariance matrix estimator may be used. Since under the null threshold parameters c_1 and c_2 are not identified and standard methods cannot be employed, the use of *SupLM* test statistics is recommended which does not depend upon the nuisance parameter ((Hansen and Seo 2002), (Seo 2003, 2253), and (Clements and Galvão 2004)):

$$SupLM_n = \sup_{\gamma \in \Gamma^* \times \Gamma^*} LM_n(\gamma), \qquad (1\text{-}7)$$

where $\Gamma^* = [c_L, c_U]$ and γ represents all admissible pairs of thresholds located between the p-th (c_L) and the $(1-p)$-th (c_U) percentiles of the threshold variable–the term spread. The statistics has a non-standard distribution so its critical and p-values are simulated through the

[2] (Seo 2003, 2253).

parametric residual bootstrap as described in Hansen and Seo (2002, 304). It is numerically equivalent to the *SupWald* statistics constructed in order to test for the following set of $[4 \times (2 + 2 \times p)]$ restrictions imposed on the parameters of model (1-4): $\mu_1 - \mu_2 = 0_{[2\times1]}$, $\alpha_1 - \alpha_2 = 0_{[2\times1]}$, $B_{1i} - B_{2i} = 0_{[2\times2]}$, $\mu_2 - \mu_3 = 0_{[2\times1]}$, $\alpha_2 - \alpha_3 = 0_{[2\times1]}$, $B_{2i} - B_{3i} = 0_{[2\times2]}$, $i = 1,2,\ldots,p$.

The estimation of thresholds is parallel to $SupLM_n$ computing. They are searched within interval $[c_L, c_U]$ formed by the sorted threshold variable z_{t-1}, with the first and the last p per cent of observations discarded and their duplicates removed. For each pair of potential thresholds threshold VECM model (1-5) is estimated by the multivariate least squares. As threshold estimates $\hat{c}_1$ and $\hat{c}_2$ such a pair of thresholds is chosen that minimizes the natural logarithm of the residual covariance matrix determinant. The optimization criterion is the same as applied by Serra and Goodwin (2003) who stress that it enables to account for a cross-equation dependence of residuals.

Finally, the primary form of threshold VECM model (1-4) is estimated with c_1, and c_2 replaced by their estimates[3], and the LR type test statistics to test the null of linear VECM model against its three-regime threshold alternative is computed:

$$LR31 = N \times [\ln(\det(\hat{\Sigma})) - \ln(\det(\hat{\Sigma}(\hat{c}_1, \hat{c}_2)))], \qquad (1\text{-}8)$$

where $\hat{\Sigma}$ is the residual covariance matrix of linear model (1-2). Since the above test statistics has a non-standard distribution, its critical and p-values are to be computed through the parametric residual bootstrap as in the case of *SupLM* statistics.

[3] The other solutions to thresholds estimation problem are also utilized. For instance, Lo and Zivot (2000), use a sequential one-at-a time algorithm, in which a single threshold is estimated for a two-regime model, and is treated as a given while determining the second threshold in a three-regime VECM. The large sample validity of such a procedure for threshold models was proven by Gonzalo and Pitrakis (2002). Earlier, Bai (1997) showed its consistency for a model with structural breaks; see also Clements and Galvão (2004, 224).

3. Empirical results

The empirical results in this paper are obtained using WIBORs collected on the Wednesdays' basis in order to avoid any possible day of the week effects in interest rates. Their performance is depicted in Fig. 1-1. The series rarely pass through their mean levels, what suggests their nonstationarity, and seem to have commoved in the period in question. Both observations find strong support in the data. The estimates of augmented Dickey-Fuller test statistics prove that all WIBORs are integrated of order one variables and their spreads are stationary. The latter is confirmed by the results of the Johansen's maximum eigenvalue and trace tests, which indicated the existence of co-integrating relations between any pair of interest rates as well as the existence of such a relations amongst their whole set. The validity of appropriate restrictions imposed on the elements of co-integrating vectors with normalization set with respect to the shorter rate confirms the co-integrating properties of the term spreads and the mean-reversion of the term structure[4].

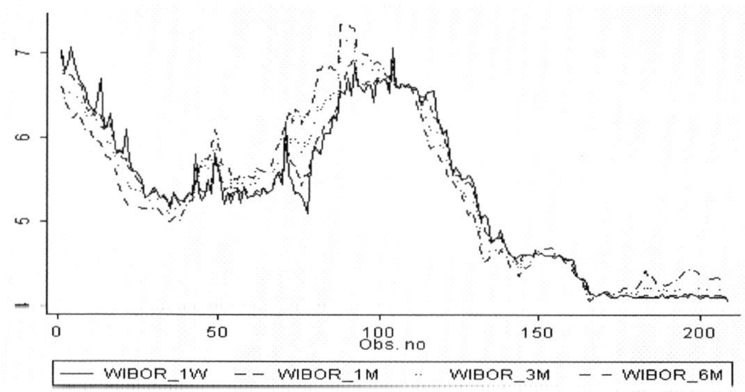

Fig. 1-1 Warsaw Interbank Offer Rates, Jan 2003-Dec 2006. Weekly observations

The predictive power of term spreads can be deducted from Fig. 1-2, 1-3 and 1-4 in which, for all pairs of interest rates, the perfect foresight spread ($PFS_t = E_t \sum_{i=1}^{k-1} \left(1 - \frac{i}{k}\right) \Delta^m R_{t+im}^{(m)}$) is plotted against the actual spread ($S_t^{(n,m)}$) indicating the existence of their possible positive linear relationship.

[4] The results of testing procedures are available from authors upon a request.

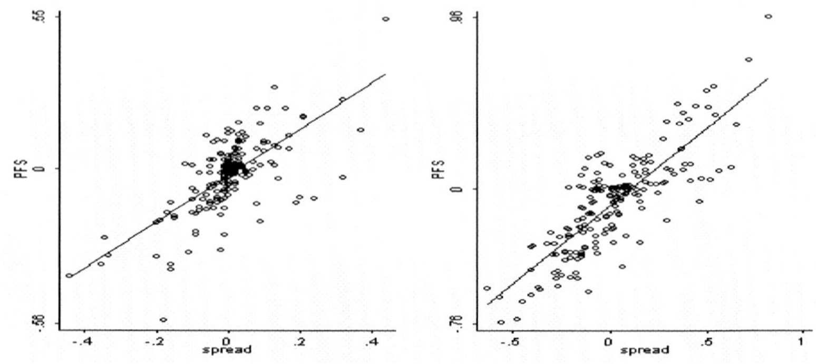

Fig. 1-2 PFSs and actual spreads for WIBOR pairs 1M-1W (left) and 3M-1W (right panel)

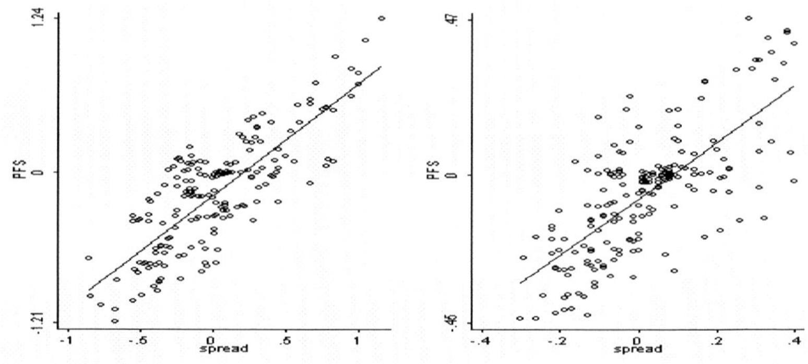

Fig. 1-3 PFSs and actual spreads for WIBOR pairs 6M-1W (left) and 3M-1M (right panel)

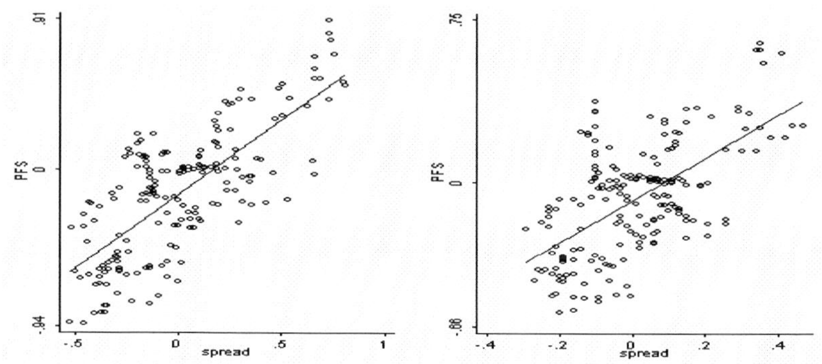

Fig. 1-4 PFSs and actual spreads for WIBOR pairs 6M-1M (left) and 6M-3M (right panel)

Prior to the estimation of model (1-4) we ascertained a nonlinear nature of mean-reversion testing for the null of linear VECM against its nonlinear but unspecified alternative by using the multivariate TAR specification test of Tsay (1998). As recommended by Obstfeld and Taylor (1997, 16) the test is run on the data arranged accordingly to both increasing and decreasing ordering of the threshold variable. The more significant value of the two test statistics is referred to. Under the null the resulting test statistics is asymptotically distributed as χ^2 variate with $2\times(k-1)+1$ degrees of freedom, where k is the number of endogenous variables (Lo and Zivot 2000, 564). Its estimates across all specifications for the pairs of WIBORs starting from 1M-1W (model M1) through 6M-3M (model M6) are gathered in Table 1-1. Interestingly, for 5 out of 6 pairs of interest rates (1M-1W, 3M-1W, 6M-1W, 3M-1M, 6M-3M) nonlinearity is accounted for. The estimates of *SupLM* test statistics and their bootstrap p-values imply that the three-regime TVECM specification for models M1 trough M4 is superior to the one-regime linear VECM specification (in the sense that the model parameters are significantly 'regime-specific'), nevertheless the estimates of $LR31$ test statistics validate this conclusion only for models M1 through M3[5]. To make picture less clear the Akaike (AIC) and the Schwarz-Bayesian (SBC) information criteria in all but the single case of model M1 favour the use of linear VECM in modelling the term structure.

[5] When estimating both test statistics the bootstrapping p values were calculated with 1000 replications.

Table 1-1 Testing for nonlinearity results and information criteria

Model	M1	M2	M3	M4	M5	M6
	WIBOR pairs					
	1M-1W	**3M-1W**	**6M-1W**	**3M_1M**	**6M-1M**	**6M-3M**
p+1	1	1	1	1	1	1
Tsay χ^2	39.689[a]	22.558[a]	9.359[a]	9.681[a]	3.821	7.624[a]
SupLM	60.138[a]	41.262[a]	50.165	30.527[b]	20.072	25.545
p-value	0.000	0.008	0.004	0.087	0.551	0.320
LR31	46.580[a]	28.380[a]	50.165[b]	30.527	13.624	15.618
p-value	0.000	0.050	0.092	0.162	0.805	0.672
SBC						
TVECM	428.733	337.512	293.193	503.665	435.883	570.679
VECM	426.793	344.672	304.517	513.178	450.421	584.221
AIC						
TVECM	436.759	345.537	301.219	511.690	443.908	578.704
VECM	433.468	351.347	311.192	519.853	457.096	590.896

NOTE: Figures marked by a (b) superscript–significant at 5 (10) per cent significance level; *p*–lag of TVECM[6].

Table 1-2 shows the estimation results for the three-regime TVECM with the VAR lag-length of one and the standard errors calculated from the Eicker-White heteroscedasticity-consistent covariance matrix estimator. In model M1 the thresholds are estimated at -0.06 and 0.05 per cent point, and $P\left(S_{t-1}^{(n,m)} \le c_1\right) = 0.149$, $P\left(c_1 < S_{t-1}^{(n,m)} \le c_2\right) = 0.827$, and $P\left(S_{t-1}^{(n,m)} > c_2\right) = 0.024$.

All adjustment coefficients of the short-term rate are positive but their magnitude is statistically significant only in regime 1. The long rate responds to the term spread only in regime 2. Thus the term spread is mean persistent in regime 3 and its predictive power disappears therein.

The conclusions drawn for other models are similar to those for M1. In all regimes it is usually either the long or the short-term rate to react to changes of the past term spread so that in only 5 out of 18 cases the term spread is persistent: once in regime 1 (model M6) and regime 2 (model M6) and 3 times in regime 3 (models M1, M2, M4). The term spread provides information on the future change in short-term rate at least in one

[6] The optimal lag *p*+1 for an unrestricted VAR model was determined with the use of the SBC criterion.

outer regime in models M1, M2, M3, M5, M6. For the long-term rate the same holds in models M4 and M5.

The level of transaction costs as measured in terms of $|c_2 - c_1|$ ranges form 0.11 (model M1) to 0.39 per cent point (model M3) and increases at diminishing rate with the magnitude of term spread. That compared to the magnitude of bid-ask spreads constrained by law to 0.2 per cent point for maturities ranging from one week onwards may suggest the existence of other sources of transactions costs at the Polish interbank market. In view of the predictive power of the term spreads in the inner regime in models M1 trough M5, however, the estimated thresholds should rather be treated as separating the regions of different adjustment speed of interest rates to their long-run equilibrium relation. Nevertheless, nonlinearity in the term structure of interest rates still applies. The time-pattern of term spread reversion within and out of the threshold bands in models M1-M6 is depicted in Fig. 1-5, 1-6 and 1-7.

The transition probabilities from one regime to another and the regime duration in each model are shown in Table 1-3. For instance, in model M1 the probability of staying in regime 2 is estimated at 0.801 and the mean duration in this regime counts to 5.04 weeks. For the shorter-end of maturity spectrum (models M1, M2, M4) staying in regime 2 is the most probable. The mean duration of staying there is relatively short (from 5.04 to 7.75 weeks) and increases with the magnitude of the term spread. For the longer-end of maturity spectrum (models M3, M5, M6) the probability of staying in regime 3 is higher than probabilities of staying in the other regimes. The mean duration of staying there is relatively long (from 16.43 to 32.67 weeks) and behaves as that of the shorter-end. Thus it can be deducted that the speed of mean reversion of the term spread depends upon the regime and the end of maturity spectrum.

Table 1-2 Estimation of threshold VECM results

Model	M1		M2		M3	
	WIBOR_1M	WIBOR_1W	WIBOR_3M	WIBOR_1W	WIBOR_6M	WIBOR_1W
α_1	0.126	1.083[a]	-0.101	0.762[a]	-0.121	0.662[a]
$S(\alpha_1)$	0.128	0.220	0.114	0.228	0.075	0.206
μ_1	-0.076[a]	-0.011	-0.090[a]	0.117[b]	-0.114[a]	0.244[a]
$S(\mu_1)$	0.027	0.043	0.035	0.069	0.038	0.100
α_2	0.778[a]	0.244	0.135[b]	0.253[b]	0.029	0.551[a]
$S(\alpha_2)$	0.217	0.402	0.076	0.136	0.141	0.238
μ_2	-0.014[a]	-0.009	-0.015[a]	-0.013	-0.020	0.071[b]
$S(\mu_2)$	0.005	0.007	0.005	0.009	0.030	0.041
α_3	-0.015	0.524	-0.027	0.347	0.045	0.170[a]
$S(\alpha_3)$	0.240	0.459	0.090	0.224	0.034	0.072
μ_3	0.055	0.023	0.044	-0.067	-0.006	-0.039[b]
$S(\mu_3)$	0.047	0.075	0.044	0.082	0.008	0.021
c_1	-0.060		-0.160		-0.370	
c_2	0.050		0.160		-0.020	
$P(z_{t-1} \leq c_1)$	0.149		0.183		0.154	
$P(c_1 < z_{t-1} \leq c_2)$	0.827		0.793		0.447	

NOTE: Figures marked by a (b) superscript–significant at 5 (10) per cent significance level.

Table 1-2 Estimation of threshold VECM results (continued)

Model	M4		M5		M6	
	WIBOR_3M	WIBOR_1M	WIBOR_6M	WIBOR_1M	WIBOR_6M	WIBOR_3M
α_1	-0.600[a]	-0.279	-0.304[b]	-0.017	-0.582	-0.169
$S(\alpha_1)$	0.229	0.233	0.165	0.134	0.390	0.363
μ_1	-0.170[a]	-0.138[a]	-0.169[a]	-0.085[b]	-0.177[a]	-0.108
$S(\mu_1)$	0.048	0.046	0.065	0.051	0.081	0.073
α_2	0.171[a]	0.102	0.007	0.208[b]	-0.032	0.086
$S(\alpha_2)$	0.065	0.085	0.071	0.123	0.165	0.127
μ_2	-0.011[a]	-0.008	-0.012	0.007	-0.015	-0.007
$S(\mu_2)$	0.004	0.005	0.009	0.014	0.010	0.009
α_3	-0.012	0.291	0.061	0.148[a]	0.136	0.220b
$S(\alpha_3)$	0.216	0.195	0.050	0.053	0.111	0.113
μ_3	0.032	-0.032	-0.006	-0.032[a]	-0.009	-0.022[b]
$S(\mu_3)$	0.069	0.056	0.013	0.012	0.014	0.013
c_1	-0.110		-0.250		-0.130	
c_2	0.110		0.080		0.030	
$P(z_{t-1} \le c_1)$	0.202		0.207		0.202	
$P(c_1 < z_{t-1} \le c_2)$	0.798		0.543		0.529	

NOTE: Figures marked by a (b) superscript–significant at 5 (10) per cent significance level.

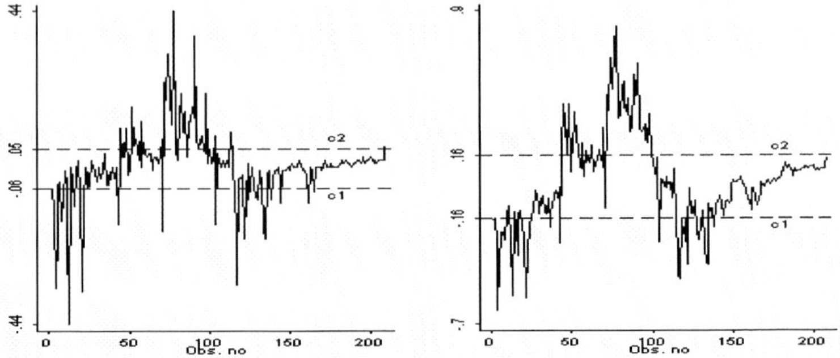

Fig. 1-5 Actual spreads and thresholds, models M1 (left) and M2 (right panel)

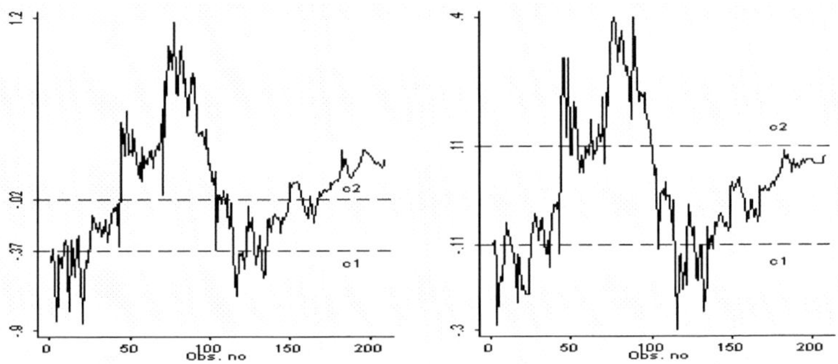

Fig. 1-6 Actual spreads and thresholds, models M3 (left) and M4 (right panel)

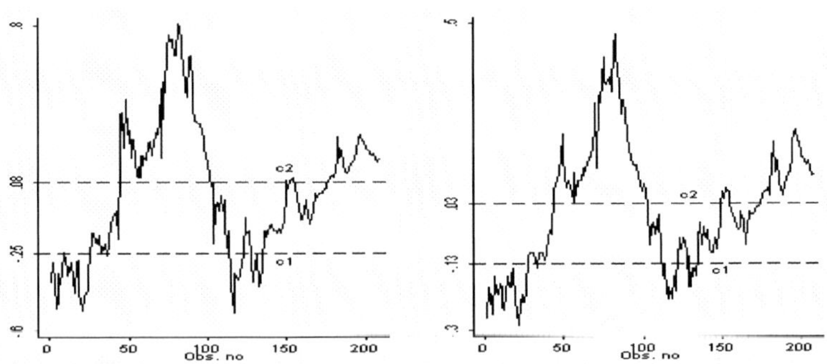

Fig. 1-7 Actual spreads and thresholds, models M5 (left) and M6 (right panel)

Table 1-3 Transition probabilities and regime duration (Transition probability $P_{ij} = P\left(S_{t-1}^{(n,m)} = i \mid S_t^{(n,m)} = j\right)$, for $i, j = 1,2,3$)

	Transition probability P_{ij}			Duration			Transition probability P_{ij}			Duration	
	$S_t^{(n,m)}$=1	$S_t^{(n,m)}$=2	$S_t^{(n,m)}$=3	**Mean**	**Median**		$S_t^{(n,m)}$=1	$S_t^{(n,m)}$=2	$S_t^{(n,m)}$=3	**Mean**	**Median**
Model 1						Model 2					
$S_{t-1}^{(n,m)}$=1	0.419	0.548	0.032	1.72	2.00	$S_{t-1}^{(n,m)}$=1	0.711	0.263	0.026	3.45	3.00
$S_{t-1}^{(n,m)}$=2	0.106	0.801	0.085	5.04	2.00	$S_{t-1}^{(n,m)}$=2	0.079	0.858	0.055	7.06	2.00
$S_{t-1}^{(n,m)}$=3	0.056	0.306	0.639	2.77	1.00	$S_{t-1}^{(n,m)}$=3	0.000	0.186	0.814	5.38	2.00
Model 3						Model 3					
$S_{t-1}^{(n,m)}$=1	0.750	0.250	0.000	4.00	3.00	$S_{t-1}^{(n,m)}$=1	0.738	0.238	0.024	3.82	1.00
$S_{t-1}^{(n,m)}$=2	0.115	0.771	0.115	4.36	2.00	$S_{t-1}^{(n,m)}$=2	0.081	0.871	0.040	7.75	2.00
$S_{t-1}^{(n,m)}$=3	0.000	0.052	0.939	16.43	2.00	$S_{t-1}^{(n,m)}$=3	0.000	0.143	0.857	7.00	2.00
Model 5						Model 5					
$S_{t-1}^{(n,m)}$=1	0.884	0.116	0.000	8.60	8.00	$S_{t-1}^{(n,m)}$=1	0.857	0.143	0.000	7.00	4.00
$S_{t-1}^{(n,m)}$=2	0.057	0.886	0.057	8.75	8.00	$S_{t-1}^{(n,m)}$=2	0.074	0.882	0.044	8.50	5.00
$S_{t-1}^{(n,m)}$=3	0.000	0.032	0.958	23.75	21.00	$S_{t-1}^{(n,m)}$=3	0.000	0.020	0.969	32.67	35.00

4. Summary and conclusions

The empirical results of testing for a nonlinear mean reversion in the term structure of interest rates at the Polish interbank market are ambiguous. On the ground of Johansen's (1988) co-integration tests we found the existence of a long run relationship in pairs of all WIBORs, showing that the term spread is mean-reverting. The significance of adjustment coefficients in the corresponding linear VECMs supports predictability of both the short and the long-term rates. Despite the strong evidence of nonlinearity in mean reversion, the use of Seo's model to capture the transaction costs at the interbank market in Poland is of little success. In particular the adjustment of either the short or the long-term interest rate takes place almost in all regimes, and the persistence of term spread is rare. We argue therefore that the estimated thresholds separate the regions of different adjustment speed of the short and the long-term interest rates to their long-run equilibrium relation and do not exhibit the shadow costs of mean reversion.

References

Bai, Jushan (1997), Estimating multiple breaks one at a time, *Econometric Theory,* 13, 315-352.

Balke, Nathan S., and Thomas B. Fomby (1997), Threshold cointegration, *International Economic Review,* 38, 627-645.

Bec, Frédérique F. and Anders Rahbek (2004), Vector equilibrium correction models with non-linear discontinuous adjustments. *Econometrics Journal,* 7, 628-651.

Campbell, John Y. and Robert J. Shiller (1987), Cointegration and tests of present value models, *Journal of Political Economy,* 95, 1062-1088.

Campbell, John Y. and Robert J. Shiller (1991), Yield spreads and interest rates movements: a bird's eye view, *Review of Economic Studies,* 58, 495-514.

Clements, Michael P. and Ana B. Galvão (2004), A comparison of tests of nonlinear cointegration with application to predictability of US interest rates using the term structure, *International Journal of Forecasting,* 20, 219-236.

Cuthbertson, Keith (1996), The expectations hypothesis of the term structure: the UK interbank market, *Economic Journal,* 106, 578-592.

Engle, Robert F. and Clive W.J. Granger (1987), Cointegration and error correction representation. Estimation and testing, *Econometrica,* 55, 251-276.

Gouveia, Pedro M. D. C. B. and Paulo M. M. Rodrigues (2004), Threshold cointegration and the PPP hypothesis, *Journal of Applied Statistics,* 31, 115-127.

Gonzalo, Jesus and Jean-Yves Pitarakis (2002), Estimation and model selection based inference in single and multiple threshold models, *Journal of Econometrics,* 110, 319-352.

Hansen, Bruce E. (1999), Testing for linearity, *Journal of Economic Surveys,* 13, 551-576.

Hansen, Bruce E. and Byeongseon Seo (2002), Testing for two-regime threshold cointegration in vector error-corrections models, *Journal of Econometrics,* 110, 293-318.

Hall, Anthony D., Heather M. Anderson, and Clive W. J. Granger (1992), A cointegration analysis of treasury bill yields, *Review of Economics and Statistics,* 74, 116-126.

Johansen, Søren (1988), Statistical analysis of cointegration vectors, *Journal of Economic Dynamics and Control,* 12, 231-254.

Jondeau, Eric and Roland Ricart (1999), The expectations hypothesis of the term structure: tests on US, German, French, and UK Euro-rates, *Journal of International Money and Finance,* 18, 725-750.

Konstantinou, Panagiotos T. (2005), The expectations hypothesis of the term structure. A look at the Polish interbank market, *Emerging Markets Finance and Trade,* 41, 70-91.

Kugler, Peter (1988), An empirical note on the term structure and interest rates stabilization policies, *Quarterly Journal of Economics,* 103, 789-792.

Lo, Ming Ch. and Eric Zivot (2001), Threshold cointegration and nonlinear adjustment to Law of One Price, *Macroeconomic Dynamics,* 5, 533-576.

Mancuso, Anthony J., Barry K. Goodwin, and Thomas J. Grennes (2003), Nonlinear aspects of capital market and real interest rate equalization, *International Review of Economics and Finance,* 12, 283-203.

Mankiw, N. Gregory and Jeffrey A. Miron (1986), The changing behaviour of the term structure of interest rates, *Quarterly Journal of Economics,* 101, 211-228.

Mankiw, N. Gregory and Lawrence H. Summers (1984), Do long-term interest rates overreact to short-term interest rates, *Brooking Papers on Economic Activity,* 1, 223-242.

Meyer, Jochen (2004), Measuring market integration in the presence of transaction costs–a threshold vector error correction approach, *Agricultural Economics,* 31, 327-334.

NBP (1998), *Średniookresowa strategia polityki pieniężnej na lata 1999-2003* (Medium range monetary policy strategy, 1993-2003), Warszawa, Narodowy Bank Polski.

—. (2005), *Założenia polityki pieniężnej na rok 2006* (Principles of monetary policy in 2006), Warszawa, Narodowy Bank Polski.

Obstfeld, Maurice and Alan M. Taylor (1997), Nonlinear aspects of goods-market arbitrage and adjustment: Heckscher's commodity points revisited, *National Bureau of Economic Research,* 6053, 1-48.

Seo, Byeongseon (2003), Nonlinear mean reversion in the term structure of interest rates, *Journal of Economic Dynamics and Control,* 27, 2243-2265.

Serra, Teresa and Barry K. Goodwin (2003), Price transmission and asymmetric adjustment in the Spanish dairy sector, *Applied Economics,* 35, 1889-1899.

Tong, Howell (1978), In Chen, C. H. (ed.), *On a threshold model, pattern recognition and signal processing*. Amsterdam, Sijhoff and Noordhoff.

Tsay, Ruey S. (1998), Testing and modeling multivariate threshold models, *Journal of American Statistical Association,* 93, 1188-1202.

Tsay, Ruey S. (2005), *Analysis of financial time series*. Hoboken, John Wiley & Sons.

Tzavalis, Elias and Michael R. Wickens (1997), Explaining the failure of the term spread models of the rational expectations of the term structure, *Journal of Money, Credit and Banking,* 29, 364-380.

Acknowledgments

We performed computations with the use of Microfit v. 4.1 and Gauss v. 8.0 packages. Parts of the Gauss source code originated from Lo and Zivot (Tsay testing procedure) and Hansen and Seo (bootstrap procedure), and were taken from http://web.stcloudstate.edu/mclo/research.html and from http://www.ssc.wisc.edu/~bhansen. The usual disclaimer applies. Financial support from the University of Gdańsk, grant BW 2330-5-01053-7, is gratefully acknowledged.

CHAPTER FOUR

SHAREHOLDER ACTIVISM AMONG PORTFOLIO MANAGERS: RATIONAL DECISIONS OR 15 MINUTES OF FAME?

LARS NORDÉN AND THERESE STRAND[1]

Abstract

This paper investigates shareholder activism by observing Swedish portfolio managers' behavior at firms' annual general meetings. Institutional shareholders' voting behavior and tendencies for raising opinions at the general meetings are related to firm characteristics, suggested by both agency theory and institutional perspectives. The results show that institutional shareholders are more likely to be active in large firms, which appear a lot in media, and have a large proportion of institutional ownership. Portfolio managers appear not to consider bad firm performance as a reason for targeting firms. Instead, managers' behavior is consistent with the institutional notion that they benefit from the activism themselves, without trying to improve target firms' performance. In view of this notion, it is rational for managers to be active

---

[1] Authors are grateful to the Jan Wallander and Tom Hedelius foundation and the Tore Browaldh foundation for research support. Therese Strand is grateful for research support from the Centre for Business and Policy Studies (SNS), within the Corporate Governance Network in Stockholm. This study has benefited from comments and suggestions by Per-Olof Berg and Steen Thomsen. We have also received valuable input from seminar participants at Stockholm University School of Business, Copenhagen Business School, the 2005 NFF Conference in Aarhus, and the 2006 Conference for Global Development of Corporate Governance in Birmingham.

in large firms, with large media coverage, achieving their 15 minutes of fame at the general meetings.

Keywords: Institutional shareholder activism; Target firms; Agency theory; Institutional theory

1. Introduction

There is a current global trend of shareholdings shifting from private individuals with direct ownership to portfolio managers and institutions holding shares for the benefit of others (Agnblad et al., 2002, Brown, 1998, Menkhoff, 2002, Sias and Starks, 1998, Smith, 1996, Useem et al., 1993). The relative increase in institutional shareholdings has altered the power structures in listed firms as well as owners' agenda of corporate governance. As a consequence, corporate governance researchers are paying increasing attention to the role and responsibility of portfolio managers holding large stakes in listed firms. Moreover, current research is showing an increasing interest in shareholder activism in general and institutional shareholder activism in particular.[2]

Institutions' shareholder activism is defined in different ways by different authors.[3] In general, shareholder activism can be categorized into either formal or informal. Formal activism is those efforts that are made publicly, as e.g. shareholder proposals, actions taken at the annual general meetings, and initiatives to public debate. Informal activism is conducted behind the scenes in terms of private negotiations, and is, thus, not publicly visible.

This paper analyzes which firms become targets of institutional activism by observing institutions' actual behavior during firms' annual general meetings in 2004 and 2005.[4] Target and non-target firm characteristics are compared using a sample of Swedish firms with substantial institutional holdings. By studying actions taken by

---

[2] In line with Murphy and Van Nuys (1994), we define an institutional shareholder as a portfolio manager who is managing capital on the behalf of others, including state pension funds, private pension funds, insurance firms, and mutual funds.
[3] See e.g. Karpoff (2001). Using a common definition, Gillan and Starks (1998) state that an activist shareholder "tries to change the status quo through "voice", without a change in control of the firm".
[4] de Jong et al. (2006) also use minutes from annual general meetings to study shareholder behavior.

shareholders at firms' annual general meetings, this study contributes to previous research since this type of activism is often neglected in studies of which firms become targets of activism. The Swedish corporate governance system is characterized by each firm having an owner-dominated nomination committee that prepares suggestions for the annual general meeting, e.g. the composition of the board of directors.[5] Since the largest owners gain substantial corporate insights and opportunities to have private negotiations with management through participation in these committees, shareholder proposals, which are one of the main tools for shareholder activism in other parts of the world, are extremely rare in Sweden. Instead, the annual general meeting is the primary arena for shareholder activism besides private negotiations in nomination committees.

We consider two measures of institutional investor activism: if an institutional owner votes against the board or another owner at the annual meeting or if the institution verbally raises an opinion at the annual meeting. Previous studies of formal institutional shareholder activism typically focus on shareholder proposals to firms' annual meetings, either by multiple shareholders, mostly institutions (Del Guercio and Hawkins, 1999, John and Klein, 1995, Johnson and Shackell, 1997, Karpoff, et al., 1996, Prevost and Rao, 2000, Rehbein, et al., 2004, Strickland, et al., 1996, Tsui, 2000, Wahal, 1996, and Woods, 1996), or from a single portfolio manager organization (Carleton, et al., 1998, English, et al., 2000, Huson, 1997, Nesbitt, 1994, Opler and Sobokin, 1995, Smith, 1996, Song and Szewczyk, 2003, and Wu, 2000). Such proposals are rare in Sweden, but institutional shareholders exercise real power through voting procedures at annual meetings if their holdings are large. In addition, they have the possibility to influence the decision-making process by asking questions and raising opinions, even in cases when they hold only smaller stakes.

In a survey article, Karpoff (2001) concludes that the empirical research is rather consistent about the characteristics of firms attracting activist efforts. However, the research on shareholder activism is traditionally based on agency theory, indicating that activism is a tool for

[5] The nomination committee is responsible for preparing and making suggestions to the annual general meeting concerning the number of board members, chairman of the board, members of the board, compensation and incentive schemes for board members, choice of auditors, level of auditor fees, as well as choice of chairman for the annual general meeting.

owners to monitor management, and thus restrict their possibilities to act in their own interests (Jensen and Meckling, 1976). Nevertheless, several studies have elaborated on the notion that other concerns than monitoring underlies the actions taken by portfolio managers (Gorton and Kahl, 1999, Kahn and Winton, 1998, Murphy and Van Nuys, 1994, Woidtke, 2002). Following DiMaggio and Powell (1983) and Meyer and Rowan (1977), we recognize that portfolio managers may possess a wider repertoire of underlying objectives than is recognized by agency theory, since they are also confined to comply with institutional pressures such as culture, societal expectations and other factors which affect their own organization. Therefore, as a further contribution to previous research, target and non-target firm characteristics are examined from a dual perspective, including both agency theory rationales such as firm performance, share price development and ownership structure, and explanatory variables emanating from institutional theory, e.g. firm size and media exposure.

Our empirical results are consistent with institutions preferring to be relatively more active in large firms that appear a lot in media, and for which the proportion of institutional ownership is relatively large. Interestingly, institutions appear not to consider bad firm performance, in terms of either stock return or accounting measures, as a reason for targeting firms for activism. Moreover, it is difficult to reconcile a large number of firms' media appearances with rational reasons for institutional owner activism, as predicted by agency theory. Instead, the activism behavior of institutions is consistent with the note from Murphy and Van Nuys (1994) who argue that portfolio managers benefit from the activism themselves, without focusing on and trying to improve target firms' performance. In view of this notion, it is rational for institutions to choose to be active in large firms with large media coverage, to get into the spotlight, appearing to care about shareholder value.

In the following section previous research on target and non-target firms is reviewed and discussed, and the characteristics of the Swedish corporate governance system are outlined. In section three, data and descriptive statistics are presented, before analyzing the regression results in section four. The final section summarizes and discusses the main conclusions in the light of the raised theoretical issues.

2. Targeting and the underlying objectives

Shareholder activism and target firm characteristics

Following an agency theoretical perspective (see Jensen and Meckling, 1976), shareholder activists are viewed as monitors whose efforts aim to solve control and incentive problems arising from owners and firm managers having different interests. Shareholders are considered to be financially rational agents seeking maximum returns on their investments. Accordingly, they engage in activism to limit management from taking aberrant actions and to ensure that decisions are made in shareholders' interests. Within this theoretical framework, shareholders' efforts should occur when expected benefits from activism exceed estimated costs (Admati et al., 1994, Pozen, 1994).

Agency theory is the dominating perspective within corporate governance research. Therefore, targeting is considered to be a monitoring effort, exerted for the purpose of increasing shareholder value to achieve maximum investment returns. Consequently, activists' efforts should primarily be directed at under-performing firms and issues where the stock price is directly at stake (Pozen, 1994). To some extent, empirical findings show diverging results on which firms become targets of activism.

Regarding stock price performance, some studies show no significant difference between targeted and non-targeted firms' market-adjusted stock returns (Carleton, et al., 1998, Smith, 1996), while others find that targeted firms' stock returns are lower than market returns (Opler and Sobokin, 1995, Strickland, et al., 1996). Analyzing control-firm adjusted stock returns, Karpoff, et al. (1996) find no differences between targeted and non-targeted firms, while Opler and Sobokin (1995) find that target firms have significantly lower stock returns than their peers.

Using accounting measures of firm performance, previous findings are also contradictory. Some studies indicate that targeted firms are poor performers with low returns to sales (Karpoff et al., 1996, Martin et al., 2000), low sales growth (Karpoff et al., 1996, Johnson and Shackell, 1997) and low growth rates in operating income (Bizjak and Marquette, 1998). Moreover, Karpoff et al. (1996) find that target firms have low market-to-book ratios, while Johnson and Shackell (1997), Smith (1996) and Strickland et al. (1996) find no significant relation between market-to-book ratios and targeting.

Several studies consider other firm characteristics than performance for determining the likelihood of a firm being targeted by shareholder activism, e.g. firms' ownership structure and size. Again, the results are mixed. Some studies report that the probability of firms being targeted with shareholder proposals is significantly affected by the percentage of portfolio managers' holdings (Bizjak and Marquette, 1998, Carleton et al., 1998, Karpoff et al., 1996, Smith, 1996), while John and Klein (1995) report a negative relation between targeting and institutional ownership. Bizjak and Marquette (1998), John and Klein (1995), Johnson and Shackell (1997), Karpoff et al. (1996), Smith (1996), and Strickland et al. (1996) all find that firm size is significantly positively related to the probability of shareholder proposals.

Karpoff (2001) argues that these divergences in empirical findings originate from different data sets and definitions of activism, but the range of motives and the underlying objectives of shareholder activism could also be wider than previously recognized. For example, Rao (2001) shows that shareholders repeatedly use activist efforts even when their holdings are trivial, few others share their concerns, and despite knowing that their actions will have little or no effect on corporate decisions. These findings strengthen the conjecture that activism is due to underlying objectives other than agency theory related monitoring. Murphy and Van Nuys (1994) argue that portfolio managers represent organizations with the same agency and incentive problems as the firms in which they invest. In line with agency theory, portfolio managers are therefore just as likely to engage in opportunism as every other manager and might use activism to pursue other goals than those beneficial for the target firms.

A competing view to agency theory is that shareholder activists target firms for other reasons than monitoring and maximizing shareholder value. Meyer and Rowan (1977) and DiMaggio and Powell (1983) postulate that organizations wish to comply with external normative pressures such as culture, law, politics, informal codes of conduct, and societal expectations to gain legitimacy as business actors. Thus, organizations must convince society and the public that they are legitimate entities worthy of support in order to survive (Mizruchi and Fein, 1999). In line with this institutional theory, Romano (1993) argues that activist efforts sometimes arise e.g. among public pension funds, where managers wish to pursue political or socially motivated objectives. Pozen (1994) reports that portfolio managers tend to direct activist efforts towards governance matters and procedural frills despite the fact that such issues prove not to be significantly correlated with either stock price or net income. Carleton et al. (1998) find that fund managers' activism is often directed at gender equality at the board of directors although the issue is associated with a decline in share value. In addition, John and Klein (1995) report that the likelihood of being targeted is significantly affected by the percentage of independent directors on the board, which according to Bhagat and Black (1998) is not unambiguously linked to firms' financial performance and development. Woidtke (2002) also elaborates on alternative agendas and finds variations in valuation effects of institutional activism depending on the institution's objective functions.

Corporate governance and shareholder activism in Sweden

Most studies of shareholder activism are conducted in Anglo-Saxon countries like the U.S. and U.K. Hence, it is interesting per se to study the subject in a governance system with other than Anglo-Saxon characteristics. Moreover, focusing on the Swedish governance system is particularly interesting because the Swedish system triggers shareholders to perform different forms of activism compared to in e.g. the U.S. or the U.K. In Anglo-Saxon countries, shareholder proposals is the dominating tool for shareholder activists while in Sweden this type of activism is virtually non-existent. The Swedish corporate governance system borrows heavily from Continental European features. Moreover, shareholder activism is conducted primarily at annual general meetings and in private negotiations with management.

Considering the system as a whole, two fundamental differences between Sweden and the Anglo-Saxon countries that affect which activist efforts are taken are highlighted. First, the structure of corporate control differs. Over the last decades, portfolio managers' relative share of the total shareholding capital has increased considerably in Anglo-Saxon as well as Continental European countries. Sweden is no exception to this development. But while the Anglo-Saxon system is characterized by dispersed ownership structures, Swedish firms exhibit very concentrated control structures with a strong separation between ownership and control. A single shareholder, a private individual or a family, often contributes with a minor part of the capital but controls a majority of the votes. This is made possible through dual-class shares and pyramid holdings. Thus, in a typical Swedish firm, portfolio managers might be providing a majority of the capital while control often is concentrated in the hands of private individuals. Portfolio managers are thereby forced to a strategy of convincing other shareholders to vote in favor of their suggestions in order to affect corporate decisions. Thus, discussions, negotiations and co-operation are crucial elements to succeed with activist efforts and the annual general meeting provides an open arena for shareholders to set the firm agenda and participate in such discussions.

Second, another fundamental characteristic of the Swedish corporate governance system is the importance of social control and informal mechanisms. Strong separation between ownership and control of firms, as is the case in Sweden, has in other countries been shown to be vulnerable to minority abuse. Still it is difficult to find examples of such violations in Sweden. Agnblad et al. (2002) argue that social status discourages abuse of minority shareholders since it is "an important, even dominant, part of the total benefits associated with control of large corporations in Sweden" (p. 252). Thus, the societal expectations on corporate owners are strong and many large shareholders, private individuals as well as portfolio managers, try to build legacy for themselves as responsible contributors to socially worthy causes. This gives mass media an important role for at least two reasons. First, it serves as a channel through which activist efforts can be promoted, and thus gives portfolio managers time in the limelight. Second, it announces the corporate issues in focus at the time, and thereby potentially makes target selection easy for activists if efforts are taken solely in order to market themselves as organizations.

The dual characteristics of the Swedish corporate governance system; the role of fund managers as providers of capital to privately control firms along with the desire to comply with strong social pressures and expectations, are two unique features which motivate studying activist efforts taken against Swedish firms.

3. Data sources and descriptive statistics

Data

The empirical analysis is based on data collected from multiple sources for the years 2004 and 2005. The occurrence of activist efforts by portfolio managers is explored through minutes from Swedish firms' annual general meetings. In line with Murphy and Van Nuys (1994), we define an institutional owner as a portfolio manager who is managing capital on behalf of others, including state pension funds, private pension funds, insurance firms, and mutual funds. The study is restricted to comprise

Swedish portfolio managers, holding shares in Swedish firms. Institutions without any employees working with governance issues are excluded, since these organizations openly state that they do not intend to practice activism, but simply rely on exit strategies. In all, the institutions in the sample hold shares with a total market value of around ten billion SEK.[6]

We select firms among all firms listed at the Stockholm Stock Exchange. To be included in the sample, each firm must have at least one institutional investor among the 25 largest owners at the time of the annual general meeting. This comprises a total number of 386 firms. Minutes from the annual general meetings are collected from each firm's webpage whenever the minutes had been posted there, and for all others by a request sent to each firm by e-mail and followed by a reminder three weeks after the first request. The sample consists of 220 minutes from 130 firms. 90 firms are in the sample for both years. Altogether, 96 minutes have been received from annual general meetings in 2004 and 124 minutes from 2005.

As a measure of a firm's media exposure, a count of how many times the firm appears in major Swedish daily and business newspaper articles is performed using the Affärsdata database. We include all articles with each firm's name in the headline that are published up to one year prior to each year's annual general meeting. In addition, data on firm characteristics are collected from firms' annual reports and the Stockholm Stock Exchange.

Descriptive statistics

Table 1 provides descriptive statistics for target and non-target firms in the sample, and for the two measures of shareholder activism. Panel A contains descriptive statistics for firms targeted by portfolio managers' acting through voting against the board or another owner, whereas Panel B encloses corresponding statistics using our wider definition of portfolio managers' activism, i.e. they are either voting against the board or another owner, or raising an opinion at the annual meeting.

Using the Panel A definition of activism, 25 firms (11.36 percent) out of our 220 sample firms are targeted by fund managers. The target and non-target firms show no significant differences in mean or median prior year's raw return or market-adjusted mean return (at the five percent

[6] The definition of institutional shareholders does not include hedge funds, simply because no hedge fund was among the 25 largest owners of the sample firms.

level). Hence, portfolio managers' target firms with on average the same performance as the corresponding non-target firms, which is inconsistent with the agency theory. Moreover, in Panel A of Table 1, the mean and median measures of accounting performance, book return on equity, and market-to-book value of equity, are not significantly different between target and non-target firms. Again, these results are not consistent with portfolio managers considering bad performance as a reason for shareholder activism.

On the other hand, portfolio managers' target firms are significantly larger than non-target firms. Mean (median) book value of assets for target firms is significantly higher than for non-target firms at a very low significance level. Moreover, target firms have a significantly higher mean and median proportion of institutional ownership than non-target firms. The mean (median) ownership proportion of all institutional investors is 0.19 (0.18) for target firms and only 0.11 (0.10) for non-target firms. In addition, the target firms on average appear significantly more often in the media relative the non-target firms, as the mean (median) occurrence in media equals 64 (19) times for the target firms and 17 (5) times for the non-target firms. The descriptive statistics in Panel A of Table 1 are supporting the view that portfolio managers are exerting activism by voting against the board or another owner at the general meetings due to other reasons than predicted by agency theory.

The descriptive statistics in Panel B of Table 1 are similar to the ones in Panel A. When activism is defined as voting against the board or another owner, or raising an opinion at the annual meeting, fund managers target 39 firms (17.73 percent) out of the 220 sample firms. Although the broader definition of shareholder activism is used, portfolio managers' target and non-target firms are not showing significantly different performance, financial or accounting based, but target firms show significantly higher proportion of institutional ownership, larger size, and higher media exposure than non-target firms. Overall, the descriptive statistics are hard to reconcile with rational behavior according to agency theory.

Table 1: Mean and median sample attributes for institutions' target and non-target firms

Panel A: Investor activism, targeting firms by voting against the board or another owner

	Target firms		Non-target firms			
Variable	Mean	Median	Mean	Median	*t*-test	*W*-test
Prior year's stock return	0.4372	0.3326	0.3464	0.2727	0.3810	0.1239
Prior year's market adjusted stock return	0.2910	0.1896	0.1868	0.1256	0.3186	0.0887
Book value of assets	1.58e+11	2.04e+10	3.91e+10	2.43e+09	0.0073	0.0002
Book return on equity (ROE)	0.0603	0.1109	0.0569	0.1183	0.9636	0.1681
Market-to-book value of equity	2.6157	1.7435	2.5806	2.1654	0.9291	0.3184
Proportion of institutional ownership	0.1896	0.1840	0.1146	0.0950	0.0001	0.0000
Number of times in media	63.680	19.000	17.37	5.0000	0.0000	0.0015
Number of firms	25	25	195	195		

Investor activism is measured in two ways: as an indicator variable equal to one if the institution has voted against the board or another owner (Panel A), and as an indicator variable equal to one if the institution has voted against the board or another owner, and/or raised an opinion at the annual meeting (Panel B). The attributes' variables are: each firm's prior year's raw and market adjusted stock returns, the firm book value of assets, each firm's market-to-book value of equity, the proportion of institutional ownership of each firm, and the number of times each firm has appeared in media during the prior year. The last two columns contain *p*-values from a *t*-test for equality between means and a Wilcoxon rank sum test for equality between medians, between the target and non-target firm values. The Wilcoxon *p*-values are based on the asymptotic normal approximation outlined in Sheskin (1997).

Table 1 (cont.): Mean and median sample attributes for institutions' target and non-target firms

Panel B: Investor activism, targeting firms by voting against the board or another owner and/or raising an opinion

	Target firms		Non-target firms			
Variable	Mean	Median	Mean	Median	*t*-test	*W*-test
Prior year's stock return	0.3506	0.2710	0.3580	0.2831	0.9311	0.7184
Prior year's market adjusted stock return	0.1979	0.1231	0.1988	0.1370	0.9918	0.6472
Book value of assets	2.20e+11	3.16e+10	1.65e+10	2.35e+09	0.0000	0.0000
Book return on equity (ROE)	0.0546	0.1020	0.0579	0.1187	0.9580	0.0844
Market-to-book value of equity	2.5664	1.8138	2.5886	2.2057	0.9459	0.2667
Proportion of institutional ownership	0.1843	0.1810	0.1099	0.0860	0.0000	0.0000
Number of times in media	58.128	18.000	14.989	5.000	0.0000	0.0000
Number of firms	39	39	181	181		

4. Regression results

To identify the relative importance of rational performance and institutional attributes that characterizes fund managers' target and non-target firms, we estimate two probit regressions, representing two measures of investor activism. In the first probit regression the dependent variable is equal to one if a fund manager has voted against the board or another owner at the firm annual meeting, and zero otherwise. Similarly, the second probit regression is run using the more broad definition of investor activism, where the dependent variable equals one if a fund manager has voted against the board or another owner, and/or raised an opinion, at the annual meeting, and zero otherwise. Both regressions contain the same set of explanatory variables, including performance and institutional attributes of the target/non-target firms. Accordingly, each measure of shareholder activism is related to two accounting measures of financial performance (book return on equity, ROE, and the ratio of market-to-book value of equity), a stock price performance measure (prior year's market adjusted stock return), firm size (the natural logarithm of book value of assets), and the proportion of institutional ownership to capture a firm governance characteristic. Moreover, we include the number of times each firm has appeared in media during the prior year, and an indicator variable for the year 2005.

Table 2 contains the results from the two probit regression estimations. For each regression model, Table 2 presents estimated coefficients, significance levels (*p*-values), and marginal effects for the explanatory variables. The first regression, where activism is measured as active voting at the firm annual meeting only (Panel A of Table 2), achieves a pseudo R-squared value of 0.33, indicating that the explanatory variables together account for 33 percent of the variability in the activism decision. Moreover, the proportion of correctly predicted outcomes using the probit model, and a classification cutoff equal to 0.5, equals 0.90. The rather high values of R-squared and the proportion correctly predicted outcomes together demonstrate an excellent model goodness of fit for explaining shareholder activism.

Portfolio managers' decisions to pursue activism by voting against the board or other owners is significantly negatively related to the annual indicator variable, at any reasonable significance level, indicating that activism was more likely to occur during the 2004 relative the 2005 annual meetings. The associated marginal effect roughly equals -0.13. Hence, ceteris paribus, the probability of this type of activism occurring in 2005 is on average 13 percent lower than the corresponding probability in 2004. Moreover, the "voting against" activism decision is not significantly related to either stock market performance, or the two accounting performance measures (ROE and market-to-book value of equity). These results suggest no evidence to support the rational view that portfolio managers target low-performing firms. On the other hand, activism is positively related to the institutional firm ownership proportion at the one percent significance level, and to firm size and firms' media appearance rate at the five percent level, confirming the results from the descriptive statistics in Panel A of Table 1.

The results from the second probit regression, where activism is measured as voting against the board or other owners and/or raising an opinion at the annual meeting, are also presented in Table 2 (Panel B). Although the explanatory power of the second regression model, as measured by both the pseudo R-squared value and the proportion of correctly predicted outcomes, is lower than for the first, most explanatory variables enter with the same signs and similar degrees of significance. The only noteworthy difference is the coefficient of media appearance variable, which is not significantly different from zero in the second regression model.

The results from Table 2 are consistent with portfolio managers choosing to be relatively more active in large firms, for which the proportion of institutional ownership is relatively large, and appear frequently in media. Interestingly, portfolio managers appear not to consider bad firm performance, in terms of either stock return or accounting measures, as a reason for targeting firms for activism. Moreover, it is difficult to reconcile a large number of firms' media appearances with agency theory related reasons for institutional owner activism. Instead, the activism behavior of institutions is consistent with institutional theory, and the note from Murphy and Van Nuys (1994) who argue that fund managers might benefit from the activism themselves, without focusing on and trying to improve target firms' performance. In view of this notion, it is rational for fund managers to choose to be active in large firms, with greater media coverage, for being in the spotlight, appearing to care about shareholder value.

Table 2: Results from the probit model of institutions' targeting of firms

Panel A: Vote against

Explanatory variables	Coefficient	Marg. Effect
Constant	-5.1023 (0.0031)	-0.4847
Indicator variable for 2005	-1.3609 (0.0007)	-0.1293
Prior year's market adjusted stock return	0.1085 (0.6595)	0.0103
Ln(book value of assets)	0.1557 (0.0407)	0.0148
Book return on equity (ROE)	0.0497 (0.8064)	0.0512
Market-to-book value of equity	0.0526 (0.3890)	0.0050
Proportion of institutional ownership	3.8938 (0.0029)	0.3699
Number of times in media	0.0039 (0.0323)	3.71e-4
Proportion correctly predicted	0.8991	
Pseudo R-squared	0.3323	

Investor activism is measured in two ways: as an indicator variable equal to one if the institution has voted against the board or another owner (Panel A, Vote against), and as an indicator variable equal to one if the institution has voted against the board or another owner, and/or raised an opinion (Panel B: Vote against and/or raise opinion) at the annual meeting. Explanatory variables in the probit model estimations are: an indicator variable for 2005 (where the base year is 2004), each firm's prior year's market adjusted stock return, the natural log of firm book value of assets, each firm's market-to-book value of equity, the proportion of institutional ownership of each firm, and the number of times each firm has appeared in media during the prior year.

Table 2: Results from the probit model of institutions' targeting of firms

Panel B: Vote against and/or raise opinion

Explanatory variables	Coefficient	Marg. Effect
Constant	-6.3849 (0.0001)	-1.2989
Indicator variable for 2005	-0.5854 (0.0152)	-0.1191
Prior year's market adjusted stock return	-0.0935 (0.6903)	-0.0190
Ln(book value of assets)	0.2226 (0.0023)	0.0453
Book return on equity (ROE)	-0.3409 (0.1850)	-0.0694
Market-to-book value of equity	0.0449 (0.4172)	0.0091
Proportion of institutional ownership	4.0050 (0.0001)	0.8147
Number of times in media	0.0027 (0.1559)	5.56e-4
Proportion correctly predicted	0.8716	
Pseudo R-squared	0.2620	

Each model uses the Huber-White quasi-maximum likelihood standard errors (see White, 1980). The estimated coefficients are presented for each explanatory variable, with *p*-values in parentheses, alongside corresponding marginal effects. Proportion correctly predicted refers to the relative number of correct classifications from each model. Accordingly, correct classifications occur if the predicted probability > 0.5, and the observed dependent variable equals one, or when the predicted probability ≤ 0.5, and the observed dependent variable equals zero. Pseudo R-squared corresponds to the measure of fit from Estrella (1998).

5. Concluding remarks

Reconsidering our empirical results we find important insights pertaining to our assumption of activist efforts being taken for other reasons than financial rationality. We find evidence of legitimacy seeking, as activism seems to be directed primarily towards large and visible firms with several institutional owners, while firm performance does not appear to be considered when making targeting decisions. Thus, the empirical data support the belief that shareholder activism is not used to monitor firm management but to gain societal legitimacy and position fund manager organizations as responsible corporate actors worthy of support.

To some extent, our results are consistent with previous research. In line with the studies of Bizjak and Marquette (1998), Carleton et al. (1998), Karpoff et al. (1996), and Smith (1996), we find that the proportion of institutional ownership is positively related to targeting. We also find that large firms attract more activism which is also the result obtained in Bizjak and Marquette (1998), John and Klein (1995), Johnson and Shackell (1997), Karpoff et al. (1996), Smith (1996), and Strickland et al. (1996). Note, however, that all of these studies use firm size merely as a control variable, without further theoretical motivation. Instead, following Murphy and Van Nuys (1994), we recognize that portfolio managers might pursue activism for their own benefits, without focusing on and trying to improve target firms' performance. In view of this notion, institutions are more likely to be active in large firms than in small firms, since the large firms' general meetings provide institutions with a relatively larger arena to promote their own organization, without necessarily allowing for a more successful influence on corporate decisions.

As an extension of previous research, we consider firm media appearance as a possible factor for triggering institutional activism. We find the media variable to be a significant determinant of activism defined as voting against board proposals at the general meeting. The support for activism being related to firm size, media exposure, and the level of institutional ownership, which is also confirmed by a majority of previous studies, while not to stock market or accounting based performance, indicates that institutional investors act based on alternative agendas than caring about shareholder value. The fact that we find no relation between firms' stock market performance and activism decisions is consistent with Carleton et al. (1998) and Smith (1996), but contrary to the results in Opler and Sobokin (1995) and Strickland et al. (1996). However, all four previous studies focus on a single portfolio manager's activism while our sample comprises a larger set of institutional investors. Moreover, since we consider both rational reasons for activism, as suggested by agency theory, and alternative explanations, consistent with institutional theory, we believe that our results are more general than those from previous studies.

On a final note, we recognize that it is not possible to exclude that actions are taken for more than one single reason. Actions can be taken with the purpose of seeking legitimacy by receiving public attention for the actions undertaken and at the same time having a monitoring effect on firm management, and vice versa. However, our empirical findings support the idea of legitimacy seeking rather than monitoring as being the first and foremost objective of activist efforts, and we conclude that agency theory assumptions of monitoring being the only reason for engaging in shareholder activism fails to explain the activism conducted and investigated in our empirical study. The findings imply that publicly visible shareholder activism is an arena for organizational positioning, where portfolio managers can receive time in the limelight to promote themselves as responsible corporate actors, even without focusing on financial rationales.

References

Admati, A., Pfleiderer, P., Zechner, J., 1994, Large Shareholder Activism, Risk Sharing and Financial Market Equilibrium, *Journal of Political Economy* 102, 1097-1130.

Agnblad, J., Berglöf, E., Högfeldt, P., Svancar, H., 2002, Ownership and Control in Sweden: Strong Owners, Weak Minorities, and Social Control. In Barca, F., Becht, M. (eds.), The Control of Corporate Europe, Oxford University Press.

Bhagat, S., Black, B., 1998, The Uncertain Relationship Between Board Composition and Firm Performance, Corporate Governance: The State of the Art and Emerging Research, In K. Hopt, M. Roe, and E. Wymeersch (eds.), Oxford University Press.

Bizjak, J., Marquette, C., 1998, Shareholder Proposals to Rescind Poison Pills: All Bark and No Bite, *Journal of Financial and Quantitative Analysis* 33, 499-523.

Brown, H., 1998. What Do Institutional Investors Really Want? *Corporate Board* 17, 5-10.

Carleton, W., Nelson, J., Weisbach, M., 1998, The Influence of Institutions on Corporate Governance through Private Negotiations: Evidence from TIAA CREF, *Journal of Finance* 53, 1335-1362.

de Jong, A., Mertens, G., Rosenboom, P., 2006, Shareholders' Voting at General Meetings: Evidence from the Netherlands, *Journal of Management and Governance* 10, 353-380.

Del Guercio, D., Hawkins, J., 1999, The Motivation and Impact of Pension Fund Activism, *Journal of Financial Economics* 52, 293-340.

DiMaggio, P., Powell, W., 1983, The Iron Cage Revisited: Institutional Isomorphism and Collective Rationality in Organizational Fields, *American Sociological Review* 48, 147-160.

English, P., Smythe, T., McNeil, C., 2000, The Role of Return Reversal in the "CalPERS Effect", *Working Paper*, Texas Tech University.

Estrella, A., 1998, A New Measure of Fit for Equations with Dichotomous Dependent Variables, *Journal of Business and Economic Statistics* 16, 198-205.

Gillan, S., Starks, L., 1998, A Survey of Shareholder Activism: Motivation and Empirical Evidence, *Contemporary Finance Digest* 2, 10-34.

Gorton, G., Kahl, M., 1999, Blockholder Indentity, Equity Ownership Structure and Hostile Takeovers, *NBER Working Paper* 7123.

Huson, M., 1997, Does Governance Matter? Evidence from CalPERS Interventions, *Working Paper*, University of Alberta.

Jensen, M., Meckling, W., 1976, Theory of the Firm: Managerial Behavior, Agency Costs and Ownership Structure, *Journal of Financial Economics* 3, 305-360.

John, K., Klein, A., 1995, Shareholder Proposals and Corporate Governance, *Working Paper*, New York University.

Johnson, M., Shackell, M., 1997, Shareholder Proposals on Executive Compensation, *Working Paper*, University of Michigan.

Kahn, C., Winton, A., 1998, Ownership Structure, Speculation and Shareholder Intervention, *Journal of Finance* 53, 99-129.

Karpoff, J., Malatesta, P., Walkling, R., 1996, Corporate Governance and Shareholder Initiatives: Empirical Evidence, *Journal of Financial Economics* 42, 365-395.

Karpoff, J., 2001, The Impact of Shareholder Activism on Target Companies: A Survey of Empirical Findings, *Working Paper*.

Martin, J., Kensinger, J., Gillan, S., 2000, Value Creation and Corporate Diversification: The Case of Sears, Roebuck & Co. *Journal of Financial Economics* 55, 103-137.

Menkhoff, L., 2002, Institutional Investors: The External Costs of a Successful Innovation, *Journal of Economic Issues* 36, 907-933.

Meyer, J., Rowan, B., 1977, Institutionalized Organizations: Formal Structure as Myths and Ceremony, *American Journal of Sociology* 83, 340-363.

Mizruchi, M., Fein, L., 1999. The Social Construction of Organizational Knowledge: A Study of the Uses of Coercive, Mimetic, and Normative Isomorphism, *Administrative Science Quarterly* 44, 653-683.
Murphy, K., Van Nuys, K., 1994, State Pension Funds and Shareholder In-Activism, *Working Paper*, Harvard Business School.
Nesbitt, S., 1994, Long Term Rewards from Shareholder Activism: A Study of the CalPERS Effect, *Journal of Applied Corporate Finance* 6, 75-80.
Opler, T., Sobokin, J., 1995, Does Coordinated Institutional Activism Work? An Analysis of the Activities of the Council of Institutional Investors, Ohio State University and Southern Methodist University Working Paper.
Pozen, R., 1994, Institutional Investors: The Reluctant Activists, *Harvard Business Review* 72, 140-149.
Prevost, A., Rao, R., 2000, Of What Value are Shareholder Proposals Sponsored by Public Pension Funds? *Journal of Business* 73, 177-204.
Rao, H., 2001, Gadflies and Corporate Behaviour, *Working Paper*, Emory University, Atlanta, CA.
Rehbein, K., Waddock, S., Graves, S., 2004, Understanding Shareholder Activism: Which Corporations Are Targeted? *Business & Society* 43, 239-267.
Romano, R., 1993, Public Pension Fund Activism in Corporate Governance Reconsidered, *Columbia Law Review* 93, 795-853.
Sheskin, D., 1997, Parametric and Nonparametric Statistical Procedures. Boca Raton: CRC Press.
Sias, R., Starks, L., 1998, Institutional Investors in Equity Markets, Working Paper, Washington State University.
Smith, M., 1996, Shareholder Activism by Institutional Investors: Evidence from CalPERS, *Journal of Finance* 51, 227-252.
Song, W-L., Szewczyk, S., 2003, Does Coordinated Institutional Activism Reverse the Fortune of Underperforming Firms? *Journal of Financial and Quantitative Analysis* 38, 317-366.
Strickland, D., Wiles, K., Zenner, M., 1996, A Requiem for the USA – Is Small Shareholder Monitoring Effective? *Journal of Financial Economics* 40, 319-338.
Tsui, R., 2000, On the Effectiveness of Pension Fund Activism, Working Paper, ULCA.
Useem, M., Bowman, E., Myatt, J., Irvine, C., 1993, US Institutional Investors Look at Corporate Governance in the 1990's, *European Management Journal* 11, 175-189.

Wahal, S., 1996, Pension Fund Activism and Firm Performance, *Journal of Financial and Qualitative Analysis* 31.

White, H., 1980, A Heteroskedasticity-Consistent Covariance Matrix Estimator and a Direct Test for Heteroscedasticity, *Econometrica* 48, 817-838.

Woidtke, T., 2002, Agents Watching Agents?: Evidence from Pension Fund Ownership and Firm Value, *Journal of Financial Economics* 63, 99-131.

Woods, J., 1996, The Effects of Pension Fund Activism on Corporate Performance: Evidence from Shareholder Proposals. *Ph.D. Dissertation*, Texas A&M University.

Wu, Yi Lin, 2000, Honey, CalPERS Shrank the Board! *Working Paper*, Hong Kong University of Science and Technology.

CHAPTER FIVE

CORPORATE GOVERNANCE AND THE COST OF DEBT

JASPER BLOM, MARC B.J. SCHAUTEN

Abstract

This paper examines the relation between the quality of corporate governance and the cost of debt. This study is based on the idea that debt holders take a firm's corporate governance into account when estimating its default risk. A higher quality would imply a lower cost of debt. The methodology of our study is comparable to Sengupta (1998). We use the Deminor Rating for the year 2000-2004 as a proxy for the quality of corporate governance performance of the 300 largest European firms (FTSE Eurotop 300). Deminor Rating bases its score on approximately 300 criteria, which can be subdivided into four corporate governance categories: rights and duties of shareholders; range of takeover defences; disclosure on corporate governance; and board structure and functioning. As a proxy for the cost of debt we use the yield of 340 bonds issued in the years 2001-2005. After adjusting for issuer characteristics, issue characteristics and market characteristics, we find that corporate governance performance is negatively related to the cost of debt. It shows that firms with strong corporate governance have lower cost of debt financing while firms with a relatively weak corporate governance performance are associated with higher cost of debt financing, with a difference of about 0.5%. The findings support the idea that debt holders use the quality of corporate governance in their assessment of risk profiles of firms. Our results imply - given the in general found positive correlation between corporate governance and equity related measures – that good corporate governance pays off for both equity and debt holders.

Keywords: corporate governance, cost of debt

1. Introduction[1]

This paper examines the relation between European firm's quality of corporate governance and their cost of debt. The results of this study show a significantly negative relation between our measure of the quality of corporate governance and the measure of the cost of debt, taking other possible determinants of the cost of debt into account. The cost of debt is measured by the yield to maturity on new debt issues. The quality of corporate governance is measured by the Deminor[2] corporate governance rating. This rating contains four different components, i.e. 1) rights and duties of shareholders 2) range of takeover defences 3) disclosure on corporate governance and 4) supervisory board structure and functioning. Especially disclosure on corporate governance has a negative impact on the cost of debt at a level that is both statistically and economically significant. This finding is in line with the results of Sengupta (1998) and Ashbaugh-Skaife, Collins and LaFond (2006).

A large body of literature already explored the influence of corporate governance on the return on equity and firm performance. A known example is the study of the CalPERS-effect (Nesbitt, 1994). CalPERS is an American pension fund with the characteristics of an active shareholder. A study into the stock returns of the firms included in CalPERS' portfolio, shows these returns to be significantly higher than the return on the S&P 500 index. Gompers et al. (2003) show a significantly positive relation between shareholders' rights (this is one component of corporate governance) and stock returns, firm value and accounting measures of performance. Bauer et al. (2004) uses the Deminor corporate governance rating and compares the performance of portfolios consisting of well-governed and poorly governed European firms. The impact of corporate governance on firm valuation is also examined. Bauer et al. (2004) find a positive relation between the variables performance and value, and corporate governance although the relationships weaken after

[1] We thank Kristof Hotiu and Jean-Nicolas Caprasse of RiskMetrics (previously Deminor) for making corporate governance data available, AAB for their data facilities and Floris Pot for his research assistance.

[2] Deminor offers since 1993 corporate governance ratings. Deminor was acquired by Institutional Shareholder Services (ISS) in 2005. ISS was acquired by RiskMetrics in 2006.

adjusting for country differences. Contrary to Gompers et al. (2003) they find a negative relation between governance standards and accounting measures of performance. Bauer et al. (2004) argue that this negative relation possibly implies that badly governed companies report less conservative earnings estimates.[3]

One of the first papers on corporate governance and the cost of debt is Sengupta (1998). He finds that firms with high disclosure quality ratings from financial analysts enjoy a lower cost of debt. His explanation is based on the argument that '... a policy of timely and detailed disclosures reduces lenders' and underwriters' perception of default risk for the disclosing firm, reducing its cost of debt' (Ibid., p.459). Bojraj and Sengupta (2003) find that bond yields are negatively associated with the percentage of shares held by institutions and the fraction of the board made up of nonofficers. Bojraj and Sengupta (2003) assume that governance mechanisms reduce potential conflicts of interest between the management and the providers of capital through effective monitoring their actions. The role that governance plays here in mitigating agency conflicts between management and stakeholders (i.e. shareholders and bondholders) is called the "management disciplining" hypothesis and has positive effects on shareholders' and bondholders' wealth (see Ashbaugh-Skaife et al.,2006, p. 207). Klock, Mansi and Maxwell (2005) find that antitakeover governance provisions are viewed favourably in the bond market. They explain this finding by the prohibition of shareholder expropriation of bondholder wealth.[4] The role governance plays here is in accordance with the "wealth redistribution" hypothesis wealth (see Ashbaugh-Skaife et al. (2006), p. 208). Ashbaugh-Skaife et al. (2006) investigate whether firms with strong corporate governance benefit from higher firms' credit ratings relative to firms with weaker governance. Ashbaugh-Skaife et al. (2006) use variables based on the four governance components from Standard & Poor's framework.[5] They find several variables related to firms' credit ratings that proxy for agency conflicts

---

[3] Other literature that investigates the effect of corporate governance from the perspective of the shareholder contains a.o.; McConnell and Serves (1990), Yermack (1996) and Karpoff, Malesta and Walkling (1996).

[4] New management could e.g. increase leverage with a negative impact on the wealth of the old bondholders as a result.

[5] S&P's four governance components are; ownership structure and influence, financial stakeholder's rights and relations, financial transparency and disclosure and board structure and processes (Standard & Poor, 2002).

between external stakeholders and management and variables that proxy for potential conflicts between bondholders and shareholders.

This research contributes to the literature in two ways. First we provide empirical evidence for European companies instead of U.S. companies. Second, our governance measure contains four different components of corporate governance from one independent source. This makes it possible to determine the relevance of each component for the cost of debt and makes our study - as Ashbaugh-Skaife et al. (2006) - more comprehensive than studies that take one aspect into account only.

The structure of the paper is as follows. Section 2 discusses prior empirical research into the relation between the quality of corporate governance and the return on equity and debt. In section 3 the hypotheses are formulated, the methodology is described and a description of the data is given. Section 4 describes the results of the empirical research and section 5 gives a brief summary.

2. Prior empirical research

This brief survey of prior research is structured in two parts. First, empirical research on the relationship between equity returns, firm value and firm performance is discussed. Second, we discuss empirical research on the association between corporate governance and the cost of debt.

CalPERS (California Public Employees Retirement System) is an American pension fund which actively monitors the firms of its investment portfolio. Nesbitt (1994) has studied the stock returns in the period 1987-1992 of 42 firms which were actively monitored by CalPERS. The research shows an average return of 52% above the return on the S&P 500. Even more striking is the fact that the average return of the 42 firms in the period 1982-1987 (CalPERS was not actively monitoring the firms in this period) was 66% below the return on the S&P 500 index. This relation is known as the CalPERS-effect.

Gompers et al. (2003) have studied the influence of corporate governance on stock returns. There are substantial differences in the field of shareholders' rights (a component of corporate governance) among firms. Using 24 antitakeover indicators, the authors compose a 'governance index', which is used to estimate the rights of approximately 1500 firms' shareholders in the period 1990-1999. A low index score implies stronger shareholder rights (weak antitakeover provisions) and a high score vice-versa. The authors find a significantly negative relation between this index and stock returns. An investment strategy, in which shares of firms with strong shareholder rights are bought and shares of firms with weak shareholder rights are sold, would have resulted in an exceptional return of 8.5% per year, during the research period. Furthermore the 'governance index ' is shown to be strongly correlated with Tobin's Q. An increase of 1 in the 1990 index is associated with a 2.4% decrease in Tobin's Q. This difference has increased enormously in 1999: an increase in the index of 1 in 1999 is associated with a 8.9% decrease in Tobin's Q. Finally, relations are shown between weak shareholder rights on the one hand and lower profit, lower revenue growth and higher capital expenditure on the other hand.

Bauer et al. (2004) perform the same kind of analysis for Europe (EMU countries versus UK) as Gompers et al. (2003) did for the U.S. Instead of using antitakeover indicators, Bauer et al. (2004) uses the Deminor corporate governance rating (total score) for 2000 and 2001 instead. Bauer et al. (2004) find some evidence that governance affects stock returns positively for UK firms but not for EMU countries. The impact of corporate governance on firm value is rather strong for EMU firms but not for the UK.[6] The results with respect to the relationship between corporate governance and firm performance are contrary to expectations, especially for the EMU countries. For the UK firms, there was no significant relation while for EMU firms a significantly negative coefficient was found for performance indicator net profit margin.[7] Bauer et al. (2004) give two possible explanations for this negative relation; 1) accounting numbers could be biased measures of firm performance and 2) possibly bad governed firms report less conservative earnings.

Klock, Mansi and Maxwell (2005) examine the relation between the Gompers et al. (2003) governance index and firm value from the view of the bondholders. According to Klock et al. (2003) the expected relation is not straight forward since antitakeover provisions might influence the value of debt in several ways. First, takeovers could reduce the cost of

[6] The strong impact for EMU firms could be due to country effects which have been documented by LaPorta et al. (1998). After country adjustments Bauer et al. (2004) find a weaker relationship.

[7] Even after adjusting for country effects.

debt as a result of coinsurance (see Billet et al., 2004).[8] Antitakeover provisions could then be interpreted as negative for the value of debt since this coinsurance effect is prohibited by the use of the provisions. Second, a takeover however could also have negative effects on bondholders' wealth and increase the cost of debt if e.g. management increases leverage or increases the payout (excess cash) to shareholders (on behalf of the shareholders) after the takeover. Third, antitakeover provisions could improve capital investment decisions[9] which have a positive influence on shareholder *and* bondholder wealth and decrease the cost of debt. Fourth, if takeover defences make managers invulnerable for the market of corporate control (Jensen and Ruback, 1983) this could have a negative impact on firm performance (because of e.g. shirking of effort) as well as on the wealth of the shareholders and bondholders. This would increase the cost of debt. Fifth, antitakeover provisions might decrease the risk of the firm and cost of debt if managers invest less in risky projects to protect their job and to reduce their human capital risk (Amihud and Lev, 1981). Klock et al. (2005) find a difference of about 34 basis points between the cost of debt of firms with the strongest management rights (strongest antitakeover provisions) and the strongest shareholder rights (weakest antitakeover provisions) and implicitly state that the positive[10] effect of the "wealth redistribution" hypothesis is stronger than the negative[11] effect of the "management disciplining" hypothesis.

Bojraj and Sengupta (2003) find that bond yields are negatively associated with the percentage of shares held by institutions and the fraction of the board made up of nonofficers, proxies for good governance.

---

[8] Klock et al. (2005), p.694, suggest there is a negative relation between the premiums shareholders of the target capture and the cost of debt. We do not agree with this assumption. First, if the shareholders of the target are paid in cash this payment negatively influences the value of the assets of the new combination. A negative relation between the premium and the cost of debt could be assumed then. Second, if the shareholders of the target are paid in new shares, the fraction the shareholders of the target get does not influence the value of the assets of the new combination which implies no relation between the premium and the cost of debt. Of course, for the shareholders of the target, antitakeover provisions are positively rewarded if management can extract higher offers from the bidder.

[9] Stein's (1988) model suggests that managers of sheltered firms are more likely to invest in R&D like projects. Harris (1990) shows that e.g. golden parachutes positively influences managerial investment in specialized human capital beneficial for the shareholders.

[10] The negative wealth transfer effect for the bondholders will be prohibited.

[11] The positive effect on firm performance will be prohibited.

Bojraj and Sengupta (2003) assume that governance mechanisms reduce potential conflicts of interest between the management and the providers of capital through effective monitoring their actions ("management disciplining" hypothesis). Bojraj and Sengupta (2003) assume that governance mechanisms reduce potential conflicts of interest between the management and the providers of capital through effective monitoring their actions. However they find that concentrated institutional ownership has an adverse impact on bond yields since the decisions made by the firm could be influenced by these institutions in their own advantage ("wealth redistribution" hypothesis).

Sengupta (1998) shows the relation between the quality of a firms' disclosure and their cost of debt.[12] The measure for the quality of the disclosure is a rating of the firm by financial analysts. The research uses two different measures for the cost of debt: 1) the yield to maturity on new issues and (2) the total interest expenses of the new issues. Results show both measures to be negatively correlated to the measure for the quality of the disclosure, taking other possible determinants of the cost of debt into account. Moreover the results imply the specific importance of disclosure to firms with insecure future prospects, using the standard deviation of daily stock returns as a measure for future insecurity.

Ashbaugh-Skaife, Collins and LaFond (2006) structure their analysis by using a framework developed by Standard & Poor's.[13] They find that firms overall credit ratings are 1) negatively associated with the number of block holders that own at least 5% ownership in the firm (this variable captures S&P's component Ownership Structure and Influence); 2) positively related to weaker shareholder rights in terms of takeover defences (S&P component Financial Stakeholder Rights and Relations); 3) positively related to the quality of working capital accruals and the timeliness of earnings (S&P component Financial Transparency); and 4) positively related to overall board independence, board stock ownership,

---

[12] The relation between disclosure and the cost of equity is analyzed by e.g. Welker (1995) and Botosan (1997). Welker (1995) documents a negative association between financial analysts' disclosure measurement the bid-ask spread set by market makers. Botosan (1997) finds for the machinery industry a negative association between disclosures in annual reports and firm's cost of equity, but only for firms with low analyst following.

[13] This framework focuses on four major components of governance: ownership Structure and Influence, Financial Stakeholder Rights and Relations, financial transparency and Board Structure and Processes (Standard & Poor, 2002).

board expertise and negatively related to CEO power on the board (S&P component Board Structure and Processes). (Ibid., p. 204.) The relations are explained by the effect of the selected variables on agency conflicts between external stakeholders (bondholders and shareholders) and management ("management disciplining" hypothesis) and potential conflicts between bondholders and shareholders ("wealth redistribution" hypothesis).

3. Hypothesis, research method and data

3.1. Hypothesis

This study is based on the philosophy that debt holders take a firm's corporate governance into account when estimating its default risk[14], therefore implying that the quality of corporate governance has an impact on the cost of debt. We assume a negative relation between the cost of debt and the quality of the components 'the degrees of transparency and responsibility towards the market' and 'Supervisory Board's structure and functioning'. Given the possible opposite effects of the "management disciplining" hypothesis and the "wealth redistribution hypothesis" for the components 'the shareholders' rights', 'range of takeover defences' we leave the prediction for these components unsigned. For the total governance score we might expect a negative relation with the cost of debt.

3.2. The research model

The influence of a firm's corporate governance quality on the cost of debt is examined by the following model[15]:

$$COD_{t+1} = f\,(COGO_t, \text{Control variables}) \qquad (1)$$

where,

[14] Prior studies of the determinants of the cost of debt present a negative relation between the firm's measures of default risk and cost of debt. In other words: the higher the default risk, the higher the cost of debt. See e.g. Fisher (1959), Jaffee (1975), Kidwell et al. (1984), and Fung and Rudd (1986).

[15] The model used by Sengupta (1998) serves as a basis for the method used in this paper.

COD_{t+1} the cost of debt issued in year t+1; as proxy for the Cost of Debt in year t+1 (COD_{t+1}) the yield to maturity on the first day of the issue in year t+1 is used. $COGO_t$ the measure for the quality of corporate governance measured over a period finishing in year t; a high score implies a high quality of corporate governance. COGO (0-40) is the total governance score or scores of the four different components (0-10).

This paper examines the possible relation between the quality of a firm's corporate governance and the firm's cost of debt. However, besides the quality of corporate governance, other determinants of the cost of debt exist. The "disturbing" effect of these factors is eliminated by incorporating control variables in the model. The selection of the control variables is based on prior research into the determinants of the cost of debt.

The following control variables have been selected by using prior research into the determinants of bond ratings and yields[16]. These studies explain bond issue costs by means of: issue characteristics; issuer characteristics; and market characteristics.

The issue characteristics are:

LNSIZE = logarithm of the issue amount (mln. €); as a result of the size-effect the measure for the cost of debt is expected to be negatively related to the issue amount. In short, the higher the issue amount, the lower the costs.

LNMATUR = logarithm of the maturity; bonds with a longer maturity are expected to have a higher yield, because of the increased exposure to interest rate risk.

CALL = 1 if the obligation is callable and 0 if the bond is not callable from the date of issue. The issuer of the bond will have to pay extra if the bond is callable; therefore a positive relation between CALL and the yield is expected.

CONVERT = 1 if the obligation is convertible into shares, otherwise 0; convertible bonds are expected to have a lower yield. Convertible bonds have a lower yield, because part of

[16] Fisher (1959), Jaffee (1975), Sorensen (1979), Boardman and McEnally (1981), Kidwell et al. (1984), Wilson and Howard (1984), Fung and Rudd (1986), Lamy and Thompson (1988), Feroz and Wilson (1992), Ziebart and Reiter (1992) and Sengupta (1998).

	the compensation for investors comes from the value of the option. A negative relation is expected.
SUBORD =	1 if the bond is subordinated, otherwise 0; subordinated bonds are expected to have a higher yield. A positive relation is expected.

The issuer characteristics are:

DE =	book value long term interest bearing debt divided by market value of equity at the end of year t; firms with a higher ratio are expected to have a higher yield;
MARGIN =	net income before preferred dividends in year t divided by net sales or revenues in year t; firms with a higher profit margin are expected to have a lower yield;
TIMES =	the sum of net income before interest and tax expense of year t divided by interest expense in year t; firms with a higher ratio are expected to have a lower yield;
LNASSET =	natural logarithm of the total assets (mln. €) at the end of year t; large firms are expected to have a lower yield;
STDRETN =	standard deviation of the daily stock return in year t corrected for dividends and stock splits. Standard deviation is a measure of total risk of equity. We assume a positive relation with the yield.

The market conditions are:

TBILL =	yield (on the bond issue date) of government bonds of the firm's country of residence with approximately the same maturity; the higher this yield, the higher the yield on the relevant bond is expected to be.
BC =	yield (on the date of the company's bond issue) on Moody's Aaa-bonds minus the yield on government bonds with the longest maturity (also on the date of issue) of the country where the company is primary listed; the yield on the issued bond is expected to increase with an increase of BC.

Next the following YIELD model is estimated[17]:

[17] The firm and time subscripts are not shown.

$$COD = \alpha_0 + \alpha_1 COGO + \alpha_2 DE + \alpha_3 MARGIN + \alpha_4 TIMES + \alpha_5 LASSET + \alpha_6 STDRETN + \alpha_7 LSIZE + \alpha_8 LMATUR + \alpha_9 CALL + \alpha_{10} CONVERT + \alpha_{11} SUBORD + \alpha_{12} TBILL + \alpha_{13} BC + \varepsilon \quad (2)$$

Where COD = YIELD

The expected signs of the coefficients are: $\alpha_1 < 0$, $\alpha_2 > 0$, $\alpha_3 < 0$, $\alpha_4 < 0$, $\alpha_5 < 0$, $\alpha_6 > 0$, $\alpha_7 < 0$, $\alpha_8 > 0$, $\alpha_9 > 0$, $\alpha_{10} < 0$, $\alpha_{11} > 0$, $\alpha_{12} > 0$, $\alpha_{13} > 0$.

An alternative is to include the credit rating (RATE) as a control variable as well. RATE is the Moody's rating (or S&P rating if Moody's was not available) attached to the particular bond. A scale has been constructed from 1 to 9 where 1 is the score for the best rated bonds and 9 for the worst. See Appendix A for the conversion table. The use of RATE as independent variable creates the risk of including the same control variables twice in the regression, as they can be determinants of RATE. To overcome this problem, the control variables are regressed on RATE, using the following equations:

$$RATE = \beta_0 + \beta_1 + \beta_2 MARGIN + \beta_3 TIMES + \beta_4 LASSET + \beta_5 STDRETN + \beta_6 LSIZE + \beta_7 LMATUR + \beta_8 CALL + \beta_9 CONVERT + \beta_{10} SUBORD + \beta_{11} TBILL + \beta_{12} BC + \varepsilon \quad (3)$$

The control variables with a significant impact on RATE will not be included in the YIELD model.[18] The regression equation of this alternative method looks as follows:

$$COD = \alpha_0 + \alpha_1 COGO + \alpha_2 RATE + \alpha_n \text{Remained n Control variables} + \varepsilon \quad (4)$$

3.3 The dataset

The original dataset consists of corporate governance ratings for European companies for the period 2000-2004. We excluded financial firms (Worldscope Industry Group code 4300) as their financing decisions are affected by somewhat different factors than those of the industrial firms (Sengupta, 1998) and some accounting variables of financial firms are difficult to compare to those of non financial firms. Information on bond issues in 2001-2005 was obtained from Bloomberg. Companies that

[18] We estimated (3) without the market conditions TBILL and BC as well.

issued bonds in either Japanese Yen or a Floating Rate Note (FRN) were removed because of their strongly deviating yields. The yield of the JPY-denominated bonds is low, and the yield of the FRN fluctuates along with the market interest rate. This complicates a comparison to the other observations. All of this finally resulted in a dataset consisting of 340 issues by 178 firms from 16 European countries. [19] A bond rating is available for 318 of the 340 bonds.

The corporate governance quality of the firms from the dataset has been measured by means of the Deminor corporate governance ratings for the years 2000-2004. Year t ratings are each year published at the beginning of year t+1. Deminor Rating annually provides independent, reliable and comparable research into European firm's corporate governance. Deminor Rating follows the FTSE Eurotop 300 index, which consists of 300 firms in 17 different countries. The corporate governance of the assessed firms has been determined using a detailed analysis of over 300 indicators. [20] From 1993 on, this network of indicators has been developed and kept up to date by Deminor Rating in cooperation with large institutional investors. The indicator can be subdivided into the following four categories: rights and duties of shareholders; range of takeover defences; disclosure on corporate governance; and supervisory Board structure and functioning.

The ratings by Deminor Rating as well as the research are based on publicly available information. When assessing a firm, Deminor Rating concludes by giving ratings for each of the above mentioned categories. The rating is scaled from 10 to 0 Deminor, where 10 Deminor is the highest score and 0 Deminor the lowest score.

---

[19] Austria (2 issues), Belgium (5), Switzerland (17), Finland (6), France (79), Germany (43), Greece (2), Ireland (2), Italy (17), Luxembourg (2), The Netherlands (25), Norway (4), Poland (1), Spain (18), Sweden (17), United Kingdom (100).

[20] The elements of the Deminor rating are based on accepted standards established by the International Corporate Governance Network, the World Bank / Organisation for Economic Cooperation and Development and the Conference Board. The criteria used by S&P for their corporate governance score are about the same (Standard & Poor's, 2002). From this fact, that all of these institutions have more or less the same ideas concerning good corporate governance, it follows that the Deminor corporate governance rating is a representative measure for the quality of a firm's corporate governance.

The issue characteristics of the 340 bonds (Size, Maturity, Callable, Convertible and Subordinated) have been obtained from Bloomberg. All the issue amounts (size) have been converted into Euro, using several exchange rates on the issue date.

The issuer characteristics are obtained from various sources. An overview of the variables used and their corresponding source and code can be found in Appendix B.

Market condition T-Bill is the yield of a comparable government bond (same maturity) in the country where the company is listed. When no matching maturity was found, the government bond with the closest maturity to the actual company bond was used. For the companies Arcelor and SES Global, which are primary based in Luxembourg, European government bonds were used because there are no government bonds available from Luxembourg. To calculate BC, Moody's Aaa-rated bonds were used. Again, when there was no matching maturity the bond with the closest maturity was taken. The longest maturity differed between the countries, but usually the longest maturity was 30 years. For Luxembourg, European government bonds with a 30-year maturity were used. Both T-Bill and BC were calculated on the day the particular company issued its debt.

This dataset has been used in a cross-section study, which examined if a high Deminor-rating in year t, resulted in a lower cost of debt in year t+1. Appendix C provides descriptive statistics and correlations among the variables.

4. Results

The hypothesis has been tested using regression equation (2). Table 7-1 summarizes the results.

Table 7-1 Results YIELD regression

Model [1] uses the total corporate governance score as one of the independent variables while model [2] uses the four separate scores instead. OLS regression is used with White's heteroskedasticity consistent standard errors. t-values are presented between parentheses.

Variables	Predicted sign	[1]	[2]
Corporate governance			
Shareholder rights	?		-0.054
			(-1.214)
Takeover defences	?		0.009
			(0.437)
Board structure	-		-0.003
			(-0.047)
Disclosure	-		-0.103
			(-2.088)**
Corporate governance total	-	-0.021	
		(-2.584)**	
Issue characteristics			
LNSIZE	-	-0.005	0.007
		(-0.122)	(0.169)
LNMATUR	+	0.514	0.546
		(4.250)***	(4.410)***
CALL	+	-0.294	-0.256
		(-1.089)	(-0.925)
CONV	-	-2.567	-2.565
		(-9.188)***	(-9.133)***
SUBORD	+	0.882	0.841
		(2.707)***	(2.685)***
Firm characteristics			
DE	+	0.380	0.414
		(4.094)***	(4.321)***
MARGIN	-	-0.004	-0.004
		(-0.809)	(-0.822)
TIMES	-	-0.002	-0.001
		(-0.219)	(-0.173)
LNASSETS	-	-0.156	-0.147
		(-3.030)***	(-2.754)***
STDRETN	+	0.440	0.418
		(5.847)***	(5.727)***
Market characteristics			
TBILL	+	0.646	0.624
		(8.659)***	(8.207)***
BC	+	0.301	0.260
		(2.963)***	(2.575)**
C		4.044	4.186
		(2.719)***	(2.867)***
Adjusted R^2		0.604	0.607
Sample Size		340	340

*,**,*** denote significance at the 0.10, 0.05, and 0.01 levels, respectively.

The results of model [1] in Table 7-1 support the hypothesis that the quality of corporate governance has a negative impact on the cost of debt. The coefficient of corporate governance total is -0.021 and is statistically and economically significant. This result indicates that an increase in the corporate governance measure with 10 points results in a 0.21% decrease in the firm's yield. Consequently, the firm with the highest corporate governance score (34 points) would have an approximately 0.546% lower yield than the firm with the lowest corporate governance score (8 points). The philosophy that debt holders include the firm's corporate governance quality in their investment decision has been confirmed. The results of model [2] in Table 7-1 show that especially the component disclosure is responsible for the relation found. The coefficient for disclosure is -0.103 and significant. This implies that the firm with the highest score for disclosure (9 points) would have an approximately 0.721% lower yield than the firm with the lowest corporate governance score (2 points) ceteris paribus. The coefficients for the components shareholder rights, takeover defences and board structure are all insignificant.

As was mentioned in section 3, the relation between YIELD and COGO has also been tested with RATE included as a control variable. To prevent inclusion of the same control variables twice, the control variables have first been regressed on RATE. This concerns a logistic regression, since RATE is an ordinal variable.

Table 7-2 Results RATE regression

Model [1] includes the market characteristics while model [2] excludes the market characteristics. This table uses ordered logistic regression with Huber/White heteroskedasticity consistent standard errors. The z-stats are presented between parentheses.

Variables	Predicted sign	[1]	[2]
Issue characteristics			
LNSIZE	-	0.297	0.309
		(2.542)**	(2.749)***
LNMATUR	+	-0.320	-0.179
		(-1.312)	(-0.729)
CALL	?	-0.156	0.007
		(-0.281)	(0.014)
CONV	?	0.640	0.413
		(0.870)	(0.546)
SUBORD	+	0.013	0.094
		(0.022)	(0.179)
Firm characteristics			
DE	+	1.023	0.926
		(3.658)***	(3.738)***
MARGIN	-	0.001	0.006
		(0.092)	(0.453)
TIMES	-	-0.116	-0.118
		(-3.916)***	(-3.903)***
LNASSETS	-	-0.828	-0.825
		(-5.832)***	(-6.113)***
STDRETN	+	0.239	0.323
		(1.507)	(2.121)**
Market characteristics			
TBILL	?	0.397	
		(2.309)**	
BC	?	-0.030	
		(-0.133)	
Sample Size		318	318

*,**,*** denote significance at the 0.10, 0.05, and 0.01 levels, respectively.

As shown in model [1] in Table 7-2 the variables LNSIZE, DE, TIMES, LNASSETS and TBILL are found to be determinants of RATE.[21]. Therefore these variables are left out, as a result of which the regression equation looks as follows:

$$COD = \alpha_0 + \alpha_1 COGO + \alpha_2 MARGIN + \alpha_3 STDRETN + \alpha_4 LMATUR + \alpha_5 CALL + \alpha_6 CONVERT + \alpha_7 SUBORD + \alpha_8 RATE + \alpha_9 BC + \varepsilon \qquad (5)$$

The results of this regression are summarized in Table 7-3. Model [1] presents the results of regression (5) where COGO is equal to the total corporate governance score. Model [2] presents the results of (5) but now including the scores of the four separate components instead of one total governance score.[22]

[21] If we exclude the market variables TBILL and BC the variable STDRETN becomes significant as well, see model [2] in Table 7-2. Models [3] and [4] in Table 7-3 contain results of equation (5) excluding STDRETN but including TBILL.

[22] Models [3] and [4] in Table 7-3 are based on the outcome of model [2] from Table 7-2 where RATE is regressed on the explanatory variables excluding the market variables TBILL and BC. Models [3] and [4] include TBILL but exclude STDRETN as explanatory variables.

Table 7-3 Results YIELD regression including RATE

Model [1] and [2] exclude variables related to RATE based on model [1] from Table 7-2, i.e. LNSIZE, DE, TIMES, LNASSETS and TBILL. Model [1] includes the total corporate governance score, model [2] the separate corporate governance scores. Model [3] and [4] exclude variables related to RATE based on model [2] from Table 7-2, i.e. LNSIZE, DE, TIMES, LNASSETS and STDRETN. Model [3] includes the total corporate governance score, model [4] the separate corporate governance scores. t-values are presented between parentheses.

Variables	E(Sign)	[1]	[2]	[3]	[4]
Corporate governance					
Shareholder rights	?		0.000 (0.009)		-0.030 (-0.710)
Takeover defences	?		0.038 (1.872)		0.013 (0.653)
Board structure	-		0.019 (0.326)		-0.074 (-1.275)
Disclosure	-		-0.131 (-2.682)***		-0.090 (-1.865)*
Corporate gov. total	-	0.002 (0.248)		-0.026 (-3.046)***	
Issue characteristics					
LNSIZE	-				
LNMATUR	+	0.874 (6.602)***	0.913 (6.873)***	0.509 (4.526)***	0.566 (5.056)***
CALL	+	0.035 (0.118)	0.080 (0.268)	-0.152 (-0.587)	-0.092 (-0.350)
CONV	-	-3.157 (-8.541)***	-3.161 (-8.346)***	-2.424 (-7.296)***	-2.462 (-7.610)***
SUBORD	+	0.853 (3.130)***	0.810 (3.058)***	0.900 (2.256)**	0.882 (2.330)**
RATE	+	0.313 (3.504)***	0.313 (3.501)***	0.316 (3.538)***	0.313 (3.513)***
Firm characteristics					
DE	+				
MARGIN	-	0.002 (0.306)	0.001 (0.186)	-0.020 (-3.015)***	-0.019 (-2.824)***
TIMES	-				
LNASSETS	-				
STDRETN	+	0.542 (6.541)***	0.501 (6.083)***		
Market characteristics					
TBILL	+			0.721 (9.214)***	0.684 (8.615)***
BC	+	0.288 (2.538)***	0.224 (1.909)*	0.358 (3.274)***	0.307 (2.880)***
C		0.547 (1.185)	1.260 (2.369)	0.136 (0.334)	0.746 (1.492)
Adjusted R^2		0.604	0.499	0.559	0.568
Sample Size		318	318	318	318

*,**,*** denote significance at the 0.10, 0.05, and 0.01 levels, respectively.

Not surprisingly, RATE proves to be a significant determinant of the YIELD. The results further show that the coefficient of the total corporate governance score becomes statistically insignificant (see model [1]). However, the coefficient for disclosure is -0.131 and remains statistically and economically significant (see model [2]). In other words, disclosure provides additional information not captured by RATE.[23]

Given the results of Bauer et al. (2004) we might expect the relation between YIELD and corporate governance to be stronger for civil law countries than for common law countries. Bauer et al. (2004) find a positive relation between value and corporate governance for civil law countries and not for common law countries (UK). This positive relation for civil law countries could be the result of a negative relation between the cost of capital (weighted average of the cost of equity and debt) and corporate governance. If we make a distinction between civil law and common law countries, first results do not show significant differences. The results for the corporate governance total score are presented in model [1] and [3] in Table 7-4 for the common law countries and civil law countries respectively. If we look at the coefficients of the different components instead of the total governance score the results remain similar, see model [2] and [4] in Table 7-4.

[23] If we include TBILL and exclude STDRETN then corporate governance total and disclosure are both negatively significant, see model [3] and [4] in Table 7-3.

Table 7-4 Results YIELD regression, common law versus civil law countries

Model [1] and [2] present the results of the yield regression for the common law countries. Model [3] and [4] present the results of the yield regression for the civil law countries. Model [1] and [3] present the coefficient for the total corporate governance score, model [2] and [4] for the four separate governance scores. OLS regression is used with White's heteroskedasticity consistent standard errors. t-values are presented between parentheses.

Variables	E(Sign)	[1]	[2]	[3]	[4]
Corporate governance					
Shareholder rights	?		0.094		-0.073
			(0.586)		(-1.499)
Takeover defences	?		-0.027		0.008
			(-0.586)		(0.388)
Board structure	-		0.112		-0.016
			(0.781)		(-0.262)
Disclosure	-		-0.106		-0.053
			(-0.433)		(-0.950)
Corporate governance total	-	0.001		-0.015	
		(0.083)		(-1.398)	
Issue characteristics					
LNSIZE	-	-0.047	-0.040	0.021	0.030
		(-0.387)	(-0.328)	(0.447)	(0.622)
LNMATUR	+	0.729	0.699	0.424	0.469
		(3.551)***	(3.284)***	(2.673)***	(2.718)***
CALL	+	0.034	0.013	-0.630	-0.612
		(0.133)	(0.048)	(-1.432)	(-1.378)
CONV	-	-2.606	-2.610	-2.590	-2.586
		(-5.611)***	(-5.564)***	(-7.187)***	(-7.240)***
SUBORD	+	0.229	0.223	1.251	1.236
		(0.770)	(0.641)	(3.053)***	(3.074)***
Firm characteristics					
DE	+	0.524	0.492	0.290	0.319
		(2.886)***	(2.351)**	(2.457)**	(2.669)**
MARGIN	-	-0.011	-0.009	-0.001	-0.003
		(-1.117)	(-0.924)	(-0.206)	(-0.397)
TIMES	-	0.014	0.011	-0.008	-0.006
		(1.194)	(0.909)	(-0.880)	(-0.667)
LNASSETS	-	-0.225	-0.216	-0.120	-0.112
		(-2.216)**	(-2.016)**	(-1.808)*	(-1.590)
STDRETN	+	0.412	0.451	0.461	0.443
		(2.956)***	(2.947)***	(4.922)***	(4.920)***
Market characteristics					
TBILL	+	0.926	0.925	0.671	0.642
		(4.961)***	(4.893)***	(8.005)***	(6.839)***
BC	+	0.319	0.295	0.339	0.297
		(2.013)**	(1.515)	(2.337)**	(1.983)**
C		3.974	3.298	2.650	2.868
		(1.050)	(0.897)	(1.519)	(1.667)
Adjusted R^2		0.636	0.627	0.606	0.605
Sample Size		102	102	238	238

*,**,*** denote significance at the 0.10, 0.05, and 0.01 levels, respectively.

However, if we include RATE in the model and exclude the control variables that were significantly related to RATE (DE, TIMES, LNASSETS and TBILL) then the coefficient for disclosure is significantly negative for civil law countries and insignificant for common law countries. See Table 7-5 model [2] and [4].[24] This finding might explain (partly) the positive relation between value and corporate governance for civil law countries and the absence of this relation for common law countries as presented by Bauer et al. (2004). A possible explanation could be that differences in creditor rights between common law and civil law countries. Because creditor rights are relatively strong in common law countries (Laporta et al., 1998) differences in corporate governance scores might have a less severe impact on the cost of debt of common law countries' firms.[25]

---

[24] If we only include DISCLOSURE as corporate governance variable then the coefficient for DISCLOSURE for common law countries' firms is -0.295 (t-value of -1.17)and for the civil law countries' firms -0.175 (t-value of -4.1).

25 The difference in findings between the non-UK and UK sample can be compared with the difference in the governance-cash holdings findings by Dittmar et al. (2003) and Harford et al. (2008). Dittmar et al. (2003) finds that corporations in countries where shareholder rights are not well protected hold more cash than firms in countries with good shareholder protection, while Harford et al. (2008) report a positive relation between the quality of governance and cash holdings for US firms.

Table 7-5 Results YIELD regression including RATE, common law versus civil law countries

Models exclude variables related to RATE based on model [1] from Table 7-2, i.e. LNSIZE, DE, TIMES, LNASSETS and TBILL. Model [1] and [2] present the results of the yield regression for the common law countries. Model [3] and [4] present the results of the yield regression for the civil law countries. Model [1] and [3] present the coefficient for the total corporate governance score, model [2] and [4] for the four separate governance scores. OLS regression is used with White's heteroskedasticity consistent standard errors. t-values are presented between parentheses.

Variables	E(Sign)	[1]	[2]	[3]	[4]
Corp.governance					
Shareholder rights	?		0.116		-0.065
			(0.706)		(-1.294)
Takeover defences	?		-0.018		0.039
			(-0.359)		(1.720)*
Board structure	-		0.109		-0.049
			(0.808)		(-0.709)
Disclosure	-		-0.377		-0.161
			(-1.389)		(-3.045)***
Corp.gov.total	-	0.008		-0.020	
		(0.434)		(-1.449)	
Issue characteristics					
LNSIZE	-				
LNMATUR	+	0.641	0.560	1.026	1.102
		(3.003)***	(2.636)***	(6.069)***	(6.712)***
CALL	+	0.506	0.427	-0.709	-0.648
		(1.951)*	(1.595)	(-1.535)	(-1.393)
CONV	-	-2.722	-2.670	-3.544	-3.569
		(-4.978)***	(-4.884)***	(-8.440)***	(-9.031)***
SUBORD	+	0.662	0.633	1.184	1.057
		(1.693)*	(1.544)	(3.326)*	(3.027)***
RATE	+	0.477	0.470	0.203	0.180
		(3.669)***	(3.454)***	(1.722)*	(1.520)
Firm characteristics					
DE	+				
MARGIN	-	0.001	0.000	0.000	-0.003
		(0.173)	(-0.030)	(0.013)	(-0.312)
TIMES	-				
LNASSETS	-				
STDRETN	+	0.399	0.377	0.626	0.548
		(2.489)**	(2.070)**	(6.578)**	(5.794)***
Market characteristics					
TBILL	+				
BC	+	0.449	0.280	0.215	0.092
		(3.147)***	(1.391)	(1.307)	(0.540)
C		0.399	2.553	0.942	2.248
		(0.417)	(1.030)	(1.332)	(2.762)***
Adjusted R^2		0.534	0.531	0.492	0.519
Sample Size		98	98	220	220

*,**,*** denote significance at the 0.10, 0.05, and 0.01 levels, respectively.

5. Summary

The results imply a statistically significant negative relation between the cost of debt and corporate governance. The negative relation with the corporate governance score 'Disclosure' is relatively strong. These findings support the philosophy that debt holders take the firm’s corporate governance into account when estimating its default risk. It can be stated that, ceteris paribus, the debt holders’ perception of a firm’s default risk is lower for firms scoring higher on corporate governance component disclosure. This might imply a lower cost of capital and a higher Tobin's Q for these firms. We further find evidence for an at least stronger negative relation for civil law countries' firms than for common law countries' firms.

References

Amihud, Y. and B. Lev (1981), Risk Reduction as Managerial Motive for Conglomerate Mergers, *Rand Journal of Economics*, 12, 605-618.

Ashbaugh-Skaife, H., D. W. Collins and R. LaFond (2006), The effects of corporate governance on firms' credit ratings, *Journal of accounting and Economics,* 42, 203-243.

Bauer, R., N. Guenster and R. Otten (2004), Empirical evidence on corporate governance in Europe: The effect on stock returns, firm value and performance, *Journal of Asset Management*, 5, 91-104.

Bhojraj, S. and P. Sengupta (2003), Effect of Corporate Governance on Bond Ratings and Yields: The Role of Institutional Investors and Outside Directors, *Journal of Business*, 76, 455-475

Billet, M., D. King and D. Mauer (2004), Bondholders wealth effects in mergers and acquisitions: New Evidence from the 1980s and 1990s, *Journal of Finance*, 59, 107-135.

Blom, J. and M. B. J. Schauten (2003), De kwaliteit van corporate governance en de kosten van vreemd vermogen, *Maandblad voor Accountancy en Bedrijfseconomie*, 11, 530-538.

Boardman, C. and R. McEnally (1981), Factors affecting seasoned corporate bond prices, *Journal of Financial and Quantitative Analysis,* 16, 207-226.

Botosan, C. (1997), Disclosure level on the cost of equity capital, *The accounting review*, 72, 323-349.

Dittmar, A., J. Mahrt-Smith and H. Servaes (2003), International corporate governance and corporate cash holdings, *Journal of Financial and Quantitative Analysis*, 38, 111-133.

Feroz, E., and E. Wilson (1992), Market segmentation and the association between municipal financial disclosure and net interest cost, *The accounting review,* 67, 480-495.

Fisher, L. (1959), Determinants of risk premiums on corporate bonds, *The Journal of Political Economy*, 67, 217-237.

Fung, W. and A. Rudd (1986), Pricing new corporate bond issues: An analysis of issue cost and seasoning effects, *Journal of Finance*, 41, 633-645.

Gompers, P., Ishii and Metrick (2003), Corporate governance and equity prices, *Quarterly Journal of Economics,* 118, 107-155.

Harford, J., S. Mansi and W. Maxwell (2008), Corporate governance and firm cash holdings in the US, *Journal of Financial Economics,* 87, 535-555.

Harris, E. (1990), Antitakeover Measures, Golden Parachutes, and Target Firm shareholder Welfare, *Rand Journal of Economics*, 21, 614-625.

Jaffee, D. (1975), Cyclical variations in the risk structure of interest rates, *Journal of Monetary Economics,* 1, 309-325.

Jensen, M. and R. Ruback (1983), The market for corporate control, *Journal of Financial Economics*, 11, 5-50.

Karpoff, J. M., P. H. Malesta and R. A. Walkling, (1996), Corporate Governance and shareholder initiatives: empirical evidence, *Journal of Financial Economics*, 42, 365-395.

Kidwell, D. S., M. W. Marr and G. R. Thompson (1984), SEC rule 415: The ultimate competitive bid, *Journal of Financial and Quantitative Analysis*, 19,183-195.

Klock, M. S., S. A. Mansi and W. F. Maxwell (2005), Does Corporate Governance Matter to Bondholders, *Journal of Financial and Quantitative Analysis*, 40, 693-719.

Lamy, R., and R. Thompson, (1988), Risk premia and the pricing of primary bond issues, *Journal of Banking and Finance*, 12, 585-601.

LaPorta, R., F. Lopez-de-Silanes and A. Shleifer, Law and Finance, *Journal of Political Economy*, 106, 1113-1155.

McConnell and Serves (1990), Additional evidence on equity ownership and corporate value, *Journal of Financial Economics*, 27, 595-612.

Nesbitt, S. (1994), Long-term rewards from shareholder activism: A Study of the "CalPERS effect", *Journal of Applied Corporate Finance*, (Winter), 75-80.

—. (1995), The "CalPERS effect": A corporate governance update, *Journal of Applied Corporate Finance*, (July), 200-209.

Sengupta, P. (1998), Corporate disclosure quality and the cost of debt, *The accounting review,* (October), 459-474.

Sorensen, E. (1979), The impact of underwriting method and bidder competition upon corporate bond interest cost, *Journal of Finance*, 34, 863-869.

Standard & Poor's (2002), Standard & Poor's Corporate Governance Scores: Criteria, Methodology and Definitions, McGraw-Hill Companies, Inc., New York.

Stein, J. (1988), Takeover Threats and Managerial Myopia, *Journal of Political Economy*, 96, 61-80.

Welker, M. (1995), Disclosure policy, information asymmetry and liquidity in equity markets, *Contemporary Accounting Research*, 11, 801-827.

Wilson, E., and T. Howard (1984), The association between municipal market measures and selected financial reporting practices: Additional evidence, *Journal of Accounting Reasearch*, 22, 207-224.

Yermack, D. (1996), Higher market valuation of companies with a small board of directors, *Journal of Financial Economics*, 40,185-211.

Ziebart, D, and S. Reiter (1992), Bond ratings, bond yields and financial information, *Contemporary Accounting Research*, 9, 252-282.

APPENDIX A

BOND RATING CONVERSION

Table 7-A1 shows the conversion between the credit ratings of Moody's and S&P, and the corresponding scale used as a measure for RATE in this research. The table is based on the papers of Blom and Schauten (2003) and Klock, Mansi and Maxwell (2005).

Table 7-A1 Bond rating conversion

Investment Grade	Moody's Rating	S&P Rating	Scale Number
Exceptional	Aaa, Aaa1, Aaa2, Aaa3	AAA, AAA-, AA+	1
Excellent	Aa, Aa1, Aa2, Aa3	AA, AA-, A+	2
Good	A, A1, A2, A3	A, A-, BBB+	3
Adequate	Baa, Baa1, Baa2, Baa3	BBB, BBB-, BB+	4
Questionable	Ba, Ba1, Ba2, Ba3	BB, BB-, B+	5
Poor	B, B1, B2, B3	B, B-, CCC+	6
Very Poor	Caa, Caa1, Caa2, Caa3	CCC, CCC-, CC+	7
Extremely Poor	Ca, Ca1, Ca2, Ca3	CC, CC-, C+	8
Lowest	C	C	9

APPENDIX B

DATA SOURCES AND CODES

Table 7-B1 shows an overview of all the variables and their corresponding source and code. The extra description provides extra codes if those codes were necessary for the acquiring of the particular variable.

Table 7-B1 Sources and Codes

Variable	Source	Code	Extra description
Yield	Bloomberg		
COGO rating	Deminor Ratings	Deminor Ratings	
Shareholder rights	Deminor Ratings	DEM1	
Takeover defences	Deminor Ratings	DEM2	
Disclosure	Deminor Ratings	DEM3	
Board structure	Deminor Ratings	DEM4	
Size	Bloomberg		
Maturity	Bloomberg		
Call	Bloomberg		
Convert	Bloomberg		
Subord	Bloomberg		
Long-term debt	Thomson financials	TF.TotalLTDebt	
Market value equity	Bloomberg	MKT_VAL_OF_EQY	
Total assets	Thomson financials	TF.TotalAssets	
Margin	Worldscope	WS.NetMargin	
Times	Worldscope	WS.FixedChargeCoverageRatio	
STDRETN	Bloomberg	STDRETN	HR (for Historical Returns)
Rate	Bloomberg	Moody's	
TBILL	Bloomberg	GGR	HP (for Historical Prices)
BC	Bloomberg	MOODCAAA	
Exchange rates	Bloomberg	CRNCY	WCV (for currency codes)

APPENDIX C

DESCRIPTIVE STATISTICS AND CORRELATIONS

Table 7-C1 Summary statistics

This table provides summary statistics of the test variables of 340 bond issues over the period 2001-2005. The variables are defined as follows: YIELD is the yield to maturity at issue date; SIZE is the size of the bond issue in € 1,000,000; LNSIZE is natural log of € 1,000,000 times SIZE; MATURITY is the number of years to maturity; LNMATURITY is the natural log of MATURITY; CALL = 1 if the debt is callable, 0 otherwise; CONVERT = 1 if the debt is convertible, 0 otherwise; SUBORD = 1 if the debt is subordinate, 0 otherwise; RATE = 1, 2,...,9 where 1 is the best rating and 9 is worst, see Appendix A for the conversion table; D/E is the book value of long term interest bearing debt at the end of year t divided by the market value of common value at the end of year t; MARGIN the sum of net income before extraordinary items and equity income of year t divided by net sales in year t; TIMES the sum of net income before interest and tax expense of year t divided by interest expense in year t; ASSET is book value of total assets at the end of year t in € 1,000,000; LNASSET is the natural log of € 1,000,000 times ASSET; STDRETN is the standard deviation of the daily stock return in year t corrected for dividends and stock splits; TBILL is the yield (on the bond issue date) of government bonds of the firm's country of residence with approximately the same maturity as the issued bond; BC is the yield (on the date of the company's bond issue) on Moody's Aaa-bonds with approximately the same maturity as the issued bond minus the yield on government bonds with the longest maturity (also on the date of issue) of the country where the company is primary listed; DEM1 is Deminor's corporate governance score for 'shareholder rights'; DEM2 for 'takeover defences'; DEM3 for 'disclosure'; DEM4 for 'board structure'; DEMTOT the sum of DEM1, DEM2, DEM3 and DEM4.

Variables	Mean	Standard deviation	Median	25%	75%
YIELD	4.84	1.41	4.90	4.02	5.75
SIZE	613.00	505.00	500.00	300	750
LNSIZE	19.82	1.15	20.03	19.52	20.44
MATURITY	8.45	5.52	7.00	5	10
LNMATURITY	2.00	0.48	1.95	1.61	2.3
CALL	0.08	0.28	0.00	0	0
CONVERT	0.09	0.29	0.00	0	0
SUBORD	0.05	0.22	0.00	0	0
RATE	3.34	0.92	3.00	3	4
D/E	0.48	0.55	0.34	0.14	0.63
MARGIN	5.26	11.85	5.35	2.37	8.82
TIMES	5.13	8.25	4.04	2.48	7.07
ASSET	38.30	47.30	20.10	10.12	44.97
LNASSET	23.80	1.05	23.73	23.04	24.53
STDRETN	2.32	0.98	2.17	1.69	2.68
TBILL	4.16	0.85	4.29	3.55	4.83
BC	1.29	0.59	1.22	0.85	1.67
DEM1	6.33	1.35	6.64	5.27	7.38
DEM2	4.09	3.72	3.89	0.75	8
DEM3	6.16	1.53	6.44	5.07	7.44
DEM4	5.07	1.54	5.33	3.75	6.45
DEMTOT	21.66	6.27	20.84	16.62	27.34

Table 7-C2 Correlations

The lower left-hand portion presents the correlations of the total sample (340 observations). The upper right-hand portion presents the correlations of the sample including bonds with a RATE score only (318 observations). Variables are defined in Table 7-C1.

		A	B	C	D	E	F	G	H	I	J	K	L	M	N	O	P	Q	R	S	T	U	V
YIELD	A		-0.08	0.12	0.24	0.31	0.01	-0.37	0.23	0.29	0.21	-0.07	-0.22	-0.06	-0.09	0.28	0.53	0.13	-0.03	0.03	-0.17	-0.12	-0.06
SIZE	B	0.08		0.74	0.01	0.09	-0.11	0.04	-0.02	0.12	0.13	-0.09	-0.09	0.16	0.17	0.23	0.08	-0.01	0.04	-0.11	-0.10	-0.21	-0.13
LNSIZE	C	0.10	0.75		0.06	0.16	-0.04	0.07	-0.03	0.17	0.04	-0.10	-0.11	0.07	0.03	0.20	0.11	-0.02	0.04	-0.05	-0.01	-0.05	-0.04
MATURITY	D	0.21	0.01	0.06		0.91	0.15	0.07	0.02	0.04	0.06	0.04	-0.07	-0.05	-0.02	-0.06	0.22	-0.01	-0.03	-0.14	0.06	0.02	-0.07
LNMATURITY	E	0.26	0.08	0.15	0.91		0.16	0.03	0.05	0.10	0.05	0.05	-0.14	-0.14	-0.11	-0.02	0.28	-0.03	-0.01	-0.12	0.03	0.02	-0.06
CALL	F	-0.06	-0.11	-0.05	0.17	0.18		0.15	0.00	0.04	0.03	-0.17	0.00	-0.04	-0.05	0.08	0.09	-0.05	0.01	-0.03	0.06	0.06	0.01
CONVERT	G	-0.41	-0.02	0.04	0.07	0.05	0.20		-0.05	0.16	-0.02	-0.17	-0.15	-0.08	-0.09	0.33	-0.03	-0.05	0.02	0.05	0.00	0.02	0.03
SUBORD	H	0.26	-0.03	-0.05	0.00	0.02	-0.02	-0.03		0.08	0.13	0.00	-0.06	-0.07	-0.06	0.10	0.10	0.03	-0.01	0.01	-0.05	0.02	0.00
RATE	I	0.29	0.12	0.17	0.04	0.10	0.04	0.16	0.08		0.27	-0.16	-0.46	-0.26	-0.32	0.35	0.22	-0.08	-0.09	0.05	-0.01	0.00	0.01
D/E	J	0.23	0.12	0.04	0.06	0.04	0.03	-0.06	0.15	0.27		-0.29	-0.32	0.19	0.24	0.26	-0.06	-0.14	0.05	-0.13	0.00	-0.16	-0.11
MARGIN	K	-0.02	-0.07	-0.08	0.06	0.07	-0.14	-0.22	-0.02	-0.16	-0.27		0.48	-0.31	-0.27	-0.43	0.07	0.09	-0.11	-0.07	-0.02	0.05	-0.06
TIMES	L	-0.15	-0.07	-0.09	-0.04	-0.08	0.00	-0.21	-0.07	-0.46	-0.26	0.56		0.05	0.08	-0.39	-0.12	0.07	0.11	-0.02	0.03	0.03	0.03
ASSET	M	-0.03	0.17	0.09	-0.05	-0.13	-0.06	-0.15	-0.08	-0.26	0.19	-0.26	0.07		0.86	0.07	-0.08	0.01	0.11	0.04	0.07	-0.08	0.05
LNASSET	N	-0.04	0.19	0.06	-0.01	-0.10	-0.08	-0.24	-0.07	-0.32	0.24	-0.17	0.12	0.86		0.02	-0.18	-0.02	-0.01	-0.11	-0.01	-0.15	-0.11
STDRETN	O	0.23	0.21	0.20	-0.06	-0.03	0.07	0.38	0.12	0.35	0.23	-0.45	-0.40	0.04	-0.05		0.17	0.01	-0.05	0.03	-0.19	-0.23	-0.09
TBILL	P	0.49	0.07	0.09	0.22	0.28	0.12	-0.04	0.09	0.22	-0.07	0.08	-0.11	-0.08	-0.16	0.13		-0.02	0.08	0.21	0.02	0.09	0.17
BC	Q	0.10	0.01	0.00	-0.01	-0.02	-0.05	-0.05	-0.03	-0.08	-0.15	0.13	0.11	0.02	0.01	0.00	-0.04		-0.04	0.11	-0.13	-0.01	0.02
DEM1	R	-0.04	0.04	0.03	-0.03	0.00	0.05	0.02	0.00	-0.09	0.05	-0.13	0.04	0.10	-0.01	-0.06	0.11	-0.06		0.50	0.17	0.14	0.59
DEM2	S	0.03	-0.11	-0.07	-0.11	-0.09	-0.01	0.01	0.02	0.05	-0.12	-0.06	-0.03	0.05	-0.10	0.00	0.23	0.10	0.48		0.35	0.44	0.89
DEM3	T	-0.14	-0.07	0.01	0.07	0.04	0.07	-0.06	-0.08	-0.01	0.01	-0.01	0.00	0.09	0.03	-0.18	0.04	-0.10	0.17	0.35		0.78	0.68
DEM4	U	-0.10	-0.18	-0.04	0.03	0.03	0.06	-0.06	-0.02	0.00	-0.14	0.07	0.03	-0.05	-0.10	-0.24	0.10	0.02	0.14	0.44	0.79		0.73
DEMTOT	V	-0.05	-0.12	-0.04	-0.05	-0.04	0.04	-0.02	-0.02	0.01	-0.09	-0.05	0.00	0.06	-0.08	-0.12	0.20	0.02	0.58	0.89	0.68	0.73	

CHAPTER SIX

A MULTIPLE CRITERIA METHODOLOGY FOR CONSTRUCTING COMMON STOCK PORTFOLIOS: AN APPLICATION FOR COMPANIES OF THE FTSE/ATHEX 140

PANAGIOTIS XIDONAS, DIMITRIOS ASKOUNIS, JOHN PSARRAS

Abstract

We propose an integrated multiple-criteria methodological framework to support decisions that concern the selection of common stock portfolios. At the first stage of the methodology, two multiple-criteria methods are employed, within the context of the outranking relations theory, towards the initial appraisal of the stocks that are examined. We then utilize a non-linear optimization model to generate portfolios comprising stocks classified as those with the optimal characteristics, during the first stage. Finally, the portfolios designed at the previous stage are evaluated by using a wide set of well-known sophisticated evaluation criteria. The preferences and experiences of professionals and experts in the field of portfolio management were taken into consideration throughout all stages of the process. The validity of the above methodology is tested through an illustrative application on the stocks that constitute the FTSE-140 index of the Athens Stock Exchange. The advantages of the proposed model against contextual approaches are finally stressed.

Keywords: multiple criteria decision analysis; outranking relations theory; portfolio construction; stock evaluation.

1. Introduction

The portfolio management process is an integrated set of stages undertaken in a consistent manner to create and maintain an appropriate portfolio (combination of assets) to meet clients' stated goals (Maginn, 2007). The three fundamental elements in managing any business process are: planning, execution and feedback. In the planning stage, investment objectives and policies are formulated, capital market expectations are formed and strategic asset allocations are established. In the execution stage, the manager constructs the portfolio and integrates investment strategies with capital market expectations to select the specific assets for the portfolio. Finally, in the feedback stage, the manager monitors and evaluates the portfolio in the light of the plan. Any changes suggested by the feedback must be examined carefully to ensure that they represent long-run considerations.

The emphasis in this article is laid on the portfolio construction phase and we focus on common stock portfolios design. The portfolio construction problem has several dimensions and the framework of multiple criteria decision making provides the solid methodological basis to resolve the inherent multicriteria nature of this problem.

The paper proceeds as follows. In Section 2 we outline the problem and analyze the portfolio management process, we review the most popular existing portfolio selection/optimization models and we stress the necessity for modelling problems of this kind by using multicriteria analysis. In Sections 3 and 4 we present the proposed methodology and the corresponding application for the Athens Stock Exchange (ASE). Finally, the concluding remarks are given in Section 5.

2. Problem setting

According to Maginn (2007), portfolio management is an ongoing process in which: (1) investment objectives and constraints are identified and specified, (2) investment strategies are developed, (3) portfolio composition is decided in detail, (4) portfolio decisions are initiated by portfolio managers and implemented by traders, (5) portfolio performance is measured and evaluated, (6) investor and market conditions are monitored, and (7) any necessary rebalancing is implemented. As stated previously, the portfolio management process is an integrated set of three stages: planning, execution and feedback (Figure 12-1).

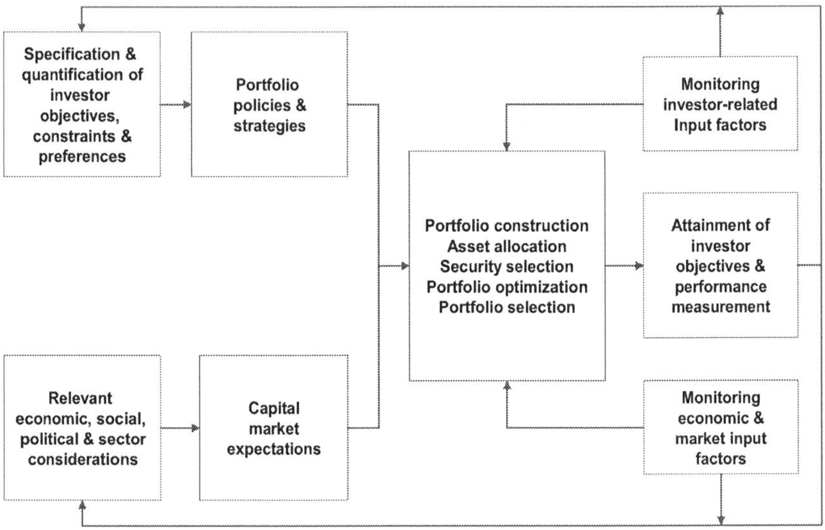

Figure 12-1: The portfolio management process (Maginn, 2007)

In the planning stage, portfolio managers formulate investment objectives and policies, assess capital market expectations and establish strategic asset allocations. The investment policy statement (IPS) serves as the foundation for the process. The investment policy statement sets out a client's return objectives and risk tolerance over that client's relevant time horizon, along with applicable constraints such as liquidity needs, tax considerations, regulatory requirements, and unique circumstances. The IPS must clearly communicate the client's objectives and constraints. The IPS thereby becomes a plan that can be executed by any adviser or portfolio manager the client might subsequently hire. A properly developed IPS disciplines the portfolio management process and helps ensure against ad hoc revisions in strategy. When combined with capital market expectations, the IPS forms the basis for a strategic asset allocation. Capital market expectations concern the risk and return characteristics of capital market instruments such as stocks and bonds. The strategic asset allocation establishes acceptable exposures to IPS-permissible asset classes to achieve the client's long-run objectives and constraints.

In the execution stage, portfolio managers initiate portfolio decisions based on analysts' inputs, and trading desks then implement these decisions (portfolio implementation decision). Subsequently, the portfolio is revised as investor circumstances or capital market expectations change; thus, the execution stage interacts constantly with the feedback stage. In making the portfolio selection/composition decision, portfolio managers may use the techniques of portfolio optimization. Portfolio optimization - quantitative tools for combining assets efficiently to achieve a set of return and risk objectives - plays a key role in the integration of strategies with expectations. The portfolio implementation decision is as important as the portfolio selection/composition decision. Poorly managed executions result in transaction costs that reduce performance. Transaction costs include all costs of trading, including explicit transaction costs, implicit transaction costs, and missed trade opportunity costs.

Finally, in the feedback stage, managers monitor and evaluate the portfolio. Any changes suggested by the feedback must be examined carefully to ensure that they represent long-run considerations. In any business endeavor, feedback and control are essential elements in reaching a goal. In portfolio management, this stage has two components: monitoring and rebalancing, and performance evaluation. Monitoring and rebalancing involve the use of feedback to manage ongoing exposures to available investment opportunities so that the client's current objectives and constraints continue to be satisfied. Two types of factors are monitored: investor-related factors such as the investor's circumstances, and economic and market input factors. Investment performance must periodically be evaluated by the investor to assess progress toward the achievement of investment objectives as well as to assess portfolio management skill. The assessment of portfolio management skill has three components. Performance measurement involves the calculation of the portfolio's rate of return. Performance attribution examines why the portfolio performed as it did and involves determining the sources of a portfolio's performance. Performance appraisal is the evaluation of whether the manager is doing a good job based on how the portfolio did relative to a benchmark (a comparison portfolio).

In order to elaborate the relationship between the decision context of the investor and the economic environment of the securities, Spronk and Hallerbach (1997) break down the investment decision process into the following stages: (1) security analysis to determine the relevant characteristics (or attributes) of the investment opportunities, (2) portfolio analysis to delineate the set of non-dominated or efficient portfolios, (3) portfolio selection to choose the optimal portfolio from the efficient set, and (4) preference analysis.

Since the pioneering work of Markowitz (1952) in the theory of portfolio analysis, based on the mean-variance formulation, several portfolio selection models have been proposed. According to this formulation, an investor regards expected return as desirable and variation of return (variance) as undesirable. On the basis of the Markowitz mean-variance formulation, many researchers developed miscellaneous new methodologies. Elton and Gruber (1987) provide a complete overview as far as these methodologies are concerned. Pardalos et al. (1994) also provide a review and some computational results of the use of optimization models for portfolio selection.

In recent years the development of new techniques in operations research and management science, as well as the progress in computer and information technologies, have given rise to new approaches for dealing with the portfolio selection problem, namely using Multiple Criteria Decision Analysis (MCDA). The multidimensional nature of the problem has been emphasized by researchers in finance, as well as by MCDA researchers (Steuer et al., 2007a, 2007b, 2006a, 2006b, 2005; Zopounidis and Doumpos, 2002; Zopounidis, 1999; Hurson and Zopounidis, 1997, 1995, 1993; Spronk and Hallerbach, 1997; Zeleny, 1982, 1981, 1977; Colson and Zeleny, 1980, 1979). In the above studies, elaborate and exhausted justifications are provided for modeling portfolio management problems within the MCDA framework.

3. Proposed methodology

The multiple criteria methodology that is proposed for constructing common stock portfolios consists of four discrete components (Xidonas et al., 2007). The first two components pertain to the security selection phase, the third component has to do with the portfolio optimization phase, while the last component fits into the portfolio selection phase. The process flow diagram of the proposed methodology is presented in Figure 12-2. In the first component (stock classification) the initial set of stocks is evaluated with stock market indicators and the multiple criteria method that is employed is the ELECTRE Tri (Yu, 1992) method, which belongs to the outranking relations theory framework. The stock market indicators that we use are (the sign in the parenthesis denotes the type of criterion scale: (+) for increasing scale and (-) for declining scale):

- *Stock market criteria*
    - Return dimension
        - Capital return (+)
        - Dividend yield (+)
    - Risk dimension
        - Standard deviation of capital return (-)
        - Beta coefficient (-)
    - Market dimension
        - Marketability (+)
        - P/E (current year) / 3-yrs Average P/E (or Relative P/E) (+) (see Martel et al. 1988)

Extended theoretical presentation of these criteria can be found in Alexander and Sharpe (1989) and Jones (1985).

In the second component (stock ranking) the improved set of stocks, i.e. the stocks that were classified in the satisfactory class during the first phase, are evaluated using the ELECTRE III method, which belongs to the outranking relations theory framework, as well [see Roy (1996) for the method's exact technical formulation]. It has to be stressed that the ranking procedure and the corresponding results provide us with useful information in terms of comparison, since we have to deal with rival companies and the relative evaluation between them is a matter of crucial importance. The financial ratios used at this stage are usually adopted in fundamental analysis:

- *Ratio analysis*
    - Profitability dimension
        - Return on assets (+)
        - Return on equity (+)
    - Management performance dimension
        - Assets turnover (+)
        - Inventories turnover (+)
    - Capital structure dimension
        - Assets to liabilities (+)
        - Liabilities to equity (-)

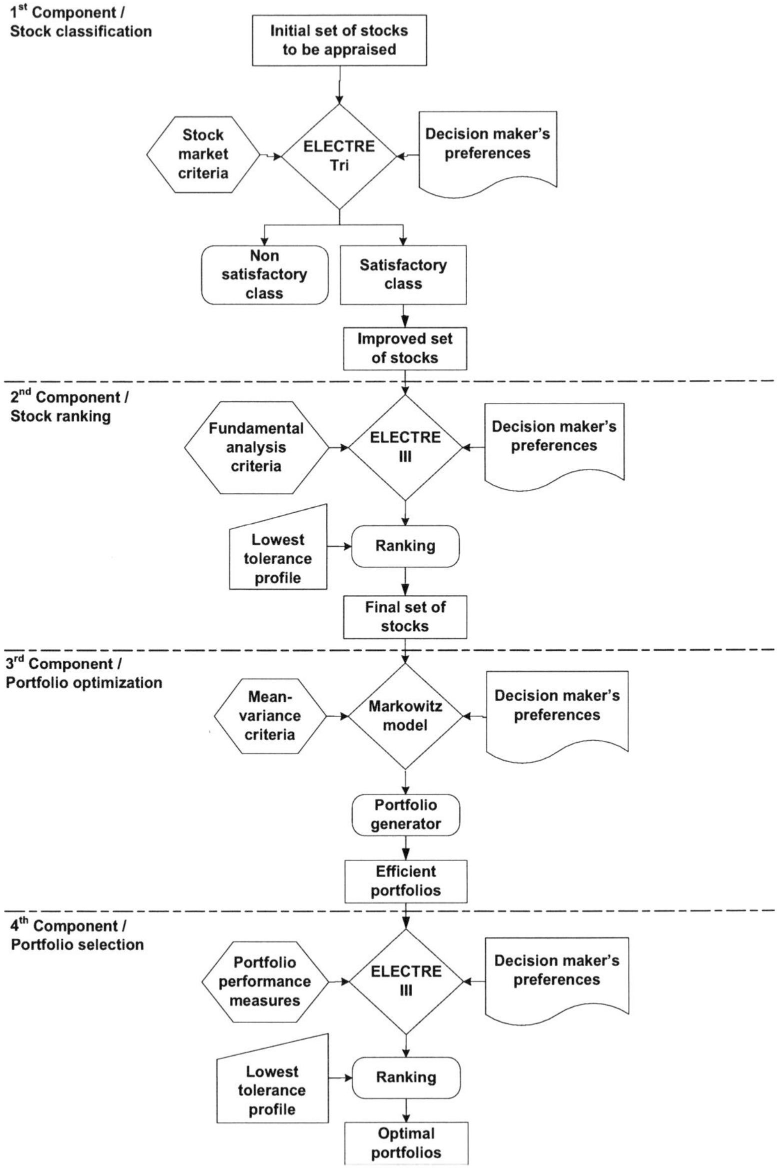

Figure 12-2: Process flow diagram of the proposed methodology

Extended theoretical presentation of these criteria can be found in Niarchos (2005). It has to be noted that despite the fact that the Assets to liabilities and the Liabilities to equity criteria provide similar information, the experts' preference was for simultaneous use of these ratios in the criteria set.

The criteria that are used above are applied only with commercial / industry companies, since our application in Section 4 is restricted to that sector (there are four accounting plans in Greece: (1) Commerce/industry companies, (2) Banks, (3) Insurance companies, and (4) Investment companies). However, this 2nd component of the proposed methodology can easily be extended to the other three accounting plans. By using different sets of indicators for each company's accounting plan we manage to make more realistic comparisons. Moreover, in order to model the lowest tolerance profile, i.e. the profile under which the stocks are considered unacceptable, a dummy stock participates in the ranking process. Samaras et al. (2007) utilize a similar formulation, named the 'lowest stock profile'. The scores of this stock in the ratios that are used are determined by the decision maker / expert and are the minimum acceptable that he tolerates.

In the third component (optimized portfolio generation), we utilize the Markowitz mean-variance formulation with additional constraints in order to construct portfolios on the efficient frontier, using the final set of stocks, as resulted from the previous stage. The details of the non-linear optimization process are:

- *Modeling optimization process*
    - Objective
        - Minimization of portfolio variance (see below for the detailed mathematical formulation).
    - Constraints
        - Basic constraints
            - Return:

              $$R_t = \left(P_t - P_{t-1} + D_t\right) / P_{t-1} \quad ,$$

              where R_t is the return on a share

in period t, P_t is the share price in period t, P_{t-1} is the share price in period *t-1* and D_t is the dividend that the share gives to the investor in period t.
    - Portfolio beta: $COV\ (R_i,\ R_m)\ /\ VAR\ (R_m)$, where R_i is the return of the share i and R_m is the return of the market portfolio (see Hurson and Zopounidis, 1995, 1997; Zopounidis et al. 1998).
    - Capital availability: The completeness constraint, which means that all the available capital is invested.
- Additional constraints
    - Dividend yield: Dividend yield of a security = Dividend in period t / Share price closed in period t.
    - Marketability: Number of transactions of shares of a company during period t / Total number of shares of a company during period t (see Hurson and Zopounidis, 1995, 1997; Zopounidis et al. 1998).
    - Upper limit investment barrier for each security.

The generic mathematical formulation of the optimization model developed follows:

Minimization of portfolio variance:

$$\text{Min } Var_p = \sigma_p^2 = \sum_{i=1}^{m} w_i^2 \sigma_i^2 + \sum_{i=1}^{m} \sum_{\substack{j=1 \\ j \neq i}}^{m} w_i w_j \sigma_{ij} = \sum_{i=1}^{m} \sum_{j=1}^{m} w_i w_j \sigma_{ij}$$

Subject to:

$$\sum_{i=1}^{m} w_i = 1$$

$$\sum_{i=1}^{m} w_i E(r_i) \geq R$$

$$\sum_{i=1}^{m} m_i w_i \geq M$$

$$\sum_{i=1}^{m} d_i w_i \geq D$$

$$\sum_{\forall i:\beta_i \leq 1} w_i \beta_i = X$$

$$\sum_{\forall i:\beta_i > 1} w_i \beta_i = Y$$

$$w_i < W, \ \forall i$$

where:

Var_p : the portfolios' variance

σ_p : the portfolios' standard deviation

σ_i : the standard deviation of returns for security i

w_i : the amount invested in security i

$E(r_i)$: the expected return of security i

m_i : the marketability of security i

d_i : the dividend yield of security i

β_i : the beta coefficient of security i

R : the portfolios' demanded expected return

M : the portfolios' demanded marketability

D : the portfolios' demanded dividend yield

X : the amount of capital invested in defensive securities

Y : the amount of capital invested in offensive securities

W : the maximum amount of capital invested in each security

In the fourth component (portfolio ranking) the portfolios that were constructed in the previous stage are evaluated with portfolio performance indicators and the multiple criteria method that is employed is, again, the ELECTRE III method. The portfolio performance indicators that we use are (the sign in the parenthesis denotes the type of criterion scale: (+) for increasing scale and (-) for declining scale):

- *Portfolio performance criteria*
    - Conventional measures
        - Portfolio return (+)
        - Portfolio variance (-)
        - Portfolio beta (-)
    - Risk adjusted measures
        - Sharpe ratio (+)
        - Treynor ratio (+)
        - Relative Value at Risk (-)

It should be noted that the simultaneous consideration of highly correlated criteria like the Sharpe or the Treynor ratio entails the risk of double counting, but in this case too the experts' preference was for simultaneous use of these ratios in the criteria set. As in the case of stock ranking, in order to model the lowest tolerance profile (LTP) (under which we consider the portfolios ranked as unacceptable), a dummy portfolio participates in the ranking process. The scores of this portfolio in the above portfolio performance criteria are determined by the decision maker and are the minimum acceptable that he tolerates.

The most crucial issue of the proposed methodology is the standardization and formulation of the decision maker's preferences, as well as the incorporation of them in all the methodology components. The decision maker's preferences are incorporated in the decision procedure through his participation in the determination of:

- 1st Component / Stock classification
    - Criteria weights (risk avert / risk seeking / moderate profile)
    - Technical parameters (indifference / preference / veto thresholds & class profile)

- 2nd Component / Stock ranking
    - Criteria weights (profitability / management performance / capital structure focus)
    - Technical parameters (indifference / preference / veto thresholds)
    - Lowest tolerance profile (LTP) (dummy benchmark stock)
- 3rd Component / Portfolio optimization
    - Beta adjustment (risk avert / risk seeking profile)
    - Optimization constraints
- 4th Component / Portfolio ranking
    - Criteria weights (risk avert / risk seeking / moderate profile)
    - Technical parameters (indifference / preference / veto thresholds)
    - Lowest tolerance profile (LTP) (dummy benchmark portfolio)

The advantages of the techniques the model embodies are summarized below:

- ELECTRE family methods
    - accepts intransitivity / incomparability
    - enjoys great scientific study frequency & popularity
    - uses techniques that are easily understandable by the decision maker
- ELECTRE Tri
    - is a perfect mean for an initial dilution of a large number of alternatives since this method does not involve pair comparison
    - provides the advantage of two assignment procedures
- ELECTRE III provides sufficient satisfactory trade off analysis
- Markowitz mean-variance model
    - does not require huge amount of information from the decision maker
    - is the market standard

4. Application

The above presented proposed methodology has been applied to the Athens Stock Exchange (ASE). The characteristics of the field of the application follow:

- 84 stocks from the commercial / industry sector of the FTSE-140 of the ASE were selected;
- 23 stocks of the index were excluded because of different accounting plans (12 stocks from the banking sector, 5 stocks from the insurance sector, and 6 stocks from the financial sector);
- 33 stocks from the commercial / industry sector stocks were also excluded because of lack of different types of data;
- Data refers to closing prices (daily closes from 2001 to 2006)
- Stock market variables (P/E, beta coefficients, marketability, dividend yields etc.) for each security (2006)
- Balance sheet and income statement items (2006)

Table 12-1 shows the specified preferences of the decision maker / expert. As we can see, as far as the 1st Component is concerned, three different investment profiles have been standardized (risk avert / risk seeking / moderate profile), while the same approach is followed for the 4th Component. As far as the 2nd Component is concerned, the focus is on three different dimensions (profitability / management performance / capital structure). Finally, two discrete profiles (risk avert / risk seeking profile) are modeled for the 3rd Component. The formulation of all the above profiles has been determined through different weighting in the key criteria, each time. On this basis, the key criteria in the 1st Component are capital return and standard deviation, the key criteria in the 2nd Component are return on assets (ROA) and return on equity (ROE), the key criterion in the 3rd Component is the beta coefficient and finally the key criteria in the 4th Component are the portfolio capital return and the portfolio variance.

Table 12-1 Decision maker's preference modeling

Stock classification		Capital return	Dividend yield	Volatility	Beta	Marketability	Relative P/E
Profile weights	Risk avert	20%	10%	40%	10%	10%	10%
	Moderate	30%	10%	30%	10%	10%	10%
	Risk seeking	40%	10%	20%	10%	10%	10%
Indifference thresholds		5%	0.5%	5%	0.1	5%	0.1
Preference thresholds		20%	2%	10%	0.4	20%	0.3
Veto thresholds		40%		30%			
Satisfactory class profile		55%	2%	35%	1	60%	1
Stock ranking		**ROA**	**ROE**	**Assets turnover**	**Inventories turnover**	**Assets to liabilities**	**Liabilities to equity**
Profile weights	Profitability	30%	30%	10%	10%	10%	10%
	Management	20%	20%	20%	20%	10%	10%
	Structure	20%	20%	10%	10%	20%	20%
Indifference thresholds		1%	3%	0.1	4	0.2	0.2
Preference thresholds		3%	6%	0.3	8	0.4	0.7
Satisfactory class profile		6%	17%	1	6	2	2.5

Table 12-1 Decision maker's preference modeling (continued)

Portfolio optimization		Beta > 1	Beta < 1	Capital availability	Marketability	Dividend yield	Investment limit
Amount to invest	Risk averse	40%	60%				
	Risk seeking	60%	40%				
Constraint 1				100%			
Constraint 2					65%		
Constraint 3						2.5%	
Constraint 4							40%
Portfolio ranking		**Portfolio return**	**Volatility**	**Portfolio beta**	**Sharpe**	**Treynor**	**Relative VaR**
Profile weights	Risk avert	20%	30%	12.5%	12.5%	12.5%	12.5%
	Moderate	25%	25%	12.5%	12.5%	12.5%	12.5%
	Risk seeking	30%	20%	12.5%	12.5%	12.5%	12.5%
Indifference thresholds		1.5%	0.5%	0.01	0.3	0.03	1000
Preference thresholds		3%	1.5%	0.03	0.6	0.06	3000
Lowest tolerance profile		30%	15%	1	2	0.3	36000

Tables 12-2 and 12-3 show the results of the 1st and 2nd component. Moreover, we can see that 30 from the 84 stocks have been classified in the satisfactory class in the 1st Component, and as far as the 2nd Component, 16 of these 30 stocks ranked above the lowest tolerance profile LTP (dummy stock).

Table 12-2 Results 1st Component / Stock classification (satisfactory class)

	Stock	Return	Dividend yield	Volatility	Beta	Mark/lity	Relative P/E
1	ELTECH	57.06	1.80	34.20	0.81	94.15	1.45
2	INLOT	84.83	2.56	37.48	1.25	68.93	1.03
3	OTE	26.59	2.48	24.13	1.00	55.42	1.05
4	AVAX	55.17	1.53	37.99	1.17	53.32	1.99
5	VSTAR	76.39	2.33	42.00	1.61	55.69	1.25
6	HERAC	73.26	5.73	32.62	1.25	24.13	1.66
7	IATR	83.22	1.05	37.48	1.26	91.45	0.88
8	LAMDA	102.2	1.64	31.57	1.33	44.40	0.15
9	MITIL	64.40	1.49	44.92	1.91	121.68	0.75
10	SIDE	181.6	1.68	57.74	0.94	68.70	1.04
11	TERNA	78.38	1.56	39.94	1.66	80.75	1.78
12	FOLI	34.23	0.40	27.48	0.78	60.23	1.01
13	FRIGO	98.38	1.43	32.86	1.09	41.85	0.89
14	AVE	89.96	1.82	45.15	1.28	66.97	1.18
15	ALMI	49.67	1.58	43.27	1.19	68.90	1.13
16	VETAN	28.88	3.88	26.63	0.61	83.35	1.53
17	BITE	40.01	2.30	39.99	0.79	54.41	1.03
18	DICHT	253.7	1.18	58.39	0.40	127.43	1.12
19	DROUK	63.47	1.74	34.50	1.50	19.51	1.29
20	EVER	34.29	2.92	41.89	0.66	85.76	1.11
21	ELTK	75.54	2.11	42.10	0.85	45.08	1.53
22	ETEM	73.45	1.62	58.15	1.13	62.84	1.12
23	KALSK	62.25	0.55	37.24	0.72	30.36	1.22
24	MOTO	35.57	5.95	32.97	0.70	24.06	1.00
25	MPTK	46.49	1.17	37.21	1.15	16.56	1.61
26	PETRO	40.59	4.28	35.21	0.26	12.59	1.70
27	PROF	108.7	1.32	32.50	1.08	94.74	0.92
28	REV	90.28	1.79	49.13	1.23	69.45	1.23
29	SIDMA	96.06	2.94	44.51	0.54	47.52	0.90
30	SPIR	62.71	0.60	35.99	1.61	30.90	1.36

Table 12-3 Results 2nd Component / Stock ranking

Ranking		Stock	Return on assets	Return on equity	Assets turnover	Inventories turnover	Assets to liabilities	Liabilities to equity
1	1	INLOT	17.2	51.3	1.3	41.3	3.0	2.5
2	2	VSTAR	5.2	10.1	0.3	92.9	2.6	1.0
3	3	FOLI	11.2	39.3	0.8	4.9	3.5	3.4
	4	FRIGO	11.3	27.0	1.2	4.6	1.5	1.1
	5	REV	4.5	12.0	8.5	154.8	1.1	2.0
4	6	EVER	6.9	16.2	1.3	40.5	1.1	1.2
5	7	LAMDA	11.3	25.9	0.1	1.6	2.6	1.0
	8	BITE	7.4	13.6	1.2	10.7	1.6	1.1
6	9	HERAC	5.7	7.4	0.7	9.5	2.8	0.3
	10	ELTK	6.9	16.2	1.1	7.9	1.9	1.5
	11	MOTO	6.8	16.9	2.0	3.7	1.6	1.5
7	12	MITIL	8.3	23.4	0.7	4.4	1.3	1.3
	13	SIDE	8.0	22.1	0.9	4.2	1.7	1.6
	14	PROF	6.8	11.2	0.7	18.2	1.6	0.7
8	15	OTE	4.9	15.7	0.5	35.1	1.5	2.1
	16	DROUK	5.7	16.7	0.9	5.8	2.1	2.3
		LTP	6.0	17.0	1.0	6.0	2.0	2.5
9	17	DICHT	7.2	26.5	0.6	26.1	1.2	3.1
	18	PETRO	4.3	11.0	1.2	5.9	1.9	1.5
	19	SIDMA	5.0	14.4	0.9	6.0	2.2	2.2
10	20	ELTECH	3.4	6.7	0.5	24.3	1.6	0.9
	21	KALSK	3.6	7.6	0.9	3.5	2.2	1.1
11	22	IATR	3.9	11.0	0.6	48.0	0.7	1.9
	23	AVE	3.9	19.0	0.4	14.4	0.7	4.3
12	24	AVAX	4.0	10.3	0.7	12.6	1.1	1.8
	25	TERNA	3.4	10.5	0.6	23.0	1.4	2.3
13	26	ETEM	1.9	4.2	0.7	3.2	2.0	1.3
14	27	VETAN	2.7	6.8	0.4	10.8	1.7	1.7
	28	MPTK	3.0	10.1	0.9	4.6	1.4	2.5
15	29	ALMI	2.0	6.3	0.7	3.2	1.4	2.1
	30	SPIR	-2.1	-3.7	0.3	1.4	1.6	0.9

Table 12-4 provides information relative to the correspondence of each security with its industry and supersector, according to the Industry Classification Benchmark (ICB) standards.

Table 12-4 Securities classified in the satisfactory class and the corresponding industry/supersector

No	OASIS Code	Name of security	Industry	Supersector
1	AVAX	J & P AVAX (CR)	Industrials	Construction and materials
2	AVE	AUDIOVISUAL (CR)	Consumer services	Media
3	ALMY	ALOUMYL MYLONAS (CR)	Basic Materials	Basic resources
4	VETAN	VETANET (CR)	Industrials	Construction and materials
5	VSTAR	BLUE STAR (CB)	Consumer services	Travel and leisure
6	BYTE	BYTE COMPUTER (CR)	Technology	Technology
7	DICHT	DIAS IXTHYOKALLIERGIES (CR)	Consumer goods	Food and beverage
8	DROUK	DROUKFARBEN (CR)	Basic Materials	Chemicals
9	EVER	EVEREST (CB)	Consumer goods	Food and beverage
10	ELTEX	ELLINIKI TEHNODOMIKI (CR)	Industrials	Construction and materials
11	ELTK	ELTRAC (CB)	Industrials	Industrial goods and services
12	ETEM	ETEM (CB)	Basic Materials	Basic resources
13	HERAC	IRAKLIS AGET (CR)	Industrials	Construction and materials
14	IATR	IATRICO ATHINON (CR)	Health care	Health care
15	INLOT	INTRALOT (CR)	Consumer services	Travel and leisure
16	KALSK	KALPINIS SIMOS (CB)	Basic Materials	Basic resources
17	LAMDA	LAMDA DEVELOPMENT (CR)	Financials	Financial services
18	MOTO	MOTODYNAMIKI (CR)	Consumer services	Retail

Table 12-4 Securities classified in the satisfactory class and the corresponding industry/supersector (continued)

No	OASIS Code	Name of security	Industry	Supersector
19	MPTK	BITROS SYMMETOHIKI (CR)	Basic Materials	Basic resources
20	MITIL	MYTILINAIOS (CR)	Basic Materials	Basic resources
21	OTE	OTE (CR)	Telecommunications	Telecommunications
22	PETRO	PETROPOULOS (CR)	Industrials	Industrial goods and services
23	PROF	PROFILE (CR)	Technology	Technology
24	REV	REVOIL (CR)	Consumer services	Retail
25	SIDE	SIDENOR (CB)	Basic Materials	Basic resources
26	SIDMA	SIDMA (CR)	Basic Materials	Basic resources
27	SPYR	SPYROU (CR)	Basic Materials	Chemicals
28	TERNA	TERNA (CR)	Industrials	Construction and materials
29	FOLI	FOLLI FOLLIE (CR)	Consumer goods	Personal and household goods
30	FRIGO	FRIGOGLASS (CR)	Industrials	Industrial goods and services

Table 12-5 shows the results of the 3rd component (optimized portfolio generation) and in Figure 12-3 one can find the corresponding efficient frontier. In total, 28 portfolios have been constructed. Again, as we can see, satisfactory diversification in the level of capitalization has been achieved.

Table 12-5 Results 3rd Component / Portfolio optimization

				1	2	3	4	…	13	14	15	16
	Stocks	MEAN	STD	INLOT	VSTAR	FOLI	FRIGO	…	SIDE	PROF	OTE	DROUK
Portfolio 1	14	0.00065	0.00750	6.1%	0.0%	11.8%	1.4%	…	0.4%	15.0%	8.6%	1.2%
Portfolio 2	14	0.00068	0.00750	6.5%	0.0%	11.8%	2.3%	…	1.1%	14.9%	8.6%	1.0%
Portfolio 3	14	0.00072	0.00754	7.1%	0.0%	11.8%	3.6%	…	2.0%	14.7%	8.5%	0.8%
Portfolio 4	14	0.00076	0.00761	7.7%	0.0%	11.8%	4.8%	…	2.9%	14.5%	8.4%	0.6%
Portfolio 5	14	0.00080	0.00770	8.0%	0.0%	11.8%	5.9%	…	3.6%	14.1%	8.3%	0.5%
Portfolio 6	15	0.00084	0.00782	8.1%	0.0%	11.6%	6.8%	…	4.1%	13.7%	8.3%	0.2%
Portfolio 7	14	0.00088	0.00796	8.0%	0.0%	11.5%	7.5%	…	4.8%	13.2%	8.3%	0.0%
Portfolio 8	13	0.00092	0.00813	7.8%	0.0%	11.5%	8.2%	…	5.5%	12.7%	8.3%	0.0%
Portfolio 9	13	0.00096	0.00832	7.6%	0.0%	11.3%	9.1%	…	6.1%	12.1%	8.1%	0.0%
…	…	…	…	…	…	…	…	…	…	…	…	…
Portfolio 23	5	0.00152	0.01369	0.0%	0.0%	0.0%	17.9%	…	21.6%	0.0%	0.0%	0.0%
Portfolio 24	5	0.00156	0.01437	0.0%	0.0%	0.0%	16.8%	…	24.7%	0.0%	0.0%	0.0%
Portfolio 25	5	0.00160	0.01512	0.0%	0.0%	0.0%	15.7%	…	27.8%	0.0%	0.0%	0.0%
Portfolio 26	5	0.00164	0.01593	0.0%	0.0%	0.0%	14.6%	…	30.8%	0.0%	0.0%	0.0%
Portfolio 27	5	0.00168	0.01678	0.0%	0.0%	0.0%	13.6%	…	33.9%	0.0%	0.0%	0.0%
Portfolio 28	5	0.00172	0.01788	0.0%	0.0%	0.0%	3.2%	…	36.1%	0.0%	0.0%	0.0%

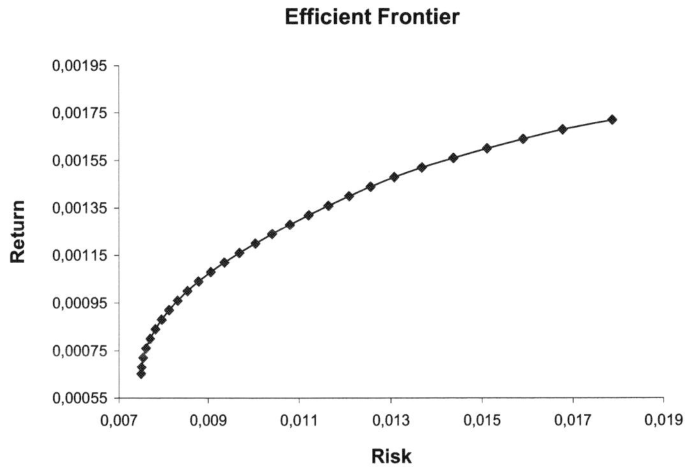

Figure 12-3: The efficient frontier

Table 12-6 shows the results of the 4th component (portfolio ranking) and Table 12-7 presents the synthesis of the acceptable portfolios. With regard to this particular component, 6 of the 28 portfolios ranked above the lowest tolerance profile LTP (dummy portfolio).

Table 12-6 Results 4th Component / Portfolio ranking

		Portfolio return	Volatility	Portfolio beta	Sharpe	Treynor	Relative VaR
1	Portfolio 6	21.0%	12.4%	0.94	1.70	0.22	28765
2	Portfolio 5	20.0%	12.2%	0.94	1.64	0.21	28332
3	Portfolio 4	19.0%	12.0%	0.93	1.58	0.20	27984
	Portfolio 13	28.0%	14.8%	0.99	1.89	0.28	34442
4	Portfolio 7	22.0%	12.6%	0.95	1.75	0.23	29285
	Portfolio 14	29.0%	15.3%	1.00	1.89	0.29	35650
5	Portfolio 8	23.0%	12.9%	0.96	1.79	0.24	29896
	Portfolio 15	30.0%	15.9%	1.01	1.89	0.30	36938
	LTP	30.0%	15.0%	1	2	0.30	36000
6	Portfolio 9	24.0%	13.2%	0.97	1.82	0.25	30595
	Portfolio 10	25.0%	13.5%	0.97	1.85	0.26	31393
	Portfolio 11	26.0%	13.9%	0.98	1.87	0.27	32305
	Portfolio 16	31.0%	16.5%	1.02	1.88	0.30	38299
7	Portfolio 12	27.0%	14.3%	0.99	1.88	0.27	33324
	Portfolio 17	32.0%	17.1%	1.03	1.87	0.31	39728
	Portfolio 18	33.0%	17.7%	1.04	1.86	0.32	41234
8	Portfolio 3	18.0%	11.9%	0.93	1.51	0.19	27740
	Portfolio 19	34.0%	18.4%	1.05	1.85	0.32	42810
9	Portfolio 21	36.0%	19.8%	1.08	1.81	0.33	46169
10	Portfolio 20	35.0%	19.1%	1.07	1.83	0.33	44446
11	Portfolio 22	37.0%	20.7%	1.09	1.79	0.34	48115
12	Portfolio 23	38.0%	21.6%	1.11	1.76	0.34	50342
13	Portfolio 24	39.0%	22.7%	1.13	1.72	0.35	52854
14	Portfolio 25	40.0%	23.9%	1.14	1.67	0.35	55611
15	Portfolio 26	41.0%	25.2%	1.16	1.63	0.35	58579
16	Portfolio 27	42.0%	26.5%	1.18	1.58	0.36	61729
17	Portfolio 2	17.0%	11.9%	0.93	1.43	0.18	27605
	Portfolio 28	43.0%	28.3%	1.27	1.52	0.34	65782
18	Portfolio 1	16.3%	11.9%	0.93	1.37	0.17	27578

Table 12-7 Portfolio synthesis of the acceptable portfolios

			1	2	3	4	5	…	12	13	14	15	16
		Stocks	INLOT	VSTAR	FOLI	FRIGO	REV	…	MITIL	SIDE	PROF	OTE	DROUK
1	Portfolio 6	15	8.1%	0 0%	11.6%	6.8%	8.0%	…	1.3%	4.1%	13.7%	8.3%	0.2%
2	Portfolio 5	14	8.0%	0 0%	11.8%	5.9%	8.5%	…	0.5%	3.6%	14.1%	8.3%	0.5%
3	Portfolio 4	14	7.7%	0 0%	11.8%	4.8%	8.9%	…	0.0%	2.9%	14.5%	8.4%	0.6%
	Portfolio 13	10	6.0%	0 0%	8.5%	13.6%	2.9%	…	9.1%	8.3%	8.5%	5.8%	0.0%
4	Portfolio 7	14	8.0%	0 0%	11.5%	7.5%	7.5%	…	2.3%	4.8%	13.2%	8.3%	0.0%
	Portfolio 14	10	5.5%	0 0%	7.8%	14.6%	2.0%	…	10.3%	8.9%	7.6%	5.1%	0.0%
5	Portfolio 8	13	7.8%	0 0%	11.5%	8.2%	6.9%	…	3.3%	5.5%	12.7%	8.3%	0.0%
	Portfolio 15	10	5.0%	0 0%	7.1%	15.7%	1.1%	…	11.5%	9.5%	6.6%	4.5%	0.0%

5. Concluding remarks

An integrated multiple-criteria methodological framework has been proposed for supporting decisions that concern the selection of common stock portfolios. At the first stage of the methodology, two multiple-criteria methods are employed, within the context of the outranking relations theory, towards the initial appraisal of the stocks that are examined. A non-linear optimization model was then developed, in order to generate portfolios that consist of the stocks that are classified as those with the optimal characteristics, during the first stage. The portfolios designed at the previous stage are evaluated in the final phase, by using a wide set of well-known sophisticated evaluation criteria. The validity of the methodology was tested through a large scale application in the Athens Stock Exchange.

The methodology that has been presented can be a useful tool for portfolio managers, financial analysts and traders in constructing and designing their portfolios. The contribution of the proposed methodology encompasses the following factors:

- The complex investment decision process in common stocks is scientifically structured
- Incorporation of the decision maker's preference system (choice among standard different investment profiles & LTPs)
- Incorporation of combination of decision support techniques and multiple decision criteria from different dimensions
- Multi-usability since the model can be utilized solely for corporate evaluation or single stock selection
- Flexibility for the decision maker since the model does not involve complex processes
- Reliable specialized stock evaluations based on each case specific accounting plan
- Minimization of time / costs & additional transparency in the whole process if incorporated into a decision support system (DSS)

Towards enhancing the proposed methodology, the issues below have to be assessed:

- Expansion of the criteria sets (stock market, ratio analysis and portfolio performance indicators)

- Embodiment of the methodology in a web-based decision information system so real-time investment decisions can be supported
- Expansion of the methodology so as to include additional asset classes

Acknowledgements

We wish to express our thanks to the two anonymous referees, whose comments on an earlier version of the paper were very helpful. We also wish to express our thanks to ICAP S.A. for the valuable financial data provided.

References

Alexander, G.J. and Sharpe, W.F., 1989. Fundamentals of Investments. Prentice Hall International, Inc., Englewood Cliffs, New Jersey.

Colson, G., Zeleny, M., 1979. Uncertain prospects ranking and portfolio analysis under the condition of partial information. Mathematical Systems in Economics, Vol. 44, Verlag Anton Hain, Maisenheim.

Colson, G., Zeleny, M., 1980. Multicriterion concept of risk under incomplete information. Computers and Operations Research 7 (1/2), 125–143.

Elton, E.J. and Gruber, M.J., 1987. Modern Portfolio Theory and Investment Analysis. 3rd edition, John Wiley and Sons Inc., New York.

Hurson, C., Zopounidis, C., 1993. Return, risk measures and multicriteria decision support for portfolio selection. In: Papathanassiou, B., Paparrizos, K. (eds.), Proceedings of the 2nd Balkan Conference on Operational Research, pp. 343–357.

Hurson, C., Zopounidis C. 1995. On the use of multicriteria decision aid methods to portfolio selection. Journal of Euro-Asian Management 1(2), 69–94.

Hurson, C., Zopounidis, C., 1997. Gestion de portefeuille et analyse multicritere. Economica, Paris.

Jones, Ch. P. (1985). Investments: Analysis and Management, John Wiley and Sons Inc., New York.

Konno, H., Shirakawa, H. and Yamazaki, H., 1993. A Mean-Absolute Deviation-Skewness Portfolio Optimization. Annals of Operations Research 45, 205–220.

Niarchos, N., 2005. Financial Statement Analysis. 2nd Edition, Stamoulis Publications, Athens.

Maginn, J.L., Tuttle, D.L., Pinto D.E., and McLeavey, D.W., 2007. Managing Investment Portfolios. 3rd Edition, John Wiley and Sons Inc., New York.

Markowitz, H., 1952. Portfolio selection. The Journal of Finance, March, pp. 77–91.

Martel, J.M., Khoury, N.T. and Bergeron, M., 1988. An application of a multicriteria approach to portfolio comparisons. Journal of the Operational Research Society 39 (7), 617–628.

Pardalos, P.M., Sandstrom, M. and Zopounidis, C., 1994. On the use of optimization models for portfolio selection: A review and some computational results. Computational Economics 7, 227–244.

Roy, B., 1996. Multicriteria Methodology for Decision Aiding. Dordrecht: Kluwer Academic Publishers.

Samaras, G.D., Matsatsinis, N.F., and Zopounidis, C., 2006. A multicriteria DSS for stock evaluation using fundamental analysis. European Journal of Operational Research, doi:10.1016/j.ejor.2006.09.020

Siskos, Y. and Zopounidis, C., 1993. Multicriteria decision support systems: Editorial. Journal of Information Science and Technology, Special Issue 2, 2, 107–108.

Spronk, J. and Hallerbach, W.G., 1997. Financial Modelling: Where to Go? With an Illustration for Portfolio Management. European Journal of Operational Research 99(1), 113–127.

Steuer, R. E., Qi, Y., Hirschberger, M., 2005. Multiple objectives in portfolio selection. Journal of Financial Decision Making 1 (1), 11-26.

Steuer, R. E., Qi, Y., Hirschberger, M., 2006a. Developments in multi-attribute portfolio selection. In: Trzaskalik, T. (ed.), Multiple Criteria Decision Making '05, Karol Adamiecki Press, Katowice, Poland, pp. 251-262.

Steuer, R. E., Qi, Y., Hirschberger, M., 2006b. Portfolio optimization: New capabilities and future methods. Zeitschrift für Betriebswirtschaft 76 (2), 199-219.

Steuer, R. E., Qi, Y., Hirschberger, M., 2007a. Portfolio Selection in the presence of multiple criteria. In: Zopounidis, C., Doumpos, M., Pardalos, M. (eds.), Handbook of financial engineering, Springer (in press).

Steuer, R.E., Qi, Y., Hirshberger, M., 2007b. Suitable-portfolio investors, nondominated frontier sensitivity, and the effect of multiple objectives on standard portfolio selection. Annals of Operations Research 152, 297-317.

Xidonas, P., Askounis, D., and Psarras, J., 2007. Towards modeling an integrated methodology for supporting common stock portfolio construction decisions. In: 7th Hellenic Operational Research Society Special Conference, Technical University of Crete, 27-28 September.

Yu, W., 1992. ELECTRE TRI: Aspect methodologiques et manuel d'utilization. Document du Lamsade, Universite Paris-Dauphine, p.74.

Zeleny, M., 1977. Multidimensional measure of risk: The prospect ranking vector. In: Zionts, S. (ed.), Multiple Criteria Problem Solving, Springer, Heidelberg, pp. 529-548.

—. 1981. Satisficing optimization, and risk in portfolio selection. In: Derkinderen, F.G.H., Crum, R.L., (eds.), Readings in Strategies for Corporate Investment, Pitman Publishing, Boston, pp. 200–219.

—. 1982. Multiple criteria decision making. McGraw Hill, New York.

Zopounidis, C., 1999. Multicriteria decision aid in financial management. European Journal of Operational Research 119 (2), 404–415.

Zopounidis, C., and Doumpos, M., 2002. Multicriteria Decision Aid in Financial Decision Making: Methodologies and Literature Review. Journal of Multicriteria Decision Analysis 11: 167-186.

Zopounidis, C., Despotis D.K., and Kamaratou, I., 1998. Portfolio selection using the ADELAIS multiobjective linear programming system. Computational Economics 11/3, 189-204.

CHAPTER SEVEN

ISLAMIC INVESTMENT: AN OVERVIEW OF ASSET CLASSES

GHASSAN CHAMMAS AND JAAP SPRONK

Abstract

Sharia compliant investors seek additional objectives beyond those pursued by the traditional or conventional investors. While common objectives remain - e.g. capital preservation, maximization of return and yield and balancing liquidity and profitability - Sharia compliant investors additionally seek to incorporate the doctrines of Sharia precepts to asset choice, linking the investment to behavioral ethics, confining the investment to legitimate goods and services and social objectives. In this paper our aim is to define the Sharia compliant investment universe. First we will describe the general mandates of Islamic finance. Then we define the set of screenings and filters that have to be applied before an asset can be included in a Sharia compliant portfolio. We will conclude by discussing different investors' perspectives to Sharia compliant investment.

Keywords: Islamic finance; Sharia compliant investment; stock markets; asset management.

1. Brief overview of Islamic finance and Sharia mandates

In the six countries of the Gulf Co-operation Council (Bahrain, Kuwait, Oman, Qatar, Saudi Arabia and the UAE) asset management is on the march. Strong liquidity resulting from high oil and gas prices, a growing maturity among investors, the repatriation of assets following 9/11 and the development of Islamic finance have all contributed to creating a thriving environment for both local and international banks. Accordingly, many are ramping up their operations and developing a strong presence on the ground. As local capital markets develop and become more open to a broader range of investors, the scope for new product development becomes more widespread.

One particular aspect of the innovative and diversified approach in this region has been the tapping of the "Islamic or Sharia compliant" investment approach. While investors still seek liquidity, capital protection and profit on their investment, some investors are also seeking Sharia compliance as well. This trend has primed a newly developed Islamic finance industry, and we have witnessed the growth of Sharia compliant investment in the past decade at a strong rate of 15-20% annually. Additionally, some 150 Islamic funds[1] and fund of funds are available in the GCC and Global market with a total capitalization of $10Bn as of 2005. All indications point to a faster expansion of this sector in particular, and many "western" banks and fund managers are entering this new field with all the financial acumen they possess and the sharp know-how of strategic assets allocations.

It has been widely accepted to denote by "Islamic finance" those financial transactions abiding by the Islamic Sharia compliance to Fiqh al Muamalat[2]. This is a set of rules and mandates, stipulated in the Holy Quran, the Sunnah and the Islamic scholars governing commercial transactions. The basic mandates of the Islamic Fiqh al Muamalat are:

The prohibition of RIBA or Interest

The conceptual framework of prohibiting Riba resides basically on the fact of banning the remuneration of money for its time value. Money is considered a transactional value of a good rather than value in itself, and the philosophy is that money does not have a value unless pegged to a certain product. Hence one can not grant a time value to money and hence interest per se is not accepted. Any instrument or transaction bearing or underpinned by any kind of interest is thus considered unlawful or Haram. This prohibition implies the application of investment based financial

---

[1] For a list of Islamic funds please see www.failaka.com

[2] Fiqh Al Muamalat: Jurisprudence of transactions. Please refer to the Glossary in appendix A for a definition of Islamic financial widely used terms.

structuring to any underlying activity to produce a distributed return and hence to create wealth in form of a Halal return or remuneration.

The prohibition of Gharar or uncertainty

In its basic form, Gharar is deceit or uncertainty, in the sense that one cannot produce wealth one-sided under conditions of advantage or deceit vis-à-vis his counterparty. A widely used academic example of Gharar is A selling his car to B for $X or €Y. This is considered uncertainty leading to dispute and hence the contract of sale of this car is Haram because it carries an element of Gharar. In the modern financial industry, the prohibition of Gharar implies the prohibition of short selling, because one is selling a item that one does not own and thus one cannot guarantee the delivery under all states of the universe of investment, the prohibition of future contract because it carries a speculative strata that can lead to deceit and dispute.

In the mathematical sense, Gharar is equivalent to a zero sum game, where the aggregate payoff the all parties is zero. In order for a transaction to be Gharar free it has to be equivalent to a positive sum game or, *ad extremis* to a mixed sum game. Debt derivatives are considered zero sum game and hence all debt derivatives are considered carrying Gharar and hence Haram.

Modern studies on quantifying Gharar have lately been published, and the seminal work of Sami al Suwailem[3] reflects the methodical approach of using binomial trees and Bayes processes to identify payoffs and hence detect Gharar through zero-sum game-like payoffs.

It should be added that Gharar includes also the sale of debt or Bai' el Dain. It is considered deceitful and uncertain to sell a debt. In fact one can "transfer" a debt entirely but without any remuneration or "penalty", and this is assimilated to a Hawala[4]. GCC scholars insist on the prohibition of Bai' al Dain but Malaysian scholars have issued many fatwas allowing the

---

[3] Al-Suwailen Sami, Towards An Objective Measure Of Gharar In Exchange, Islamic Economic Studies Vol. 7, Nos. 1 & 2, Oct. '99, Apr. 2000

[4] Not to be confused with the widely used Hawala or money transfer. A Hawala is the transfer of a debt from one debtor to another, with the consent of all parties. No remuneration or penalty is applied and the terms and conditions of the initial debt agreement should be conserved.

"slicing" of a debt and its sale. Islamic indexes and funds do not, however, include a sold debt into their portfolio.

The prohibition of Maisir or gambling

Gambling is any activity that involves an arrangement between two or more parties, each of whom undertakes the risk of a loss where a loss for one means a gain for the other, as it is common for gambling activities. The gain accruing from these games is unlawful in Islam. Gambling is also a zero sum game scheme and hence carries a double sided prohibition. It should be mentioned however that although stock trading is a zero sum game at the level of the complete system, it is not considered so at the individual level and hence is totally allowed, as long as it obeys the rules of investment that we shall describe later in this paper.

The prohibition of dealing with unlawful products and industries

Islam considers some products or industries as unlawful. Activities related to Alcohol, gambling, arms and armaments, financial and insurance institutions, pornography, tobacco industries, hotels and immoral entertainment, pork food and alcohol serving restoration are prohibited. Hence any investment related to these activities is considered banned or Haram. Financial Sharia compliance and the modern enterprise.

2. Financial Sharia compliance and the modern enterprise

The Sharia prohibitions described in Section 1 of this paper relate to some general concepts governing commercial activities. Historically, sales, rents, hiring and in general lending were centered around some primitive activities, mainly agriculture and some basic handcraft industries.

Modern days market place is much more complicated and the surge of organized stock markets paved the way to more sophisticated investment schemes and complicated portfolio structures that presented a real challenge to Sharia compliant investors. Investors in general trade in assets and assets classes usually involving a bundle of individual and simple underlying commercial and financial activities. The need for a holistic Sharia compliant approach to "investment" surged and the basic mandates governing the Islamic transactions were projected on a broader substrate.

Ranging from commodities trading to stocks and from derivatives to funds, Sharia scholars transposed the major prohibitions into a set of filters and screenings to cover the modern days financial trading activities.

Most conservative *ulemas* would categorically prohibit dealing with any company or enterprise undertaking any *haram* or unlawful activity[5]. Apart from ruling out companies dealing with unlawful products, investors are faced with an investing dilemma: it is rare to find any enterprise or company not dealing with any form of conventional banking, whether it is from the placement or from the financing side.

Sharia scholars are mainly concerned about 3 major financial issues:

a. Indebtedness of the company
b. Interest and other "impure" earnings of the company
c. Extent of cash and receivables with the company.

a) Indebtedness of the company

Theoretically any debt contracted by an enterprise gives rise to interest payment and hence contravenes the Sharia mandate of prohibition of Riba. When an investor acquires a share of an indebted enterprise he is actually incurring in two major prohibitions:

i) The investor is trading in debt (Bai' el dain)

ii) The investor is acquiring a portion of an enterprise dealing in Riba

Scholars widely acknowledge the presence of debt in almost all modern enterprises and many Fatawas (jurisprudence) were issued dealing with the permissibility of such a transaction under certain well observed conditions, which we will discuss in the next section of this paper.

Conventionally the ratio to measure the indebtedness of a company is the gearing or the debt to equity ratio (D/E). Alternatively, some argue that a proper indication would be the debt to total capitalization and also the debt to total market capitalization, in an approach to measure the severity of the level of debt to the acquired value of the equity share. We shall discuss these variations in the next chapter.

---

[5] Yaqubi, Nizam, October 2000.*Participation and trading in equities of companies whose main business is primarily unlawful. Paper presented to the fourth Harvard Islamic Finance Forum, October 2000.*

b) Impure or impermissible earnings of the company

Normally, all cash flows of a modern enterprise flow through a bank and hence might generate interest. Some companies recur to investment in securities and commercial papers for short term excess liquidity management. The accrued interest on these deposit are considered to be unlawful and would eventually tan the total income of the company with impure proceeds. Again, a cut-off level was considered by Sharia scholars to facilitate trading in equity shares of such companies. The ratio of interest income to total income is usually used to gauge the proportion of impermissible income in a company, and the admissible ratio can vary between 5% and 15% as discussed in the next chapter.

c) Extent of cash and receivables with the company

Sharia stipulates that cash and debts cannot be traded except at par value. However, the valuation process of a company involves the projection of cash flows including its assets and liabilities value as they appear in its balance sheet, including fixed assets, investments, cash, inventory, receivables, payables and debts. The traded price of its equity represents the expected future value paid for the underlying assets and liabilities and not its book value. This issue remains very sensitive in the light of the unlawfulness of trading in debt and in future expectations of cash and receivables which are only permitted to be traded at par value. The consensus of Sharia scholars is to place a limit on the proportion of current assets in the total assets of the company.

The parameter most commonly used to judge compliance on this score is the ratio of current assets or receivables or net current assets to total assets (or total capitalization) of the company. The cut-off value of the parameter is usually set in the range of 40% to 50%, as discussed in the next chapter.

3. Stock selection criteria: industry and financial screening

Different Islamic banks, investment companies and Islamic funds have their own investment strategy and norms for stock selection and compliance. Each of these institutions has a Sharia board that sets and oversees the compliance criteria. Some independent investors rely on widely used indexes and funds for the Sharia compliance criteria.

Among the most popular Islamic indexes are the Dow Jones Islamic Index DJIMI, the Islamic FTSE index and the MSCI Global Islamic index. Each index has its Sharia board and applies different financial criteria for admission of a security in its portfolio.

Additionally, the Securities and Exchange Commission of Malaysia, the SEC Malaysia, has established a different approach to the selection criteria. In this section we will briefly discuss each of these selection methods.

3.1 The Dow Jones Islamic index[6] financial screening

Industry screening

Based on revenue allocation, if any company has business activities in the Sharia inconsistent group or sub-group of industries it is excluded from the Islamic index universe. The DJIMI Sharia Supervisory Board established the following broad categories of industries as inconsistent with Sharia precepts: alcohol, pork related products, conventional financial services (banking, insurance, etc.), hotels, entertainment (casinos/gambling, cinema, pornography, music, etc.), tobacco, and weapons and defense industries.

Debt to market capitalization ratio

Excludes all companies of which the ratio of 'Debt' to 'The twelve-months' average trailing market capitalization' exceeds **33%**. The main reason behind the exclusion of highly geared companies resides in the Sharia concepts discussed earlier. In fact, if a company is highly geared, transacting with its shares is assimilated to trading a debt and its income is impure with a high ratio of Riba transactions.

Liquid assets to market capitalization

Excludes all companies of which the ratio of 'Cash and interest bearing securities' to 'The twelve-months' average trailing market capitalization' exceeds 33%.

Receivables to market capitalization

Excludes all companies of which the ratio of 'Accounts receivables' to 'The twelve-months' average trailing market capitalization' exceeds **33%**.

---

[6] www.djindexes.com

3.2 The FTSE SGX[7] Sharia Global Equity index selection criteria

The FTSE SGX index uses the 'Total assets' of the company in the denominator to establish the financial ratios screening cut-off threshold, in contrast with DJIMI that uses 'The twelve-months' average trailing market capitalization'. The FTSE SGX introduces an additional layer of non-Sharia income threshold to its screening criteria.

Industry screening

Similar to DJIMI, the FTSE SGX excludes all Sharia non-compliant industry activities.

Debt to Assets ratio

Excludes all companies of which the ratio of 'Debt' to 'Total assets' exceeds **33%**.

Liquid assets to total Assets

Excludes all companies of which the ratio of 'Cash and interest bearing securities' to 'Total assets' exceeds **33%**.

Receivables to total Assets

Excludes all companies of which the ratio of 'Accounts receivables' to 'Total assets' exceeds **50%**.

Impure income to total revenues

Excludes all companies of which the ratio of 'Total interest + non-compliant activities' income' to 'Total revenues' exceeds **50%**.

This additional screening criterion applies a higher level of stringency vis-à-vis the core business activity of the company and its reflection on its income. It implies a purified "dividend" based on total revenues of the firm.

---

[7]http://www.ftse.com/Indices/FTSE_Shariah_Global_Equity_Index_Series/Downloads/FTSE_Shariah_Index_Series_Ground_Rules.pdf

3.3 MSCI Global Islamic[8] index

Similar to FTSE SGX indices, the MSCI Global Islamic indices use the 'Total assets' in the denominator to establish its financial ratios. Additionally, the MSCI Global Islamic indices apply a total interest purification from the dividends as compared to an accepted level of 5% with FTSE SGX.

Industry screening

Similar to DJIMI and the FTSE SGX, MSCI Global Islamic indices exclude all Sharia non-compliant industry activities.

Debt to Assets ratio

Excludes all companies of which the ratio of 'Debt' to 'Total assets' exceeds **33%**.

Liquid assets to total Assets

Excludes all companies of which the ratio of 'Cash and interest bearing securities' to 'Total assets' exceeds **33%**.

Receivables to total Assets

Excludes all companies of which the ratio of 'Accounts receivables' to 'Total assets' exceeds **70%**

.

Impure income total depuration

All reflections of "impure income" in the total revenues are to be depurated donating them to charity at the time of dividend reception. This trade-off between the absence of cut-off threshold (all levels are accepted as compared to 5% of impure income to total income with FTSE SGX) and dividend depuration presents a flexible rule to managing the indices or funds based on MSCI Global Islamic indices at the expenses of P/E ratio and total fund performance. It remains to be investigated whether this rule improves on the diversification of the portfolio and hence whether the hypothetical lower risk derived from wider diversification is traded-off against relative lower return due to this absolute depuration criterion.

[8]http://www.msci.com/gimi/islamic/MSCI_Global_Islamic_Indices_IndexSummary_July2007.pdf

3.4 Screening Criteria of Securities And Exchange Commission (SEC)[9], Malaysia

Screening for Sharia compliant stocks is done at central level by the Sharia Advisory Council (SAC) of the Securities and Exchange Commission (SEC). A list of permissible stocks is issued by the SAC twice a year. The screening criteria are mainly activity or income based. No debt or liquidity screens are used. Thus screening requires income statements but not the balance sheets of the companies. Individual funds or investment companies do not make their own Sharia screening criteria.

Core Activities

The core activities of the companies should be Sharia compliant. Therefore companies having the following as their core business activities are excluded: Financial services based on Riba (interest); gambling; manufacture or sale of non-Halal products or related products; conventional insurance; entertainment activities that are non-permissible according to Sharia; manufacture or sale of tobacco-based products or related products; stock-broking or share trading in Sharia non-approved securities; and other activities deemed non-permissible according to Sharia.

Mixed Activities

For companies with activities comprising both permissible and non-permissible elements, the SAC considers two additional criteria:

a. The public perception or image of the company must be good and

b. The core activities of the company are important and considered Masalahah (in the public interest) to the Muslim Ummah (nation) and the country. The non-permissible element is very small and proven unavoidable.

Benchmarks of Tolerance

The benchmarks of tolerance apply in case of mixed activities. If the contributions in turnover or profit before tax from non-permissible activities of a company exceeds the benchmark, the securities of the company are classified as Sharia non-approved. The benchmarks are:

- The **5%** Benchmark

[9] http://www.sc.com.my

Applied to assess the level of mixed contributions from the activities that are clearly prohibited such as Riba (interest-based companies like conventional banks), gambling, liquor and pork.

- The **10%** Benchmark

Applied to assess the level of mixed contributions from the activities that involve the element of 'Umum Balwa" which is a prohibited element affecting most people and difficult to avoid. For example, interest income from fixed deposits in conventional banks.

- The **25%** Benchmark

This benchmark is used to assess the level of mixed contributions from the activities that are generally permissible according to Sharia and have an element of Maslahah (public interest), but there are other elements that may affect the Sharia status of these activities. For example, hotel and resort operations, share trading etc., as these activities may also involve other activities that are deemed non-permissible according to the Sharia.

- Debt and Liquidity

No restrictions on the proportion of debt or proportion of liquid assets in total assets.

4. Islamic Investment Universe: Asset classes

It is a fair to conclude that the Islamic investment Universe could eventually be a subset of the complete "conventional" investment universe for all possible states of the market in consideration. More precisely, if we consider all the shares of companies listed in a given market or markets as the investment universe, and if we rule out the "impure" assets and shares, we obtain the Islamic investment universe with shares complying with the Sharia filters only and hence the chosen or accepted titles are indeed a subset of the complete investment universe of the chosen market or markets:

- Shares of companies that comply with the screening criteria of industry and financial ratios.

- Fixed income instruments: Bonds are excluded because the underlying asset is a debt rather then tangible and because the coupon represents a fixed amount regardless of the performance of the underlying activity, which is Gharar. Only Sukuks are included. Sukuks are Islamic bonds with a tangible underlying asset and hence could be considered as collaterized. Moreover, Sukuks returns or "coupons" are not fixed and are usually a percentage of the underlying asset performance. This will eventually admit a fluctuating coupon value ranging from zero to a maximum. Even in the case of Sovereign Sukuks, the underlying asset should be tangible and hence they also are considered as collaterized.

- Derivatives: Derivatives are not allowed in the Islamic Investment Universe because of its reliance on Gharar (case of options) and on Riba (case of swaps). Besides derivative are considered speculative (especially when no delivery of underlying asset occurs) and are judged to be a kind of gambling or Maisir, for which reasons they are ruled out. Hedging is however possible and available, through a newly introduced Sharia compliant and option like instrument called Urboun or Ourboun. Urboun is not very widely used and it is not tradable. It can be transferred at par and to the date of delivery of this paper, the authors do not know of any exchange or secondary market for Urbouns, if at all.

- Money markets and FX. No Riba instruments or papers are allowed in an Islamic Investment Universe. Some equivalent Murabaha certificates or Murabaha funds exist to simulate a short term liquid instrument. FX operations are allowed on spot basis only. It is not permitted to use futures or forward contracts on FX or on any commodity or share. Islam prohibits the future sale of any good because of Gharar. Islam allows the sale of goods and values already in legal and physical possession of the offering counterparty. For this reason shorting is not allowed and it is assumed speculative and Gharar-full to short-sell or short-buy any security.

- Real estate and commodities. The dealing with real estate and commodities is permitted in Islam as long as the underlying asset exists and is in possession of the offering party. Many commodity Murabahas are already commonly used for short term liquidity management, using a spot purchase and physical possession of a commodity, usually platinum or palladium, and its subsequent sale at deferred payment with a mark-up. Many fund managers use this instrument to manage excess or shortage of liquidity. It's common name is Tawarruq, although scholars did not reach a consensus on the legitimacy and compliance of such an instrument.

- Private Equity. Private equity is also a major ingredient of any Islamic oriented investment, as long as it obeys the screening and filtering rules. Fund managers tend to avoid this class of security because of the difficulty of liquidation at the moment of exit. But in theory PE is an accepted class of investment for Sharia scholars.

- Funds and fund of funds. Sharia compliant funds are gaining increased acceptance among investors. The growth rate of Islamic funds surpasses 20% per annum in assets and in number as well[10]. An Islamic fund pools assets and asset classes that pass the screening rules on an individual level. Sharia scholars do not allow any netting or cross cancellation of debt or receivable within a given fund. The Sharia compliance screening is carried on each and every individual asset and asset class included in the fund, and the cut-off threshold for the financial ratios is observed on individual asset level and not on the fund level.

Islamic fund structure

By definition, an Islamic fund is a pool of assets complying individually with Sharia mandates and the management and trading principles of which obey the Sharia prohibition of Riba, Gharar, Maisir, short selling and sales of debt. In this sense, an Islamic fund is a restricted conventional fund , admitting those assets belonging to what we defined earlier as Islamic Investment Universe.

However, and because of the *sui generis* structure of the basic Islamic financial instruments, some additional and non-conventional asset classes are included in this Investment Universe, like Murabaha funds, Murabaha-Mudaraba funds and Ijara funds.

Mostly closed ended, those funds rely on pooling investors cash and investing them, through an SPV in "plain vanilla" Islamic instruments like Murabahas (cost+ margin sales) of commodities or leasing the real assets of the SPV through Ijara (lease) structure, as shown below:

[10] Source: www.failaka.com

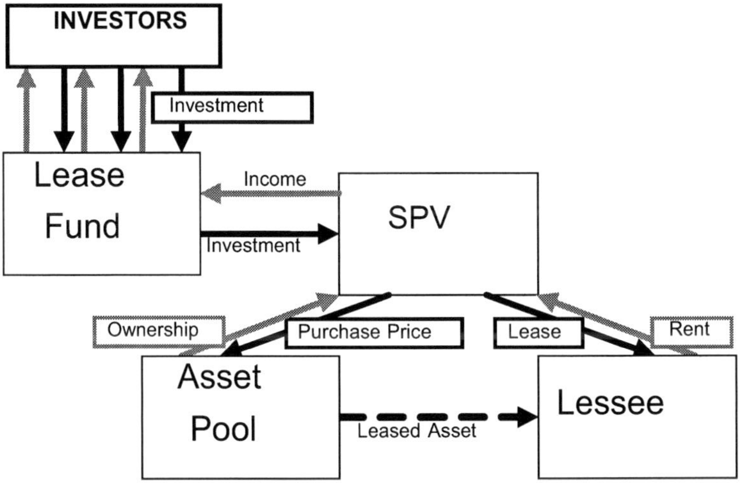

References

Al-Rifai Tariq (2003), "An Overview of Islamic Finance and The growth of Islamic Funds", *Islamic equity Funds: Workshop.*

Al-Suwailen Sami (200), "Towards An Objective Measure Of Gharar In Exchange", *Islamic Economic Studies Vol. 7, Nos. 1 & 2.*

Ausaf, Ahmad (2000), research division, "Instruments of regulation and control of Islamic banks by the central banks", *Islamic Development Bank Islamic Research and Training Institute.*

Chapra, M Umer & Khan, Tariqullah (2004), « Règlementation et Contrôle des Banques Islamiques », *étude spéciale No3, Banque Islamique de Développement Institut Islamique de Recherches et de Formation.*

Chapra, Muhammad Umer (1997), *Vers Un Système Monétaire juste*, Série de traduction de travaux en économie Islamique No.10, Banque Islamique de Développement Institut Islamique de Recherches et de Formation, Djeddah, Arabie Saoudite.

Dr Hussein A., Khaled (2004), "Banking efficiency in Bahrain: Islamic vs. Conventional Banks", paper no.68, *IDB publications.*

Duncan, Michael & Desai, Bimal, & Rieger, Julie (2004), "Islamic bankers take role on international projects", *International Financial Law Review 23 No5 52-4.*

El-Gamal, Mahmoud Amin (2000), *a Basic Guide to Contemporary Islamic Banking and Finance,* Rice University.

Esty, Benjamin (2004), « Why Study Large Projects? An Introduction to Research on Project Finance", *European Financial Management, Vol. 10, No 213-224.*

Euromoney 34, No 413 (September 2003), "Shariah-compliant banking takes centre stage", *Euromoney Institutional Investors PLC.*

Euromoney 35 38-40, 32-3, "Islamic finance needs solid foundations", *Euromoney Publications.*

Euromoney 35 Guide4-Guide6 (2004), "A New Generation of Services from Gulf Finance House", *Publications PLC.*

Hume, James (2004), "Islamic finance: provenance and prospects", *International Finance Law Review 23 no5 48-50.*

Khan, M. S., and Mirakhor, A. (1989). Islamic Banking: Experiences in the Islamic Republic of Iran and Pakistan. (IMF Working Paper No. wp/89/12). Washington DC: International Monetary Fund. (JEL Classification Nos. 3116; 3120; 314). p. 1

Munawar, Iqbal & Ausaf, Ahmad & Tariqullah, Khan (First Edition 1998), "Challenges Facing Islamic Banking", paper *n°1*, *Islamic Development bank Islamic Research and Training Institute*.

Rosly, Saiful Azhar (2005), *Islamic Banking and Financial Markets*, Dinamas, Kuala Lumpur, Malaysia.

Wilson, Rodney. (1983*). Banking and Finance in Arab Middle East.* London: Macmillan Publisher Ltd.

Yaqubi, Nizam, October 2000. *"Participation and trading in equities of companies whose main business is primarily unlawful.". Paper presented to the fourth Harvard Islamic Finance Forum, October 2000.*

www.failaka.com

www.sc.com.my

www.msci.com/gimi/islamic/

www.ftse.com/Indices/FTSE_Shariah_Global_Equity_Index_Series/

www.djindexes.com

Appendix A – Glossary

Al -kharaj bildaman:	the Islamic legal principle that means entitlement to revenue follows assumption of responsibility. Profits, therefore, are based on the ownership of, and responsibility for, capital
Bai al-dayn:	sale of debt or receivables
Bai al-inah:	a loan in the form of a sale, called *inah* (façade) because it is a sale in appearance only. This is accomplished by one's buying back what one has sold for a lower price than that for which one originally sold it. The difference, ostensibly profit, is actually a loan.
Bai al wafa':	a sale with the right of redemption, literally, a sale of honour. Typically, such a sale takes place when a commodity is sold on the condition that the seller be allowed to redeem the commodity upon paying its price; and the buyer agrees to honour the condition
Bai bithaman ajil	differed payment sale, credit sale
Daman/Kafala	guaranty or surety
Fatwa	an authoritative legal opinion based on the Sharia (Islamic law)
Fiqh	practical jurisprudence or human articulations of divine rules encompassing both laws and ethics. As such, *fiqh* may be understood as the jurists' understanding of the Sharia, or jurists' law
Fiqh al mu'amalat	Islamic commercial jurisprudence or the rules of transacting in a Sharia compliant manner
Fuqaha:	pl. of *faqih*, qualified specialists in *fiqh*, or jurists

Gharar: uncertainty in a contract of exchange as to the existence of the subject-matter of the contract and deliverability, quantity or quality of the subject-matter. It also involves contractual ambiguity as to the consideration and the terms of the contract. Such ambiguity will render most contracts void.

Hadith: the narrative record of the, sayings, doings, and implicit approval or disapproval of the Prophet, peace be upon him. The world is sometimes used in English as a collective noun; sometimes an "s" is added to make the plural

Halal: lawful; one the five major Sharia categorizations of human acts

Hamish gedyyah: security deposit. An amount of money paid by the purchase order upon request of the seller to make sure that the orderer is serious in his order of the asset. However if the promise in binding and the purchase ordered declines to purchase the asset, the actual loss incurred to the seller shall be made good from this amount

Haram unlawful; one of the five major Sharia categorizations of human acts

Ijara the transfer of ownership of a service for a specified period for an agreed upon lawful consideration

Ijara mountahia bittamleek: this is a form of leasing contract used by Islamic financial institution which includes a promise by the lessor to transfer the ownership of the leased property to the lessee, either at the end of the term or the lease period or by stages during the term of the contract. In this form of leasing contract, the title to the lease is executed by means of a promise to give it as a gift for no consideration or as a gift contingent upon the payment of the remaining installments or a promise to sell for a token or other consideration, or by accelerating the payment of the remaining installments or by paying the marked value of the leased property

Ijm'a: the consensus of jurists; considered a binding legal indicator (*dalil*) in the classical jurisprudence

Ijtihad: effort or toil (literally) as a legal term it means the effort of a qualified Islamic jurist to interpret sources of Islamic law. Thus, while every toiler or *mujtahid* is a jurist (*faqih*), not every jurist is a *mujtahid*. This is because many jurists serve merely to bear on convey *fiqh*, while others (through *ijtihad*) actually produce it

Ihtikar: monopoly

Ikhtilaf: divergence of opinions among jurists

Istihsan: judicial preference for one legal analogy over another, usually in view of the public welfare

Istisna'a: a contract of sale of specified goods to be manufactured, with an obligation of the manufacturer to deliver them upon completion. It is a condition in *istisna'a* that the seller provides either the raw material or cost of manufacturing the goods.

Jahala: lack of knowledge or ambiguity in the terms of a contract

Khiyar al-shart: an option in a sale contract concluded at the time of signing the agreement, giving one of the two parties to the contract a right to cancel the sale within a stipulated time

Manfaa: usufruct or benefit derived from an asset

Maqasid: the general objectives of Islamic law

Mudaraba: a partnership in profit between capital and work. A *Mudaraba* is typically conducted between investment account holders, as providers of funds, and the Islamic bank as a *Mudarib* (see below). The Islamic bank announces its willingness to accept the funds of investment account holders, the sharing of profits being as agreed between the two parties, and the losses being borne by the provider of funds, except in case of managerial misconduct, negligence or violation of the conditions agreed upon the Islamic bank. A *Mudaraba* contract may also be concluded between Islamic bank, as a provider of funds, on behalf of itself or on behalf of investment account holders, and business owners and other craftsmen, including farmers, traders, etc

Mujtahid: legal expert, or a jurist who expends great effort in deriving a legal opinion or interpreting the sources of law

Mudarib: the managing partner in a Mudaraba (see above)

Murabaha: sale of goods with an agreed upon profit mark-up on the cost. There are two types of *murabaha* sale. In the first, the Islamic bank purchases the goods and makes them available for sale without any prior promise from a customer to purchase it and is termed a normal or spot murabaha. The second type typically involves the customer's promise to purchase the item from the institution, which is called murabaha to the purchase orderer. It is distinguished from the normal type of murabaha which does not involve such a promise by the customer. The murabaha to the purchase order is the sale of an item by the institution to a customer (the purchase orderer) for a pre-agreed selling price, which includes a pre-agreed profit mark-up over its cost price, this having been specified in the customer's promise to purchase. Normally, a *murabaha* to the purchase order transaction involves the institution granting the customer a *murabaha* credit facility. A *murabaha* to the purchase order transaction typically involves deferred payment terms, but such deferred payment is not one of the essential conditions of such transactions. A murabaha can be arranged with no deferral of payment. In this case, the mark-up will only include the profit the institution will receive for a spot sale and not the extra charge it will receive for deferral of payment

Musharaka: a form of partnership between the Islamic bank and its clients whereby each party contributes to the partnership capital in equal or varying degrees to establish a new project or to share in an existing one. Each of the parties becomes an owner of the capital on a permanent or declining basis and shall have his due share of profits. Losses, however, are shared in proportion to the contributed capital. It is not permissible to stipulate otherwise

Qard Hassan a loan *per amore* in which there is no interest. In Islamic law, all loans are gratuitous contracts

Qura'n: thc Book of Divine Revelation that was delivered to humankind by the Prophet Mohammed, peace be upon him.

Rab al-mal: investor or owner of capital in a Mudaraba contract

Riba: interest; sometimes, equated with usury, though its means is somewhat broader. Its prohibition is meant to distinguish an unlawful exchange (in which there is a clear advantage to one on the contracting parties) from a lawful, mutually beneficial exchange and lawful loan

Salam: a contract for the purchase of a commodity for deferred delivery in exchange for immediate payment according to specified conditions

Sharia the term Sharia has two meanings: Islamic law, and the totality of divine categorizations of human acts (*Islam*). The second meaning of the term means Sharia rules do not always function as rules of law in the western sense, as they include obligations, duties and moral considerations not generally thought of as "law". Sharia rules, therefore, admitting of both a legal and a moral dimension, have as their purpose the fostering of obedience to the Almighty. In the legal terminology, Sharia means the law as extracted by the *mujtahids* from the source of law.

Sukuk: participation securities; coupons, investment certificates

Sunnah: the way of the Prophet Mohammed, peace be upon him, including his sayings, deeds, approvals or disapprovals as preserved in the *Hadith* literature: the second of the two sources of revelation

Takaful: a Sharia-compliant system of insurance in which the participants donate part or all of their contributions, which are used to pay claims for damages suffered by some of the participants. The company's role is restricted to managing the insurance operations and investing the insurance contributions

Ulema: pl. of 'alim, Sharia scholars or jurists

Urboun: earnest money. It is the amount paid by the client (orderer) to the seller after concluding a contract of sale, with the provision that the contract is completed during the prescribed period. The *urboun* amount will be kept by the seller if the buyer fails to execute the contract

Usul al-fiqh: Islamic legal theory

Wadia: safe-keeping/resale of goods with a discount on the original stated cost.

Wakala: agency. An agency contract which may include in its term a fee for the agent

Zakah: literally, it means blessing, purification, increase, or cultivation of good deeds. In Sharia, it is an obligation in respect of funds paid for a specified type of purpose and for specified categories. It is a specified amount prescribed by Allah Almighty for those who are entitled to *Zakah* as specified in the Qur'an. The word *Zakah* is also used to indicate the amount paid from the funds that are subject to *Zakah*.

CHAPTER EIGHT

APPLICATION OF DYNAMIC RANKINGS TO PORTFOLIO SELECTION

ANDRZEJ M.J. SKULIMOWSKI

Abstract

In this paper we will present the theoretical background and an application of dynamic ranking approach to pick stocks and bonds to an equity portfolio. The same approach can also be applied to rank and select real investment projects. We will investigate a class of multicriteria portfolio management problems, namely the dynamic stock picking based on rankings, where an equity ranking can be regarded as the result of a sequence of multicriteria analysis problems. Based on a dynamic programming model, we present the way the dynamic ranking of projects to be financed can be used, and which actions are to be taken when the priorities change in a response to an external event or as a result of achieving certain goals. While solving the stock-picking problem there arises a bi-level multicriteria ranking problem: at the first level equities are assessed making use of a set of expected future performance criteria, which base on current financial indicators, trends, and a set of anticipated events. As ranking criteria we considered a.o. the expected 1-month P/E, and P/BV ratios, EBITDA, expected mean volume, expected variation of volume. At the second level, the portfolios arisen by stocks (and bonds) picking are assessed according to the criteria of expected risk, and expected decision flexibility. We provide also a procedure to determine how the rankings are to be applied to allocate the available budget. Finally, using the above sketched approach, we have adopted the REFSET (cf. Skulimowski, 1997) outranking method, with the reference sets defined as reference portfolios, financial planning targets and the evidence from earlier portfolio investment processes.

Keywords: Multicriteria decision support; portfolio management; preference structures; dynamic multicriteria rankings.

1. Introduction

In this paper we will present the theoretical background and the resulting practical approach to solve a relevant class of multicriteria financial decision problems occurring when assigning funds to equities in an equity portfolio, and which can also be used to rank real investment projects in a project portfolio or in a mixed real-investment/equity portfolio. The approach is based on dynamic rankings of investment objects under consideration and can be regarded as a generalization of stock picking when the underlying information and preferences are changing (for other approaches and an introduction to portfolio optimization see e.g. Groenendijk, Spronk, 1999; Spronk, Steuer, and Zopounidis, 2005; Steuer, Qi and Hirschberger, 2005; Skulimowski, 1996b). Among the motivations to introduce this kind of models we should mention a generally positive experience in using asset rankings to build a portfolio as well as failures of approaches based on the statistical forecasts only. Moreover, supporting financial decisions with long-term obligations and impact gives often an opportunity to apply the qualitative results of foresight, scenarios and priority analysis in particular. The same kind of information is used here to establish dynamic portfolio rankings, serving thus also as a source of additional preference information to solving portfolio selection problems.

For the clarity's sake, in the sequel we will concentrate on presenting the theory for equity portfolios, having in mind that the applications for real investments or project portfolios can be equally covered by the theory presented, with a different set of real-life examples.

Let us recall that a *multicriteria optimisation problem* can be formulated as:

$$(F : U \rightarrow E) \rightarrow min(\theta) \tag{1}$$

where U and E are the decision and criteria spaces, respectively. One usually assumes that E is a complete vector space ordered by a closed, convex and pointed cone θ. The partial order in E introduced by the cone θ will be denoted by $\leq_\theta$, by definition, $x \leq_\theta y \Leftrightarrow y - x \in \theta$. The set of *nondominated points* in the problem (1) will be denoted by P(U,F,θ), by definition $x \in P(U,F,\theta)$ iff for every $y \in U$, $[y \leq_\theta x \Rightarrow x=y]$. In the most common case and throughout this paper, $E = \mathbb{R}^n$ with $F = (F_1, F_2, \ldots F_n)$ and θ the positive orthant $\mathbb{R}^n_+$ in $\mathbb{R}^n$, or θ is isomorphic to $\mathbb{R}^n_+$ and $\eta(\mathbb{R}^n_+) \subset \theta$ for certain isomorphism η (cf. Skulimowski, 1996). The latter conditions allows to investigate the sets of nondominated points to (1) which were defined using trade-off coefficient constraints.

2. Problem formulation

The *outranking problem* over the set X_0 may be formulated as a sequence of multicriteria decision-making problems:

$$(F_k: X_k \rightarrow \mathbb{R}^n) \rightarrow \min(\theta) \tag{2a}$$

$$(\varphi_k : P(X_k,F_k,\theta) \rightarrow \mathbb{R}) \rightarrow \min \tag{2b}$$

$$X_k := X_{k-1} \backslash \operatorname{argmin}\{(\varphi_{k-1} \circ F_{k-1})(X_{k-1})\}, \text{ for } k=1,\ldots,K-1 \tag{2c}$$

where:

(2a) is a multicriteria optimisation problem,

$X_0 := X$ is a finite set of feasible alternatives (stocks; bonds, convertibles, index derivatives), with $\#X \geq K$, where $\#X$ denotes the cardinality of X, $K \in \mathbb{N}$,

$F_0 := F = (f_1,\ldots f_n),\ldots,F_k = (f_{1,k},\ldots f_{n,k})$ are the vector criterion functions for the *k-th* optimisation/decision problem (2a)-(2c), k=1,…,K, describing the fundamental and technical characteristics of equities as well as external economic circumstances (appearing usually as sector criteria) and ecological preferences of investors,

θ_k is the convex cone defining the ordering in $\mathbb{R}^n$,

and

φ_k is the *k-th* multicriteria value function reflecting the additional social, economic, ecological preferences of the stakeholders as well as the degree of achievement of decision-maker's targets for k=1,…N.

Definition 1. *A*ny sequence of solutions to (1b), ***R***, will be called a *simple ranking*. A simple ranking is *complete*, iff #X=K.

To assure the *fairness of choice*, we will assume that

$$\text{for all } k=1,\ldots,K,\ F_k = F,\ \varphi_k := \varphi \text{ on } X_0, \text{ and } \theta_k=\theta. \tag{3}$$

Definition 2. An outranking problem (2) fulfilling (3) will be called *fair*.

Fair outranking in our case corresponds to the situation, when all equities considered are treated by the same evaluation procedure. This is realistic as long as the investment portfolio is constructed at once, i.e. it is likely to be fulfilled in equity portfolios, but may be questioned when building large real investment portfolio over a long period of time. Specifically, fair ranking assumes solving problems (2a)-(2c) in such a way that it 'forgets' relations between equities, while an equity ranking has a clear goal of selecting the best group of n elements, rather than a set of n isolated best alternatives. Therefore we will formulate below a groupwise ranking problem - a sequence of multicriteria decision problems:

$$(F_k : X_k \to IR^n) \to \min(\theta) \text{ for all } k=0,\ldots,K\text{-}1 \tag{4a}$$

$$(G : 2^X \to IR^m) \to \min(\xi) \tag{4b}$$

$$(\psi_k : [2^X \text{ x } P(X_k,F_k,\theta)] \to IR) \to \min \tag{4c}$$

[*aggregated risk-adjusted earnings prospect*] for all $k=1,\ldots,K$

$$X_k := X_{k-1} \backslash \text{argmin}\{(\psi_{k-1} \circ F_{k-1})(X_{k-1})\}, \text{ for } k=1,\ldots K\text{-}1;\ X_0:=X \tag{4d}$$

where:

X is the finite set of all basic feasible alternatives (stocks; bonds, convertibles, index derivatives, $\#X \geq K$),

$F_0:=F=(f_1,\ldots f_n)$, $F_k=(f_{1,k},\ldots f_{n,k})$ is the vector criterion function for the k-th problem, with the same interpretation as in problem (2), optimized with respect to θ - the partial order relation in IR^n.

ξ is a partial order in the family of all compositions of portfolios 2^X,

and

ψ_k (Y,x) is the multicriteria conditional value function reflecting the additional preferences of the decision makers to include x into a portfolio Y, for k=1,…N.

Definition 3. By a *group ranking* ***R*** we will mean any sequence of solutions to (4a)-4d).

Similarly to the fairness for simple rankings, we can define the *groupwise fairness of choice* assuming that for all k, $F_k = F$, and $\psi_k := \psi$.

Since the priority in an equity ranking does not translate immediately in the amount of money to be assigned to each n-th place winner, the first task of the decision-support expert is to redefine this notion in terms of mid-term goals, quantitative indicators such as earnings or risk, and – if appropriate - the estimated social and/or ecological benefit functions. Next, the amount to be assigned and the prospective economic and financial parameters for the planning period are to be taken into account as constraints. To make the priority ranking meaningful, we have to determine precisely how the rankings influence the way the priorities elicited are applied to allocate the budget according to the investment rules and the competences of the investors concerned. Funds allocation may often be coped with defining the temporal relevance of alternatives, i.e. higher-ranked priorities correspond to the acquisition/sale decision made earlier than those less preferred.

Example 1. Let us define for a selected capital market the stock picking criteria as

$F=(f_1,\ldots f_n)$=(4Q-income trend, P/E, P/BV, EBITDA, FST-S, PTP-S, 45-Session trend, SP-sector prospect),

and the other elements of the preference structure of the problem (4):

G: $X^2/R \ni (s_1 , s_2) \rightarrow corr(s_1,s_2)$ - the real function which assigns the correlation coefficient between the quotations of equities s_1,and s_2,

S(0,K) – initial portfolio consisting of K solutions to the problem (2b),

$$\Psi: (Y, P(X_k,F_k,\theta))\rightarrow Y\cup\{x: G(Y\cup\{x\}) \text{ is } \xi\text{-minimal}\}$$

R(0,K1) – initial portfolio obtained by the groupwise ranking procedure (4a)-(4d) from S(0,K).

Then the auxiliary portfolio optimization problem can be formulated as:

$$(H : \bigcup [S(i) \times IR^{i-1}] \rightarrow IR^{p}) \rightarrow \min(\rho), \quad (5)$$

where H is an assignment of weights to equities, and the preference ordering ρ corresponds to a usual risk aversion measurement. The next steps for solving the dynamic equity ranking and portfolio selection problem consists in constructing scenarios and using R(0,K1) as an input to dynamic ranking.

The major drawback of the approach presented above consists in the fact that once the assignment priorities are determined and approved, there is no mechanism to adjust them to the needs of the changing (financial market, but also social, environmental, legal) situation. The common approach used by the investors is twofold: once, the procedures, goals, and strategies are being re-defined each time after a relevant change takes place, based on new market studies or expert advice. The latter may be based on foresight exercises, such as finding market scenarios, involving further experts in a Delphi-like procedure. However, the translation of expert advice to quantitative procedures and long-term strategies is very vague, and loosing the essential findings of the decision support is likely. Furthermore, it is obvious that the investment targets achieved so far influence the conditions to achieve the next targets, for instance by re-investment opportunities in a multi-step investment processes. Despite of it, alternative scenarios are often considered as having no links between each other, thus future deviations from the most expected situation may surprise the decision-makers.

Motivated by the need of ranking investment projects, which are to be assigned funds paid in temporarily distributed instalments, such as large portfolio investments distributed over time due to limited liquidity, in this paper we investigate the problem of dynamic ranking of portfolios, based on the dynamic ranking of equities. The novelty of the *dynamic ranking approach* consists in the fact that the mutual impact of events forming and influencing the future scenarios are taken into account in one model jointly. Mutual dependence of events is modelled as a controlled discrete-event system, allowing thus to represent the network of future events and the causal relations between them as a multigraph with the time-dependent structure. The vertices of this multigraph are interpreted as the achieved states of the object (portfolio structures), parameterised by the values of all criteria to be optimised (usually risk and earnings). The edges correspond to the decisions (sale/buy/hold) made and are quantified in a natural way.

3. Dynamic rankings in the foresight setting

The foresight methodology, which will be applied to find a compromise distribution of funding allocation, has been initially used to assess the development of military technologies, and now it is gaining rapidly the popularity as the strategic decision support approach at the (over)national, regional and the company level. One of the possible goals of foresight, at all its levels, is to recommend strategic policy priorities to the decision-makers for a relatively long period of time, usually within the range of 15-50 years. In this paper we will refer to foresight methods first to situate the portfolio management and fund allocation strategies within the macroeconomic, political, technological and research environment. It is assumed that portfolio management priorities are the results of foresight-based advices and, usually in form of recommendations and relative importance rankings, trends, and scenarios, and of the real-time external event inflow. It is to be noted that similarly as in case of individual projects rankings, an investment priority is not a well-defined term, so that the notion of priority must again be linked to a plan of concrete actions, taking into account the socio-economic and political boundary conditions.

The above setting leads to formulating a hierarchical multicriteria decision problem that explores results of external advice (foresight-based) with a set of independent criteria describing the social, economic, ecological preferences of the stakeholders as well as the degree of achievement of long-term investment targets defined by the fund supervisory authorities. Some of the latter preferences may coincide with some from the first group, but in most cases the investment policy targets may generate independent criteria as well.

In the sequel we will focus our attention on a hierarchical fund assignment problem: at the higher level dynamic ranking is used to rank the investment policies, which follow from the foresight exercises or supervisory authorities decisions. Such general recommendations may have the form of sector, size, or regional preferences concerning stocks, or may regard the portfolio structure. The decision-making goal at the lower level is to rank the portfolios taking into account the higher-level policy ranking and using additional equity characteristics (each stock may be included in several different portfolios that satisfy the higher-level conditions). Finally, the rankings will be implemented as portfolio management rules, by assigning funds to equity acquisitions on the stock exchange. Each assignment is a function of time and of external logical variables, the latter representing the changes in higher-level ranking and the states of external political, socio-economical and ecological environment.

A characteristics feature of the approach presented that links it even closer to the foresight methodology is the use of scenarios to establish the future rankings in an adaptive mode. Namely, based on the feasible scenarios found at moment t_0, we calculate the feasible future rankings for $t= t_0+1, t_0+2,\ldots, t_0+k$. This allows inputting into the fund planning and assignment essentially more ex-post knowledge than in a usual static approach.

Below we give an illustrative example:

Example 2. Portfolio managers in an investment fund follow general policy rules defined by the Fund's Supervisory Council that recommended investing in oil stocks and in environmentally friendly companies, then to balance the portfolio by other stocks with positive market prospect up to 30% value and use hedging up to 4% of invested funds. These recommendations change usually once a year or in a case of emergency, and follow from systematically updated foresight exercises. The managers follow the news, and classify them as events that can influence the higher-level rankings, and consequently, the investment policies and investment operational decisions. The influence mechanism consists in integrating incoming external events with the events forming scenarios and trends that served to establish earlier rankings, and by recalculating the rankings. The new higher-level priorities, coped with the fund allocation, define a preference structure in the set of available equities and the admissible portfolios. If – in the above starting situation – the news agency announces a pollution of a sea by the tanker belonging to the oil company X, after processing this information in the dynamic ranking – recommendation generating engine, the portfolio managers may get a new ranking, and a new operational recommendation to do not increase, or to reduce the shares of X. In a longer perspective, the criteria of expected earnings, expected risk, and a synthetic measure of satisfying the higher-level recommendation will be confronted to yield a consensus trade-off. The fund allocation algorithm (e.g. buy or keep m-highest ranked stocks unless all are mutually positively correlated with $\rho>0,3$) need not be changed when updating the rankings.

Beyond rationalising the ranking and financing of portfolios and projects, in real-life circumstances the higher-level investment policy ranking may also assist to determine the organisational structure and the characteristics of the human resources of the portfolio management department, further, the budgetary needs over future periods, and the actions to be taken when the priorities change in a response to an external event. They may also serve to derive other rankings at a lower (operational) decision level, such as technologies to be developed, directions of the market expansion, preventive actions to be taken, municipal investment strategies etc.

An example of application of the above outlined approach to establish a dynamic ranking of the energy-sector-related investment projects and the corresponding portfolio acquisition is provided in Sec. 4. The dynamic policy rankings are used there together with the MREF (cf. Skulimowski, 1996, Chapter 6; 1997) outranking method to derive the time-dependent assignment of funds. The impact of the assignment to be implemented on the ecological and national security criteria values is taken into account as well.

4. An outline of the methodology of dynamic equity rankings (DER)

Mutual dependence of events and an impact of an external decision-maker can be modelled as a controlled discrete-event system (cf. Ramadge and Wonham, 1987; Skulimowski, 1991), allowing thus to represent the network of future events and the causal relations between them as a multigraph with time-dependent structure and the vertices interpreted as the achieved state of the governed object, parameterised by the values of all optimisation criteria.

Let us recall that a *discrete-event system* is a 5-tuple:

$$P=(Q,V,\delta,Q_0,Q_m) \tag{6}$$

where:

Q – is the set of system's states,

V – is the set of admissible operations over the system,

$\delta : V \times Q \rightarrow Q$ – the transition function governing the results of operations over states,

Q_0 - the set of (potential) initial states of the process,

Q_m – set of marked (or final) states.

A pair of states $e:=(q_1,q_2)$, such that $q_2=\delta(v,q_1)$will be called *an event.* The set of all admissible events in the system (6) will be denoted by E. We assume that the operations V may be either external decision-maker's actions over Q or may occur spontaneously as a result of a random process. In the first case the operations will be called *controls*. Furthermore, we assume that there exists a set X(Q) of quantitative or ordinal characteristics of the set of states Q, which can be deterministic, interval, stochastic, fuzzy etc. Similarly, to the events may be associated a set of criteria $G=(G_1,\ldots,G_k):E\rightarrow\mathbb{R}^k$. One of the coordinates of G may (but not need to) be identified with time. *An elementary scenario s* is a sequence of events $(e_1,\ldots,e_p)$, such that if $e_i=(q_i,q_{i+1})$ *then* $e_{i+1}=(q_{i+1},q_{i+1+2})$. Remember that an arbitrary sequence of states does not necessarily represent a trajectory of the system (6) as the subsequent states need not form events.

To conform to the usual foresight meaning of scenarios, let us note that by a scenario a foresight expert means usually a cluster of elementary scenarios, where the clustering is implied by additional similarity rules applied to elementary scenarios. In addition, a scenario is usually identified with the values of X(Q) for a certain moment of time or a prescribed set of future moments.

Discrete-event systems may govern the evolution of causal systems, thus giving a tool to construct scenarios, which appear as trajectories to (6). Consequently, when using the discrete event systems approach to generate nondominated scenarios, strategies or policies, we can apply a generalisation of the multicriteria shortest-path algorithm (*msp*). The features of the algorithms are taken directly from Bellman dynamic programming principle to deal with the variable structure networks that appear in optimal control of discrete-event systems (cf. Skulimowski, 1991; 1996 Chapter 8). Further, for each moment of time we can use an outranking method to rank the states of the governed object, taking into account the quantitative characteristics evaluated by the *msp* algorithm. Assigning additionally probabilities to each external event and each scenario under consideration, we are able to derive the expected ordering of priorities for each moment of time. As the priorities are shown on an ordinal scale, this can be presented in form of a chart (an example is given in Fig. 1 in Skulimowski, 2008).

The main steps of the decision support procedure yielding both quantitative (the anticipated future values of indicators within each scenario) and qualitative (ranking of priorities) results are presented below:

- The policy targets and indicators are to be elicited during the knowledge-acquisition phase of the exercise

- They are to be initially ranked using an end-user-selected multicriteria analysis method and discussed with the decision-makers. Specifically, we have used the multiple reference point methods, MREF and REFSET, the Controlled Goal Attainment method, cf. Skulimowski, 1996, Chapters 6,7, respectively, as well as other commonly used outranking methods;

- Policy areas are to be defined, then initial *Relative Importance Factors* are to be assigned to each policy area based on the guidelines approved by the authorities and in force at the time the exercise is started;

- Target ranking dynamics is to be considered, taking into account the momentary state of development of the factors and indicators considered in the exercise, and the cross-impact analysis of targets;

- Quantitative forecasts of the human resources development, economic growth, future budget available, and qualitative social preferences are elaborated using nonlinear trend analysis and the official statistical data;

- External events, which may influence the implementation of the policies, and their characteristics are to be specified;

- Future scenarios and their cross-impact are to be constructed.

Building a ranking, which is a part of the above procedure can thus be presented as

Algorithm 1.
Step 1. Define the objects (equities) to be ranked (this may be a part of the previous stages of a foresight exercise)
Step 2. Define the criteria and associate them to the objects, and select an outranking method to be used in the next steps.

Step 3n. Gather and represent the knowledge about the future (trends, scenarios, experts' assessments, forecasts, and their mutual relations)
Step 4n. Build the ranking NOW to be applied in FUTURE using the selected outranking method
Step 5n. Translate the quantitative results into the experts' recommendations to be presented to the decision-makers
Repeat Steps 3n-5n after every change of market situation or external circumstances (a reaction threshold is to be defined first).

5. Applications of the DER method

Using the above outlined procedure with a pre-selected outranking method, one can derive the time-dependent relative priority importance chart showing the rankings on an ordinal scale. The chart does not show the social and economical impact of achieving each combination of the policy targets, as this has been already evaluated in the 'impact modelling' phase of the method. In the experiments made so far we have used the REFSET-based outranking methods (cf. Skulimowski, 1996 Chapter 6; 1997) as well as the Controlled Goal Attainment method (Skulimowski, 1996, Chapter 7) and the well-known interactive trade-off coefficients approach. Other outranking methods can be used as well, as long as they comply with the information structures available in the equity selection problems.

Thus the Algorithm 1 can be improved by including the dynamic features sketched in Sec. 4 above. It results in the following:

Algorithm 2. (Dynamic priority ranking approach)
Step 1. Define the objects to be ranked (equities or their groups) and their transformation dynamics during the planning period
Step 2. Associate the criteria (as functions of time) to the objects
Step 3. Assign the initial Relative Importance Factors to the ranked objects, based on external sector criteria or ratings
Step 4. Gather and represent the knowledge about the future (trends, scenarios, experts' assessments, forecasts, and their mutual relations, and describe quantitatively the dependence of (n+1)th moment priorities on the n-th one quantitatively
Step 5. Build the portfolio ranking (problem (4)) and ranking update rules every time after an intermediate goal is attained (take profit moment) or when relevant external events occur

Step 6. Translate the quantitative results into the experts' recommendations to be presented to the portfolio managers, including the potential results of the prior attainment of certain targets
Step 6a. Present the temporal preference structure of the portfolio selection targets to be attained (if any).

The above approach can be applied in the following portfolio management - fund allocation procedure:

Algorithm 3.
Step 1. Find the set S(0) of initial scenarios of the future states of the economic environment
Step 2. Derive the rankings (scenario-dependent)

$$R(0, S(0)):=\{p1,0(t),\ldots,pk(0),0(t)\}\ (S(0))$$

of projects to be financed for $t=t_0$
Step 3. Derive and apply the transaction (sell/buy/swap) rules h to {p1,0(t),…,pk(0),0(t)} (s), for the scenario s (f(p,s) is a k(0)xT matrix)
Step 4. Find the value of the aggregated criteria φ,ψ and G
Register external events and apply the control rule δ to events forming all scenarios resulting in a set of scenarios S(n)
Step 6n. Derive the rankings (scenario-dependent)

$$R(n, S(n)):=\{p1,0(t),\ldots,pk(0),0(t)\}\ (S(0))$$

of equity portfolios for $t=t_0$
Step 7n. Find the value of the assignment quality criteria G(n).
If $G(n)\leq G(n-1)$
- investigate the trade-off between the value of $G(n)-c(n,S_a(n))+g(n, S_a(n))$ and G(n-1), find a compromise value
- apply the actions $(v(1,1),\ldots,v(1,k)\in V$ yielding a selected updated scenario and the new value G'(n)

Step 8n. Derive and apply the money allocation rule f to {p1,n(t),…,pk(n),n(t)} (s), for the updated scenario s (observe that f(p,s) is a k(n)xT matrix)
Step 9. Repeat the steps 5n-8n during the portfolio management period
Step 10. Calculate the values of the final portfolio management assessment criteria.

6. Final remarks concerning applications to portfolio selection

Before running a decision-support-type implementation of the above algorithms one has to interpret in quantitative terms and include the impact of the technological and financial prospects on the equities, groups of equities, or real projects into the multicriteria optimization model.

An example of the resulting dynamic priority elicitation scheme is shown below:

Solution scheme 1.
Step 1. Solve the problem (2) ('Ex-Ante ranking')
Step 2. Solve the problem (4) for an initial groupwise ranking
Step 3. Construct the scenarios based on the external event observations, trends, and control
Step 4. Elaborate the action planning for significant events in each scenario
Step 5. Perform the scenario-dependent dynamic ranking planning

Following a similar approach in case of ranking real investment projects (cf. Salo et al., 2006; Skulimowski, 2008), their dynamic ranking, can be elaborated in a similar way as stocks. Therefore one can consider mixed real-investment – traded-equity portfolios in a homogeneous way.

The first-level criteria are selected empirically from a larger set of fundamental and technical indicators, so that expected periodic earnings, and expected decision flexibility are maximized. Although the problem of feature selection can be regarded as a relevant 0-level optimization problem itself (cf. e.g. Dombi, Zsiros, 2005; Doumpos, Zopounidis, 2004) and the set of relevant features may depend on time, to present the ranking approach it suffices to consider a fixed set of characteristic equity features. Specifically, as basic ranking criteria we consider a.o. the expected 1-month P/E, and P/BV ratios, EBITDA, expected mean volume, expected variation of volume. The external events can be related to new technologies implemented, new products appearing on the market, mergers and acquisitions, or to the company sales and distribution markets directly.

At the second level, the portfolios arisen by stocks (and bonds) picking are assessed according to the criteria of expected risk and expected decision flexibility. As the mutual correlations are not taken into account at the first level, the second-level assessment allows for a more appropriate risk estimations. The inclusion of equity derivatives as risk-management tools can also be performed at this level of optimization without interfering with the dynamic rankings performed at level one.

In the above case the *dynamic ranking approach* consists in finding the relation between the preceding and current rankings based on market trends and on the impact of external events forming the scenarios that influence the ranking criteria. There arises a bi-level multicriteria ranking problem: at the first level equities are assessed making use of a set of expected future performance criteria, which base on current financial indicators, trends, and a set of anticipated events. The latter are modeled as a controlled discrete-event system (6), allowing thus to represent the network of future events and the causal relations between them as a multigraph with the time-dependent structure and the vertices interpreted as the achieved state of the objectives describing the stocks and bonds.

In the approaches to portfolio selection by stock picking, the position of an equity in a ranking does not translate immediately into the relative share of this instrument in the portfolio. To make this portfolio selection method constructive, we provide a procedure to determine precisely how the rankings are applied to allocate the available budget. Finally, using the above approach to derive the time-dependent assignment of funds, we have adopted the reference-set-based outranking method, with the reference sets defined as reference portfolios, financial planning targets (target points), and the evidence from earlier portfolio investment processes (status-quo and anti-ideal points, depending on their assessment). The approach presented allows defining concrete market moves to be taken at each planning period as well as to optimize large transactions that are to be distributed over certain time. The foresight methodology applied to determine the anticipated events and scenarios that influence rankings assists in a more precise planning of actions to be taken when managing an equity portfolio.

Finally, observe that, besides of equity and project portfolios, the models of structure of orders on a stock exchange (Skulimowski, 1999) and of evolution of any discrete population (Skulimowski, 1994) often include ordering structures that can be described by dynamic rankings. Moreover, it is to be observed that a tailored architecture of multicriteria decision support with a knowledge base has to be designed for each class of applications. Such DSS can be applied to the analysis of the investment results, and to update the goals and portfolio composition rules when needed.

References

Dombi, J., Zsiros, A. (2005). Learning multicriteria classification models from examples: Decision rules in continuous space. *European Journal of Operational Research*, 160, 2005, 663-675.

Doumpos M., Zopounidis C. (2004). A multicriteria classification approach based on pairwise comparisons, *European Journal of Operational Research*, 158, 2004, 378-389.

Groenendijk, A., Spronk, J. (1999). Portfolio performance through the eyes of monkeys. In: M. Bonilla, T. Casasus, R. Sala (Eds.), Financial Modelling, Springer Verlag, 1999.

Ramadge P.J., W.M. Wohnam (1987). Supervisory control of a class of discrete event processes. *SIAM J. Control*, 25, No.1, 206-230.

Salo A., Mild P., and Pentikäinen T. (2006). Exploring causal relationships in an innovation program with Robust Portfolio Modeling. *Technological Forecasting and Social Change*, 73, 1028-1044.

Skulimowski A.M.J. (1991). Optimal Control of a Class of Asynchronous Discrete-Event Systems. In: Automatic Control in the Service of Mankind. Proceedings of the 11th IFAC World Congress, Tallinn (Estonia), Aug. 1990, Vol.3, pp. 489-495; Pergamon Press, London.

—. (1994). Optimizing the Structure of a Partitioned Population. In: J. Henry and J.-P. Yvon (Eds.) System Modelling and Optimization; *Lecture Notes in Control and Information Sciences*, Vol. 197, Springer-Verlag, Berlin-Heidelberg-New York, pp. 771-782.

—. (1996a). Decision Support Based on Reference Sets, AGH University Publishers, Series: Automatics, No. 40, p.165.

—. (1996b). Dynamic portfolio optimization based on reference trajectories. In: System Modelling and Optimization, Proceedings of the 17th IFIP TC7 Conference on System Modelling and Optimization, July 1995; Chapman & Hall, 1996, pp. 171-178.

—. (1997). Methods of Multicriteria Decision Support Based on Reference Sets In: R. Caballero, F. Ruiz, R.E. Steuer (Eds.) Advances in Multiple Objective and Goal Programming, *Lecture Notes in Economics and Mathematical Systems*, 455, Springer-Verlag, Berlin-Heidelberg-New York, pp. 282-290.

—. (1999). A Discrete-Control-System Model of Order-Driven Capital Markets; In: Financial Modelling – Proceedings of the 23rd Meeting of the EURO WG on Financial Modelling, Progress & Business Publishers, Kraków, Dec. 1999, pp. 322-339.

—. (2008). Applications of dynamic multicriteria rankings in technological forecasting. *Reports of the Department of Mathematical Information Technology. Series A. Collections*, No. A 1/2008, 139-148.

Spronk, J., Steuer, R. E., and Zopounidis C. (2005). Multicriteria decisionaid/analysis in finance. In Figueira J., Greco S., Ehrgott M., (Eds.), Multiple Criteria Decision Analysis: State of the Art Surveys, Springer Science, 2005, 799-857.

Steuer R.E., Qi Y., and Hirschberger M. (2005). Multiple objectives in portfolio selection. *J. Financial Decision Making*, 1 (1), 11-26.

CHAPTER NINE

CROSS-SECTIONAL LIQUIDITY INTERACTIONS FROM INTRADAY PERSPECTIVES

EMANUEL KOPP, MICHAEL HUETL,
OTTO LOISTL AND JOHANNES PRIX

Abstract

This is the first empirical study on non-idiosyncratic liquidity components that investigates different intraday time periods during the trading session based on complete tick-by-tick order book data from the *Xetra* electronic trading system of the *Frankfurt Stock Exchange* (FSE). We apply non-overlapping cost of round-trip measures, which allows capturing liquidity in different regions of the entire limit order book. To extract common factors in liquidity, we rely on cross-sectional principal components analysis (PCA). Since PCA provides no interpretation of the extracted systematic factors, we propose a robust multi-stage PCA and regression approach to investigate cross-sectional liquidity determinants and their interactions in detail. We detect considerable influence of market-wide liquidity and furthermore show which factors count for the intraday variation in liquidity commonality. Moreover we can empirically demonstrate that systematic liquidity is strongly related to common factors in stock returns, and also to market-wide buying or selling pressures.

Keywords: financial markets, commonality in liquidity, limit order book

1. Introduction

The structure of established asset pricing models indicates that the market-wide context of liquidity has been disregarded for many years. But the topic has regained attention. Today it is well documented in the academic literature that the liquidity of individual stocks in a market is considerably determined by latent market-wide factors.

This strong evidence of *commonality in liquidity* has far-reaching consequences for financial theory, exchange organizations, regulators, and individual market participants. For individual traders, commonality in liquidity means that some part of liquidity risk is systematic and, hence, cannot be diversified. Consequently, conventional asset pricing models that do not consider the second moment of liquidity fail to correctly assess liquidity risk. Finally, the understanding of these systematic liquidity factors is essential for effectively regulating and stabilizing the financial system.

Detailed intraday order book data has not been available until recently. In particular the early studies on market-wide liquidity usually applied price or quote data in monthly, weekly, or daily frequency obtained from the *ISSM Transactions File Database* or the *NYSE Trade Quotation (TAQ) Database*. Since traders are most severely exposed to changes in market-wide liquidity risk if there is a need to trade high volumes during the trading session, an investigation of market-wide liquidity in the sense of *tradability aspects* should also be studied by the use of *intraday data*.

One shortcoming of most existing papers is the almost exclusive concentration on liquidity around the spread. But the liquidity at best bid and best ask is only a small part of the liquidity provided by limit orders in the order book. For instance, Kempf and Mayston (2005) show that more than twenty percent of all transactions in the Xetra system walk up the order book. Hence, there is also valuable trading information about liquidity beyond best bid and best ask. To adress this shortcoming, we apply different non-overlapping tradability measures of liquidity that allow the investigation of liquidity in different areas of the order book.

Our empirical analysis is based on high-frequency order book data from the *Xetra* trading system. The dataset consists of each tick-by-tick Xetra order book entry for all *DAX-30* stocks during the period 6-13 December 2006. Xetra operates as an open limit order book. Compared to the Paris stock exchange, not only the best five quotes are displayed to the traders. In contrast to the *NYSE*, every trader has insight into the complete order book[1]. Each trader can easily compute how far his or her order would have to walk up the book to get fully executed. Hence, our data set is especially appropriate for an *intraday* investigation of liquidity commonality in the *entire* limit order book.

First, we address the question whether also market-wide factors determine the liquidity of individual stocks. For this purpose, we conduct cross-sectional principal components analysis (PCA) on the liquidity measures applied in this study. Since the results obtained from conventional PCA approaches can be strongly affected by the presence of outliers in the sample, we apply a much more robust method that arises from the *Projection-Pursuit* principle (see Huber (1985)).

Unfortunately, a PCA methodology only allows examining if common factors *exist*, but offers no economic (or causal) interpretation of the latent determinants. To get to an interpretation of the systematic liquidity components, we propose a multi-stage PCA and regression approach using non-overlapping cost-of-roundtrip measures.

To examine whether also the systematic factors of different liquidity variables are correlated cross-sectionally, we run canonical correlations analysis between the systematic components of the different variables in the cross-section. From this investigation we can demonstrate that also also the systematic factors of different and non-overlapping liquidity measures are correlated in the cross-section. The correlations are highest in neighboring regions of the order book.

In addition, we apply several other trading-related measures and study (canonical) correlations between their market-wide determinants and the systematic factors in liquidity. Most interestingly, systematic return co-movements and market-wide volume imbalances are strongly related to common factors in liquidity.

To investigate how commonality behaves during the trading session, we analyze three different time periods during continuous trading. From regression analysis we additionally find out which determinants count for

[1] Exceptions are hidden orders (iceberg orders).

the intraday-variation of the different measure-independent systematic liquidity components.

The paper is organized as follows: Section 2 discusses the existence and consequences of systematic market-wide liquidity factors and briefly surveys the literature on market-wide liquidity. Section 3 informs about the Xetra trading system of the Frankfurt Stock Exchange (FSE) and reports the structure of our data-set. The description of liquidity measurement and Projection-Pursuit PCA can be found in section 4. In section 5, we conduct several principal components and canonical correlation analysis between the systematic factors extracted from different measures. Section 6 analyzes whether also measure-independent systematic liquidity factors exist. Based on measure-specific systematic factors in liquidity, we extract *global* systematic liquidity factors and study factor interactions across different PCA stages. Section 7 summarizes the most important results of this study and concludes.

2. Market-wide liquidity

2.1. Literature overview and recent developments

Until the end of the 1990ies, researchers focused almost exclusively on the liquidity of individual stocks.[2] Hasbrouck and Seppi (2001) state that "[u]ntil recently, however, little direct empirical research has been conducted on the magnitudes of cross-stock interactions at the microstructure level. [...] This focus on stocks in isolation has, however, left us ignorant of even the most basic facts about cross-sectional interactions between stocks."[3]

Probably the most prominent empirical papers that investigate the time-variation of market-wide liquidity are Chordia et al. (2000) and Hasbrouck and Seppi (2001). For instance, Chordia et al. (2000) apply different spread measures and quoted depths to measure liquidity on NYSE listed stocks during 1992, and show that individual liquidity measures of different stocks co-move with each other. They argue that *commonality in liquidity* empirically manifests in time-series co-movement in liquidity because of latent common determinants across

[2] For instance, O'Hara (1995) provides a survey on the literature on liquidity from a single-asset perspective.

[3] Hasbrouck and Seppi (2001), p. 384.

stocks, and apply a market model that relates individual stock liquidity to market liquidity, which is similar to the CAPM, but for liquidity. Concretely, they run regressions to measure the sensitivity of individual stock liquidity to market liquidity, which they define as the average of all stocks' liquidity (see Chordia et al. (2000)). They conclude that inventory effects[4] and asymmetrically distributed information might be the sources of market-wide liquidity co-movements. Different from the market-model approach, Hasbrouck and Seppi (2001) rely on principal components analysis (PCA) of different liquidity measures separately to extract latent, market-wide factors that systematically drive the liquidity of individual stocks. In recent years, the use of PCA has become the predominant methodology to study cross-sectional liquidity commonality. Hasbrouck and Seppi (2001) apply bid-ask spreads, depths, and quote-slope measures to the thirty Dow-Jones stocks during 252 trading days in 1994. While Chordia et al. (2000) report that the extracted liquidity determinants explain more than thirty percent of daily changes in liquidity, the results of Hasbrouck and Seppi (2001) are less supporting. They do not detect significant evidence of commonality in the applied liquidity measures. Conversely, they find strong evidence for the existence of market-wide factors in order-flows and stock returns.

The latest developments in the literature on market-wide liquidity factors are the investigation of different aspects of liquidity, a shift towards a demand/supply perspective of liquidity, and the use of higher data frequency. The most recent development in the commonality literature is the investigation of order-driven market structures, also due to better availability of order book data.[5]

For instance, Domowitz and Wang (2002) investigate an order data-set of the Australian ASX during 2000 and argue that liquidity commonality

[4] Chordia et al. (2000) argue that the inventory explanation of liquidity suggests that more trading leads to smaller spreads, since inventory risks per trade can be maintained at lower levels.

[5] One of the most important recent developments in stock exchanges information management systems is the real-time provision of full-displayed order book data to market participants. For instance, the London Stock Exchange has already introduced such services to interested clients. This evolution, which also represents an improvement in market transparency, offers considerably more detailed order book information to stock market traders than ever before. This additional trading information may also work as input data into trading algorithms and event stream processing systems.

is due to supply and demand co-movements. They measure liquidity as a functional of supply and demand schedules, and liquidity commonality is measured by functional co-variance. The liquidity measure they apply is the gap, or distance, between a stock's supply and demand schedules. Korajczyk and Sadka (2008) estimate a measure of systematic liquidity risk across a set of eight liquidity measures (spread measures, share turnover, components of price impacts, and a return/volume measure). They use 18 years of intraday data for NYSE-traded companies from the ISSM Transactions database and the TAQ database, and estimate monthly time-series for the liquidity measures. Korajczyk and Sadka (2008) apply an asymptotic principal components method and find supportive evidence of common liquidity factors, which is strongest for spreads and the (fixed) components of price impacts. The first three components they compute count for more than 50 percent of the variation in individual stocks' spreads.

In contrast to the investigation of liquidity commonality across stocks, Beltran-Lopez et al. (2005) investigate liquidity commonalities in price-depth pairs in stock-specific, reconstructed Xetra order books. They apply PCA and measure liquidity by (hypothetical) price-impacts during the first three months of 2004 and confirm the existence of commonality in liquidity based on Xetra order book data. Beltran-Lopez et al. (2005) show that the first two principal components for price-impacts explain even more than 94 percent of the total variation on the individual stock level. Beltran-Lopez et al. (2005) perform PCAs on price-impacts on the bid- and ask-side of the order book separately, and find out that the two sides of the market are driven by different latent factors that drive price-impacts.

Both Kempf and Mayston (2005) and Brockman and Chung (2002) investigate order-driven markets based on a similar methodology like Chordia et al. (2000), i.e. a market model for liquidity. Also Kempf and Mayston (2005) detect very strong evidence for commonality in liquidity in some stocks of the Xetra limit order market based on the PCA methodology. They stress that one shortcoming of existing studies on liquidity commonality is that only the liquidity at best bid and best ask is considered. Kempf and Mayston (2005) show that even in highly liquid order books, 20% of all orders walk up the book. Hence, there is also valuable information about liquidity beyond the first stage, in particular if there is a need to trade large volumes, where the associated orders necessarily have to walk up the order book.

2.2. Existence of systematic liquidity and its consequences

The existence of market-wide liquidity co-movements has far-reaching consequences for traders, stock exchanges, regulators, and financial theory. If the liquidity of individual stocks is at least partly determined by common (market-wide) factors, shocks to these liquidity factors influence the entire market. For the individual market participant the existence of market liquidity commonality implies that some part of liquidity risk is systematic and, hence, cannot be diversified. Market-wide liquidity (risk) becomes a priced factor. But such a market-wide liquidity (risk) factor is usually disregarded in conventional asset pricing models. Consequently, traditional diversification strategies that do not consider the second moment of liquidity, fail to diversify liquidity risk effectively (see also Domowitz and Wang (2002)). Future asset pricing models will have to take into account the cross-sectional dynamics of liquidity.

Since commonality shocks have consequences for individual stocks in the market, the understanding of these market-wide liquidity determinants is important for the functioning and stabilizing of financial markets in general. Therefore, market-wide liquidity (risk) is also a policy- and regulation-issue.

3. Market structure and data

The *Deutsche Börse AG* runs the *Frankfurt Stock Exchange (FSE)*, which is the definitely the most important among the eight German stock exchanges, and offers floor trading as well as fully-electronic trading on the *Xetra* system. While many of the *DAX-30* stocks are also listed on other exchanges, 97% of all trading of these stocks takes place in the Xetra system (see Deutsche Börse AG (2005)). Xetra operates as an open limit order book. Compared to the Paris stock exchange, not only the five best orders are displayed to the traders. In contrast to the *NYSE*, every trader has insight into the complete order book. Hence, the Xetra order book is an ideal laboratory to investigate common liquidity determinants in the entire *Xetra* order book beyond the best-quote perspective of liquidity .
The order data-set we apply is not limited to best bid and ask limits or best quotes. It consists of each single *Xetra* order book entry during the period 6-13 Dec 2006. Each of these tick-by-tick entries comprises time stamp, order number, order limit, order volume, trader and order restrictions, an indication of buyer or seller initiation, type of order entry (insertion,

cancellation, execution, partial execution, system insertion/deletion), and an indication of the trading phase.

In the Xetra trading system, four main types of orders are made available: *Limit Orders* comprise by far the largest proportion of orders in the Xetra order book. A limit order is an order to buy or sell a security at a specified price. Orders with a higher (lower) price limit for a bid (ask) order get higher priority for execution. In the case of a *Market Order*, there are no restrictions on the price the submitter is willing to accept. They are executed immediately, usually generate trades, and may also walk up the order book. A *Market-to-Limit* order combines features of both market order and limit order. Similar to market orders, the best order of the opposite site is matched, if completely filled. If this type of order is not completely filled at the best limit on the other side, the unexecuted part enters the order book as a limit order with exactly that limit. *Iceberg Orders* split up the invisible total order volume into visible parts of smaller size and only display this fraction as a limit order at each time point. As soon this visible fraction is completely filled, a new limit order of the same size is entered automatically.

For limit and market orders, three additional restrictions (or flags) are provided: The *Fill-or-Kill* restriction will cause the system to check whether the order can be completely matched immediately. If possible the order is executed. If not, the order is deleted immediately. The *Immediate-or-Cancel* restriction causes the system to execute all matches that are possible at the arrival time of the order. Any part that can not be matched immediately is deleted immediately. The *Triggered-Stop Order* is automatically entered into the order book as soon as pre-defined stopping conditions are met (see Prix et al. (2007)).

Table 1 gives the importance of different order types concerning number of orders and money volume traded, respectively, during the period 6-13 Dec 2006. The most important order type is definitely type limit order with 92% of number of orders submitted. These orders count for more than 85% of traded money-volume during this time period. The relative number of market orders is as expected relatively low[6], but also the money-volume they caused to trade is only around 6% of the total money volume traded. Iceberg orders are an order type that is typically

[6] This is due to the fact that limit orders usually have lower volumes than market orders or iceberg orders.

used to trade large volumes with a single order, where only a fraction of the total money is displayed. They count for around 6% of submitted orders, and also for in about 6% of traded money volume. Market-to-Limit (*MtL*) orders are responsible for only a small fration of traded money volume and number of orders. Limit orders therefore play the key-role in both, number of orders and money volume traded. Moreover, limit orders in the book constitute the displayed part of provided liquidity. Hence, we concentrate on limit orders in this study. For an investigation of iceberg orders see, for instance, Mönch (2005).

Table 1:
Importance of different order types concerning number of orders and money volume traded in the time 6-13 Dec 2006

	Number of orders submitted[2]				Money volume traded[3]			
Res.[1]	Limit	Market	MtL	Iceberg	Limit	Market	MtL	Iceberg
N	88.68%	1.99%	0.11%	5.87%	78.44%	7.54%	0.35%	6.22%
F	0.01%	0.00%	0.00%	0.00%	0.04%	0.06%	0.00%	0.00%
I	3.28%	0.00%	0.00%	0.00%	0.01%	0.00%	0.00%	0.00%
S	0.01%	0.04%	0.00%	0.00%	7.33%	0.00%	0.00%	0.00%
Tot. (%)	**91.98%**	**2.03%**	**0.11%**	**5.87%**	**85.82%**	**7.60%**	**0.35%**	**6.22%**

Notes: Observation period was the time from December 6th December 13th of 2006. A total of 2,650,641 orders were examined. Percentage of the money volume and number of orders belonging to each category are shown above.

[1] Restrictions: 'N' means that there is no restriction. Order restriction 'F' means Fill-Or-Kill, Order restriction 'I' means Immediate-or-Cancel and 'S' means Triggered-Stop-Order.

[2] The left part of the table shows the relative frequency of each order type entered into the Xetra system in conjunction with each order restriction. 100 percent corresponds to all orders submitted. Thus, in the left part of the table all orders are counted, regardless of whether they are executed or cancelled. The total percentage figures do not sum up to 100% due to rounding effects.

[3] The right part of the table shows the relative amount of money volume traded using each order type in conjunction with each order restriction. Money volume was computed using the size of the execution in shares times the price of the transaction per share. Thus, if the price is better than a possible limit supplied, the transaction price was used for the computation. The cancelled part of any order is disregarded in this part of the table. 100 percent in the right part of the table corresponds to the total money volume traded on Xetra in the observation period. The total percentage figures do not sum up to 100% due to rounding effects.

For our investigation, we take one-minute snapshots of the data that was originally time-stamped in 1/100-second intervals. Since the call auction phases at 09:00 o'clock and 13:00 o'clock follow an entirely different trading mechanism than continuous trading (i.e. a call auction), we exclude the time around auctions from the sample. Finally, we end up with a data-set consisting of 2394 observations for each liquidity measure during 6-13 Dec 2006. Despite the high computational effort, we run all calculations for the entire *DAX-30* market and do not exclude any stocks from the sample. If systematic *market-wide* liquidity is investigated, the cross-section of all stocks in a market should be cosidered in co-variation analysis. Table 2 gives the intraday time periods investigated in this study:

Table 2
Intraday time periods

Time period	Time [hh:mm:ss.hs]
Morning	10:00:00.00 - 11:59:59.99
Noon	12:00:00.00 - 12:50:00.00 13:10:00.00 - 14:59:59.99
Afternoon	15:00:00.00 - 16:59:59.00
Total	10:00:00.00 - 12:50:00.00 13:10:00.00 - 16:59:59.00

4. Liquidity measurement and extraction of systematic liquidity factors

4.1. Liquidity measurement from order book data

At each time t the order book for a stock i consists of the set of available ask volume A_t and the set of available bid volume B_t given by

$$A_t = \{(l^a_{tj}, v^a_{tj}) \mid j = 1,2,3,...,n_a; l^a_{t1} < l^a_{t2} < ... < l^a_{tn^a}\} \quad (1)$$

$$B_t = \{(l^b_{tj}, v^b_{tj}) \mid j = 1,2,3,...,n_b; l^b_{t1} > l^b_{t2} > ... > l^b_{tn^b}\} , \quad (2)$$

where the stock index i is omitted. l^a_{tj} (l^b_{tj}) is the j-th best ask (bid) limit in the order book and v^a_{tj} (v^b_{tj}) denotes the total available volume at this ask (bid) limit at time t. $l^a_{tn^a}$ ($l^b_{tn^b}$) is the highest (lowest) ask (bid) limit in the order book at time t.

We measure liquidity in terms of *round-trip costs*, i.e. the costs of buying K Euros of the stock at time t and selling the stocks immediately after the purchase also at time t. Like Irvine et al. (2000), we refer to the *immediate supply of liquidity*, i.e. the cost of an immediate round-trip of K Euro money-volume against the order book at time t.[7] The costs of a round-trip $RTC_{it}(K)$ of trading K Euro of stock I at time t are given by

$$RTC_{it}(K) = \frac{K}{\sum_{j=1}^{J^a} v_{itj}^{a}} - \frac{K}{\sum_{j=1}^{J^b} v_{itj}^{ib}}, \tag{3}$$

where J^a and J^b fulfill

$$\sum_{i=1}^{J^a} v_{itj}^{a} l_{itj}^{a} = \sum_{j=1}^{J^b} v_{itj}^{b} l_{itj}^{b} = K. \tag{4}$$

Figure 1
Order book illustration and cost attribution

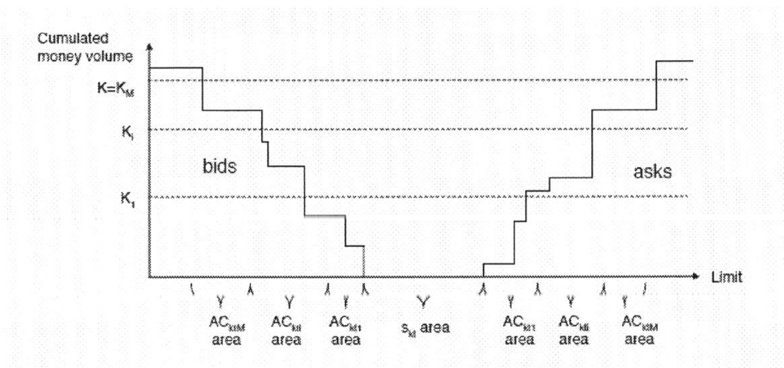

For our investigation, we attribute the round-trip costs to *different areas of the order book* as shown in Figure 1, which illustrates the roundtrip cost attribution for stock i at time t: spread s_{it}, additional roundtrip costs AC_{itK_m} for trading a money volume of $K_m - K_{m-1}$ additional to already traded K_{m-1} Euros. The attributed part of the roundtrip costs

[7] Cost of roundtrip measures are also proposed by Irvine et al. (2000), Gomber et al. (2004), and Beltran-Lopez et al. (2005).

RTC_t *(K)* which is independent of the targeted trading volume K at a certain time t is given by the (absolute) bid-ask spread s_{it}, i.e. by

$$s_{it} = l^a_{it1} - l^b_{it1}. \tag{5}$$

The remaining roundtrip costs dependent on K given by

$$RTC_{it}(K) - s_{it} \tag{6}$$

are attributed by considering different trading volumes. We calculate *additional roundtrip costs* AC_{itK_m} for stock i of trading $K_m - K_{m-1}$ Euros additional to the already traded K_m Euros at time t:

$$AC_{itK_m} = \begin{cases} RTC_{it}(K_1) - s_{it} & m = 1 \\ RTC_{it}(K_m) - RTC_{it}(K_{m-1}) & m > 1 \end{cases} \tag{7}$$

For the *additional round-trip cost measures* we consider $M = 5$ different volumes ranging from K = 25.000 to K = 1.000.000 Euro. To summarize, we study the following five *non-overlapping* liquidity measures in this paper:

Table 3
Liquidity measures

Liquidity measure	Money-volume [Euro]	Symbol
Bid-ask spread		s_{it}
AC 25.000	K_1 = 25.000	AC_{it25}
AC 50.000	K_2 = 50.000	AC_{it50}
AC 100.000	K_3 = 100.000	AC_{it100}
AC 500.000	K_4 = 500.000	AC_{it500}
AC 1.000.000	K_5 = 1.000.000	AC_{it1000}

4.2. Robust principal components analysis

The PCA methodology has become the predominant method to measure latent determinants in studies on commonality in liquidity, and is also suited for an intraday investigation of the systematic part of individual stock liquidity. This method allows to judge how much systematic liquidity the applied measures show. When we run a PCA, we extract linear combinations of all individual variables according to the total variability they explain. These linear combinations are contained in the eigenvectors of the covariance matrix. But it is well documented that the results of conventional principal components analysis can be strongly influenced by the presence of outliers in the data sample (see for instance Filzmose and Fritz (2007), and Croux and Ruiz-Gazen (2005)). More robust PCA methods arise from the *Projection-Pursuit* (PP) principle, which was first proposed by Huber (1985). In a nutshell, PP methods find structures in multivariate data by *projecting* the original high-dimensional data on a lower-dimensional subspace. The data is projected on a lower-dimensional space such that a *robust measure of variance of the projected data will be maximized.* Following Croux et al. (2007), also principal components analysis is a PP method:[8] Consider a data matrix X and n observations, and all of these observations are column vectors of dimension p. The variance is denoted by S^2. The first principal components can be extracted by finding the unit vector a that maximizes the variance of the data that gets projected. The principal components are computed by maximizing

$$a_1 = arg\, max\, S^2(a^t x_1,...,a^t x_n). \tag{8}$$

From this step, univariate data $a^t x_1, ..., a^t x_n$ is obtained by projecting the (multivariate) data in the direction a_1. If we apply the variance of the sample as projection index, a_1 is the eigenvector of the sample covariance matrix of the data corresponding to the largest eigenvalue (see Croux et al. (2007)). Since we apply the median as projection index, an approximative algorithm is needed to compute the principal components my maximizing equation (8). The algorithm of Croux and Ruiz-Gazen (2005) is applied because it works best in cases where the sample size is relatively large compared to the number of variables. The trial directions the algorithm considers are pointing in the directions where the data is. For an exhaustive description of the algorithm see Croux and Ruiz-Gazen (2005).

In our case the data matrix X comprises the time-series (n) of a particular liquidity measure for all thirty *DAX* stocks (p) in the sample. If we run a PCA on this matrix, we obtain a market-wide liquidity vector M that is measure-specific. We repeat this procedure for each measure to get the corresponding vectors $M_{1,...,n}$ for n different measures. To extract *measure-independent* systematic liquidity factors from a second step, we

---

[8] The notation is leaned on Croux et al. (2007).

again rely on Projection-Pursuit PCA (PP-PCA) for the estimation of measure-independent systematic factors. We can now differentiate systematic liquidity factors that are not only non-idiosyncratic, but also independent of the underlying non-overlapping liquidity measures.

5. Measure-specific systematic liquidity factors

5.1. Cross-sectional PCA on non-overlapping liquidity measures

We denote the mean adjusted spread of stock i at time t by s_{it} and the mean adjusted additional trading costs for this stock by $AC_{it25}, \ldots, AC_{it1000}$. As we consider the DAX-30 stock market, $i = 1, \ldots, 30$. For investigating commonality in liquidity we aggregate n stock liquidity measures in a first step over all stocks such that we have $M + 1$ corresponding K-dimensional market wide liquidity measure vectors for each t which k-th component is given by

$$s_t^k = \sum_{i=1}^{30} \lambda_{ik}^s s_{it} \tag{9}$$

$$AC_{t25}^k = \sum_{i=1}^{30} \lambda_{ik}^{25} AC_{it25} \tag{10}$$

$$AC_{t50}^k = \sum_{i=1}^{30} \lambda_{ik}^{50} AC_{it50} \tag{11}$$

$$AC_{t100}^k = \sum_{i=1}^{30} \lambda_{ik}^{100} AC_{it100} \tag{12}$$

$$AC_{t500}^k = \sum_{i=1}^{30} \lambda_{ik}^{500} AC_{it500} \tag{13}$$

$$AC_{t1000}^k = \sum_{i=1}^{30} \lambda_{ik}^{1000} AC_{it1000}, \tag{14}$$

where the λ_{ik}s denote the corresponding discriminant scores of component k for stock i.

Table 4 gives the results of the intraday cross-sectional principal components analysis for the six liquidity measures applied. The table shows the proportions of explained and cumulative explained variance for the first three systematic factors of each liquidity measure for three intraday time periods during 6-13 Dec 2006. The results are obtained using

PP-PCA. Individual stock liquidity is considerably driven by latent market-wide factors. Regardless which measure we apply, the first three systematic factors explain more than 40% of the (measure-specific) liquidity variation in individual stocks. Note that we considered all the entire *DAX-30* market and did not exclude any stocks in analysis.

Since most researchers that apply PCA on liquidity-related measures rely on bid-ask spread measures, we discuss our PCA results for the bid-ask spread in more detail. The first three common liquidity factors resulting from PCA on individual stocks' bid-ask spreads explain more than 40% of the total variation in individual stocks' spreads. Hasbrouck and Seppi (2001) find an explanatory power above 50% of the total variation for the first three components. Also Korajczyk and Sadka (2008) detect supportive evidence of common liquidity factors in the case of spread measures. Also in their study, the first three components count for more than 50% of the variation in individual stocks' bid-ask spreads.

Table 4

(Cumulated) explained variances of market-wide liquidity factors during different intraday time-periods based on PP-PCA

	Morning			Noon			Afternoon		
	k = 1	k = 2	k = 3	k = 1	k = 2	k = 3	k = 1	k = 3	k = 3
S	16.9 (16.9)	15.9 (32.8)	15.8 (48.7)	16.4 (16.4)	14.2 (30.6)	14.0 (44.6)	17.5 (17.5)	15.0 (32.5)	14.1 (46.7)
AC^k_{25}	16.9 (16.9)	13.1 (30.0)	13.1 (43.1)	16.2 (16.2)	15.9 (32.1)	12.9 (45.0)	15.9 (15.9)	14.0 (29.9)	13.9 (43.8)
AC^k_{50}	21.5 (21.5)	20.1 (41.7)	11.5 (53.1)	19.4 (19.4)	19.2 (38.6)	16.8 (55.4)	18.4 (18.4)	17.6 (36.0)	16.6 (52.6)
AC^k_{100}	26.1 (26.1)	24.9 (51.1)	9.4 (60.4)	19.0 (19.0)	18.3 (37.3)	13.9 (51.1)	20.4 (20.4)	19.3 (39.7)	11.2 (50.9)
AC^k_{500}	20.9 (20.9)	19.4 (40.3)	13.0 (53.4)	22.4 (22.4)	15.5 (37.9)	12.2 (50.0)	21.7 (21.7)	18.9 (40.5)	12.6 (53.2)
AC^k_{1000}	20.9 (20.9)	17.9 (38.8)	10.3 (49.1)	19.7 (19.7)	16.2 (35.9)	11.5 (47.4)	21.3 (21.3)	14.2 (35.4)	13.4 (48.8)

Notes: Proportion of variance (cumulated proportion of variance) in percent [%]. The summary table shows the proportions of explained and cumulative explained variance for the first three principal components, i.e. systematic factors, k = 1,2,3 of each particular liquidity measure during the period 6-13 Dec 2006. The calculation is based on projection-pursuit principal component analysis (PP-PCA) using the Croux and Ruiz (2005) algorithm. Morning period is during 10:00-11:59, the noon period is 12:00-12:50 and 13:10-14:59, the afternoon period is 15:00-16:59, and the total period is during 10:00-12:50 and 13:30-16:59.

Concerning the systematic components extracted from additional roundtrip costs *AC*, we find even stronger stronger commonality deeper in the order book. In more detail, explained variances are higher for liquidity in the areas AC_{50}, AC_{100}, AC_{500}, and get lower in the deepest order book region AC_{1000}. Hence, the influence of market-wide factors in liquidity is stronger for liquidity beyond the best bid and ask limits. However, the proportions of cumulative explained variances stay highly stable throughout the trading session. Hence, we can conclude from the investigation of different time periods during continuous trading that there are fluctuations in the variance the different systematic factors explain. But, overall, the cumulated proportions remain quite stable throughout the trading day.

Table 5

(Cumulated) explained variances of market-wide liquidity factors during different intraday time-periods based on conventional PCA

	Morning			Noon			Afternoon		
	k = 1	k = 2	k = 3	k = 1	k = 2	k = 3	k = 1	k = 3	k = 3
S	17.4 (17.4)	14.6 (32.0)	11.2 (43.2)	15.4 (15.4)	13.9 (29.3)	11.5 (40.8)	17.7 (17.7)	14.3 (32.0)	10.6 (42.6)
$\mathbf{AC^k_{25}}$	38.1 (38.1)	13.4 (51.5)	11.0 (62.4)	33.3 (33.3)	12.0 (45.3)	9.3 (54.5)	44.5 (44.5)	13.5 (58.0)	6.1 (64.1)
$\mathbf{AC^k_{50}}$	29.5 (29.5)	19.9 (49.3)	7.4 (56.7)	19.4 (19.4)	19.2 (38.6)	16.8 (55.4)	25.2 (25.2)	14.2 (39.3)	9.6 (48.9)
$\mathbf{AC^k_{100}}$	42.3 (42.3)	17.3 (59.6)	6.3 (65.0)	32.9 (32.9)	15.3 (48.2)	8.9 (57.2)	37.9 (37.9)	15.6 (53.4)	7.9 (61.4)
$\mathbf{AC^k_{500}}$	30.8 (30.8)	14.2 (45.1)	7.1 (52.2)	29.8 (29.8)	12.9 (42.7)	7.7 (50.4)	27.1 (27.1)	13.7 (40.8)	10.1 (51.6)
$\mathbf{AC^k_{1000}}$	30.2 (30.2)	9.6 (39.8)	8.7 (48.5)	28.7 (28.7)	9.0 (37.7)	8.8 (46.5)	27.1 (27.1)	13.1 (40.3)	7.9 (48.2)

Notes: Proportion of variance (cumulated proportion of variance) in percent [%]. The summary table shows the proportions of explained and cumulative explained variance for the first three principal components, i.e. systematic factors, k = 1,2,3 of each particular liquidity measure during the period 6-13 Dec 2006. The calculation is based on conventional principal components analysis. Morning period is during 10:00-11:59, the noon period is 12:00-12:50 and 13:10-14:59, the afternoon period is 15:00-16:59, and the total period is during 10:00-12:50 and 13:30-16:59.

Table 5 gives the results obtained from conventional PCA. One pattern that can be identified is that in most cases the first systematic component captures more variance than in Projection-Pursuit PCA, while the subsequent components count for less variance than in PP-PCA. Cumulated explained variances of the first three systematic liquidity factors are quite similar. An illustrative example of how the presence of outliers influences conventional PCA is shown by the first systematic factor in the area AC_{25} during the total time period. This single factor captures more than 60% of variation in individual stocks.

5.2. Canonical correlations between systematic liquidity factors

From PP-PCA we have already extracted latent market-wide determinants of the liquidity of individual stocks in the market. One question that arises is whether the measure-specific systematic factors extracted by the use of PCA are related to each other, i.e. do the systematic liquidity factors show correlation in the cross-section. Therefore, we conduct canonical correlation analysis on the different systematic liquidity factors to get a more detailed picture of interactions across different liquidity measures.

For instance, canonical correlation analysis is also applied by Hasbrouck and Seppi (2001) and Korajczyk and Sadka (2008). While Hasbrouck and Seppi (2001) compute the canonical correlations between order imbalances and stock returns to examine if the the two variables show commonality, we study co-variation across systematic liquidity factors. Similar to Korajczyk and Sadka (2008), we investigate the systematic factors' correlations across each pair of the different liquidity measures.

Canonical correlation analysis allows investigating the relation between two sets of variables.[9] As in factor analysis, there may be more \than one significant dimension, i.e. canonical correlation, where each one represents an orthogonally separate pattern of relationships between the two latent variables. Let E_t and F_t denote the two sets of variables, which are in our case the discriminant scores of the systematic components for

[9] Another measure for the conformity of two data sets in *redundancy*, which is a weighted mean of canonical correlations. Rencher (2002) argues that redundancy is less productive, and recommends canonical correlation analysis. Canonical correlation places the fewest restrictions on the types of data on which it operates. Because other techniques impose more rigid restrictions, it is generally believed that the information obtained from canonical correlation analysis is of higher quality and may be presented in a more interpretable manner (see e.g. Hair et. al. (1998)).

each pair of liquidity measures. The canonical coefficients, $a_1,a_2,...,a_n$ for the nE variables and $b_1,b_2,...,b_m$ for the mF variables are selected such that the correlation between CV_{E1} and CV_{F1} is maximized:

$$CV_{E1} = a_1E_1 + a_2E_2 + ... + a_nE_n \tag{15}$$

$$CV_{F1} = b_1F_1 + b_2F_2 + ... + b_mF_m \tag{16}$$

CV_{E1} and CV_{F1} are the first pair of canonical variates. The pairs of canonical variates are representing superordinate constructs. For each pair this construct is estimated as a linear combination of the variables, where the only criterion for choosing one linear combination over another is maximizing the correlation between the two canonical variates. The first canonical correlation is always the one which explains most of the relationship.[10]

Table 6

First three canonical correlations between each pair of systematic liquidity factors

	AC_{25}	AC_{50}	AC_{100}	AC_{500}	AC_{1000}
S	0.29	0.57	0.35	0.38	0.21
	0.25	0.29	0.34	0.36	0.17
	0.19	0.25	0.31	0.31	0.15
AC_{25}		0.56	0.57	0.31	0.29
		0.42	0.31	0.18	0.22
		0.36	0.21	0.16	0.16
AC_{50}			0.83	0.35	0.22
			0.54	0.17	0.16
			0.51	0.16	0.13
AC_{100}				0.43	0.29
				0.32	0.20
				0.29	0.18
AC_{500}					0.38
					0.35
					0.26

Notes: The table reports the first three canonical correlations between each pair of (measure-specific) systematic liquidity factors during the period 6-13 Dec 2006. Canonical correlations of 0.18 and 0.13 correspond to statistical significances of 1% and 5%, respectively.

---

[10] The canonical correlations are interpreted the same as Pearson's r. Their square is the proportion of variance in the canonical variate of one set of variables explained by the canonical variate for the other set along the dimension represented by the given canonical correlation.

Table 6 gives the first three canonical correlations between each pair of systematic (measure-specific) liquidity factors. Levels of statistical significance of 1% and 5% correspond to canonical correlations of 0.18 and 0.13, respectively. The most obvious, and also the most interesting result is that changes in the systematic factors of the different liquidity measures are correlated. Or, put different, the systematic components of different measures are correlated across different measures of liquidity. A pattern that can be identified is that systematic factors that drive liquidity in neighboring areas of the order book are stronger correlated. The highest canonical correlations can be found between the different *AC* measures, and strongest correlated are the market-wide factors of AC_{25} and AC_{100}, where even the third canonical correlation is still above 0.50. Conversely, the weakest correlations are between the factor scores of bid-ask spread and AC_{1000}, probably due to the fact that the two variables measure liquidity in areas, which are far away from each other. Hence, the common factors that drive individual stock liquidity in the anterior fractions of the order book are (more) different from the systematic factors that influence liquidity deep in the book, i.e. for higher target volumes. The finding that the changes in the systematic part of different liquidity measures are correlated across measures are in a line with the results of Acharya and Pedersen (2005) and Korajczyk and Sadka (2008).

5.3. Canonical correlations with other trading-related measures

In this section, we investigate whether the latent liquidity determinants already extracted are also related to the systematic components of other trading-related variables. First, we investigate a volume-based measure that informs about the maximum money-volume of stock *i* that is *immediately tradable* at time *t*, where the associated order does not eat into the order book, i.e. the cost of the trade is only the bid-ask spread. This trading-related measure is defined as the aggregated money-volume of all shares quoted at best bid and best ask at time *t*

$$VS_{it}^{max} = n_{it}^{b} l_{it}^{b} + n_{it}^{a} l_{it}^{a}, \tag{17}$$

where n_{it}^{b} (n_{it}^{a}) is the number of shares at best bid (ask), and l_{it}^{b} (l_{it}^{a}) denotes the best bid (ask) limit for stock *i* at time *t*.

As a return/volume measure we apply a variable that was originally inspired by the *Illiquidity Measure* proposed by Amihud (2002). He measures daily illiquidity as the "[...] average ratio of daily absolute return on the (dollar) trading volume on that day."[11]. He argues that this ratio gives the "daily price impact of the order flow."[12] Conversely, we apply an *intraday price/volume measure* PV_{it} in one-minute intervals. This ratio for stock i at time t is given by

$$PV_{it} = \frac{l_{it}^{mid}}{\bar{l}_{it}^{a} A_{it} + \bar{l}_{it}^{b} B_{it}} \tag{18}$$

where $\bar{l}_{it}^{a}$ ($\bar{l}_{it}^{b}$) is the average, i.e. the arithmetic mean, of all limits on the ask-side (bid-side) of the order book, and A_{it} (B_{it}) is the total ask side (bid side) money-volume. The mid-limit, which we apply as a return measure, l_{it}^{mid} is the mid-point between best bid and best ask for stock i at time t:

$$l_{it}^{mid} = \frac{l_{it}^{a} - l_{it}^{b}}{2}. \tag{19}$$

Since we compute all measures dynamically, i.e. by changes, the intraday price/volume measure PV_{it} captures the percentage change of the mid-limit in relation to the quoted volumes weighted by the average limit on both sides of the order book in one-minute intervals.

The next trading-related measure we consider is relative *volume imbalance* IM_{it}, which we define as the relative difference between the total ask-side volume and the total bid-side volume of the order book at time t. Chordia and Subrahmanyam (2004) argue that "[...] there are at least two reasons why order imbalances can provide additional power beyond trading activity measures such as volume in explaining stock returns. First, a high absolute order imbalance can alter returns as market makers struggle to re-adjust their inventory. In addition, order imbalances can signal excessive investor interest in a stock [...]."[13] We also argue that imbalances between the two sides of the market may offer valuable information about stock or market sentiment. Imbalances between the two sides of the order book, or massive shifts in imbalance mean that there exist buying- or selling-pressures, which may indicate a (future) rise or fall in transaction prices. While Chordia and Subrahmanyam (2004) examine

---

[11] Amihud (2002), p. 34.

[12] Amihud (2002), p. 34. Hasbrouck (2005) notes that Amihud's *Illiquidity Measure* works better than other measures in capturing the price impact parameter λ proposed by Kyle (1985), i.e. the response of price to order-flow.

[13] Chordia and Subrahmanyam (2004), p. 486.

imbalances in the number and the money-volume of *transactions* and investigate the time-series relation between order imbalances and individual stock returns, we measure *imbalances in bid and ask money-volumes* provided by limit orders at each time *t*. The variable we apply captures selling- or buying-pressure considering all limit orders supplied in the book. We define (relative) money-volume imbalance for stock *i* at time *t* as the difference between the volumes on bid and ask side of the order market, relative to the total money volume placed in the order book, i.e. by

$$IM_{it} = 2\frac{A_{it} - B_{it}}{A_{it} + B_{it}}, \tag{20}$$

where B_{it} (A_{it}) is the total order volume on the bid (ask) side of the order book of stock *i* at time *t*.[14]

Table 7 shows the first three canoncial correlations between the systematic liquidity factors in the bid-ask spread, the roundtrip-based liquidity measures and the systematic factors of other trading-related measures.[15] Canonical correlations between the bid-ask spread and the four trading-related measures are partly significant, but relatively weak compared to correlations with market-wide factors in *AC* liquidity measures. The canonical correlations between the money-volume placed at the spread *VS*, i.e. the maximum money-volume that is immediately tradable where the price of the trade is only the bid-ask spread, and the changes in the bid-ask spread are only weak, but mostly significant around 5%. Overall, the money-volume quoted at the bid-ask spread does not correlate considerably with the *AC* liquidity measures. Conversely, we detect a strong relation between systematic factors in the price/volume measure *PV* and the systematic factors of all roundtrip-based measures applied. The strong relation between systematic factors in order imbalances between the two sides of the market and the market-wide determinants of additional round-trip costs is one of the most important findings of this section. This empirical finding means that *changes in market-wide buying or selling pressures are strongly related to changes in the systematic part of individual stocks' liquidity*. The correlations are

[14] The ratio is multiplied by the factor 2 due to reasons of numerical computation.
[15] Note that we extract the systematic factors of these trading-related variables using projection-pursuit PCA that, again, relies on the Croux and Ruiz (2005) algorithm for estimating the systematic factors.

considerably higher in the anterior regions of the order book, i.e. AC_{25}, AC_{100}, where most orders activities take place.

Table 7
Canonical correlations between systematic factors in liquidity and market-wide factors in trading-related measures

Measure	s	AC_{25}	AC_{50}	AC_{100}	AC_{500}	AC_{1000}
Money-Volume at Spread *VS*	0.15	0.15	0.15	0.15	0.13	0.14
	0.13	0.12	0.10	0.12	0.12	0.12
	0.12	0.10	0.08	0.11	0.11	0.10
Price/Volume *PV*	0.18	0.61	0.40	0.48	0.55	0.53
	0.15	0.54	0.40	0.34	0.51	0.46
	0.13	0.34	0.25	0.27	0.47	0.44
Volume Imbalance *IM*	0.13	0.41	0.37	0.45	0.26	0.25
	0.11	0.38	0.26	0.17	0.17	0.22
	0.09	0.30	0.13	0.12	0.13	0.17
Mid-Limit l^{mid}	0.16	0.90	0.54	0.70	0.41	0.32
	0.14	0.63	0.42	0.46	0.23	0.29
	0.12	0.54	0.19	0.15	0.14	0.20

Notes: The summary table reports the first three canonical correlations between the systematic liquidity components of five liquidity-measures and four trading-related variables during the period 6-13 Dec 2006. Canonical correlations of 0.18 and 0.13 correspond to statistical significance of 1% and 5% respectively.

Concerning systematic changes in mid-limits l^{mid}, which we consider as a return measure, we find out that there is only weak correlation with the systematic factors exhibited in the most popular liquidity measure bid-ask spread. But we detect very strong correlations between the market-wide determinants of individual stocks' mid-limit changes and systematic changes in *AC* liquidity measures. Consequently, we conclude that *the systematic fraction of individual stocks' returns is strongly related to changes in systematic liquidity*, and that this relation is even more severe with systematic liquidity in the anterior regions of the order book, and still considerable (and statistically significant) for liquidity deep in the book.

We summarize section 5 with the following findings: (1) Based on highly robust cross-sectional principal components analysis on six non-overlapping liquidity measures, we detect heavy-weighting market-wide liquidity determinants. Regardless which liquidity measure we apply, the first two or three principal components explain more than 40% of the variation in individual stocks' liquidity in the market. This finding also holds during different continuous trading phases. So, the single-asset perspective on liquidity is inable to effectively examine liquidity (risk) and, therefore, to be questioned. From the erspective of asset pricing, future models need to also consider cross-sectional liquidity interactions in a market. (2) From canonical correlations analysis we show that also the systematic liquidity components are correlated across different non-overlapping liquidity measures. (3) Concerning the additionally applied trading-related measures, we find out that the systematic liquidity factors are highly correlated with changes in market-wide buying- or selling pressures. Moreover, we detect strong correlations between the market-wide determinants of individual stocks' mid-limit changes (i.e. returns) and systematic changes in liquidity in the anterior areas of the order book. The canonical correlations reach even up to 90%.

6. Global systematic liquidity

6.1. Aggregation of measure-specific systematic liquidity factors

Most researchers study commonality with a single measure or with different measures *separately*. Such approaches only allow to detect common liquidity factors that are dependent on the particular facet of liquidity the applied measure is able to capture. Well, some researchers examine market-wide liquidity (risk) factors over several overlapping liquidity variables (p.e. Korajczyk and Sadka (2008)). An estimation of systematic liquidity from overlapping measures is problematic and may give deceiving results that lead to misinterpretations. In respect to the requirement of clean liquidity measurement, we examine whether there are also market-wide liquidity determinants extractable, which are not only stock-independent but also independent of the underlying *non-overlapping* liquidity measures. To distinguish these factors from those obtained from the first PCA stage, we call these latent determinants *global systematic liquidity factors* in the following.

6.2. Global systematic liquidity factors

We aggregate the six measure-specific market-wide liquidity measure vectors s, AC_{25}, ..., AC_{1000} to a multi-dimensional *global* market-wide liquidity vector G. To extract *measure-independent* systematic liquidity factors, we again rely on PP-PCA for the estimation of the latent factors. First, we isolate the time-series of the discriminant scores of the different measures' first three market-wide liquidity factors obtained from the first cross-sectional PCA. The input into the second PCA is a matrix containing the discriminant scores' time-series of the first three systematic factors of each of the six non-overlapping liquidity measures. This step gives the global systematic liquidity factors G^h with $h = 1,...,n$, which are (1) stock-independent, and (2) also independent of the underlying measure. Therefore, the h-th component of the H-dimensional *global* market-wide liquidity vector G_t is given by

$$G_t^h = \sum_{k=1}^{K} \xi_{hk}^{s} s_t^k + \sum_{k=1}^{K} \xi_{hk}^{AC_{25}} AC_{t25}^k + ... + \sum_{k=1}^{K} \xi_{hk}^{AC_{1000}} AC_{t1000}^k \tag{21}$$

$$\begin{aligned} &= \sum_{k=1}^{K} \left(\xi_{hk}^{s} \sum_{i=1}^{30} \lambda_{ik}^{s} s_{it} + \xi_{hk}^{AC_1} \sum_{i=1}^{30} \lambda_{ik}^{AC_{25}} AC_{it25} + ... + \xi_{hk}^{AC_{1000}} \sum_{i=1}^{30} \lambda_{ik}^{AC_{1000}} AC_{it1000} \right) \\ &= \sum_{i=1}^{30} \left(s_{it} \sum_{k=1}^{K} \xi_{hk}^{s} \lambda_{ik}^{s} + AC_{it25} \sum_{k=1}^{K} \xi_{hk}^{AC_{25}} \lambda_{ik}^{AC_{25}} + ... + \sum_{k=1}^{K} \xi_{hk}^{AC_{1000}} \sum_{i=1}^{30} AC_{it1000} \lambda_{ik}^{AC_{1000}} \right) \\ &= \sum_{i=1}^{30} \left(s_{it} \gamma_{hi}^{s} + AC_{it25} \gamma_{hi}^{AC_{25}} + ... + AC_{it1000} \gamma_{hi}^{AC_{1000}} \right) \end{aligned} \tag{22}$$

where the ξs denote the corresponding factors loadings of the market-wide liquidity vectors s, AC_{25}, ..., AC_{1000}.

Table 8 reports the factor loadings of each of the first three principal components of measure-specific systematic liquidity factors towards the three global systematic liquidity factors G^1, G^2, and G^3. Concerning the *first global liquidity factor* G^1, the market-wide factors of s^1, AC_{500}^1, and AC_{500}^2 show the strongest correlations with G^1 (> 0.40). Weaker, but also considerable loadings towards G^1 can be found in the factors AC_{100}^2, AC_{500}^3, AC_{1000}^1, and AC_{1000}^2. Concerning the *second global factor* G^2 the strongest relations can be found in s^1, AC_{500}^1, and AC_{500}^2, which are all above |0.40|. Consideble factors loadings with G^2 are exhibited in s^3, and AC_{500}^1. Note that the loadings of the systematic liquidity factors AC_{25} and AC_{1000} show only very little loadings towards the second global liquidity factor G^2. In the case of the *third global global liquidity factor* G^3 the picture changes. The highest loadings can be found in the systematic factors of s, AC_{500}, and AC_{1000}, whereas AC_{25} and AC_{100} show very weak loadings towards G^3.

Table 8
Loadings towards global systematic liquidity factors

		G^1	G^2	G^3
Measure	**Loading**	$h = 1$	$h = 2$	$h = 3$
S^1	ξ^{s}_{h1}	0.3667	-0.4467	-0.3365
S^2	ξ^{s}_{h2}	0.0112	-0.0974	0.2862
S^3	ξ^{s}_{h3}	-0.0400	-0.2191	-0.0772
AC^1_{25}	$\xi^{AC\,25}_{h1}$	-0.0252	0.0021	0.0187
AC^2_{25}	$\xi^{AC\,25}_{h2}$	0.0033	0.0077	-0.0313
AC^3_{25}	$\xi^{AC\,25}_{h3}$	0.0110	-0.0018	0.0089
AC^1_{50}	$\xi^{AC\,50}_{h1}$	-0.0095	-0.0281	-0.0108
AC^2_{50}	$\xi^{AC\,50}_{h2}$	-0.0410	-0.0092	0.0043
AC^3_{50}	$\xi^{AC\,50}_{h3}$	-0.0096	-0.0025	0.0080
AC^1_{100}	$\xi^{AC\,100}_{h1}$	-0.0141	-0.1328	-0.0123
AC^2_{100}	$\xi^{AC\,100}_{h2}$	0.1109	-0.0385	0.0111
AC^3_{100}	$\xi^{AC\,100}_{h3}$	0.0190	-0.066	0.0136
AC^1_{500}	$\xi^{AC\,500}_{h1}$	-0.5477	-0.6329	0.0223
AC^2_{500}	$\xi^{AC\,500}_{h2}$	0.6765	-0.1993	0.4833
AC^3_{500}	$\xi^{AC\,500}_{h3}$	-0.1869	0.4973	0.1622
AC^1_{1000}	$\xi^{AC\,1000}_{h1}$	-0.2102	-0.1490	0.6983
AC^2_{1000}	$\xi^{AC\,1000}_{h2}$	0.1071	0.0733	-0.2008
AC^3_{1000}	$\xi^{AC\,1000}_{h3}$	0.0003	-0.0878	-0.0919

Note: Factor loadings of the first three systematic liquidity factors of the five liquidity measures and the global systematic liquidity factors during the period 6-13 Dec 2006.

Table 9 gives the results from gobal systematic factor estimation, which is based on PP-PCA on the first three systematic (measure-dependent) factors of each liquidity measure applied. Explained and cumulative explained variance as well as the systematic factors' standard deviations are reported in the table for different time-periods during the trading session. The *morning period* is during 10:00-11:59, the *noon period* comprises the periods 12:00-12:50 and 13:10-14:59, the *afternoon period* is during 15:00-16:59, and the *total* time-period comprises the periods 10:00-12:50 and 13:10-16:59. The most important result is that we can demonstrate that there are systematic liquidity factors, which are also independent of underlying non-overlapping liquidity measures. The first three global systematic liquidity factors we extract explain around 70% of the total variation in the first three measure-specific common factors in liquidity.

Table 9
Explained variances of global systematic liquidity factors

Time Period		G^1	G^2	G^3
Morning Period	Standard Deviation	8.77	7.27	6.19
	Proportion of Variance	33.63%	23.13%	16.74%
	(Cum.)	(33.63%)	(56.76%)	(73.50%)
Noon Period Standard	Standard Deviation	6.17	5.98	5.24
	Proportion of Variance	25.43%	23.89%	18.31%
	(Cum.)	(25.43%)	(49.15%)	(67.63%)
Afternoon Period	Standard Deviation	8.60	7.39	7.30
	Proportion of Variance	27.55%	20.33%	19.72%
	(Cum.)	(27.55%)	(47.90%)	(67.60%)
Total	Standard Deviation	7.33	6.51	5.66
	Proportion of Variance	29.63%	23.39%	17.67%
	(Cum.)	(29.63%)	(53.02%)	(70.68%)

Notes: The summary table shows the proportions of explained and cumulativeexplained variance for the global principal components during the period6-13 Dec 2006, and the systematic factors' standard deviations. The calculation is based on projection-pursuit principal components analysis using the Croux and Ruiz (2005) algorithm.

Concerning the *different time periods* during the trading session, the picture is comparable to the results obtained from the first PCA stage. While the proportions of variance the single systematic factors explain vary during the day, the cumulative proportion of variance the first three global systematic factors explain stays very stable, and varies only between 67.60% during the noon period and 73.50% during the morning hours. A finding that longs for a more detailed investigation is that the explanatory power of G^1 falls considerably from 33.63% during the morning period to only 25.43% during the noon time period, while the variance the other two factors explain stays relatively stable throughout the trading day.

6.3. Systematic liquidity factors and global liquidity factors

To get a more detailed picture of the relations between systematic, measure-specific liquidity factors and the global liquidity factors, we next conduct regression analysis between the measure-dependent, market-wide liquidity factors (resulting from first-stage PCA) and the global systematic liquidity measures (resulting from the second PCA). Since the first three systematic factors of the different liquidity measures explain in about the half of the total liquidity variation in individual stocks, we again concentrate on these most influential factors. In more detail, we regress the systematic market-wide liquidity factors exhibited in the different liquidity measures on each of the first three global liquidity factors extracted in the second stage cross-sectional PCA.

Table 10
Regressions summary statistics

	G1			*G2*			*G3*		
	Coef	*Sig*	*R2*	*Coef*	*Sig*	*R2*	*Coef*	*Sig*	*R2*
S^1	0.77	***	0.17	-0.46	***	0.10	-0.33	***	0.08
S^2	-0.15	***	0.01	-0.41	***	0.07	0.39	***	0.09
S^3	-0.31	***	0.02	-0.54	***	0.11	-0.02	-	0.00
AC^1_{25}	-0.12	.	0.00	-0.12	*	0.00	0.16	***	0.00
AC^2_{25}	-0.02	-	0.00	-0.08	*	0.00	0.09	**	0.00
AC^3_{25}	-0.15	*	0.00	-0.21	***	0.00	0.13	**	0.00
AC^1_{50}	-0.91	***	0.03	-0.90	***	0.05	-0.27	***	0.01
AC^2_{50}	-1.35	***	0.08	-0.68	***	0.03	-0.26	***	0.01
AC^3_{50}	-0.35	**	0.00	0.00	-	0.00	-0.03	-	0.00
AC^1_{100}	-0.73	***	0.08	-0.83	***	0.16	-0.20	***	0.01
AC^2_{100}	1.03	***	0.14	0.26	***	0.02	0.27	***	0.02
AC^3_{100}	0.32	**	0.00	-0.16	*	0.00	0.20	**	0.00
AC^1_{500}	-0.82	***	0.58	-0.65	***	0.61	-0.02	-	0.00
AC^2_{500}	1.05	***	0.68	0.00	-	0.00	0.30	***	0.14
AC^3_{500}	-0.25	***	0.02	0.81	***	0.31	0.10	***	0.01
AC^1_{1000}	-0.52	***	0.13	-0.23	***	0.04	0.70	***	0.56
AC^2_{1000}	0.54	***	0.06	0.28	***	0.03	-0.57	***	0.17
AC^3_{1000}	-0.02	-	0.00	-0.18	***	0.01	-0.20	***	0.02

Notes: Univariate regressions of the first three measure-dependent systematic liquidity factors on the first, second, and third global systematic liquidity factor, respectively. 'Coef' ... regression coefficient; 'Sig' ... stat. significance; 'R2' ... coefficient of determination (= square of correlation coefficient).

Table 10 reports univariate regression results of market-wide liquidity factors on the global liquidity factors G^1, G^2, and G^3, i.e. (univariate) regression coefficient (*Coef*), statistical significance (*Sig*), and coefficient of determination (*R2*). The significance codes for *Sig* follow the denotation: 0.001 '***'; 0.01 '**'; 0.05 '*'; 0.1 '.'; 1 '-'.

From regression analysis we get a clear picture of which factors dominate (the variation of) the global liquidity factors. The variation in G^1 is primarily driven by the systematic components AC^1_{500} with a R^2 of 0.58, and by AC^2_{500} with a R^2 of 0.68, respectively. The corresponding regression coefficients are at the highest level of statistical significance, i.e. at 0.001. If we regress the same market-wide liquidity factors on the *second and on the third global liquidity factors*, we also find clear patterns. The market-wide liquidity factor that shows the highest explanatory power of G^2 is AC_{500}^{1} with coefficient of determination of 0.61. The regression coefficient is highly significant. Lower, but considerable explanatory power is exhibited in the systematic liquidity factor AC_{500}^{3} with R^2=0.31. The influence of all other common liquidity components is rather negligible. In the case of the third global systematic liquidity factor G^3 it is the systematic component AC_{1000}^{1} that explains the largest proportion of variation in G^3 (R^2=0.56). Hence the extraordinarily high variation of the first global liquidity factor G^1 during the trading session is determined by latent, market-wide liquidity components exhibited in high-volume orders where the targeted volume K is half a million Euro. The same pattern can be idenified for G^2. Conversely, G^3 is most importantly influenced by a systematic factor that influences individual stocks' liquididy in the deepest area of the book investigated.

We conclude section 6 with the findings that (1) measure-independent *global systematic liquidity factors* exist, and that the first three global liquidity factors we extract explain around 70% of the total variation on the sub-level. (2) From the investigation of different time periods during the trading session, we conclude that also the global systematic liquidity factors vary in their proportion of explained variance throughout the trading day: While the proportion of variance the single factors explain fluctuate during the day (in particular G^1), the cumulative proportion of variance the first three global factors explain stays quite stable throughout the trading session. (3) Another interesting finding from the systematic liquidity factors' factor loadings towards the global liquidity factors is that the latent factors that drive the bid-ask spreads of individual stocks show stronger correlations than the systematic parts of the AC measures that capture liquidity in the anterior regions of the order book. For targeted volumes > 500.000 Euro the factor loadings are considerably higher than for systematic factors associated with orders that only eat into anterior areas of the order book. (4) From regression analysis we can show that the variation in global systematic liquidity factors is primarily determined by latent market-wide factors that drive the liquidity of individual stocks in deep order book regions, i.e. AC_{500} for G^1 and G^2, and AC_{1000} in the case of G^3. Hence, latent measure-specific determinants exposed in price-impacts of large order volumes count for the intraday variation in global systematic liquidity factors.

7. Summary

To overcome the methodological drawbacks of existing studies on market-wide liquidity co-variation, we propose a multi-stage PCA and regression approach. Using a highly robust principal components analysis method based on the Projection-Pursuit principle, we are able to extract reliable common factors in liquidity. The advantage of the application of non-overlapping liquidity measures, which refer to the cost of an immediate trade of different money-volumes, is that we are able to measure commonality in liquidity in a 'cleaner', and also more plausible manner.

From several cross-sectional Projection-Pursuit PCAs on different non-overlapping liquidity measures we detect heavy-weighting latent factors that determine the changes in the liquidity (measures) of individual stocks in the market. Regardless which liquidity measure we apply, the first three systematic liquidity factors explain more than 40% of the total (measure-specific) variation in individual stocks' liquidity.

The second PCA stage allows extracting systematic liquidity factors that are not only non-idiosyncratic, but also independent of the underlying, non-overlapping measures. From this step we obtain global systematic liquidity components, where the first three of them count for more than 70% of the variation on the sub-level.

We argue that traders are most severely exposed to changes in market-wide liquidity when there is a need for trading high order volumes during the trading session. Therefore, we investigate three different time periods during continuous trading, and show that there is a variation in the proportions of liquidity variance the single factors explain, while the cumulative proportion of variance the first three systematic factors explain stays quite stable throughout the day. These results hold for both PCA stages, i.e. for measure-dependent systematic liquidity determinants and also for the global systematic factors. The intraday-variation of gobal systematic liquidity factors is due to the influence of common liquidity factors across stocks that influence liquidity areas in deep areas of the order book.

The investigation of the canonical correlations between the systematic factors of different liquidity measures leads us to the conclusion that also the market-wide liquidity factors of the different non-overlapping liquidity measures are correlated in the cross-section. The correlations are strongest between variables that measure liquidity in neighboring areas of the order book.

Additionally, we apply four trading-related measures and investigate their relations to the the liquidity measures. Here we detect high correlations between the intraday price/volume measure and the cost of round-trip measures. A highly intersting result is the strong relation between the latent determinants of order-volume imbalances between buy- and sell-side of the market and the systematic factors exhibited in additional round-trip cost liquidity measures. This empirical finding means that changes in market-wide buying- or selling-pressures are strongly related to systematic changes in individual stocks' liquidity. These correlations are strongest in the anterior regions of the order book where the major part of order activities take place. As a return-related measure we also study systematic changes in mid-limits and find formidable correlations with changes in systematic factors of additional round-trip costs of up to 90%.

The latest developments in the literature on market-wide liquidity, in particular the results obtained from the investigation of high-frequency order book data, have shown that latent market-wide factors exist, and that these factors systematically drive the liquidity of individual stocks. In most studies, more than the half of the variation of individual stocks' liquidity can be explained by the first three systematic factors. This convincing evidence of commonality in liquidity indicates that the predominant single-stock perspective on liquidity is no longer sustainable. The fact that the liquidity of individual stocks is such severely driven by latent market-wide factors longs for enhanced asset pricing models that also consider the second moment of liquidity.

References

Acharya, V. and L. Pedersen (2005), Asset pricing and liquidity risk., *Journal of Financial Economics*, 77, 275-310.

Amihud, Y. (1998), Illiquidity and stock returns: Cross-sectional and time-series effects, *Journal of Financial Markets*, 5, 31-56.

Beltran-Lopez, H., P. Giot and J. Grammig (2005), Commonalities in the order book, *CORE Discussion Paper*, available at: ssrn.com/abstract=884363.

Brockman, P. and D. Chung (2002), Commonality in liquidity: Evidence from an order-driven market structure, *Journal of Financial Research*, 25, 521-539.

Chordia, T., R. Roll and A. Subrahmanyam (2000), Commonality in liquidity, *Journal of Financial Economics*, 56, 3-28.

Chordia, T. and A. Subrahmanyam (2004), Order imbalance and individual stock returns: Theory and evidence, *Journal of Financial Economics*, 72, 485-518.

Croux, C., P. Filzmoser and M. Oliveira (2007), Algorithms for projection-pursuit robust principal component analysis, chemometrics and intelligent laboratory systems, *SSRN Working Paper Series*, available at: papers.ssrn.com/sol3/papers.cfm?abstract_id=968376.

Croux, C. and A. Ruiz-Gazen (2005), High breakdown estimators for principal components: The projection-pursuit approach revisited, *Journal of Multivariate Analysis*, 95, 206-226.

Deutsche Börse AG (2005), Order_Book_Statistics_Xetra_Close-1.xls. *Online Publication*, available at: http://deutsche-boerse.com.

Domowitz, I. and X. Wang (2002), Liquidity, liquidity commonality and its impact on portfolio theory, *SSRN Working Paper Series*, available at: ssrn.com/sol3/papers.cfm?abstract_id=296870.

Filzmoser, P. and H. Fritz (2007), Exploring high-dimensional data with robust principal components, *Forschungsbericht Vienna University of Technology*, CS-2007-2.

Gomber, P., U. Schweickert and E. Theissen (2004), Zooming in on liquidity, *SSRN Working Paper Series*, available at: papers.ssrn.com/sol3/papers.cfm?abstract_id=559406.

Hair, J., R. Anderson, R. Tatham and W. Black (1998), *Multivariate Data Analysis*, Prentice Hall, USA.

Hasbrouck, J. (2005), Trading costs and returns for US equities: The evidence from daily data, *Stern School Working Paper*, available at: papers.ssrn.com/sol3/papers.cfm?abstract_id=38836

Hasbrouck, J. and D. Seppi (2001), Common factors in prices, order flows, and liquidity, *Journal of Financial Economics*, 59, 383-411.

Huber, P. (1985), Projection pursuit, *The Annals of Statistics*, 06/04.

Irvine, P., G. Benston and E. Kandel (2000), Liquidity beyond the inside spread: Measuring and using information in the limit order book, *SSRN Working Paper Series*, available at: ssrn.com/sol3/papers.cfm?abstract_id=229959.

Kempf, A. and D. Mayston (2005), Commonalities in liquidity in pure order-driven markets, *SSRN Working Paper Series*, available at: search.ssrn.com/sol3/papers.cfm?abstract_id=67696.

Korajczyk, R. and R. Sadka (2008), Pricing the commonality across alternative measures of liquidity, *Journal of Financial Economics*, forthcoming.

Kyle, A. (1985), Continuous auctions and insider trading, *Econometrica*, 53, 1315-1335.

Mönch, B. (2005), *Strategic Trading in Illiquid Markets*, Springer, Berlin.

O'Hara, M. (1995), *Market Microstructure Theory*, Blackwell Publishers, Cambridge, USA.

Prix, J., O.Loistl and M. Huetl (2007), Algorithmic trading patterns in Xetra orders, *European Journal of Finance*, 13, 717-739.

Rencher, A. (2002), *Methods of Multivariate Analysis*, Wiley Series in Probability and Statistics, Wiley & Sons, New York.

Acknowledgements

We are thankful to *Deutsche Börse AG* for generously providing complete order book data from the electronic trading system *Xetra*. We also like to thank the participants of the XLI EWGFM Meeting (Lisbon, Portugal) and the participants of the 11th Conference of the Swiss Society for Financial Market Research (Zurich, Switzerland), in particular Mr. Marc van Achter, for fruitful inputs to improve the paper. A previous version of this study is also presented at the 2008 FMA Annual Conference (Dallas, U.S.A.), the 2008 FMA Asian Conference (Tokio, Japan), and the 2008 EFMA Conference (Athens, Greece). The authors are grateful to Mr. Joaquim P. Pina for helpful comments and for guiding the publication process.

CHAPTER TEN

PRICE LIMITS, VOLATILITY, LIQUIDITY AND OVERREACTION: AN EVENT STUDY FROM THE ATHENS STOCK EXCHANGE

THEODOROS STAMATIOU

Abstract

Price limits are automated mechanisms that pre-specify the maximum daily percentage range – upwards and downwards – in which stock prices are allowed to move within a single day. I examine if the price limits (+/- 8 %) of the Athens Stock Exchange (ASE) for the "bubble" period 1998-2001 had an effect on volatility, liquidity and abnormal returns by testing three conjectures. The first is that price limits cause a decrease in volatility the day(s) following a price limit hit. The second is that price limits cause an increase in liquidity the day(s) following a price limit hit and the third is that price limits cause market overreaction the day(s) following a price limit hit against the alternative. I use daily data for the period 01/06/1998- 31/05/2001. The open to close volatility and the liquidity hypothesis are new to the price limits literature. My results are against price limits. The volatility and liquidity conjectures are rejected while the overreaction conjecture is rejected for the Up limits only.

Keywords: price limits, volatility, close to open volatility, illiquidity, overreaction

1. Introduction

Informational efficiency - the concept of how much information is revealed by the price process - is central to the analysis of financial economics. According to Fama (1970) a market in which prices always fully reveal all available information is called efficient and moreover prices change only in response to relevant new information.

The above statement gives no role to the direction and / or the magnitude of price changes in response to new information. Nevertheless, the magnitude of price change - irrespective of the direction - is a crucial parameter in which stock markets around the world focus their attention. This is based on the fact that (large) price changes are not welcomed by market participants. Hence large price changes are banned from the daily picture of stock markets. This ban takes the form of a price limit which is a market mechanism that specifies the upward or downward price movements in which stock prices are allowed to move within a single day. The allowed price change can take the form of a percentage change on the previous day's price. This percentage may be fixed but in same cases maybe a varying one.

Price limits are a common case in stock markets around the world but their use is recent[1]. After the October 1987 crash, the Brady Report (1988) suggested that price limits might be useful in preventing excess market volatility. The adoption of price limit mechanisms became apparent. Currently, the stock market of all the EU countries (except UK), Taiwan, Thailand, Japan, China etc. use various forms of price limit mechanisms[2].

Even though in actual markets price limits are a common case there is a strong academic debate concerning their usefulness. The first argument in favour of price limits is that in days of high uncertainty in the market they stop the price resolution process and therefore they give time to market participants to "digest" new information and reassess their investment decisions. The second argument in favour of price limits is concerned with high market volatility. In days of high market uncertainty

---

[1] Price limits exist in future markets for a long time in the past. Japan used futures contracts price limits in the eighteenth century while for the US future contract price limits were first established on 1917. Brennan (1986), Chodhry and Nanda (1998) and Kodres and O'Brien (1994) develop theoretical rationales for the existence of price limits in future markets.

[2] Kim and Yang (2004) distinguish between automated and non-automated circuit breakers. The former are usually referred as price limits while the latter are referred as trading halts. In addition they examine market wide trading halts. Table 1 of Kim and Yang (2004) presents various price limits in futures markets while Table 2 includes a list of (outdated) price limits regulations from various stock markets around the world.

price limits define the bounds of price movement and hence they construct artificial bounds for volatility.

Empirical evidence in favour of price limits is scant. Ma, Rao and Sears (1989) examine price overreaction in Treasury Bonds, silver, corn and soybean future contracts using event study methods. Their results are in favour of the price overreaction hypothesis. There is no price change between pre and post limit hit days or at least prices reverse in the post limit hit day.

It is obvious from the above discussion that the arguments in favour of the price limits mechanism abstract from the full informational efficiency hypothesis of Fama (1970) and are based on a behavioural approach, i.e. rational and behavioural traders coexist in the market and price limits exist so as to set boundaries for the behaviour of the latter. With respect to that Harris (1998) mentions the psychological power that price limits might have. The empirical results do not agree with the behavioural approach. Several studies (Gay, Kale, Kolb and Noe (1994), Chen (1988) find no support for systematic overreaction by market participants. Moreover, Kim and Rhee (1997) using an event study approach for the Tokyo Stock Exchange (TSE) price limit mechanism find evidence of price continuation after a price limit hit.

For the volatility reduction hypothesis results are also not encouraging. Only Ma, Rao and Sears (1989) find volatility reduction the day following a price limit hit. However, according to Harris (1998) the volatility result is statistical and not due to the price limits use (i.e. high volatility days are followed by low volatility days - mean reversion in volatility). In addition, Kim and Rhee (1997) find abnormally high volatility in days following a price limit hit. The volatility reduction hypothesis is not supported either by Chen (1993), Phylaktis et al. (1999), Kim (2001), Henke and Voronkova (2005) and Stamatiou (2005).

The basic argument that underlies all these papers is that price limits only delay the price discovery process (Fama (1989)). If the price change is due to new fundamental information, a price limit hit will only delay the price from reaching its equilibrium level for one (or more in the case of successive price lit hits) day(s). Moreover, as Fama(1989) argues, rational prices are not necessarily less volatile prices. As long as price volatility comes from rational responses to changes in fundamental values, high volatility per se in not a bad thing for the market. Again the difference is between rational and behavioural approaches to the market.

This difference is not answered by the theory studies on price limits either. Subrahmanyam (1994) builds a model with risk neutral traders, risk averse market makers and liquidity traders. His result shows that price limits increase volatility and act like magnets. This happens because informed traders place their trades in such a way so as the price limit mechanism will not affect their ability to trade. As a result even if the stock price won't hit its price limit the existence of it will increase volatility. In the event that prices are close to their limits then the behaviour of the informed traders will induce them to hit their limits. This is defined as a magnet or gravitational effect.

In a recent paper Abad and Pascual (2007) empirically examine for the Spanish Stock Exchange (SSE) if the existence of an (intraday) price limit causes more aggressiveness in part of investors as the stock price reaches close to its limit. Their results are against the magnet effect. There is no sign of investor aggressiveness as stock prices reach close to their limit. Even though their results might be due to the institutional arrangements of the SSE intraday price limits it is still important.

Brunnermeier and Pedersen (2005) examine the behaviour of predatory traders and derive results in favour of price limits. "Predators" buy (sell) shares when their "prey" buys (sells) hence they drive the price upwards and when the latter stops buying (selling) they sell (buy) and hence they gain the difference. This is achieved because the "predator" drains liquidity from the market. The introduction of price limits permits other traders to enter the market in the opening clearing mechanism and as result liquidity draining stops. That leads to the break-up of the predatory game if only a single "predator" exists or to decreased profits for the surviving "predators" in the case of multiple predators.

My paper now has three main objectives. The first one is to test if the price limit mechanism causes a decrease in volatility the day(s) following a price limit hit. For this I am using the event study approach of Kim and Rhee (1997) for a sample of stock prices from the Athens Stock Exchange (ASE) for the period 1998-2001. The main advantage of this approach is the examination of volatility not only for the stocks that hit their price limit but also for the stocks that reached their limit but did not hit it. The control groups permit the distinction between the excess volatility that comes from general market conditions and the one that comes from the price limit mechanism. I use close to close volatility and close to open volatility. The formers use is not new to the literature but it is the first time it is used in the ASE. The latter type of volatility is new to the price limit literature and originates from the Amihud and Mendelson (1991) study of the TSE trading system.

Note here that the event study approach is used instead of an ARCH, GARCH specification because the former captures in a better way the effects that price limits might have in the trading days around the limit hit. The time series approach captures long run volatility and therefore the effects of price limits might disappear or at least be ambiguous (Kim (2001)). My work follows the line of research of Chen(1993), Kim and Rhee (1997), Kim (2001) and not that of Phylaktis et al. (1999), Veld-Merkoulova (2003), Henke and Voronkova (2005) and Stamatiou (2005). Nevertheless, the latter using a GARCH(1,1) volatility specification and for the ASE finds evidence against the price limit implementation.

The second objective of the paper is to test if price limits cause increased liquidity the day after a price limit hit. This arises from Brunnermeier and Pedersen's (2005) argument that liquidity is increased after a price limit hit. I measure liquidity using Amihud's (2002) illiquidity measure. Again I use the control groups described above. The liquidity objective is new - at least in my knowledge - in the price limit literature.

The third objective of the paper is to test if the price limit mechanism causes price overreaction in the ASE. I am using the abnormal returns approach of Warner and Brown (1985). Diakogiannis et al. (2005) used a similar method for the ASE. Compared with theirs my analysis has two advantages. First, my sample period includes the "bubble" period of 1999-2000 and price limits are mechanisms made to work in such environments. Diakogiannis's et al. (2005) sample period was 1995-1998 a relatively calm period for the ASE. Second, I use control samples - as in Kim and Rhee (1997) - so as to control their abnormal returns behaviour with those of the stocks that hit their limit.

In summary the decreased volatility conjecture the day(s) following a price limit hit is rejected for stocks that hit their up or down price limits. For the liquidity results are not better either. The increased liquidity conjecture is not rejected for the single hit up limits case while it is rejected for all the other cases. The overreaction conjecture cannot be rejected for up limit case while is rejected for the down limit cases.

The reminder of the paper goes as follows. Section 2 gives some details for the ASE during the sample period and also presents the descriptive statistics of the sample stocks. Section 3 includes the testing of the excess volatility hypothesis. Section 4 presents the liquidity conjecture and Section 5 shows the price continuation hypothesis. Finally Section 6 concludes the paper.

2. The ASE and the Sample Stocks

The ASE is the sole official stock market in Greece. For the sample period ASE operated from Monday to Friday between 10.45 and 1.30 p.m. The opening price of each day was determined by a preopening period between 10.15 and 10.45. Limit and market orders enter the system. During the trading session the electronic system is used on the matching of orders according to price and time priorities. An order was executed whenever a counter order existed at the same price with the first order entered into the system executed first.

Price limits were first imposed on the ASE on August 1992. Initially there was a +\- 4 % price limit for heavily traded stocks and a +\- 8% for less heavily traded stocks. The percentage was based on the previous day closing price. In the following years for all the stocks listed in the ASE the +\- 8% was adopted. Phylaktis et al. (1999) work refers to that regime. My sample period belongs to the +\- 8% regime also.

From 1998 to September 1999 there was a tremendous increase in the ASE stock prices. The General Index (GI) of the ASE was 2060 units in 01/04/1998 and reached 6335 units in 17/09/1999. This was due mainly to the expectations that were created after the devaluation of the drachma in March 1998. This, in turn, created expectations that Greece will join the EURO in 2001 and also created great expectations concerning the future growth of the Greek economy. At the same time the convergence of this period inflation and interest rates to the EU levels, created an excess demand for risky assets.

Obviously there was a self-fulfilling expectation element in all the above that led to the creation of a "bubble environment" in the ASE. The turning point was in 17/09/1999 which was the higher level ever reached by the GI. From there a gradual decrease started that accelerated from mid-2000 onward. As a result the GI reached its 1998 levels in 2001.

The sample period of the paper covers the time span from 1/6/1998 to 31/5/2001. The stocks that are included in the analysis satisfy the following criteria:

- Positive number of price limits (either upwards or downwards).
- Stocks first entered the ASE before the start of the sample period.
- There is sufficient trading for the stocks in the sample period.

There is no need to state why the first criterion is needed (it's a price lit analysis after all). The second criterion is needed not only because it help us to avoid problems by IPOs etc. but also because in Section 4 a control period of 90 days is needed before the price limit hit. The third criterion is needed because after the "bubble" crash of the 17th of September 1999 the trading volume of - almost all - the small capitalization stocks dropped to zero. Only 168 of the 376 ASE stocks satisfy the above criteria.

There is no database that records the price limit hits therefore an indirect method is used. The first step is to find the days for which $P_{i,t} \geq P_{i,t-1} + 0.079P_{i,t-1}$ for the Up limits or $P_{i,t} \leq P_{i,t-1} - 0.079P_{i,t-1}$ for the Down limits where $P_{i,t}$ is the price of stock i on day t. The price data come from Datastream. The second step is to observe in the ASE database if on day t the closing bid price and the respective volume was zero for the Up limits or the closing ask price and the respective volume was zero for the Down limits.

Moreover for each day t for which we have an Up or Down price limit hit - following Kim and Rhee(1997) - I construct four additional groups, two for the Up limits and two for the Down limits. For the Up limits the first group consists of the stocks that on day t at least reached the 90 percent of their price limit but did not hit it i.e. the stocks for which the following relation holds on day t:

$$P_{i,t} < P_{i,t-1} + 0.079P_{i,t-1} \text{ and } P_{i,t} \geq P_{i,t-1} + 0.90 * 0.079P_{i,t-1}$$

The second group consists of the stocks that at least reached the 80 percent of their price limit but where smaller from the 90 percent of their limit.

$$P_{i,t} < P_{i,t-1} + 0.90 * 0.079 P_{i,t-1} \text{ and } P_{i,t} \geq P_{i,t-1} + 0.80 * 0.079 P_{i,t-1}$$

For the Down limits the 90 and 80 percent groups are those that satisfy the following relations respectively.

$$P_{i,t} > P_{i,t-1} - 0.079 P_{i,t-1} \text{ and } P_{i,t} \leq P_{i,t-1} - 0.90 * 0.079 P_{i,t-1}$$

$$P_{i,t} > P_{i,t-1} - 0.90 * 0.079 P_{i,t-1} \text{ and } P_{i,t} \leq P_{i,t-1} - 0.80 * 0.079 P_{i,t-1}$$

Table 1 presents the summary statistics for the sample of the identified (Up or Down) price limit cases and the respective 90 and 80 percent groups. This sample is important because it is the first time it is constructed for the ASE and also for a small emerging market in a "bubble" period. Observe that the number of the Up price limits (3234) is almost double that of the Down limits (1617). This is similar with that of Kim and Rhee (1997). Price limits prevent more stock price increases than decreases.

In addition for the Up limit cases Group 80 cases (11463) are greater than Group 90 cases (7351) and the latter are greater than Group Hit cases (3233). This does not hold for the Down limit cases. There Group 80 cases (3161) are less than Group 90 (13280) cases and the latter are greater than Group Hit cases (1617). This combined with the number of Up and Down price limits may be attributed to the existence of asymmetric feedback effects as in Shen and Wang (1998). Asymmetric feedback traders tend to believe that prices will be higher in the near future when prices go up while when prices go down they tend to believe that prices will decrease in the near future but at a slower rate.

Table 1

Number of Events and Control Groups

	HIT-UP	90	80	HIT-DOWN	90	80
1-day	1992	4202	5111	1208	9600	1516
2-days	629	1235	3355	248	1886	492
3-days	249	420	1238	79	596	246
4-days	112	246	660	29	299	660
5-days	113	984	843	29	645	98
6-days	30	85	168	9	84	26
≥ 7-days	109	229	28	15	170	123
Total	3234	7401	11403	1617	13280	3161

Note: The left-hand side (right-hand) of the table presents the case of the Up Limits (Down Limits). The criteria for the selection of the limits are:

- $P_{i,t} \geq P_{i,t-1} + 0.079P_{i,t-1}$ (Up limits) or $P_{i,t} \leq P_{i,t-1} - 0.079P_{i,t-1}$ (Down Limits).
- if on day t the closing bid price (ask price) and the respective volume was zero for the Up Limits (Down Limits).

For the Hit-Up and Hit-Down columns only the first price limit is considered as an event. The columns labeled 90 and 80 include the stocks that reached at least the 90 percent (80 percent respectively) of their limit but did not hit it (where below the 90 percent respectively). The criteria for the inclusion are the following:

- $P_{i,t} < P_{i,t-1} + 0.079P_{i,t-1}$ and $P_{i,t} \geq P_{i,t-1} + 0.90 * 0.079P_{i,t-1}$ (Group 90) and $P_{i,t} < P_{i,t-1} + 0.90 * 0.079P_{i,t-1}$ and $P_{i,t} \geq P_{i,t-1} + 0.80 * 0.079P_{i,t-1}$ (Group 80) for the Up Limits.
- $P_{i,t} > P_{i,t-1} - 0.079P_{i,t-1}$ and $P_{i,t} \leq P_{i,t-1} - 0.90 * 0.079P_{i,t-1}$ (Group 90) and $P_{i,t} > P_{i,t-1} - 0.90 * 0.079P_{i,t-1}$ and $P_{i,t} \leq P_{i,t-1} - 0.80 * 0.079P_{i,t-1}$ (Group 80) for the Down Limits.

Using the above three groups in what follows I will examine if there is:

- a decrease in - close to close and / or close to open - volatility the day(s) following a limit hit. (***Conjecture 1***)
- an increase in liquidity the day(s) following a limit hit. (***Conjecture 2***)
- no overreaction the day(s) following a limit hit. (***Conjecture 3***)

3. Price Limits and Volatility in the ASE

3.1 Price Limits and Close to Close Volatility

As already mentioned one of the basic arguments in favour of the price limit mechanism is the reduction of volatility in times of high market turbulence. To test this, an event study approach is used similar with Kim and Rhee (1997). A window of ten days is constructed around the hit day for the group that hit its price limit (Group Hit) and for the groups that reached their price limits on Day 0 but did not hit it.

For each day volatility is calculated using the following formula:

$$V_t = (r_{i,t}^{CC})^2$$

where $r_{i,t}^{CC}$ is the close to close return for stock i between day $t-1$ and t. This volatility event study is similar to the one used by Kim and Rhee (1997) and Nath (2004). Differences in volatility across the three groups may lead to results concerning the implementation of the price limit mechanism in the ASE. More specifically increased volatility the days following Day 0 for the Group Hit might be translated as volatility spillover from Day 0 to the following days. This evidence will be reinforced if the volatility spillover for the Group Hit will be significantly greater from the respective volatilities of the 90 and 80 Groups for the days following the price limit hit.

Table 2:

Up Limits and Close to Close Volatility

	Panel A: Case One UP					Panel B: Case Two UP				
Days	**Group Hit**		**Group90**		**Group80**	**Group Hit**		**Group90**		**Group80**
-10	1.614	>>	1.733		1.292	1.694		1.751		1.635
-9	1.631		1.467		1.504	1.760	>	1.168		1.626
-8	1.475		1.363		1.087	1.646		1.739		1.245
-7	1.666		1.679	>>	0.926	1.867		2.161		2.063
-6	1.564		1.124		1.288	1.617		1.146	>>	1.588
-5	1.661	>>	1.882		1.402	1.83		2.013		1.618
-4	1.826		2.309		1.919	1.938		1.903		2.551
-3	1.751		1.569		2.001	1.791		1.636		1.631
-2	1.912		1.908	>>	1.467	2.065		2.709	>>	1.689
-1	1.809		2.582		1.712	1.875	>>	3.017		1.770
0	**5.911**	>>	**5.264**	>>	**4.311**	**5.894**	>>	**5.261**	>>	**4.33**
1	2.156	>>	1.885		1.052	3.353	>>	2.549		1.924
2	2.112	>	2.003		2.061	2.833	>>	2.209		1.936
3	2.148	>>	2.766		3.127	2.652	>>	2.682	>>	2.080
4	1.973		2.178	>>	1.273	2.296		2.374		1.984
5	2.165		2.198		2.467	2.333		2.053		2.207
6	2.205	>>	2.692		3.331	2.379	>>	2.808		2.670
7	1.877		1.937		1.479	2.149		2.007		1.532
8	5.669	>	1.736	>	3.174	4.624	>>	1.620		2.041
9	2.185		2.247		2.382	2.428		2.838		2.457
10	2.189		2.060	>>	3.325	2.205	>>	1.566		1.818

Note: For the three stock groups I calculate the close to close volatility for a window of -10 to +10 around the event according to: $V_{i,t} = (r_{i,j}^{CC})^2$. Only events with no limit hits for the [-10,-1] period are used for the control groups. Panel A (Panel B) presents the case of a single price limit (successive price limits). Volatility is multiplied by 10^3. The symbols >> and > indicate that the left-hand side figure is greater than the right-hand figure at the 0.01 and 0.05 levels of significance using the Wilcoxon signed-rank test.

Table 3:

Down Limits and Close to Close Volatility

	Panel A: Case One DOWN					Panel B: Case Two DOWN				
Days	**Group Hit**		**Group90**		**Group80**	**Group Hit**		**Group90**		**Group80**
-10	2.680		2.010		1.579	3.522		2.099	>	1.422
-9	2.522		1.632		1.415	2.546		1.715	>>	1.363
-8	2.286		1.830		1.655	2.470		1.838		1.781
-7	2.838		2.803	>>	2.187	2.843		2.819		2.312
-6	6.663		2.247	>	1.830	6.024		2.317		1.856
-5	3.263	>>	4.432		1.955	3.373	>>	5.304		1.718
-4	2.909		3.118		1.870	3.012		3.536		1.819
-3	3.022		2.417		2.196	3.179	>>	2.066		2.383
-2	2.794	>>	1.635		1.817	2.976		1.864		1.791
-1	2.538		2.509		1.940	2.512		2.435		2.078
0	**7.100**	>>	**5.986**	>>	**4.942**	**7.026**	>>	**5.991**	>>	**4.933**
1	2.747	>>	1.941		4.247	3.533	>>	2.388		4.8676
2	3.666	>>	3.711		3.100	3.567		3.899		3.253
3	2.843		3.015	>>	2.026	3.153	>>	3.018	>	2.122
4	3.493	>>	2.757	>>	3.751	3.603	>>	2.951	>	3.546
5	3.174	>>	3.538		2.942	3.433		3.294		2.891
6	2.838	>>	2.547		2.584	3.016	>>	2.305		2.659
7	2.917		3.362		3.182	2.918		2.902		3.262
8	2.289	>>	3.501	>>	2.888	2.508		2.884		3.109
9	2.709		2.849		2.619	2.712		2.596		2.763
10	2.838		2.659		2.390	2.842		2.373		2.522

Note: For the three stock groups I calculate the close to close volatility for a window of -10 to +10 around the event according to: $V_{i,t} = (r_{i,j}^{CC})^2$.

Only events with no limit hits for the [-10,-1] period are used for the control groups. Panel A (Panel B) presents the case of a single price limit (successive price limits). Volatility is multiplied by 10^3. The symbols >> and > indicate that the left-hand side figure is greater than the right-hand figure at the 0.01 and 0.05 levels of significance using the Wilcoxon signed-rank test.

I include in the analysis that follows price limit cases that:

- Experienced no limit hits from Day -10 to Day -1.
- Had similar volatility with group Hit volatilities for Days -10 to -1.

I distinguish both Up and Down limit cases in two groups. The first one includes cases with only one limit hit (Day 0) and the second includes cases with successive limit hits. There I count only the first price limit as the event (Day 0). This distinction is made because I want to examine if the single hit cases have similar behaviour with the successive hit cases. Table 2 presents the results for the Up limits close-to-close volatility. Volatility is multiplied by 103. Panel A presents the simple limit hit case while Panel B presents the successive limit hits case. The first column presents the volatility from Day -10 to Day 10 for the group of stocks that hit their price limits (Group Hit). The second and third columns present the respective volatilities for the groups that reached the 90 (Group90) and the 80 (Group80) percent of their price limits. The symbols >> and > indicate that the left-hand side figure is greater than the right-hand figure at the 0.01 and 0.05 levels of significance using the Wilcoxon signed-rank test.

From Panel A note that on Day 0 volatility for Group Hit is greater than volatility for Group 90 and the latter is significantly greater than the respective volatility for Group 80. But this is a trivial result. The three volatilities have this ordering by construction. The interesting results of the analysis lay before and after Day 0.

Observe that there is a substantial decrease in volatility from Day 0 to Day 1. Volatility continuous a decreasing pattern for Days 2 and 3. Group 90 volatility from Day 0 to Day 1 shows a substantial decrease also. Moreover volatilities for Days 1 to 3 are significantly greater for Group Hit than for Group 90. Since the only difference between the two groups is the price limit hit of the first one the previous result provides evidence that cannot reject the hypothesis that price limits cause excess volatility. The fact that excess volatility of Group Hit relative to Group 90 is attributed to price limit hits is reinforced from the pattern of volatilities of the two groups for Days -10 to -1. During this period both groups have similar daily volatilities (means) and for five days volatilities are significantly greater for Group Hit and for the rest period are greater for Group 90. In addition observe that there is no pattern in the behavior of Group 80 towards Group 90. For the [-10,10] period only Day -7, Day -2 and Day 10 are significantly grater for Group 90 than for Group 80.

From Panel B note that the same pattern with the single hit case exists for the Day 0 volatilities of the three groups. The crucial point here is that again a decrease in volatility is observed for Days 1 to 3 for Group Hit. The same behavior holds for Group 90. Volatilities for Group Hit are significantly higher than volatilities for Group 90. This pattern does not hold for the volatilities between Group 90 and Group 80.

Table 3 presents the results for the down limits close-to-close volatility. Volatility is multiplied by 103. In Panel A case the Day 0 trivial result of Table 2 is also true. This pattern of behavior holds also for Days 2 to 6 – except Day 2 – while it is not true between Groups 90 and 80. From Panel B the trivial result for Day 0 volatilities holds. For Day 1 volatile is decreased for both Group Hit and Group 90 with the former being significantly greater than the latter. In addition for Days 3, 4 and 6 volatilities for Group Hit are significantly greater than those of Group 90. The greater volatilities of Group Hit from the respective of Group 90 in the post limit hit days for both panels are attributed to the limit hit and not to the price increase. From Table 3 I conclude that there is enough evidence for rejecting Conjecture 1. This rejection is similar to the results of Kim and Rhee (1997) for the TSE and only partially differs from Nath (2004) for the NSE.

Table 4

Up Limits and Close to Open Volatility

	Panel A: Case One UP					Panel B: Case Two UP				
Days	**Group Hit**		**Group90**		**Group80**	**Group Hit**		**Group90**		**Group80**
-10	2.895	>>	1.388		1.34	2.746	>	3.832		1.134
-9	2.335	>>	1.246	>>	1.089	2.949		5.432		1.091
-8	2.031		1.424		0.957	3.131		3.906		1.764
-7	2.051		1.475		1.095	3.191		3.192		1.111
-6	2.207		1.987		1.555	3.722		0.785	>>	0.765
-5	1.959		1.859		1.493	4.281		1.450		0.966
-4	1.950		1.888		1.521	4.488	>>	0.466	>>	2.299
-3	2.067		1.965		1.888	3.635		0.374		1.517
-2	2.16		1.701		2.082	3.689		0.813		1.349
-1	2.112	>>	2.696	>>	1.759	3.505		0.954		0.864
0	**1.83**	>>	**2.159**	>>	**1.469**	**2.768**	>>	**0.676**	>>	**2.115**
1	2.585	>>	2.062		1.079	2.875	>>	1.414		2.19
2	2.87	>>	2.021		0.95	2.857		2.495		1.678
3	3.241	>	3.227		1.16	2.973	>>	1.837		1.506
4	3.693	>>	5.565		1.519	2.942	>>	2.238		1.656
5	2.379	>>	4.652		1.483	2.985		1.984		0.971
6	2.18		2.282		1.904	3.155	>>	1.797		1.192
7	1.95		2.176		1.795	3.148		1.236		0.951
8	1.659	>	2.115	>	1.974	2.78	>>	1.672	>>	0.759
9	1.953		2.589		2.047	2.881		1.808		0.904
10	1.797	>	1.751	>>	1.784	3.114		1.87		1.78

Note: For the three stock groups I calculate the close to close volatility for a window of -10 to +10 around the event according to: $V_{i,t} = (r_{i,j}^{CO})^2$.

Only events with no limit hits for the [-10,-1] period are used for the control groups. Panel A (Panel B) presents the case of a single price limit (successive price limits). Volatility is multiplied by 10^3. The symbols >> and > indicate that the left-hand side figure is greater than the right-hand figure at the 0.01 and 0.05 levels of significance using the Wilcoxon signed-rank test.

Table 5

Down Limits and Close to Open Volatility

	Panel A: Case One DOWN					Panel B: Case Two DOWN				
Days	**Group Hit**		**Group90**		**Group80**	**Group Hit**		**Group90**		**Group80**
-10	2.746	>	3.832		1.134	2.793		4.463		1.337
-9	2.949		5.432		1.091	2.943		5.843		1.165
-8	3.131		3.906		1.764	3.097		4.926		1.529
-7	3.191		3.192		1.111	3.158		3.988		0.964
-6	3.722		0.785	>>	0.765	3.717		0.819		0.723
-5	4.281		1.45		0.966	4.326		1.415		1.012
-4	4.488	>>	0.466	>>	2.299	4.66	>>	3.69		2.2
-3	3.635	>>	0.374	>>	1.517	3.876	>>	0.322	>>	1.496
-2	3.689		0.813		1.349	3.985		0.703		1.142
-1	3.505		0.954		0.864	3.873		0.783		0.752
0	**2.768**	>>	**0.676**	>>	**2.115**	**2.874**	>>	**0.609**	>>	**1.828**
1	2.875	>>	1.414		2.19	2.728	>>	1.159		1.894
2	2.857		2.495		1.678	2.841		2.064		1.544
3	2.973	>>	1.837		1.506	3.052	>>	1.373		1.321
4	2.942		2.238		1.656	3.002		2.006		1.544
5	2.985		1.984		0.971	2.858		1.698		0.944
6	3.155	>>	1.797		1.192	2.964	>>	1.578	>>	1.109
7	3.148		1.236		0.951	2.99		1.182		0.924
8	2.78	>>	1.672	>>	0.759	2.766	>>	1.697	>>	0.642
9	2.881		1.808		0.904	2.872		1.999		0.843
10	3.114		1.87		1.78	2.946		1.855		1.637

Note: For the three stock groups I calculate the close to close volatility for a window of -10 to +10 around the event according to: $V_{i,t} = (r_{i,j}^{CO})^2$.

Only events with no limit hits for the [-10,-1] period are used for the control groups. Panel A (Panel B) presents the case of a single price limit (successive price limits). Volatility is multiplied by 10^3. The symbols >> and > indicate that the left-hand side figure is greater than the right-hand figure at the 0.01 and 0.05 levels of significance using the Wilcoxon signed-rank test.

3.2 Price limits and Close to Open Volatility

Another approach for testing the effect of price limits on volatility is the one using the close-to-open volatility. This concept - at least in my knowledge - is new to the price limits literature and originates from Amihud and Mendelson (1991) study of the TSE trading system. They use among other things close-to-open volatility so as to examine the periodic clearing mechanisms and the closing transactions of the various TSE trading sessions. The basic idea behind their analysis is that any differences between volatilities it might be attributed - excluding new information - to the price disturbances among them resulting from trading frictions. In other words the framework will be the same with close-to-close volatility.

For each day volatility is calculated using the following formula:

$$V_t = (r_{i,t}^{CO})^2$$

where $r_{i,t}^{CO}$ is the close to open return for stock i between day $t-1$ and t. One caveat of the close to open volatility analysis has to do with data availability. There are no opening prices data available prior to September 1999. Hence I have to exclude a large portion of the initial sample described in Table 1 above.

Nevertheless, Table 4 presents the Up Limits close to open volatility. Volatility is multiplied by 103. Again results of the single limit hit are shown on Panel A. There for Day 0 volatility for Group Hit is significantly greater than Day 0 volatility for Group 90 and the latter is significantly greater than Day 0 volatility for Group 80. Again this is a trivial result made by the construction of the three groups.

Observe that close-to-open volatility for Group Hit increases from Day 0 to Day 1 and this increase continuous until Day 4. A decrease in close-to-open volatility starts from Day 5 downwards. One might argue here that this increase is in favor of the price limits implementation. In other words close-to-open returns do not have a price limit and so their volatility increases. This is not true. Close-to-open volatility for Group 90 decreases from Day 0 to Days 1 and 2. Even though there is an increase in volatility for Days 3 and 4 the decreasing pattern continuous from Day 5 downwards. Moreover volatility for Days 1 to 5 of Group Hit is significantly greater than volatility for Days 1 to 5 for Group 90. This pattern of behavior can not be observed for Group 80. According to Amihud and Mendelson (1991) the greater volatility of Group Hit it might be attributed to the difference of the trading system between these groups. The only difference between Group Hit and Groups 90 and 80 is the limit hits of the first group. Note that there is no difference between post Day 0 days for Group 90 and Group 80. From Panel B the Day 0 trivial results also holds. Moreover, close-to-open volatility decreases for Group Hit from Day 0 to Day 1 and this decrease continuous downwards. For Group 90 volatility decreases from Day 0 to Day 1 and there is no clear pattern of behaviour from Day 2 downwards. Group Hit volatility is significantly greater than Group 90 volatility while this is not true between Group 90 and Group 80. Again the result is that the post Day 0 difference in volatilities for Group Hit and Group 90 is attributed to the limit hit of Group Hit. As a result Conjecture 1 is rejected for both single and successive Up limits.

Table 5 presents the results for the Down Limit close-to-open volatility. Volatility is multiplied by 103. From Panel A for the single limit hit the trivial result for Day 0 also holds. Close-to-open volatility increases from Day 0 to Day 1 and it follows a more or less increasing pattern from Day 2 downwards for Group Hit and Group 90 with the former being significantly greater than the latter in most cases. This is not true between Group 90 and Group 80. Again the result is that the post Day 0 difference in volatilities for Group Hit and Group 90 is attributed to the limit hit of Group Hit. From Panel B except from the Day 0 trivial result close-to-open volatility for Group Hit decreases from Day 0 to Day 1 and there is no clear pattern downwards. On the other hand close-to-open volatility increases from Day 0 to Day 1 for Group 90 and Group 80 and here too there is no clear pattern for the following days. Group Hit close-to-open volatility is significantly greater than the respective volatility of Group 90 but this is not true between Group 90 and Group80. Again the result is that the post Day 0 difference in volatilities for Group Hit and Group 90 is attributed to the limit hit of Group Hit. For both single and successive Down price limits Conjecture 1 is rejected.

Table 6

Up Limits and Illiquidity

Days	Group Hit		Group90		Group80
Panel A: Case One UP					
-5	2.000	>>	5.400	>>	1.470
-4	5.700		4.920		3.400
-3	2.150		0.814		1.480
-2	1.780		1.240		1.330
-1	1.530		1.750		1.070
0	1.610	>	2.500	>	1.410
1	0.892	>>	0.384	>>	0.620
2	1.420		0.396		1.120
3	1.200		0.321		1.010
4	1.160	>>	0.185	>>	0.948
5	0.929		0.620		0.978
Panel B: Case Two UP					
Days	**Group Hit**		**Group90**		**Group80**
-5	2.270	>	3.380		1.720
-4	4.580		3.110		2.890
-3	1.990	>>	0.589	>>	1.470
-2	1.870		0.885		1.420
-1	1.510		1.310		1.110
0	1.680	>>	1.760	>>	1.470
1	1.170	>>	0.391		0.898
2	1.360		0.359		1.070
3	1.210	>>	0.328		0.950
4	1.190	>>	0.223		0.977
5	0.907	>	0.531		0.908

Note: For the three stock groups I calculate the close to close illiquidity for a window of -5 to +5 around the event according to the following formula:

$$illiq_t = \frac{\left| r_{t,j}^{CC} \right|}{vol_{t,j,€}}$$

where $\left| r_{t,j}^{CC} \right|$ is the absolute value of close to close return for stock i between day t-1 and t and $vol_{t,j,€}$ is the respective daily volume in euros (€). I include in the analysis stocks that experienced no price limit hits for the (-10,-1) period and also had similar illiquidities across the three groups. Panel A (Panel B) presents the case of a single price (successive price limits). Illiquidity is multiplied by 10^7.. The symbols >> and > indicate that the left-hand side figure is greater than the right-hand figure at the 0.01 and 0.05 levels of significance using the Wilcoxon signed-rank test.

4. Price Limits and Liquidity

Brunnermeier and Pedersen's (2005) argument in favour of price limits is that "predators" cannot gain from their "prey" under a price limit mechanism. This happens because "predators" gain from their "prey" by draining liquidity from the market. A price limit hit first stops liquidity draining on the limit hit day and second the day after limit hit the open clearing mechanism of the trading session permits all market participants to provide liquidity in the market. Therefore it stops or reduces the "predators" impact on price and thus eliminates or at least reduces their profits. As a results Brunnermeier and Pedersen (2005) conclude that price limits will lead to increased liquidity - or in other words decreased illiquidity - the day (s) after a limit hit.

There are two issues arising for the price limit analysis from the Brunnermeier and Pedersen (2005) argument. The first is that a predator (or a group of predators) is needed. There is no explicit answer in this paper for this. Only an implicit answer on the existence of predators might be given. During the 1999 ASE "bubble" period rumours circulated in the market concerning the growth, investment plans, possible mergers and acquisitions of a large number of the firms of my sample. One can find this rumours, tips etc. in the Greek Financial/Economic Press of that period. A big part of these rumours started from insiders of the firms and after the bubble some of them were prosecuted by the Greek Exchanges and Securities Commission.

The second issue that arises here is liquidity measurement. Usually in studies of liquidity and asset returns intraday data are used because they capture trade by trade liquidity. This gives more information on the behaviour of traders around the price limit hit. For example if in the period before an Up limit hit there are successive buy trades with high volume that push the price upwards which is followed with sell-trades after the limit hit (the following day) than there are evidence on the existence of a "predator" as the one described by Brunnermeier and Pedersen (2005). In fact the intraday study on the magnet effect of Abad and Pascual (2007) uses a similar framework. Nevertheless intraday ASE data are not available for the sample period under question. To circumvent this problem I use daily data and the illiquidity measure proposed by Amihud (2002) which is described as the absolute (percentage) price change per euro of daily trading volume and is given by the following formula:

$$illiq_{i,t} = \frac{\left| r_{i,t}^{CC} \right|}{vol_{i,t,€}}$$

where $\left| r_{i,t}^{CC} \right|$ is the absolute value of close-to-close return for stock i between day $t-1$ and t and $vol_{i,t,€}$ is the respective daily volume in euros (€). The illiquidity measure is closely related with Kyle's (1985) result for liquidity i.e. the order flow necessary to induce prices to rise or fall by one euro (€) .

Table 6 presents the results for the Up limits illiquidity. From Panel A illiquidity for Group Hit is significantly grater from Day 0 illiquidity for Group 90 and the latter is significantly greater than Day 0 illiquidity for Group 80. Observe that the Day 0 illiquidity is greater from Day -1 illiquidity for all three groups. This is similar with Brunnermeier and Pedersen's (2005) result that "predators" drain market from liquidity - and thus creating illiquidity - before the price limit hit. For Group Hit, Group 90 illiquidity for Day 1 compared with Day 0 is decreased which again agrees with Brunnermeier and Pedersen (2005). Illiquidity decreases also for Group 80 from Day 0 to Day 1. In addition Group Hit Day 1 illiquidity is significantly greater than Group 90 Day 1 illiquidity but the latter is also significantly greater than Group 80 Day 1 illiquidity. Consequently it is not possible to determine if the increased illiquidity between Group Hit and Group 90 is due to the price limit mechanism or to the difference in price increase between the groups. From Panel B Day 0 illiquidity follows the repective pattern of Panel A Day 0 illiquidity. Again there is an increase between Day -1 and Day 0 illiquidity and a decrease in illiquidity from Day 0 to Day 1 for all three groups. But this time only Group Hit Day 1 illiquidity is significantly greater than Group 90 Day 1 illiquidity. As a result the liquidity conjecture cannot be rejected for the single Up limit case while it is rejected for the successive Up limit case.

Table 7

Down Limits and Illiquidity

Panel A: Case One DOWN

Days	**Group Hit**		**Group90**		**Group80**
-5	1.490		0.382		1.220
-4	2.060	>>	0.021	>>	1.420
-3	1.410		0.232		1.250
-2	1.360		0.158		0.968
-1	1.260		0.141		1.150
0	**6.920**	>>	**0.364**	>>	**7.890**
1	2.650		0.435		3.150
2	3.260	>>	0.145	>>	3.710
3	2.470	>>	0.095		2.640
4	2.180	>>	0.029		2.170
5	2.460		0.388		2.810

Panel B: Case Two DOWN

Days	**Group Hit**		**Group90**		**Group80**
-5	1.75		0.382		1.520
-4	1.99	>>	0.021		1.470
-3	1.38		0.232		1.220
-2	1.29	>	0.158		0.977
-1	1.22		0.141		1.170
0	**6.28**	>>	0.364	>>	7.390
1	3.13		0.435		3.620
2	3.18	>>	0.145		3.670
3	2.54	>>	0.0948		2.690
4	2.11	>>	0.0289	>>	2.140
5	3.15		0.388		3.640

Note: For the three stock groups I calculate the close to close illiquidity for a window of -5 to +5 around the event according to the following formula:

$$illiq_t = \frac{\left| r_{t,j}^{CC} \right|}{vol_{t,j,€}}$$

where $\left| r_{t,j}^{CC} \right|$ is the absolute value of close to close return for stock i between day t-1 and t and $vol_{t,j,€}$ is the respective daily volume in euros (€). I include in the analysis stocks that experienced no price limit hits for the (-10,-1) period and also had similar illiquidities across the three groups. Panel A (Panel B) presents the case of a single price (successive price limits). Illiquidity is multiplied by 10^7.. The symbols >> and > indicate that the left-hand side figure is greater than the right-hand figure at the 0.01 and 0.05 levels of significance using the Wilcoxon signed-rank test.

Table 7 presents the results for the Down limits illiquidity. The behavior of Day's 0 illiquidity is as before. Moreover from Day -1 to Day 0 there is a substantial increase in illiquidity while for Day 1 there is a decrease in illiquidity for all three groups. For Days 2 to 4 illiquidity decreases for Group Hit and is significantly greater from the respective illiquidity for Group 90 while this is not true between Groups 90 and 80. From Panel B the previous result for Days 0 illiquidity holds. Again there is an increase from Day -1 to Day 0 and a decrease for Day 1 for all three groups. Finally for Day 2 to 4 illiquidity for Group Hit is greater from illiquidity for Group 90 while this is not true between Groups 90 and 80. Therefore the liquidity conjecture is rejected for both single and successive Down limit cases.

In summary, the liquidity conjecture is not rejected for the single hit price limits case while it is rejected for all the other cases. Illiquidity is increased - and hence liquidity is decreased - the day after a price limit hit.

5. Price Limits and Overreaction

In this section the question of whether the price limits mechanism causes stock price overreaction or not will be answered. By the term overreaction I mean that the behaviour of stock prices surrounding an event - a price limit hit in this analysis - can be decomposed in two terms. The first ones describe the normal behaviour of stock prices and the second term describes the "non-normal" behaviour of stock prices. The normal behaviour could be addressed either by a statistical or an economic model (MacKinley (1999)). The statistical model might be the mean stock returns or the market adjusted returns (Brown and Warner (1985)) or an economic model for example the Capital Asset Pricing Model (CAPM) of Sharpe (1964) and Lintner (1965). Usually economic models have more constraints than the statistical ones making the analysis of overreaction more complicated.

The "non-normal" term of stock prices behaviour can be attributed to investor cognitive biases as those described by Kahneman and Tversky (1982) or by the limits to arbitrage literature as is reviewed in Barberis and Thaler (2002). The former provides psychological reasoning while the latter an economic argument on the existence of "non-normal" returns. In fact the Subrahmanyam (1994) and Brunnermeier and Pedersen (2005) papers belong to the limits of arbitrage area. In what follows I will not try to relate "non-normal" returns with a theory model. Rather I will try to examine if these returns exist using an event study methodology as the one described by Brown and Warner ((1980), (1985)) and MacKinley (1999).

Usually in studies of this form the efficient market price is disturbed either upwards or downwards by an information driven event. Then the speed of adjustment to the fully informational price is examined. According to Fama (1970) this adjustment is instantaneous. But according to the behavioural (psychological or limits to arbitrage) approach this adjustment is slower and may give ways of profits for informed investors.

The key difference of the common event studies with what follows is the nature of the event. Usually the events are information driven (earnings announcements, stock splits etc.) and so the event study is a semi-strong test of the efficient market hypothesis (Dimson et al (1998)). Here the price limit hit is not information driven but it can be considered as containing information (or at least noise) implicitly. Fama (1989) argues that the limits only delay the price adjustment process after the new information while the arguments in favour state that limits give time to investors to "digest" this information.

In what follows the sample of the 168 stocks from the ASE is used. An event window of -10 to 10 days around each price limit and an estimation window of 200 days is used also. I use all the price limit cases with up to 4 price limit hits without excluding those that hit their price limit from Day -10 to -1. This is done because I want to include as many price limits cases as possible in the abnormal returns analysis and because using the single and successive hit samples of the analysis above gives no different results. Nevertheless for the successive price limit cases only the first limit is counted as an event.

For the estimation period the market model is used with $r_{m,t}$ being the return of the General ASE index for the estimation window. The market model takes the form:

$$r_{i,t}^{estw} = \alpha_i + b_i r_{m,t} + e_{i,t}$$

With $E[e_{i,t}] = 0$ and $Var[e_{i,t}] = \sigma_e^2$. The "abnormal returns" are given by:

$$r_{i,t}^{abn} = r_{i,t}^{estw} - (\overline{\alpha}_i + \overline{b}_i r_{m,t}^{evw})$$

Where $r_{i,t}^{estw}, r_{m,t}^{evw}, r_{i,t}^{abn}$ are the actual returns for the estimation period, the actual market returns for the event window and the abnormal returns respectively.

Table 8 gives the results for the abnormal returns. Note that the asterisk denotes significance of the abnormal return using a t-test as this is described in Brown and Warner (1985) and MacKinley (1999). The symbols >> (<<) and > (<) denote that the left hand figure is greater (less) than the right-hand figure at the 0.01 and 0.05 levels of significance using the Wilcoxon signed rank test.

From Panel A for the Up Limit case Group Hit Day 0 abnormal returns are positive and significantly different from zero and this also holds for Group 90 and Group 80 Day 0 abnormal returns. For Group Hit Day 0 returns are positive and significantly greater than zero while this is not true between Group 90 and Group 80 abnormal returns. For Group Hit Day 1 abnormal returns are positive and significant while this is not true for Group 90 or Group 80 Day 1 abnormal returns. For Group Hit and for Days 3 to 10 abnormal returns are negative and significant while this is not true for the abnormal returns of the other two groups. By observing Group Hit I can conclude that an overreaction exists.

In addition from the Wilcoxon test Group Hit Day 0 abnormal returns are significantly greater than Group 90 Day 0 abnormal returns and the latter are significantly greater than Group 80 Day 0 returns. Abnormal returns of Group Hit for Day 1 are greater from the respective returns of Group 90 and this does not hold between Group 90 and Group 80. Moreover for Days 3 to 10 - the reversal period for Group Hit - abnormal returns of Group Hit are significantly less than abnormal returns of Group 90 while there is no difference between returns of Group 90 and Group 80.

All these lead to the result that Conjecture 3 - no overreaction exists for Group Hit - is rejected for the Up Limits case and this is attributed to the price limit hit.

Table 8

Price Limits and Abnormal Returns

	Panel A: Case One UP					Panel B: Case Two UP				
Days	**Group Hit**		**Group90**		**Group80**	**Group Hit**		**Group90**		**Group80**
-10	-2.466		-2.123		-2.182	-1.242		-2.318		-2.629
-9	-2.723	>>	-2.164		-1.93	-2.787		-3.088		-3.719
-8	-1.662		-2.195		-1.504	-3.928		-3.751		-4.272
-7	-1.988		-2.471		-2.161	-3.676		-4.23		-3.774
-6	-2.047		-2.521		-2.4	-2.498		-3.894		-3.618
-5	-2.122		-2.307		-2.379	-3.323		-3.889		-3.167
-4	-1.744		-2.129		-1.835	-4.194		-4.364		-4.286
-3	-1.974		-1.331		-0.951	-3.202		-6.148		-5.991
-2	-0.212		0.525		0.762	-6.581*	<<	-8.990**	<	-8.406**
-1	0.202		3.447		3.247	-8.441**	<<	-9.834**	<<	-9.461**
0	**9.770****	**>>**	**5.328***	**>>**	**4.698**	**-17.623****	**<<**	**-11.113****	**<<**	**-10.446****
1	**4.326****	>>	1.821*		1.196	-6.794**	<<	-7.069**	<<	-6.509**
2	0.149		-0.399		-1.367	-7.314**	<<	-6453		-6.466
3	-2.947*	<<	-1.383		-2.483	-6.458*		-5.233		-5.534
4	-3.216*	<	-1.958		-3.112	-4.948		-3.814		-3.974
5	-3.292*	<<	-1.877		-3.016	-3.933		-2.973		-3.168
6	-3.237*	<<	-1.898		-3.265	-2.877		-3.331		-3.072
7	-3.154*	<	-2.25	>	-3.406	-4.427		-4.095		-4.194
8	-3.316**	<<	-2186		-3.253	-3.367		-4.436		-4.276
9	-3.110*	<<	-2.174	>>	-3.19	-4.129		-4.196		-3.539
10	-3.553**	<<	-2.136		-3.241	-3.566		-4.231		-3.814

Note: I calculate abnormal returns according to Brown and Warner [35], MacKinley [25]. I include in the analysis stocks that experienced no price limit hits for the (-10,-1) period and also had similar abnormal returns across the three groups. Panel A (Panel B) presents the case of the Up Limits (Down Limits). Both single and successive price limit hits are included. Abnormal returns are multiplied by 10^3. The asterisk denotes significance of the abnormal return using a t-test as this is described in Brown and Warner [35] and MacKinley [25]. The symbols >> (<<) and > (<) denote that the left hand figure is greater (less) than the right-hand figure at the 0.01 and 0.05 levels of significance using the Wilcoxon signed rank test.

From Panel B for the Down Limits case Group Hit Day 0 abnormal returns are negative and significant and this also holds for Group 90 and Group 80 Day 0 abnormal returns. But Day -2 and Day -1 results are negative and significant for Group Hit and Groups 90 and 80. For Group Hit abnormal returns are negative and significant for Days 1 to 3 while for Group 90 and Group 80 only Day 1 abnormal returns are negative and significant. In addition there is no reversal pattern for all three groups since returns from Day 4 downwards are insignificant for Group Hit and this is also true for Group 90 Day 2 and Group 80 Day 2 downwards.

From the Wilcoxon test Group Hit Day 0 abnormal returns are significantly less than Group 90 Day 0 returns and the latter are significantly less from Group 80 abnormal returns. For Group Hit abnormal returns are less than abnormal returns of Group 90 for Days -2 and -1 and this also hold between Group 90 and Group 80. Group Hit Day 1 abnormal returns are significantly less than Group 90 abnormal returns and this also holds between Group 90 and Group 80 Day 1 abnormal returns. For Group Hit Day 2 abnormal returns are significantly less than Group 90 Day 2 abnormal returns but there is no difference between Group 90 and Group 80 abnormal returns. As a result Conjecture 3 is not rejected for the Down Limit cases.

Hence overreaction is present for the case of Up Limits and is not present for the Down Limits. This result is consistent with the general notion of a "bubble" where the frenzy usually takes place in the upward side and is consistent with the asymmetric feedback effect mentioned by Shen and Wang (1998). In other words traders buy stocks when prices go up but are more reluctant to sell stocks when prices go down.

6. Conclusion

Even though the use of price limits is widespread in stock markets around the world their usefulness is doubtful. My results support this position. In summary two out of the three conjectures that were posed at the beginning of the paper were rejected while the third was at least half rejected. In other words there is no decrease in - close-to-close or close-to-open - volatility after a (Up or Down) price limit hit. At the same time there is no increase in liquidity the day following a price limit – with the exception of the Up single limit case. Finally, overreaction exists only for the case of the Up price limits while this is not true for the Down limits.

In addition there are a number of additional features of the analysis that need to be mentioned. First of all is the large sample of price limit hits and the groups that reached but did not hit their limits. The main characteristic of this sample is that it refers to a volatile "bubble" period and includes much more price limit cases than that of Kim and Rhee (1997). The "bubble" period is important because price limits are mechanisms made especially for such environments. The tightness of the price limit mechanism +/- 8% contributes also to the great number of price limit cases.

The second contribution of the paper is the introduction of the close-to-open volatility and liquidity measures. The former gives new insights to an old question on price limits that of the reduction of volatility the day following a price limit hit. At the same time it does not carry the price limit bounds that close-to-close volatility carries. The liquidity measure on the other hand gives an answer to a newly posed question concerning price limits that of Brunnermeier and Pedersen (2005) that price limits increase liquidity the day after a price limit hit under a "predatory" setting. In this direction Amihud's (2002) illiquidity measure helps in circumventing the lack of intraday data and at the same time it captures Kyle's (1985) definition of liquidity i.e. the order flow necessary to induce prices to rise or fall by one euro (€).

Among the weaknesses of the paper is the lack of opening prices for the entire sample period and the lack of intraday data. The conjecture concerning asymmetric feedback traders remains without answer also. Nevertheless the result on price limits is not encouraging. Price limits seem to fail serving the purposes for which they were made for.

References

Abad, D., Pascual, R., (2007), On the Magnet Effect of Price Limits, *European Financial Management*, 13, 833-852

Amihud, Y., (2002), Illiquidity and Stock Returns: Cross-Section and Time-Series Effects, *Journal of Financial Markets*, 5, 31-56

Amihud, Y., Mendelson, H., (1991), Volatility, Efficiency, and Trading: Evidence from the Japanese Stock Market, *Journal of Finance*, 46, 1765-1789

Barberis, N., Thaler, R., (2002), A Survey of Behavioral Finance, *NBER Working Paper* No. 9222

Brady Commision, (1988), Report of the Presidential Task Force on Market Mechanisms.

Brennan, M.J., (1986), A Theory of Price Limits in Futures Markets, *Journal of Financial Economics*, 16, 213-233

Brunnermeier, K.M., and Pedersen, H,L., (2005), Predatory Trading, *Journal of Finance*, LX,4, 1825-1863

Chen, H., (1988), Price Limits, Overreaction and Price Resolution in Futures Markets, *The Financial Review*, 37, 243-263

Chen, Y.M., (1993), Price Limits and Stock Market Volatility in Taiwan, *Pacific-Basin Finance Journal*, 1, 139-153

Chodhry, B., Nanda, V., (1998), Leverage and Market Stability: The Role of Margin Rules and Price Limits, *Journal of Business*, 71, 179-210

Diakogiannis, P. G., Patsalis, N., Tsangarakis, V.N., Tsiritakis, D.E., (2005), Price Limits and Overreaction in the Athens Stock Exchange, *Applied Financial Economics*, 15, 53-61

Dimson, E., Mussavian, M., (1998), A Brief History of Market Efficiency, *European Financial Management*, 4, 91-193

Fama, E.F., (1970), Efficient Capital Markets: A Review of Theory and Empirical Work, *Journal of Finance*, 25, 383-417

—. (1989), Perspectives on October 1987, Or, What Did We Learn from the Crash?, (Eds) Kamphuis, R.W.Jr., Kormendi, R.C., Watson, J.W.H., Black Monday and the Future of Financial Markets, Chicago: Mid America Institute for Public Policy Research

Gay. G., Kale, J., Kolb, R., Noe, T., (1994), Fads in Asset Prices:Evidence from the Future Market, *Journal of Futures Markets*, 14, 243-263

Harris, L., (1998), Circuit Breakers and Program Trading Limits: What have we learned, *Brooking - Wharton Papers on Financial Services*, 17-63

Henke, H., Voronkova, S., (2005), Price Limits on a Call Auction Market: Evidence from the Warsaw Stock Exchange, *International Review of Economics and Finance*, 14,.439-453

Kahneman, D., Tversky, A., (1982), Judgement under Uncertainty: Heuristics and Biases, (Eds) Kahneman,D., Slovic, P., Tversky A., Cambridge University Press, London, pp.3-20

Kim, A.K., (2001), Price Limits and Stock Market Volatility, *Economics Letters*, 71, 131-136

Kim, A.K., Rhee, G.S., (1997), Price Limit Performance: Evidence from the Tokyo Stock Exchange, *Journal of Finance*, 52, 865-901

Kim, H.Y., Yang, J.J., (2004), What Makes Circuit Breakers Attractive to Financial Markets? A Survey, *Financial Markets, Institutions and Instruments*, 13, 109-146

Kodres, L.E., OBrien, D.P., (1994), The Existence of Pareto Superior Price Limits, *The American Economic Review*, 84, 919-932

Kyle, S. A., (1985), Continuous Auctions and Insider Trading, Econometrica, Vol. 53, 1315-1336

Lintner, J., (1965), The Valuation of Risk Assets and the Selection of Risky Investments in Stock Portfolios and Capital Budgets, *The Review of Economics and Statistics*, 47, 13-37

MacKinlay, A. G., (1999), Event Studies in Economics and Finance, *Journal of Economic Literature*, 35, 13-39

Ma, K.C., Rao,P.R., Sears, R.S., (1989), Volatility, Price Resolution, and the Effectiveness of Price Limits, *Journal of Financial Services Research*, 3, 165-199

Nath P., (2004), Are Price Limits Always Bad?, *Journal of Emerging Market Finance*, 4, 281-313

Phylaktis, K.,Kavussanos, M., Manalis, G., (1999), Price Limits and Stock Market Volatility in the Athens Stock Exchange, *European Financial Management*, 5, 69-84

Sharpe, F.W., (1964), Capital Asset Prices: A Theory of Market Equilibrium under Conditions of Risk, *Journal of Finance*, 19, 425-442

Shen, C.-H., Wang, L.-R., (1998), Daily Serial Correlation, Trading Volume and Price Limits: Evidence from the Taiwan Stock Market, *Pacific-Basin Finance Journal*, 6, 251-273

Subrahmanyam A., (1994), Circuit Breakers and Market Volatility: A Theoretical Perspective, *Journal of Finance*, 49, 232-254

Stamatiou, T., (2005), Price Limits, Volatility and Price Continuation in the Athens Stock Exchange, *Manuscript*, University of Piraeus

Veld-Merkoulova, V.Y., (2003), Price Limits in Futures Markets: Effects on the Price Discovery Process and Volatility, *International Review of Financial Analysis*, 12, 311-328

Warner,B.J., Brown,S.J., (1980), Measuring Security Price Performance, *Journal of Financial Economics*, 8, 205-258

Warner,B.J., Brown,S.J., (1985), Using Daily Stock Returns: The Case of Event Studies, *Journal of Financial Economics*, 14, 3-31

Acknowledgments

I am especially thankful to Gikas Hardouvelis, and also to Nikitas Pittis, Dimitris Malliaropoulos, Theodoros Diasakos, Kostas Koufopoulos, Timotheos Angelidis, Christos Tsoumas, Antonis Antypas and Giannis Sarantis. I would like to acknowledge an anonymous referee whose comments improved the paper and gave me new insights for further research on the subject. I am grateful for comments by Dan Galai and seminar participants at the XLI-Euro Working Group on Financial Modelling Conference (Lisbon, 2007) and to Emilios Galariotis and seminar participants at the HFAA-2007 Conference (Patras, Greece).

CHAPTER ELEVEN

EFFECTS OF INCREASED LIQUIDITY ON THE RETURNS OF SMALL-CAP EQUITIES: EVIDENCE FROM THE ISTANBUL STOCK EXCHANGE

SERKAN ARAN

Abstract

Thanks to the improvement in investment environment in Turkey, foreign participation in Turkish equity markets has doubled these last years. However, liquidity still is a problem in small-cap stocks. In this paper, we examine the liquidity of selected small-cap companies and the reaction of these stocks to the changes in liquidity, relating the variations in market value to the variations in trading volume. We find significant relation between volume variations and return performance, though asymmetrical in positive and negative periods.

Keywords: liquidity impact, trading volume

1. Introduction

In order to address the feedback received from international investors about the difficulties in Turkey's investment environment, the Government of Turkey has launched a Reform Program to improve administrative procedures. The first step taken was to launch the "Decree on Improving the Investment Environment in Turkey" in December 2001, as a part of a national strategy to increase the overall level of income and productivity and to raise the level of competitiveness of firms operating in Turkey.

With the end of the 'coalition governments' after the election in

November 2002, Turkey began to attract more foreign direct and portfolio investments. The Central Bank of Turkey data clearly show that the amount of Foreign Direct Investments increased dramatically between 2000 and 2006 from $0,95 billion to $9,67 billion in 2005 and to $20,2 billion in 2006. Political stability and economic performance have also brought portfolio investments to the country, which also increased dramatically in the same period from $11, 98 billion to $66 billion. Foreign institutional investors' holdings on the free float of Turkish companies increased from 37.66% to 71.36% between July-2000 and July-2007. Increase in foreign participation has also brought some problems for foreign investors, as Turkish investors are sometimes not capable to allow foreign investors to liquidate their positions.

A number of theories in finance rely on the market's appropriateness for equity holders to trade a large amount of stock without affecting the price. However, there exist several frictions such as liquidity, currency rate volatility, short sale restrictions that impact price formation.

Liquidity can be defined as the ability to buy or sell large quantities of an asset quickly and at low cost. The vast majority of equilibrium asset pricing models do not consider the issues related to trading and thus ignore the time and cost of transforming cash into financial assets or vice versa. Recent financial crises, however, suggest that, at times, market conditions can be severe and liquidity can decline or even disappear.

The main reason behind studying liquidity is that liquidity affects the "exit price", that is, the price an investor pays when closing a position. For example, if trading volume is low, then the stock is harder to sell especially in bearish markets and the bid-ask spread becomes wide. However, spreads usually do not widen in Turkish market because Istanbul Stock Exchange (ISE) has a "price tick system" that already renders quite high the spread between the bid and the ask prices.

We mainly find high variations in daily and monthly trading volumes and returns of small-cap stocks, without major differences as to company size. Besides, variations in volume and returns are positively correlated. Furthermore, there is an asymmetry in this relation. When returns are negative, the relation between the volume variation and return becomes more prominent.

The paper is organized in the following way. Next section gives the literature review and possible contribution. Section 3 and Section 4 describe the dataset and the model. Section 5 presents the empirical results and the last section concludes.

2. Literature review and contribution

Liquidity shocks are a potential channel through which asset prices are influenced. Amihud and Mendelson (1986) and Jacoby, Fowler, and Gottesman (2000) provide theoretical arguments to show how liquidity impacts financial market prices. Amihud and Mendelson (1986) estimate that the most illiquid stocks could gain 50% in value if, all else equal, their liquidity raised to the level of the most liquid stocks.

Alternatively, Baker and Stein (2002) explain that there is a class of irrational investors who under-react to the information contained in order flows and that there are short-sales constraints. In this framework, the presence of irrational investors lowers the price impact of trades and boosts liquidity, while the short-sales constraints imply that irrational investors will be most active in the market when their valuations are higher than those of rational investors. Thus, high liquidity is a sign that the sentiment of irrational investors is positive and that expected returns are therefore abnormally low.

In their theoretical research Bagehot (1971) and Glosten and Harris (1988), have shown that adverse selection costs are the primary cause of illiquidity in financial markets. This provides additional justification for a negative return-liquidity relationship.

Bekaert, Harvey and Lundblad (2003) examine the effects of liquidity on expected returns for a set of emerging markets. Bekaert, G., C. R. Harvey and C. Lundblad, (2007) examined the liquidity matters for expected returns in emerging markets where liquidity ought to be particularly important. They started by proposing a measure of liquidity and transaction costs: the proportion of daily zero firm returns averaged over the month and found that the zero measure significantly predicts returns, and unexpected liquidity shocks are positively correlated with returns and negatively correlated with dividend yields. For emerging markets, there is the additional complication that the market may be segmented or integrated. Many of the markets they examined underwent a liberalization process and liberalization may affect the dynamic relation between returns and liquidity.

Chordia, Sarkar and Subrahmanyam (2003) study the effect of flows on forecasting stock and bond liquidity. Hasbrouck and Seppi (2001) examine factors in Prices, such as order flows and liquidity. Avramov, Chordia and Goyal (2005) explore liquidity and autocorrelations in individual stock returns. Robert Dubil (2002) models the optimal behaviour of an individual or trustee who decides to liquidate a position in an asset.

Brennan and Subrahmanyam (1996) and Datar et al. (1998) also find that stock returns are a decreasing function of various measures of liquidity -such as turnover, which is the liquidity measure used in this paper.

Sang-Gyung Jun, Achla Marathe and Hany A. Shawky (2003) find in their studies in which they used data of 27 emerging equity markets for the period January 1992 through December 1999 that, stock returns in emerging countries are positively correlated with aggregate market liquidity as measured by turnover ratio, trading value and the turnover–volatility multiple. The results hold in both cross-sectional and time-series analyses, and are quite robust even after they control for world market beta, market capitalization and price-to-book ratio. The positive correlation between stock returns and market liquidity in a time-series analysis is consistent with the findings in developed markets. However, the positive correlation in a cross-sectional analysis appears to be at odds with market microstructure theory that has been empirically supported by studies on developed markets. Their findings regarding the crossectional relation between stock returns and liquidity is consistent with the view that emerging equity markets have a lower degree of integration with the global economy.

Viral V. Acharyaa, and Lasse Heje Pedersen (2005) dealt with a simple equilibrium model with liquidity risk. In their liquidity-adjusted capital asset pricing model, a security's required return depends on its expected liquidity as well as on the co variances of its own return and liquidity with the market return and liquidity. In addition, a persistent negative shock to a security's liquidity results in low contemporaneous returns and high predicted future returns. Lack of liquidity causes an important cost while trading equities. Smaller size trades are often executed within a reasonable range [e.g., Petersen and Fialkowski (1994) and Knez and Ready (1996)], larger trades more often face prices far inferior from the market prices.

Beyond the previous research in the field, this paper tries to understand the relationship between the liquidity increase in small-cap companies in the ISE and its effect on the price performance. That may also be used in setting trading strategies for small cap companies whose "exit price" is generally 'abused' by illiquidity, hence the timing of the decision to sell becomes important to improve "exit price performance". To the best of our knowledge, no any academic paper exists in this particular area.

3. Data

Obtained from the Istanbul Stock Exchange (ISE) and the Central Registry Agency Inc. of Turkey (CRA), our dataset contains the volume-weighted average price (VWAP), total number of shares traded and market capitalizations on a daily basis of all the stocks traded in the Istanbul Stock Exchange (ISE) for a period of eight years from 3 April 2000 to 15 April 2008 during which foreign institutional investors' holdings in the ISE widened. We then apply the following methods to select small cap stocks and ensure the accuracy of the data.

-Select all the stocks that have never been included in the ISE 100 Index, the main index for the stocks with the highest capitalisation and liquidity level, during the period of the analysis.

-Exclude seven other stocks due to abnormal variations.

-Multiply by two the volume figures of the days in which only one trading session was held instead of both morning and afternoon sessions (typically in pre-holiday days).

-For the stock-based analysis, for each stock, we also exclude those days for which daily price variation exceeds 21% (following the rule of price limits in ISE) and for which total trading volume in YTL is higher than 200% or lower than 10% of the average volume for that stock (a very large trading volume indicating a probable block trade and very low levels of trading volume indicating a probable trading halt in that stock).

Thus, we end up with 103 stocks and 2014 days of observation.

We use the variables below in our analysis:

For day t and stock i,

- $VWAP_{it}$: Daily volume-weighted average price

- VOL_{it}: Daily trading volume in New Turkish Lira (YTL), i.e. the number of shares traded times the VWAP

- $MKTCAP_{it}$: Daily market capitalization at VWAP

In addition to the variables above, we create a synthetic index called Small-Cap Index (SCI) such that

$$SCI_t = 100 \times \left(\sum_{i=1}^{N} w_{it} \times p_{it} \right)$$

where N is the number of stocks in the index and w_i and p_i show weight and price based on a base price, respectively. These are defined as

$$w_{it} = MKTCAP_{it} / MKTCAP_{mt} \quad \text{such that} \quad \sum_{i=1}^{N} w_{it} = 1 \quad \text{and}$$

$$p_{it} = MKTCAP_{it} / MKTCAP_{i0}$$

where $MKTCAP_i$ and $MKTCAP_m$ designate the market capitalizations of stock i and of the overall small-cap stocks, respectively. $MKTCAP_{i0}$ is the base price of stock i, i.e. the VWAP of the day the first time stock i appeared in the dataset. Hence, the first day value of SCI is 100.

The Augmented Dickey-Fuller tests on SCI, MKTCAP and VOL series as defined above revealed nonstationarities. Therefore, after calculating 20-day averages of these variables (which corresponds roughly monthly data), we take their percentage variation to make estimations. This makes 100 observations in each series (99 observations in variation series) and thus we obtain smoother data with the characteristics allowing ordinary least squares (OLS) estimation.

4. Modelling the price impact of liquidity

Although liquidity has several definitions and measures, volume usually is the first indicator that comes into minds. High volume shows an intensive activity of trading. Investors can have more confidence in stocks that are traded more. Therefore, we use volume as a proxy of liquidity throughout the paper.

We investigate the price impact of liquidity in two ways. The first consists of a study at the stock level and the second is at the market level, aggregating the data for all the 103 stocks.

4.1. The Relation between Volume and Returns at Stock Level

We model the impact volume may have on returns with the simple OLS regression below.

$$\Delta MKTCAP_{it} = \alpha_i + \beta_i \, \Delta VOL_{it} + \varepsilon_{it} \quad (1)$$

where $\Delta MKTCAP_{it}$ and ΔVOL_{it} are percentage variations in average market capitalization and in average daily trading volume of stock i in period t, respectively.

4.2. The Relation between Volume and Returns at Market Level

Similarly, we define the market returns both as percentage change in the Small-Cap Index (SCI) and in MKTCAP (for the whole 103 stocks).

$$\Delta SCI_{st} = \alpha_s + \beta_s \, \Delta VOL_{st} + \varepsilon_{st} \quad (2)$$

$$\Delta MKTCAP_{mt} = \alpha_m + \beta_m \, \Delta VOL_{mt} + \varepsilon_{mt} \quad (3)$$

Secondly, in order to see whether positive and negative shifts in volume symmetrically affect returns, we distinguish between positive and negative variations in volume by the equations below.

$$\Delta MKTCAP^{+}_{mt} = \alpha^{+}_{m} + \beta^{+}_{m}\,\Delta VOL^{+}_{mt} + \varepsilon^{+}_{mt} \qquad (4)$$

$$\Delta MKTCAP^{-}_{mt} = \alpha^{-}_{m} + \beta^{-}_{m}\,\Delta VOL^{-}_{mt} + \varepsilon^{-}_{mt} \qquad (5)$$

As both the explanatory and dependent variables are in the form of percentage change, these equations can be considered as *volume elasticity of returns*.

5. Results

Similarly, we can handle our empirical results in two categories: results at the stock level and results at the market level.

5.1. Results at the stock level

We run the regression in (1) with each of 103 stocks and obtain the results summarized in Table 1.

Table 1. Summary Results of Stock-Based Regressions

	Min	Max	Median	Avg	Std	<0,05	<0,01	>1,65	>0,10	>0,20
Total *(N=103)*										
C	-2,56	2,78	0,28	0,26	1,14					
P-value (C)	0,01	0,99	0,57	0,58	0,24	2	1			
beta	0,00	0,12	0,04	0,04	0,03					
P-value (beta)	0,00	0,75	0,00	0,02	0,11	96	88			
R2	0,00	0,88	0,18	0,19	0,13				80	40
AdjR2	-0,01	0,88	0,17	0,19	0,14				78	36
DW	1,05	2,05	1,64	1,62	0,22			53		
Large companies *(N=26)*										
C	-1,19	1,98	0,71	0,61	0,84					
P-value (C)	0,13	0,96	0,50	0,53	0,20	0	0			
beta	0,01	0,09	0,03	0,04	0,02					
P-value (beta)	0,00	0,05	0,00	0,00	0,01	26	23			
R2	0,04	0,41	0,18	0,18	0,09				21	7
AdjR2	0,03	0,40	0,18	0,18	0,09				20	5
DW	1,06	2,05	1,66	1,64	0,24			11		
Small Companies *(N=77)*										
C	-2,56	2,78	-0,04	0,14	1,21					
P-value (C)	0,01	0,99	0,58	0,60	0,26	2	1			
beta	0,00	0,12	0,04	0,04	0,03					
P-value (beta)	0,00	0,75	0,00	0,03	0,12	70	64			
R2	0,00	0,88	0,18	0,20	0,15				58	32
AdjR2	-0,01	0,88	0,17	0,19	0,15				57	30
DW	1,05	2,02	1,61	1,61	0,22			42		

According to this table, average constant coefficient is 0,26 but is almost never significant. On the other hand, beta coefficient is 0,04 on average and its significance is quite high with 96 stocks out of 103 having a P-value below 0,05. Explanatory power is not very high (Adjusted R^2 nearly 0,19) but this is normal with such time series.

In the second and third panel of the table, we give the same statistics separately for larger and smaller companies although by definition all are less liquid and low capitalized stocks. One can notice that there is not much difference between these two categories.

5.2. Results at the market level

In order to have an idea about the movement of indicators of these 103 stocks during last eight years, one can look at Graph 1. From this chart, it is clear that aggregate market volume varies markedly much more than the aggregate market cap or the SCI.

Figure 1. Monthly Movement of Aggregate Market Indicators

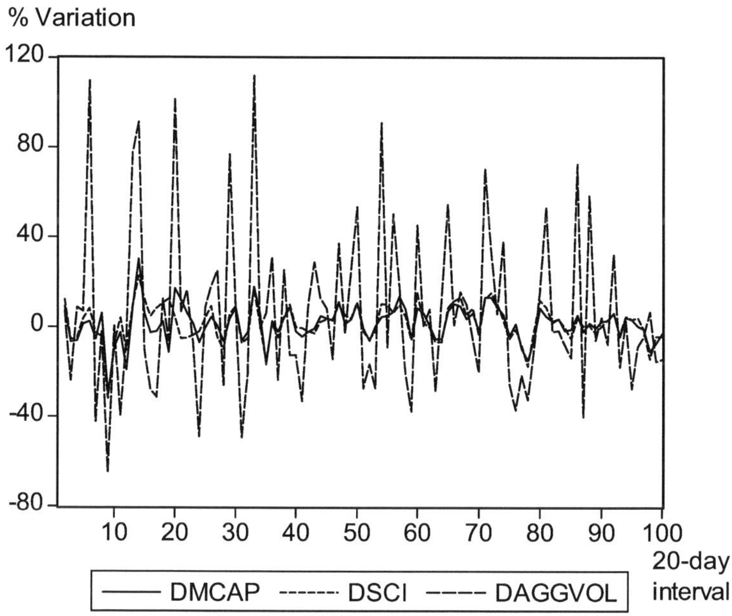

DMCAP: Percentage change in aggregate market capitalization
DSCI: Percentage change in SCI
DAGGVOL: Percentage change in aggregate trading volume in YTL

Table 2 gives the results of the regressions modelled in Equations 2 to 5. In all the four cases in different panels, both constant coefficient and beta coefficient are positive but only the latter is significant at a very high confidence interval. Results in Panel A and Panel B are qualitatively the same, but as for the returns, the explanatory power of MKTCAP is higher than SCI, as R^2 proves higher. Moreover, DW statistic of 1,41indicates a positive autocorrelation for the first regression.

Table 2. Estimation Results of the Regressions of Variations in Aggregate Volume on Variations in Aggregate Market Capitalization and in SCI

PANEL A

Dependent Variable: DSCI

Method: Least Squares

Sample: 199

Variable	Coefficient	Std. Eror	t-Statistic	Prob
C	-3.22E-16	0.692066	-4.65E-16	1,0000
DVOL	0.124565	0.019207	6,485342	0,0000
R2	0.302458			
Adj. R2	0.295267			
D-W stat	1,416504			

PANEL B

Dependent Variable: DMKTCAP

Method: Least Squares

Sample: 199

Variable	Coefficient	Std. Eror	t-Stat	Prob
C	-1.01E-15	0.646002	-1.56E-15	1,0000
DVOL	0.138863	0.017929	7,745304	0,0000
R2	0.382125			
Adj. R2	0.375755			
D-W stat	1,763123			

PANEL C

Dependent Variable: PVDMKTCAP

Method: Least Squares

Sample (adjusted): 143

Variable	Coefficient	Std. Eror	t-Statistic	Prob
C	1,119069	1,320150	0.847683	0.4015
DVOL	0.107023	0.030032	3,563624	0.0009
R2	0.236491			
Adj. R2	0.217869			
D-W stat	2,130673			

PANEL D

Dependent Variable: NVDMKTCAP

Method: Least Squares

Sample (adjusted): 156

Variable	Coefficient	Std. Eror	t-Statistic	Prob
C	1,668751	1,6	1,040697	0.3027
DVOL	0.213209	0.056290	3,787658	0.0004
R2	0.209907			
Adj. R2	0.195275			
D-W stat	1,908284			

The comparison of Panel C and Panel D is interesting. While the beta coefficient for the whole market is 0,14 (in Panel A), it is 0,11 and 0,21 in Panel C and Panel D, respectively. This means beta and the impact of volume is asymmetrical across the periods when volume accelerates or decelerates.

From the table, we can infer that a 1% increase in volume is associated with a 0,14% increase in returns on average. However, if the volume goes down by 1%, the returns would go down by 0,21%.

6. Conclusion

In addition to the existing research, this paper tries to understand the relationship between the liquidity increase in small cap companies in the Istanbul Stock Exchange and its effect on small cap companies' price performances by using a dataset over a period from April 2000 to April 2008. The analysis helps us to enhance our understanding of the behaviour of prices, and also sheds useful light on how increase in small cap trading volume affects small-cap stock prices.

Main findings are as follows.

Both trading volumes and returns of small-cap companies remarkably fluctuate at a monthly and daily basis. Total volume of trading at market level is sometimes doubled from one month to the next.

There is not much of a difference between the 103 stocks investigated as for the company size. Both larger and smaller companies show similar patterns in terms of the relation between volume and returns.

Variations in volume and returns are correlated. Returns become higher in periods when volumes are higher too. This result supports the idea that volume brings strength, that is, it sustains returns, as suggested by some technical analysts.

Upward and downward movements in volume have an asymmetrical impact on returns. When volume accelerates, returns are higher too, but when volume decelerates, returns go down much faster than they go up in good periods. This may imply that investors attribute a higher importance to liquidity decreases than liquidity booms. They hurry up to close their positions when liquidity shrinks. That is why any investor should take into account the liquidity of the asset in which he/she invests.

Acknowledgements

I am especially thankful to Professor Gulnur Muradoglu for her encouragement throughout and to all the other participants at the XLI EWGFM meeting for useful comments. The analyses, opinions and findings of this paper represent the views of the author. The author gratefully acknowledges funding from Is Investment, Istanbul - Turkey.

References

Acharyaa, V. and L. H. Pedersen (2005), Asset pricing with liquidity risk, *Journal of Financial Economics*, 77, 375-410.

Admati, A. R., and Paul Pfleiderer (1988), A theory of intraday patterns: Volume and price variability, *Review of Financial Studies* 1, 3-40.

Amihud, Y. and Mendelson (1986), Asset Pricing and the Bid-Ask Spread, *Journal of Financial Economics,* 17, 223-249.

Avramov, D., Chordia, T. and Goyal, A. (2005), Liquidity and Autocorrelations in Individual Stock Returns, *working paper,* University of Maryland, Emory University.

Baker, M. and J.C. Stein (2002), Market liquidity as a sentiment indicator. *Discussion Paper,* Harvard Institute of Economic Research, N1977.

Bekaert, G., Harvey, C.R., and C. Lundblad (2003), Liquidity and Expected Returns: Lessons from Emerging Markets, *working paper*, Columbia University, National Bureau of Economic Research, Duke University, Indiana University.

Bekaert, G., C. R. Harvey and C. Lundblad (2007), Liquidity and expected returns: Lessons from emerging markets, Review of Financial Studies, *forthcoming.*

Breen, W.J., Hodrick, L.S. and Korajczyk, R.A. (2000), Predicting Equity Liquidity, *working paper*, Kellogg Graduate School of Management, Northwestern University, Graduate School of Business, Columbia University.

Brennan, M. J., and Avanidhar Subrahmanyam (1996), Market microstructure and asset pricing: On the compensation for illiquidity in stock returns, *Journal of Financial Economics,* 41, 441-464.

Brennan, Michael J., Tarun Chordia, and Avanidhar Subrahmanyam (1998), Alternative factor specifications, security characteristics, and the cross-section of expected stock returns, *Journal of Financial Economics,* 49, 345-373.

Chordia, T., Roll, R. and Subrahmanyam A. (2000), Market Liquidity And Trading Activity, *working paper*, Vanderbilt University, UCLA.

Chordia, T., Sarkar, A. and Subrahmanyam A. (2001), Common Determinants of Bond and Stock Market Liquidity: The Impact of Financial Crises, Monetary Policy, and Mutual Fund Flows, *working paper*, Emory University, Federal Reserve Bank of New York, University of California.

Chordia, T., Sarkar, A. and Subrahmanyam A. (2003), An Empirical Analysis of Stock and Bond Market Liquidity, *Staff Reports*, 164, Federal Reserve Bank of New York

Datar, Vinay T., Narayan Y. Naik, and Robert Radcliffe (1998), Liquidity and stock returns: An alternative test, *Journal of Financial Markets,* 1, 203-219.

Dubil, R. (2002), How quickly should you liquidate your vested stock?, *working paper*, University of Connecticut.

Glosten, L. and L Harris (1988), Estimating the components of the bid-ask spread, *Journal of Financial Economics,* 21, 123-142.

Hasbrouck, J., Seppi, D.J. (1999), Common Factors in prices, Order Flows and Liquidity, *working paper*, Stern School of Business, Carnegie Mellon University.

Hisata Y. and Yamai Y. (2000), Research Toward the Practical Application of Liquidity Risk Evaluation Methods, *working paper*, Institute for Monetary and Economic Studies, Bank of Japan.

Hong, H. and Rady, S. (2000), Strategic Trading and Learning About Liquidity, *working paper*, Stanford University, University of Munich.

Jacoby, G., D. Fowler, and A. Gottesman (2000), The Capital Asset Pricing Model and the Liquidity Effect: A Theoretical Approach, *Journal of Financial Markets*, 3, 69-81.

Jankowitsch, R., Mösenbacher, H. and Pichler, S. (2002), Measuring the Liquidity Impact on EMU Government Bond Prices, *working paper*, Vienna University of Technology, Bank Austria, CCEFM.

Piqueira, N.S. (2000), Trading Activity, Illiquidity Costs and Stock Returns, *working paper*, University of Houston.

Sang-Gyung Jun, Achla Marathe and Hany A. Shawky (2003), Liquidity and Stock Returns in Emerging Equity Markets, *Emerging Markets Review*, 4, 1-24.

Sias, R.W., Starks, L.T. and Titman S. (2001), The Price Impact of Institutional Trading, *working paper*, Washington State University, University of Texas.

CHAPTER TWELVE

THE VOLATILITY-VOLUME RELATION AROUND TAKEOVER ANNOUNCEMENTS: A FRENCH EVIDENCE

DORRA MEZZEZ HMAIED

Abstract

This paper focuses on the relation between stock prices volatility and trading volume around takeover announcements for targets listed on the Paris Bourse. We examine if the positive volatility-volume relation well documented in empirical studies is affected by specific information arrivals. The relation is explored before and after the announcement of the takeover by separating the volume effect on conditional volatility into its pre and post-announcement components. Moreover, we check if the relation depends on the mean of payment.

The results confirm the positive volatility-volume relation before and after the takeover announcement. In addition, they show that information revealed by the takeover announcement affect trading volume and volatility differently depending on the mean of payment. The post-announcement relation differs significantly from cash to share-exchange offers. The volatility-volume relation is stable for share exchange offers but it is found to be weaker for cash offers for post-bid than pre-bid.

Keywords: takeover announcements, conditional volatility, trading volume, cash offers, share exchange offers.

1. Introduction

The growing number of takeovers all over the world has attracted increasing attention from academic researchers. Much of the work devoted to the market for corporate control has focused on the behaviour of target stocks around the announcement of takeover bids, either on a daily basis (see e.g. Jensen and Ruback (1983), Murray (1994), or using intraday data (Jennings (1994)).[1] These studies find strong evidence that target shareholders earn substantial excess returns around takeover announcements. Empirical studies examining trading volume of target stocks around this event show different reactions of volume (see e.g. Jarrell and Poulsen (1989) and Ascioglu *et al.* (2002)). Fewer studies have been interested in the price volatility of takeover targets and the findings are inconclusive (Lee *et al.* (1994), Smith *et al.* (1997) and Hutson & Kearney (2001)).

While previous research on takeovers has studied share price and trading volume behaviour around the announcement, separately, the relation between the two has not yet been examined for the market for corporate control. The existence of a positive relation between price volatility and trading volume is well documented in empirical studies of equity, foreign exchange and futures markets.[2] However, there is no consensus about what drives the relation observed empirically. Karpoff (1987) argues that the price-volume relation provides insight on how the information is disseminated and the extent to which market prices convey the information. Therefore, the price-volume relation will depend on the rate of information flow to the market. In addition, this relation can be used to measure changes in the variance of the price process from non event to event time.

The aim of this paper is to investigate the volatility-volume relation around the announcement of takeover bids. The announcement of a takeover constitutes a major corporate event that reveals unanticipated news to the market providing thus a good opportunity to study how the market reacts to information. The literature on financial markets suggests that volume and prices contain useful information about the trading process. Foster and Viswanathan (1993) show that higher trading volume and volatility should be related to unexpected news. Kim and Verrecchia (1991) report that post-announcement volume is a function of the absolute price change accompanying the announcement and the extent to which

[1] Jensen and Ruback (1983) provided a review of empirical studies examining the behaviour of target stocks around the announcement of takeover bids.

[2] Karpoff (1987) offers a comprehensive review of empirical and theoretical research on the relation between price changes and trading volume in financial markets.

information precision changes across traders who are heterogeneously informed. However, Smith et *al* (1997) state that takeover announcements vary greatly in terms of the information they convey and thus the response of traders should vary across different news releases. They argue that takeover announcements may lead to different levels of volatility and volume depending on the method of payment and the outcome of the bid.[3] They suggest thus that the positive link between volatility and volume may not apply to the dynamics involved in takeover announcements.

Using daily price and volume data on 72 French takeover targets listed on the Paris Bourse for the period from April 1997 to December 2005, we examine if the volatility-volume relation for target stocks is affected by the announcement of the takeover. We explore the relation before and after the announcement, delineating the sample by the mean of payment to cash and securities offers.[4] Examining this relation may shed light on the price formation process for takeover targets and may help to understand how traders react to takeover announcements. It is interesting to know if the positive volatility-volume relation is stable through time or may be affected by specific information arrivals. The results confirm the positive volatility-volume relation before and after the takeover announcement. However, the relation is affected differently by the nature of the information conveyed to the market. In fact, the post-announcement relation differs significantly from cash to share-exchange offers.

The main contributions of the paper are the following. This study is the first, to our knowledge, examining the volatility-volume relation around the announcement of takeovers. Second, this study considering jointly price changes and trading volume provides additional evidence on prices and trading volume reactions to takeover announcements.[5] In fact, in addition, we use conditional volatility as a measure of price changes.[6] Third, we examine this relation for a long time before the announcement and over the full bid period. Studies examining volume and volatility on

---

[3] Expected payoffs for target shareholders are uncertain. Excess returns are higher in cash offers than in share exchange offers and in the case of competing bids and successful offers.

[4] It is interesting also to distinguish successful and unsuccessful bids but it was not possible to do because the sample of unsuccessful bids was too small.

[5] The findings of previous studies are not unanimous on these reactions.

[6] Hutson and Kearney (2001) is the only study examining conditional volatility for takeover targets.

target stocks were limited to some days surrounding the announcement or focused only on the day following the announcement.

This paper is structured as follows: section 2 reviews previous empirical work and the relevant theoretical literature. Section 3 presents the features of the French market for corporate control, the data set and summary statistics. Section 4 describes methodological issues and section 5 presents the results. The final section concludes the paper.

2. Theoretical background and previous empirical research

Theoretical literature proposed two, mainly complementary, hypotheses explaining the positive relation between trading volume and volatility: the mixture of distributions models (Clark (1973), Epps and Epps (1976)) and differences in opinion models (Shalen (1993), Harris and Raviv (1993)).

The mixture of distributions hypothesis states that trading volume and price movements result from new information arrivals. Mixture of distributions models use information as mixing variable that determines both volatility and volume.[7] Clark (1973) argues that the volatility-volume relation occurs because of randomness in the number of intraday transactions. Considering the daily price change as the sum of a random number of intraday price changes, the trading volume is related positively to the variability of price changes as it is positively related to the number of intraday transactions. Epps and Epps (1976) argue that the intraday price changes reflect the average of changes in traders' reservation prices and the trading volume is positively related to the degree of dispersion in traders' reservation prices. Then, an increase in the extent to which traders disagree is associated with a larger absolute price change.

Dispersion of beliefs theories relate unusual volume and extremes of volatility to differences in trader beliefs. Dispersion of beliefs is a lack of consensus about the fundamental value of a stock that should result from revealed information. Harris and Raviv (1993) assume that even though all

[7] Jones et *al* (1994) designate the average transaction volume and the number of transactions as mixing variables and show that the positive volatility-volume relation reflects the positive relation between volatility and the number of transactions.

traders receive the same information, they differ in the way in which they interpret this information.

Hutson and Kearney (2001) apply a mixture of distributions model to takeover targets using the variance components model a la Tauchen and Pitts (1983). They interpret the bid price as the common informational component and the likelihood of success of the bid as the specific informational component. The model predicts that for targets of takeover bids that are ultimately successful the dispersion in traders' beliefs about the value of the stock will diminish during the course of the bid and the conditional price volatility will consequently decline.

Empirical work on corporate takeovers has examined the effect of takeover announcements on trading volume and volatility, separately. Most studies were interested in trading volume behaviour before takeover announcements. Market for corporate control literature offers different explanations to increased trading volume before takeover announcements: insider trading (Keown and Pinkerton (1981)); market anticipation hypothesis (Jensen and Ruback (1983)); liquidity clustering (Admati and Pfleiderer (1988)) and arbitrage (Harris and Raviv (1983)). Jennings (1994) finds weak evidence of increased trading volume before takeover announcements and concludes the absence of informed trading for the NYSE. Moreover, Vandelanoite (2002b) finds no evidence for the presence of informed traders on the Paris Bourse. Gao and Oler (2004) find that significantly high trading volume precedes high share price movement by about seven days for U.S. targets. They argue that heavy trading without price change is consistent with the arbitrage explanation.

Fewer studies are interested in the post-announcement volume. Smith *et al.* (1997) focus on the first trading day following a takeover announcement. They find that post-takeover intraday volume is abnormally high although decreasing throughout the first five hours after the reopening of trading which confirms the evidence of Jennings (1994) who examines the first five trades after the announcement and finds high trading volume just after the announcement.

Little attention has been directed to targets' stocks volatility around takeover announcements. Lee et *al* (1994), for the NYSE, and Smith *et al.* (1997), for the Toronto stock exchange, found that intraday unconditional stock price volatility is abnormally high but decreasing on the day of a takeover announcement. These studies are though limited to the announcement day. Hutson and Kearney (2001) have examined the conditional price volatility of Australian target stocks over the bid period and find that it declines after the takeover announcement. They argue that this decline reflects a convergence of trader opinion regarding target stock value.

Moreover, Smith et *al* (1997) examine whether differences in the nature of information released during takeover announcements affect target firm stock volatility and trading volume. They find that the level of post announcement volatility is significantly related to the type of payment method and the likelihood of a takeover contest. Post-announcement volume is significantly higher where there is a large post-announcement price change and the takeover offer is contested.

Table 1 provides a summary of empirical studies examining trading volume and/or volatility around takeover announcements.

3. The French market for corporate control and the Dataset

3.1 Features of the French market for corporate control

Under French tender offers regulation, a full takeover bid (100% of voting shares) must be launched if an individual or company holds less than 50% of voting shares. A normal procedure is then applied to the takeover. A simplified bid can be launched if the acquirer holds at least 50% of voting shares. The means of payment can be cash, securities or a combination of both.

Table 1 – Summary of empirical studies on trading volume and volatility around takeover announcements

	Sample And data	Volatility	Trading volume	
			Before announcement	After announcement
Jennings (1994)	Targets listed on the NYSE Intraday data		Weak evidence of increased trading volume	High trading volume during the first five trades
Vandelanoite (2002a)	Targets listed on the Paris Bourse Daily data		No increased trading volume	A high increase is noted, then a decrease lasting 6 days
Gao & Oler (2004)	US targets Daily data		High volume is observed seven days before stock price variation	
Lee et al (1994)	Targets listed on the NYSE Intraday data	Volatility is abnormally high, decreasing on the day of the announcement		
Smith et al (1997)	Targets listed on the Toronto S.E Intraday data			Volume is high, decreasing throughout the first five hours
Hutson & Kearney (2001)	Australian targets Daily data	Conditional price volatility declines during the bid period		

On the Paris Bourse, target firms are suspended before the formal announcement of the takeover in order to prevent informed trading, to ensure better information and to protect investors. Trading in target stocks is suspended on average for 5 trading days from the submission of the offer by the acquirer until the publication of the admissibility of the offer by the French securities market regulator (AMF).[8] This period allows traders to collect and treat information about the offer and no private information will be produced after announcements.[9] Bids remain open for a minimum of 25 trading days (a maximum of 35 trading days can be allowed by AMF). This enables target shareholders to have enough time and information to decide if the offer is relevant. The bid period is reduced in the case of simplified tender offers, 10 (15) trading days for cash bids (share-exchange or mixed bids). For simplified offers, targets shares are sold directly on the market.

3.2 Sample and Data

Our sample consists of 72 French targets listed on the Paris Bourse and involved in tender offers from April 1997 to December 2005. Tender offers information (the official announcement date, the suspension date, the bid period: open and conclusion dates and the offer outcome) is checked for each target company in the notices published by the "AMF Website". Daily closing prices and volumes (number of shares traded) are obtained from the "abc bourse" database and from "Euronext Website" for a period beginning 250 days before the announcement day until the conclusion of the bid.

We first consider all French target firms on the study period. We removed from the initial sample bids for which competing offers were launched, mixed bids and stock repurchase bids. We removed also targets for which data were not available, those that were not listed for the full prior year or that were not frequently traded.[10] [11]

---

[8] AMF is the abbreviation of "Autorité des Marchés Financiers".

[9] Contrary to the French market, there is no systematic trading halt on takeover target stocks for other markets. For the NYSE, trading on target stocks is rarely suspended or not suspended at all.

[10] Data are not available because targets are delisted after a going private offer or listed on the *Marché Libre* for instance.

[11] Targets for which trading is frequently suspended and observations series are very short.

3.3 Summary statistics

Table 2 provides summary statistics for target stock returns (mean and standard deviation) and the log of trading volumes. The statistics are delineated by the mean of payment (cash and share-exchange offers) and reported for the pre and post-announcement periods. The pre-bid period runs from 250 days to the day before the takeover announcement and the post-bid period begins the day of the announcement to the formal conclusion of the bid.

Table 2 - Summary statistics for target stock returns and volume

	Sample size	Mean Return	Standard Deviation	Log (volume)
Pre-bid period				
Total	72	0,001	0,033	7,96
Cash	54	0,001	0,031	7,11
Share-exchange	18	0,001	0,041	10,48
Post-bid period				
Total	72	0,003	0,033	9,36
Cash	54	0,004	0,032	8,93
Share-exchange	18	-0,001	0,037	10,64
Percent variation (p-value)				
Total	72	200 (0,09)	0 (0,48)	18 (0,00)
Cash	54	300 (0,02)	3 (0,41)	26 (0,00)
Share-exchange	18	-229 (0,31)	-10 (0,36)	2 (0,42)

Notes: The pre-bid period runs from 250 days to 1 day before the takeover announcement. The post-bid period begins the day of the announcement to the formal conclusion of the bid. The figures are cross-sectional averages of the statistics calculated for each target in time series. The percent variation (*p*-value) reports the results for the one-tailed *t*-test which tests if there are significant differences between pre and post announcement mean returns, standard deviations and trading volumes.

The average return for the full sample increases significantly from 0.1% for the pre-bid period to 0.3% for post-bid using *t*-test (*p*-value=0.09). In addition, target stock returns are significantly higher for cash offers than for share exchange offers after the takeover announcement. The difference between pre-bid and post-bid unconditional volatility of target stocks is not significant for all samples (total, cash and share-exchange offers). For the total sample, the volume increases by 18% after the announcement of the takeover (*p*-value=0.00). The increase is significant and more pronounced for cash offers (26%) but no increase is noted for share exchange offers.

4. Hypotheses and Methodology

We predict a change in the volatility-volume relation from pre-bid to post-bid as trading volume and volatility may be affected differently after a takeover announcement. The suspension of trading on target stocks specific to the Paris Bourse may lead to higher volume and lower volatility than on other markets. The inability to trade during the suspension period will lead to increased trading volume after the reopen of trading. However, trading suspension allows traders to collect and treat information about the offer which may lower volatility. Moreover, volatility will be higher for share-exchange offers than for cash offers.

The volatility-volume relation is estimated using a two step procedure similar to Jones et al (1994). We specify a two-equation model for the return and the conditional volatility of target stocks.

$$R_t = \alpha_0 + \sum_{k=1}^{5} \alpha_{1,k} R_{t-k} + \alpha_2 AN_t + \varepsilon_t \qquad (1)$$

where R_t is the return on day t, the lagged returns are used to estimate short term movements in conditional expected returns. The dummy variable AN is included to capture any spike in the return series that might occur on the announcement of the takeover. It is equal 1 for the announcement day and 0 otherwise. The residual ε_t is an estimate of the unexpected return on day t.

$$|\hat{\varepsilon}_t| = \gamma_0 + \sum_{k=1}^{5} \gamma_{1k} |\hat{\varepsilon}_{t-k}| + \gamma_2 V_t \cdot PRE_t + \gamma_3 V_t \cdot POST_t + \mu_t \qquad (2)$$

We then use the absolute value of the residuals estimated from Eq. (1) as the dependent variables in Eq. (2).

The absolute value of the residual ε_t constitutes our measure of the conditional volatility. The lagged values of $|\hat{\varepsilon}_t|$ are used to control for the persistence in volatility. V_t is the log of the trading volume on day t, PRE and POST are two dummy variables to refer to the pre-announcement period and the post-announcement period. PRE is equal 1 before the announcement day and 0 otherwise; POST is set to unity from the announcement day to the conclusion of the bid. These variables are included to examine whether there is a change in the volatility-volume relation after the takeover announcement.

In estimating our models, the pre-announcement period begins 250 days before the takeover announcement and ends at the market close the day before the announcement. The post-announcement period runs from the market open after the announcement to the formal conclusion of the bid. The regressions are run for each firm then the parameter estimates are averaged across firms. We estimate Eq. (1) and (2) using OLS as Jones et al (1994).[12] [13] [14]

5. Results

The model described in Eqs. (1) and (2) has been estimated for each of the 72 target stocks in our sample. The equations perform quite well, the R^2 statistics explain between 4% and 36% of the conditional volatility and the F statistic is significant at the 1% level for 92% of the equations estimated. Tables 2 and 3 summarize the important findings and report the means of the coefficient estimates.

Table 3 reports the average values of the announcement dummy coefficient obtained from the estimation of Eq. (1). Column 2 reports the proportion of each group for which the announcement dummy variable is

[12] We use White method to correct for heteroscedasticity.

[13] OLS estimation provides consistent but not efficient estimators of the parameters. However this does not pose inference problems as pointed out by Jones et al (1994).

[14] Chan & Fong (2000) and Naes & Skjeltorp (2006) use the same estimation method.

positive and statistically significant at the 10% level or better. The results confirm the excess returns obtained by target shareholders at the announcement of a takeover. The average excess return for the announcement day is 5.7% and it is significant at the 10% level or better for 64% of the sample. When delineating the sample by the mean of payment, the findings support previous research in that excess returns are higher for cash offers (6.6%) than for exchange-security offers (3.2%). The sign test confirms the positive excess returns (significant at the 1% level) for the total sample and for cash offers.

Table 3 – Announcement-day returns for takeover targets

	Average value α_2	Percent (+) significant	Sign test
Total	0,057	64	4.00*
Cash	0,066	65	3.81*
Share-exchange	0,032	61	1.41

The average value reported in the table is the cross-sectional average of the dummy coefficient α_2 in the return Eq. (1) estimated for 72 target stocks. The column 2 reports the percentage of the sample where the dummy coefficient is significantly positive. An asterisk means that the Signtest is statistically significant at the 1% level.

Table 4 documents the effect of takeover announcements on the volatility-volume relation. The volume effect in Eq. (2) is separated into its pre and post-bid components using the dummy variables PRE and POST. The results exhibit a standard volatility-volume relation documenting a positive relation between the conditional volatility and volume for both the pre-bid and the post-bid periods.

Looking at the total sample, we note a reduction after a takeover announcement in both the average value of the volume coefficient and the number of cases in which the volume is found to be significant. For the pre-bid period, the average value of the volume coefficient (γ_2) is 0.0046 and it is statistically significant at the 10% level or better in 79% of cases. The average value of (γ_3) is 0.0035 and it is significant in only 57% of the sample. The reduction of 24% is not significant at usual statistical significance levels using the parametric *t*-test. Using the non parametric

Mann-Whitney test which compares the medians of two independent samples, the reduction is significant at the 1% level. The post-announcement volume coefficients are thus different from pre-announcement coefficients.

For targets of cash offers, the average value of γ_3 is 0.001 and is 58% smaller than γ_2. The proportion of significant positive coefficients declines from 74% before the takeover announcement to 46% for the post-bid period. This represents a highly decline of the effect of volume on the conditional volatility of target stocks. The change in the relation between volume and volatility from pre-bid to post-bid is statistically significant at the 1% level using the Mann-Whitney test. Trading volume related to cash offers targets seems to explain less price changes during the bid period. Smith et *al* (1997) find a weak relationship between abnormal target firm volatility and relative market volume in the post-takeover period.[15] They explain this by the fact that the specific risk of a target becomes more important than systematic risk during the post takeover announcement period.

For share-exchange offers, the results do not show any change in the volatility-volume relation before and after a takeover announcement. The positive relation between volatility and volume holds for 94% of the sample before the announcement and for 89% of cases after with a value of 0.011 for both γ_2 and γ_3. In addition, we test if there is a difference between the post-bid volume coefficients (γ_3) for cash and share-exchange offers using the two tailed *t*-test. We find that the post-announcement volatility-volume relation is significantly different for cash and share-exchange bids (*p*-value=0.00). We document then a change in the volatility-volume relation especially for cash offers.

Hutson and Kearney (2001) note a positive relationship between volume and volatility for Australian takeover targets even when they delineate the sample by the outcome of the bid or the method of payment. Although they included the volume to explain the conditional volatility, they do not focus on the relation itself and they do not report the volume coefficients.

---

[15] They regress abnormal absolute returns on the abnormal market volume among other variables.

Table 4 – The volatility-volume relation for pre and post bid periods

	Pre-bid		*Post-bid*		Percent variation (p-value)	Mann-Whitney test
	Average value γ_2	Percent (+) significant	Average value γ_3	Percent (+) significant		
Total	0,0046	79	0,0035	57	-24 (0,23)	-2.40*
Cash	0,0024	74	0,0010	46	-58 (0,20)	-3.03*
Share-exchange	0,0113	94	0,0110	89	-3 (0,45)	-0.42

Notes: The pre-bid period runs from 250 days to 1 day before the takeover announcement. The post-bid period runs from the day of the announcement to the formal conclusion of the bid. The average value reported in the table is the cross-sectional average of the volume coefficients (γ_2 and γ_3) in the conditional volatility Eq. (2) estimated for 72 target stocks. Columns headed *percent (+) significant* report the percentage of the sample where the volume coefficients are significantly positive. Percent variation is the difference between pre and post-bid volume coefficients and p-values are given by the one-tailed t-test which tests if post-bid coefficients are lower than pre-bid ones. The last column reports values of Mann-Whitney test which tests if the samples of the coefficients γ_2 and γ_3 are different. An asterisk means that the difference is statistically significant at the 1% level.

To further explain the post-announcement change in the volatility-volume relation, we examine trading volume and conditional volatility after the takeover announcement.

Post-bid trading volume

Fig. 1 reports the evolution of targets' trading volume around takeover announcements (30 days before the announcement until the conclusion of the bid) for takeover bids delineated by the mean of payment, cash and security exchange bids delineated by the type of the offer "normal" and "simplified", respectively.[16] [17]

Fig. 1 shows an increase in the post bid trading volume for cash offers with the highest level at the announcement day. The trading volume is 26% higher after the takeover announcement than before but no significant variation is noted for share exchange bids (Table 1). The increase in trading volume after the takeover announcement is observed even when we separate cash offers into "normal" and "simplified" offers. The post-bid trading volume is significantly higher than the pre-bid using the one tailed *t*-test for "simplified" cash offers (OPAs) (p-value = 0.00) and for "normal" cash offers (OPA) (p-value = 0.07). The increase is more pronounced for OPAs because selling target shares occurs on the market during the bid period. However, no variation in trading volume is observed following the announcement of a share exchange bid neither for "normal" offers (OPE) nor for "simplified" offers (OPEs).

Looking at the full bid period, we observe a tendency to decrease the trading volume beginning the day following the announcement towards the conclusion date for cash bids. The post-bid level of trading volume does not reach the pre-bid level rapidly, it takes some days for OPA and no return to normal for OPAs is observed because shares are still sold on the market as the bid is open. Our results confirm the findings of Vandelnaoite (2002 a) on the French market for the period 1995-2000. She finds that the trading volume for the announcement day increased and the increase is more pronounced for cash offers than for share-exchange offers. A decrease in the trading activity is observed thereafter (lasting 6 days) confirming the progressive return to a normal level of activity.

---

[16] See section 3.1 for definitions of the two types of offers.

[17] The post-bid period varies considerably across offers.

Figure.1: Average trading volume across takeover targets

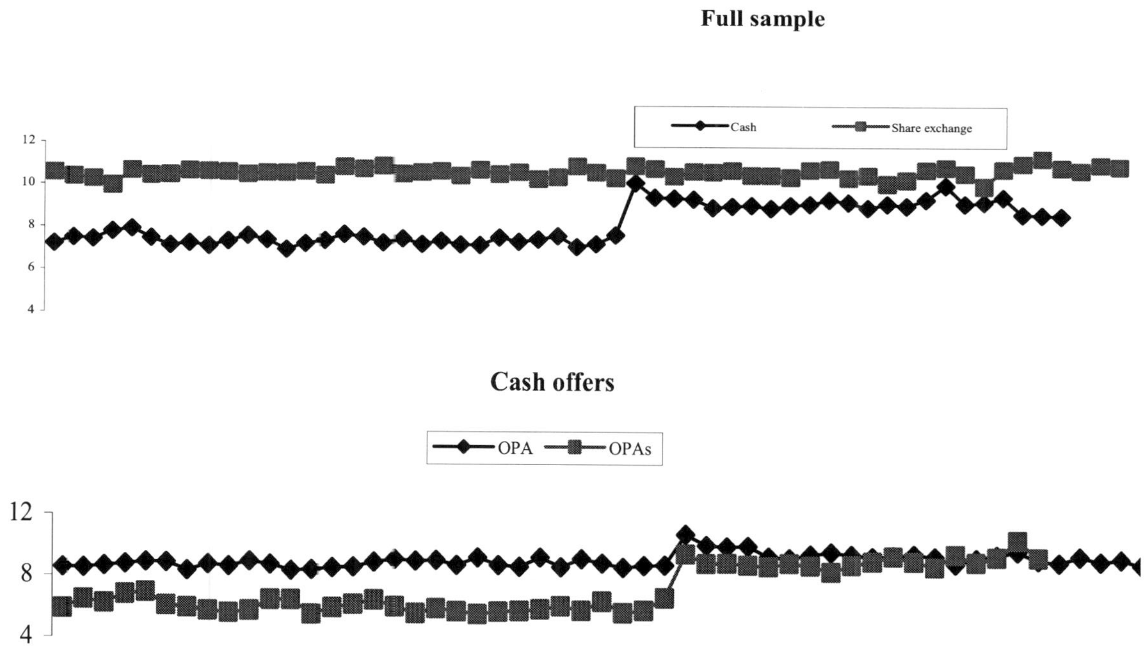

Share exchange offers

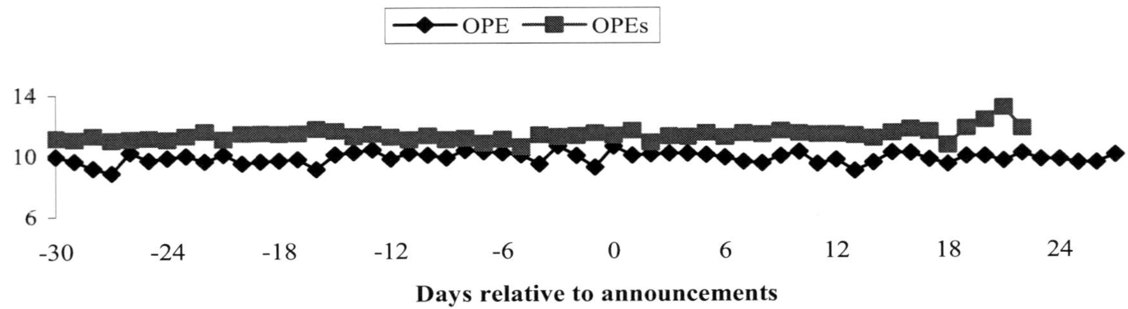

Notes: Average trading volume is computed for each trading day from 30 days before the announcement to the formal conclusion of the bid. OPA (OPAs) and OPE (OPEs) refer to normal (simplified) cash and share exchange offers respectively.

Hutson (2000) finds that trading in Australian targets tends to decline as the conclusion of the bid approaches.

The high increase in trading volume just after the cash takeover announcement is predictable since investors are eager to trade on target stocks after waiting for one week trading suspension in average, especially after the target stock price proposed by the acquirer becomes known to the public. This trading activity can be either for speculative or portfolio management purposes. It can be also related partly to dispersion in traders' beliefs about the fundamental stock value of the target. Hutson (2000) argues that dispersion in traders' beliefs drives speculative trading activity. The decrease observed thereafter may be explained by a decrease in information asymmetry as the bid progresses. Several studies give evidence of low information asymmetry after takeover announcements. Vandelanoite (2002 b) examines changes in information asymmetry on French target firms value around takeover announcements through the adverse selection component of the bid-ask spread. The author finds that adverse selection costs decrease after the takeover announcement confirming the reduction of information asymmetry about target's value.[18]

Post bid conditional volatility

Fig. 2 reports the conditional volatility of target stocks (absolute residuals of Eq. (1)) around the takeover announcement from 30 days before the announcement until the conclusion of the bid, for cash and share-exchange offers, respectively.

For cash offers, the mean conditional volatility is slightly lower for the post-bid period than pre-bid (p-value = 0.11). The reduction in volatility is pronounced for cash offers towards the conclusion of the bid. However, for share-exchange offers, we do not observe a change in the mean conditional volatility (p-value = 0.29). Moreover, Fig. 2 shows a high target stock volatility around the announcement for share-exchange than for cash offers.

---

[18] Conrad and Niden (1992) and Draper and Paudyal (1999) observe also a reduction in the bid-ask spread after takeover announcements. Jennings (1994) finds that the bid-ask spread of target firm shares is abnormally high immediately following the takeover announcement but falls rapidly thereafter.

Figure 2. Conditional target stocks volatility

Cash offers

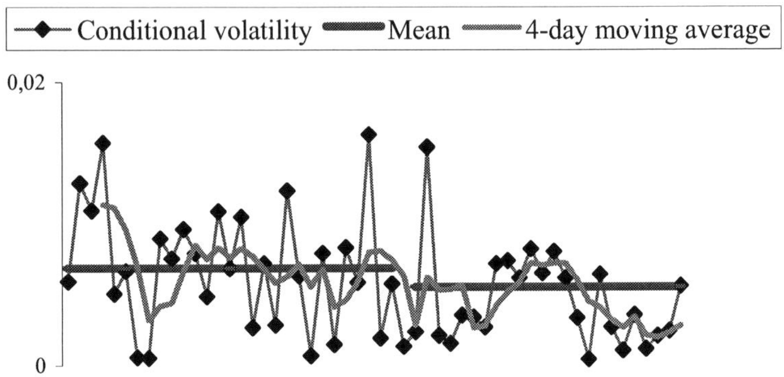

Share-exchange offers

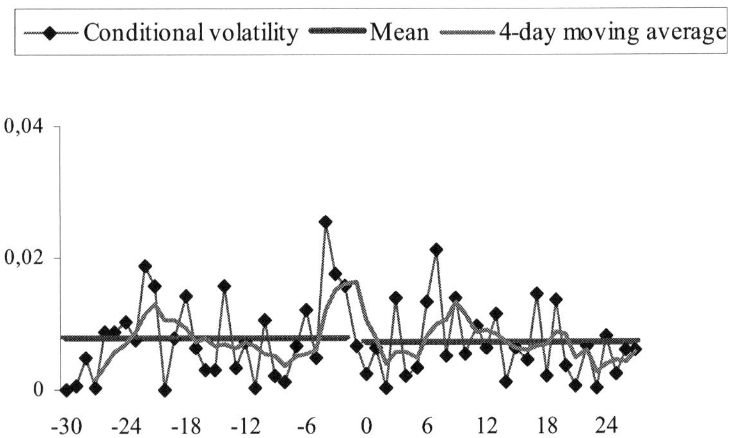

Notes: Conditional volatility is computed across targets for each trading day beginning 30 days before the announcement until the formal conclusion of the bid.

To examine if the change in volatility is significant from pre-bid to post-bid period, we regress the absolute residuals of Eq.(1) on a dummy variable POST to examine whether there is a post announcement change in the conditional price volatility of target stocks and on lagged values of $|\hat{\varepsilon}_t|$ to control for the persistence in volatility.

Table 5 reports the results for the effect of a takeover announcement on conditional volatility. The dummy coefficient of volatility for the post-bid period is negative and statistically significant at the 10% level or better in 71% of cases for the total sample. For cash bids, volatility decreases in average by 0.,4% and this slight decrease is significant in 76% of cases. For share exchange offers, the average reduction in volatility is lower than for cash offers and is significant only in 55% of the sample.

Table 5 – Post-bid volatility

	Average value λ_2	Percent (-) significant
Total	-0,0038	71
Cash	-0,0040	76
Share-exchange	-0,0033	55

$|\hat{\varepsilon}_t|$ is the absolute value of the residual obtained from the estimation of Eq. (1). The post-bid period runs from the day of the announcement to the formal conclusion of the bid. The average values reported are the cross-sectional averages of the post-bid dummy variable (λ_2). The last column reports the percentage of the sample where the post-bid dummy coefficients are significantly negative.

This result supports the findings of Hutson and Kearney (2001) and Smith et *al* (1997). Hutson and Kearney (2001) find that the reduction in volatility of Australian target stocks is smaller for share-exchange bids than for cash bids. In addition, the reduction is found to be significant for 71% of cash offers and only for 31% of share-exchange offers. Smith et *al* (1997) find that share exchange offers produce greater target firm stock unconditional volatility than cash offers for the Toronto stock exchange.

They argue that volatility is higher for share-exchange bids because the payoff involving bidder shares is uncertain. [19]

A decrease in volatility is generally interpreted as a reduction in the dispersion of traders' beliefs regarding target's stock value. As the bid progresses, the outcome of the offer becomes more apparent. There is a convergence of opinions about the target stock value which is determined largely by the market's assessment of the likelihood of success of the takeover bid. Especially for the French market, investors have a period of some days to analyse the news during the suspension of trading on the target stocks but even after the reopening of trading, the agents may have different opinions regarding the target value, the probability of takeover success and other variables This may explain that we have find a slight reduction in volatility over the bid period.

The changes observed for volume and volatility after the takeover announcement enlighten the post-bid volatility-volume relation. The relation is stable for share-exchange bids, post-bid volume and volatility do not change significantly from pre-announcement levels. However for cash offers, the post-bid volatility-volume relation has changed considerably from pre-bid relation. We have observed a tendency to decrease over the bid period for trading volume and conditional volatility but the effect of volume on conditional volatility is found to be weaker after the announcement. Cash offers targets experience then a change in their price formation process from pre-announcement to post-announcement. The weak effect of volume on price changes after the announcement denotes that post-announcement volume does not affect prices because it does not convey the arrival of new information. Price variations observed are then the result of prices' correction in order to converge to the fundamental stock value of the target.

Our findings for the effect of takeover announcements on the volatility-volume relation corroborates the argument of Smith et al (1997) that takeover announcements may lead to different levels of volatility and volume depending on the information they conveyed and how traders interpret this information. In addition, Karpoff (1987) argues that the price-volume relation depends on the rate of information flow to the market.

---

[19] For share-exchange offers, the bid price varies with the bidder's share price.

6. Conclusion

This paper examines the volatility-volume relation for French takeover targets around the announcement of the bid. Although there is strong evidence that the volatility-volume relation is positive, previous work does not examine this relation for the corporate control market. We explore the relation before and after the announcement of the takeover by separating the volume effect on conditional volatility into its pre and post-announcement components. Moreover, we check if the relation depends on the mean of payment.

We find support of the mixture of distributions model as our results show a positive relation between volatility and volume for both pre and post-bid period. When delineating the sample by the mean of payment, we find that the relation is stable for share-exchange offers but it changes for cash offers from pre-announcement to post-announcement period. There is a weak evidence of a significant positive relation for cash offers and the effect of volume on conditional volatility is found to be lower after a takeover announcement. Moreover, the post-announcement relation for cash offers and share-exchange offers is significantly different.

A closer look to trading volume and conditional volatility before and after the takeover announcement shows that the change in the relation is explained by the volatility and volume behaviour after the announcement. We find a significant high level of trading volume after the announcement of cash offers which declines thereafter and a slight decrease in the post conditional volatility. Information revealed by the announcement lead thus to different levels of volatility and volume depending on how traders interpret this information.

Future research on the issue must examine the volatility-volume relation for other markets to check if institutional features of the corporate control market such as trading suspension on target stocks or microstructure features i.e. how information is conveyed to the market via the announcement of the offer have impact on this relation since they are different across markets.

References

Admati, A. R. and P. Pfleiderer (1988), A theory of intraday Patterns: volume and price variability, *The Review of Financial Studies,* 1, 3-40.

Ascioglu, N. A., T. H. McInish and R. A. Wood (2002), Merger announcements and trading, *The Journal of Financial Research,* 25, 263-278.

Chan, K. and W. M. Fong (2000), Trade size, order imbalance and the volatility-volume relation, *Journal of Financial Economics,* 57, 247-273.

Clark, P. K. (1973), A subordinated stochastic process model with finite variance for speculative prices, *Econometrica,* 41, 135-155.

Conrad J. and C. Niden (1992), Order flow, trading costs and corporate acquisition announcements, *Financial Management*, winter, 22-31.

Draper P. and K. Paudyal (1999), Corporate takeovers: mode of payment, returns and trading activity, *Journal of business, Finance and Accounting,* 26 (5-6), 521-558.

Epps, T. W. and M. L. Epps (1976), The stochastic dependence of security price changes and transaction volumes: implications for the mixture of distributions hypothesis, *Econometrica,* 44, 305-321.

Foster, F. D. and S. Viswanathan (1993), The effect of public information and competition on trading volume and price volatility, *Review of Financial Studies,* 6, 23-56.

Gao, Y and D. Oler (2004), Trading in target stocks before takeover announcements, Working paper.

Harris, M. and A. Raviv (1993), Differences of opinion make a horse race, *The review of financial studies,* 6, 473-506.

Hutson, E. (2000), Takeover targets and the probability of bid success: evidence from the Australian market, *International Review of Financial Analysis,* 9, 45-65.

Hutson, E. and C. Kearney (2001), Volatility in stocks subject to takeover bids: Australian evidence using daily data, *Journal of Empirical Finance,* 8, 273-296.

Jarrell, G. and A. Poulsen (1989), Stock trading before the announcement of tender offers: insider trading or market anticipation?, *Journal of Law, Economics and Organizations,* 5, 223-248.

Jennings, R. H. (1994), Intraday changes in target firms' share price and bid-ask quotes around takeover announcements, *The Journal of Financial Research,* 17, 255-270.

Jensen, M. and R. S. Ruback (1983), The market for corporate control: the scientific evidence, *Journal of Financial Economics,* 11, 5-50.

Jones, C. M., G. Kaul and L. M. Lipson (1994), Transactions, volume and volatility, *The Review of Financial Studies,* 7, 631-651.

Karpoff, J. (1987), The relation between price changes and trading volume: a survey, *Journal of Financial and Quantitative Analysis,* 22, 109-126.

Keown A. J. and J. M. Pinkerton (1981), Merger announcements and insider trading activity: an empirical investigation, *Journal of Finance,* 36, 855-869.

Lee, C. M. C., M. J. Ready and P. J. Seguin (1994), Volume, volatility and New York Stock Exchange trading halts, *Journal of Finance,* 49, 183-214.

Murray, P.G. (1994), Pre-announcement share price run-ups and abnormal trading volume in takeover target's shares: a test of the market speculation hypothesis, *Pacific-Basin Finance Journal,* 2, 319-348.

Naes, R. and J. A. Skjeltorp (2006), Order book characteristics and the volume-volatility relation: empirical evidence from a limit order market, *Journal of Financial Markets,* 9, 408-432.

Shalen, C. T. (1993), Volume, volatility and the dispersion of beliefs, *The review of Financial Studies,* 6, 405-434.

Smith, B. F., R. White, M. Robinson and R. Nason (1997), Intraday volatility and trading volume after takeover announcements, *Journal of Banking and Finance,* 21, 337-368.

Tauchen, G. E. and M. Pitts (1983), The price variability-volume relationship in speculative markets, *Econometrica,* 51, 485-505.

Vandelanoite S. (2002a), Les modalités de transmission et d'incorporation de l'information sur les marchés financiers, PHD thesis – Université Paris-I, La Sorbonne.

—. (2002b), Takeover announcements and the components of the bid-ask spread, Working paper n° 02-079 – Université Paris I, La Sorbonne.

Acknowledgments

I thank anonymous referees for helpful comments. The opinions and findings and errors of this paper are those of the author.

CHAPTER THIRTEEN

WHAT "HIDES" BEHIND SOVEREIGN DEBT RATINGS?

ANTÓNIO AFONSO, PEDRO GOMES
AND PHLIPP ROTHER

Abstract

In this paper we study the determinants of sovereign debt credit ratings using rating notations from the three main international rating agencies, for the period 1995-2005. Using linear methods and ordered response models we employ a new specification that allows us to distinguish between short and long-run effects, on a country's rating, of several macroeconomic and public governance explanatory variables. Our results point to a good performance of the estimated models, across agencies and across the time dimension, as well as a good overall prediction power. Relevant explanatory variables for a country's credit rating are: GDP per capita, GDP growth, government debt, government effectiveness indicators, external debt, external reserves and default history.

Keywords: credit ratings; sovereign debt; rating agencies; panel data; random effects ordered probit

1. Introduction

Sovereign credit ratings are a condensed assessment of a government's ability and willingness to repay its public debt both in principal and in interests on time. In this, they are forward-looking qualitative measures of the probability of default put forward by rating agencies. Naturally, one should try to understand the determinants of credit ratings, given its relevance for international financial markets, economic agents and governments. Indeed, sovereign credit ratings are important in three ways.

First, sovereign ratings are a key determinant of the interest rates a country faces in the international financial market and therefore of its borrowing costs. Second, the sovereign rating may have a constraining impact on the ratings assigned to domestic banks or companies. Third, some institutional investors have lower bounds for the risk they can assume in their investments and they will choose their bond portfolio composition taking into account the credit risk perceived via the rating notations. For instance, the European Central Bank when conducting open market operations can only take as collateral bonds that have at least a single A rating attributed by at least one rating agency.

In this paper we perform an empirical analysis of foreign currency sovereign debt ratings, using rating data from the three main international rating agencies: Fitch Ratings, Moody's, and Standard & Poor's. We have compiled a comprehensive panel data set on sovereign debt ratings, macroeconomic data, and qualitative variables for a wide range of countries starting in 1990. In this context, the use of panel data is appealing because it allows examining not only how the agencies attribute a rating, but also how they decide on upgrades and downgrades.

Our main contributions to the existing literature are the discussion on the econometric issues and the innovation in both the method and in the specification used. Indeed, the fact that a country's rating does not have much variation across time raises some econometric problems. While fixed effects type of specification is uninformative as the country dummy captures the average rating, a random effects specification will also be inadequate due to the correlation between the country specific error and the regressors. We salvage the random effects approach by means of modelling the country specific error, which in practical terms implies adding time-averages of the explanatory variables as additional time-invariant regressors. This setting will allow us to make the constructive distinction between short or long-run effects of a variable on the sovereign rating.

Regarding the empirical modelling strategy, we follow the two main strands in the literature. We make use of linear regression methods on a linear transformation of the ratings and we also estimate our specifications using both ordered probit and random effects ordered probit methods. The latter is the best procedure for panel data as it considers the existence of an additional normally distributed cross-section error. This approach allows both to determine the cut-off points throughout the rating scale as well as to test whether a linear quantitative transformation of the ratings is, in fact, a good approximation. Furthermore, we perform robustness check by allowing for a sub-period analysis and for a differentiated high and low rating analysis.

The results show that in particular six core macroeconomic variables have a consistent impact on sovereign ratings. These are the level of GDP per capita, real GDP growth, the public debt level and government effectiveness, as well as the level of external debt and external reserves. A dummy reflecting past sovereign defaults is also found significant as well as, in most cases, the fiscal balance. It is noteworthy that fiscal variables turn out to be more important than found in the previous literature.

The paper is organised as follows. In Section Two we give an overview of the rating systems and review the relevant related literature. Section Three explains our methodological choices, specifically regarding the econometric approaches employed. In Section Four we report on the empirical analysis, notably in terms of the estimation and prediction results. Section Five summarises the paper's main findings.

2. Rating systems and literature

2.1. Overview of rating systems

We use sovereign credit ratings by the three main international rating agencies, Moody's, Standard & Poor's (S&P) and Fitch Ratings. Although these agencies do not use the same qualitative codes, in general, there is a correspondence between each agency rating level as shown in Table 1.

Table 1 – S&P, Moody's and Fitch rating systems and linear transformations

Characterization of debt and issuer (source: Moody's)		Rating			Linear	
		S&P	Moody's	Fitch	Scale 21	Scale 17
Highest quality		AAA	Aaa	AAA	21	17
High quality	Investment grade	AA+	Aa1	AA+	20	16
		AA	Aa2	AA	19	15
		AA-	Aa3	AA-	18	14
Strong payment capacity		A+	A1	A+	17	13
		A	A2	A	16	12
		A-	A3	A-	15	11
Adequate payment capacity		BBB+	Baa1	BBB+	14	10
		BBB	Baa2	BBB	13	9
		BBB-	Baa3	BBB-	12	8
Likely to fulfil obligations, ongoing uncertainty	Speculative grade	BB+	Ba1	BB+	11	7
		BB	Ba2	BB	10	6
		BB-	Ba3	BB-	9	5
High credit risk		B+	B1	B+	8	4
		B	B2	B	7	3
		B-	B3	B-	6	2
Very high credit risk		CCC+	Caa1	CCC+	5	
		CCC	Caa2	CCC	4	
		CCC-	Caa3	CCC-	3	
Near default with possibility of recovery		CC	Ca	CC		
				C	2	
Default		SD	C	DDD		1
		D		DD	1	
				D		

We build a ratings database with sovereign foreign currency rating attributed by the three above-mentioned main rating agencies. For the rating notations we covered a period from 1970 to 2005. The rating of a particular year is the rating that was attributed at 31st of December of that year. In 2005 there are 130 countries with a rating, though only 78 have a rating attributed by all three agencies.

2.2. Literature review

Sovereign ratings are assessments of the relative likelihood of default. The rating agencies assess the risk of default by analysing a wide range of elements from solvency factors that affect the capacity to repay the debt, but also socio-political factors that might affect the willingness to pay of the borrower.

A first study on the determinants of sovereign ratings by Cantor and Packer (1996) concluded that the ratings can be largely explained by a small set of variables namely: per capita income, GDP growth, inflation, external debt, level of economic development, and default history. Further studies incorporated more variables, for instance, macroeconomic performance variables like the unemployment rate or the investment-to-GDP ratio. In papers focussing on the study of currency crises several external indicators such as foreign reserves, current account balance, exports or terms of trade seem to play an important role. Moreover, indicators of how the government conducts its fiscal policy, budget balance and government debt can also be relevant, as well as variables that assess political risk, like corruption or social indexes.

Regarding the econometric approach, there are two major strands in the literature. The first uses linear regression methods on a numerical representation of the ratings. The early study by Cantor and Packer, applies OLS regressions to a linear representation of the ratings, on a cross section of 45 countries. This methodology was also pursued by Afonso (2003), Alexe et al. (2003) and Butler and Fauver (2006), while Mellios and Paget-Blanc (2006) use principal component analysis. Using OLS analysis on a numerical representation of the ratings is quite simple and allows for a straightforward generalization to panel data by doing fixed or random effects estimation (Monfort and Mulder, 2000; Eliasson, 2002).

Although estimating the determinants of ratings using these approaches has in general a good fit and a good predictive power it faces some critiques. As ratings are a qualitative ordinal measure, using traditional estimation techniques on a linear representation of the ratings is not the most adequate framework of estimation. First, it implies the assumption that the difference between two rating categories is equal for any two adjacent categories, which would need to be tested. Furthermore, even if this assumption was true, because of the presence of elements in the top and bottom category, the estimates are biased, even in big samples. Nevertheless, Eliasson (2002) argues that given the existence of many categories one can treat the rating variable as continuous and to overcome the criticism of the assumption of an even distance between steps, it is possible to use different quantitative transformations. For instance, Reisen and Maltzan (1999) apply a logistic transformation of the ratings and Afonso (2003) applies both a logistic and an exponential transformation of the ratings. In that case, the differences between categories are not constant, but are still imposed *a priori*.

The other strand of the literature uses ordered response models. These methods will themselves determine the size of the differences between each category. For example, this procedure was used by Hu et al. (2002), Bissoondoyal-Bheenick (2005) and Bissoondoyal-Bheenick et al. (2006). Although this should be considered the preferred estimation procedure it is not entirely satisfying. The crucial point is that the ordered probit asymptotic properties do not generalise for a small sample, so if we estimate the determinants of the ratings using a cross-section of countries, we would have too few observations. It is therefore imperative to try to maximize the number of observation by using panel data, but when doing so, one has to be careful. Indeed, the generalization of ordered probit to panel data is not completely straightforward, due to the existence of a country specific effect. Furthermore, within this framework, the need to have many observations makes it harder to perform robustness analysis by, for instance, partitioning the sample.

3. Methodology

Using a linear scale we grouped the ratings in 17 categories, by putting together in the same bucket the few observations below B-, given that the bottom rating categories have very few observations (see Table 1).

3.1. Explanatory variables

Building on the evidence provided by the existing literature, we identify a set of main macroeconomic and qualitative variables that may determine sovereign ratings.

GDP per capita – positive impact on rating: more developed economies are expected to have more stable institutions to prevent government over-borrowing and to be less vulnerable to exogenous shocks.
Real GDP growth – positive impact: higher real growth strengthens the government's ability to repay outstanding obligations.

Inflation – uncertain impact: on the one hand, it reduces the real stock of outstanding government debt in domestic currency, leaving overall more resources for the coverage of foreign debt obligations. On the other hand, it is symptomatic of problems at the macroeconomic policy level, especially if caused by monetary financing of deficits.

Unemployment – negative impact: a country with lower unemployment tends to have more flexible labour markets making it less vulnerable to changes in the economic environment. In addition, lower unemployment reduces the fiscal burden of unemployment and social benefits while broadening the base for labour taxation.

Government debt – negative impact: a higher stock of outstanding government debt implies a higher interest burden and should correspond to a higher risk of default.
Fiscal balance – positive impact: large fiscal deficits absorb domestic savings and also suggest macroeconomic disequilibria, negatively affecting the rating level. Persistent deficits may signal problems with the institutional environment for policy makers.
Government effectiveness – positive impact: high quality of public service delivery and competence of bureaucracy should impinge positively of the ability to service debt obligations.

External debt – negative impact: the higher the overall economy's external indebtedness, the higher becomes the risk for additional fiscal burdens, either directly due to a sell-off of foreign government debt or indirectly due to the need to support over-indebted domestic borrowers.
Foreign reserves – positive impact: higher (official) foreign reserves should shield the government from having to default on its foreign currency obligations.
Current account balance – uncertain impact: a higher current account deficit could signal an economy's tendency to over-consume, undermining long-term sustainability. Alternatively, it could reflect rapid accumulation of fixed investment, which should lead to higher growth and improved sustainability over the medium term.

Default history – negative impact: past sovereign defaults may indicate a great acceptance of reducing the outstanding debt burden via a default. The effect is modelled by a dummy variable indicating the past occurrence of a default and by a variable measuring the number of years since the last default. This variable measures the recovery of credibility after a default and can be expected to influence positively the rating score.

3.2. Linear regression framework

A possible starting point for our linear panel model would follow Monfort and Mulder (2000), Eliasson (2002), generalizing a cross section specification to panel data,

$$R_{it} = \beta X_{it} + \lambda Z_i + a_i + \mu_{it}, \quad (1)$$

where we have: R – quantitative variable, obtained by a linear or by a non-linear transformation; X_{it} is a vector containing time varying variables that includes the time-varying explanatory variables described above and Z_i is a vector of time invariant variables that include regional dummies.

In (1) the index i (i=1,…,N) denotes the country, the index t (t=1,…,T) indicates the period and a_i stands for the individual effects for each country i (that can either be modelled as a error term or as N dummies to be estimated). Additionally, it is assumed that the disturbances μ_{it} are independent across countries and across time.

There are three ways to estimate this equation: pooled OLS, fixed effects or random effects estimation. In *standard conditions* all estimators are consistent and the ranking of the three methods in terms of efficiency is clear: a random effects approach is preferable to the fixed effects, which is preferable to pooled OLS. What we mean by *standard conditions* is whether or not the country specific error is uncorrelated with the regressors $E(a_i| X_{it}, Z_i)$=0. If this is the case one should opt for the random effects estimation, while if this condition does not hold, both the pooled OLS and the random effects estimation give inconsistent estimates and fixed effects estimation is preferable.

In our case, it seems more natural that the country specific effect is correlated with the regressors.[1] Given this scenario one should be tempted to say that the "fixed effects estimation" is the best strategy, but that has a problem. Because there is not much variation of a countries rating over time, the country dummies included in the regression will capture the country's average rating, while all the other variables will only capture

[1] This idea can easily be checked by doing some exploratory regressions. We estimated equation (1) using random effects and performed the Hausman test; the Qui-Square statistisc was in fact very high, and the null hypothesis of no correlation was rejected with p-values of 0.000.

movements in the ratings across time. This means that, although statistically correct, a regression by fixed effects would be seriously striped of meaning.

There are two ways of rescuing a random effects approach under correlation between the country specific error and the regressors. One is to do the Hausman-Taylor IV estimation but for that we would have to come up with possible instruments that are not correlated with a_i, which does not seem an easy task. In this paper we will opt for a different approach that consists on modelling the error term a_i. This approach, described in Wooldridge (2002), is usually applied when estimating non-linear models, as IV estimation proves to be a Herculean task but, as we shall see, the application to our case is quite successful. The idea is to give an explicit expression for the correlation between the error and the regressors, stating that the expected value of the country specific error is a linear combination of time-averages of the regressors $\overline{X}_i$. This follows Hajivassiliou and Ioannides (2007) and Hajivassiliou (2006).

$$E(a_i \mid X_{it}, Z_i) = \eta \overline{X}_i . \quad (2)$$

If we modify our initial equation (1), with $a_i = \eta \overline{X}_t + \varepsilon_i$ we get

$$R_{it} = \beta X_{it} + \lambda Z_i + \eta \overline{\mathrm{X}}_\mathrm{i} + \varepsilon_i + \mu_{it} , \quad (3)$$

where ε_i is an error term by definition uncorrelated with the regressors. In practical terms, we eliminate the problem by including a time-average of the explanatory variables as additional time-invariant regressors. We can rewrite (3) as:

$$R_{it} = \beta(X_{it} - \overline{\mathrm{X}}_i) + (\eta + \beta)\overline{\mathrm{X}}_i + \lambda Z_i + \varepsilon_i + \mu_{it} . \quad (4)$$

This expression is quite intuitive. $\delta = \eta + \beta$ can be interpreted as a long-term effect (e. g. if a country has a permanent high inflation what is the respective effect on the rating), while β is a short-term effect (e. g. if a country manages to reduce inflation this year by one point what would be the effect in the rating). This intuitive distinction is useful for policy purposes as it can tell what a country can do to improve its rating in the short to medium-term. We will estimate equation (4) considering random effects, but we also estimate the fixed effects version and a simple OLS. The way we modelled the error term can be considered successful if the coefficients of $\overline{X}_i$ are significant and if the Hausman test indicates no correlation between the regressors and the new error term.

3.3. Ordered response framework

Alternatively we estimate the determinants of sovereign debt ratings in a limited dependent variable framework. As we mentioned before, the ordered probit is a natural approach for this type of problem, because the rating is a discrete variable and reflects an order in terms of probability of default. The setting is the following. Each rating agency makes a continuous evaluation of a country's credit-worthiness, embodied in an unobserved latent variable R^*. This latent variable has a linear form and depends on the same set of variables as before,

$$R^*_{it} = \beta(X_{it} - \overline{X}_i) + \delta\overline{X}_i + \lambda Z_i + \varepsilon_i + \mu_{it}\,. \qquad (5)$$

Because there is a limited number of rating categories, the rating agencies will have several cut-off points that draw up the boundaries of each rating category. The final rating will then be given by

$$R_{it} = \begin{cases} AAA\ (Aaa) & if \quad R^*_{it} > c_{16} \\ AA+\ (Aa1) & if \quad c_{16} > R^*_{it} > c_{15} \\ AA\ (Aa2) & if \quad c_{15} > R^*_{it} > c_{14} \\ \vdots & \\ < CCC+(Caa1) & if \quad c_1 > R^*_{it} \end{cases} \qquad (6)$$

The parameters of equation (5) and (6), notably β, δ, λ and the cut-off points c_1 to c_{16} are estimated using maximum likelihood. Since we are working in a panel data setting, the generalization of ordered probit is not straightforward, because instead of having one error term, we now have two. Wooldridge (2002) describes two approaches to estimate this model. One "quick and dirty" possibility is to assume we only have one error term that is serially correlated within countries. Under that assumption one can do the ordered probit estimation ignoring the additional error term, but a robust variance-covariance matrix estimator is needed to account for the serial correlation. The second possibility is the random effects ordered probit model, which considers both errors ε_i and μ_{it} to be normally distributed, and the maximization of the log-likelihood is done accordingly. This second approach should be considered the best one, but it has as a drawback the quite cumbersome calculations involved. In STATA this procedure was created by Rabe-Hesketh et al. (2000) and substantially improved by Frechette (2001a, 2001b), and we will use such procedures in our calculations.

4. Empirical analysis

4.1. Data

Regarding the rating data we use the sovereign foreign currency rating attributed by the three main rating agencies and given overall data availability we cover the period from 1995 to 2005. The rating of a particular year is the rating that was attributed at 31st of December of that year.[2] The variables inflation, unemployment, GDP growth, fiscal balance and current account entered as a 3-year average, reflecting the agencies' approach to take out the effect of the business cycle when deciding on a sovereign rating. The external debt variable was taken from the World Bank and is only available for non-industrial countries, so for industrial countries it was attributed the value 0, which is equivalent to having a multiplicative dummy. As for the dummy variable for European Union, we consider that the rating agencies anticipated the EU accession. Thus we tested the contemporaneous variable as well as up to three leads. We find that for Moody's and S&P the variable enters with two leads, while for Fitch we find no anticipation of EU accession.[3]

4.2. Linear panel results

Full sample

The results generated by the panel regressions point to broadly similar regression models across the three rating agencies (see Table 2). In view of the analytical considerations above the discussion will focus on the random effects estimations. This is supported by the Hausmann tests

---

[2] The full historical rating dataset that we compiled, including foreign and local currency ratings as well as credit rating outlooks, is available from the authors on request.

[3] See Afonso et al. (2007) for a full list of variables used in the estimations as well as their specification and data sources, notably IMF World Economic Outlook, World Bank Aggregate Governance Indicator and Jaimovich, Panizza (2006) for government debt.

reported at the end of each table pointing to the acceptability of the random effects approach, and pooled OLS results are not reported here.

Table 2 – Random effects estimation

	Moody's		S&P		Fitch	
	(1)	(2)	(3)	(4)	(5)	(6)
Constant	3.431	8.291	4.347	7.421***	4.409	7.179***
	(0.95)	*(12.49)*	*(1.25)*	*(15.11)*	*(1.19)*	*(13.16)*
GDP per capita	1.779***	1.789***	1.411***	1.403***	1.697***	1.667***
	(7.61)	*(8.03)*	*(7.12)*	*(7.67)*	*(8.83)*	*(9.51)*
GDP per capita Avg.	0.650		0.450		0.375	
	(1.46)		*(1.05)*		*(0.87)*	
GDP growth	8.643***	8.768***	8.125***	8.256***	3.385	4.110*
	(3.07)	*(3.26)*	*(3.50)*	*(3.72)*	*(1.39)*	*(1.74)*
GDP growth Avg.	5.237		-1.907		3.220	
	(0.46)		*(-0.20)*		*(0.26)*	
Unemployment	0.014		0.055**	0.056***	0.017	
	(0.52)		*(2.53)*	*(2.73)*	*(0.61)*	
Unemployment Avg.	-0.072*	-0.073*	-0.018		0.027	
	(-1.78)	*(-1.70)*	*(-0.45)*		*(0.50)*	
Inflation	-0.124*	-0.145**	-0.235***	-0.229***	-0.107	
	(-1.79)	*(-2.11)*	*(-6.17)*	*(-6.13)*	*(-1.24)*	
Inflation Avg.	-0.360*	-0.347**	-0.427***	-0.353**	-0.150	
	(-1.84)	*(-2.00)*	*(-2.65)*	*(-2.44)*	*(-0.66)*	
Gov Debt	-0.014**	-0.014**	-0.033***	-0.033***	-0.022***	-0.027***
	(-2.38)	*(-2.53)*	*(-6.61)*	*(-7.22)*	*(-3.82)*	*(-7.30)*
Gov Debt Avg.	-0.011	-0.014**	-0.010	-0.012**	-0.007	
	(-1.49)	*(-2.24)*	*(-1.34)*	*(-1.97)*	*(-0.69)*	
Gov Balance	7.740***	6.991***	4.387**	4.411**	4.371	
	(2.77)	*(2.54)*	*(1.97)*	*(2.01)*	*(1.37)*	
Gov Balance Avg.	7.893		5.144		5.220	
	(0.80)		*(0.59)*		*(0.69)*	
Gov Effectiveness	0.242		0.370**	0.362**	0.787***	0.887***
	(1.18)		*(2.36)*	*(2.47)*	*(4.54)*	*(5.34)*
Gov Effectiveness Avg.	1.906***	2.470***	2.370***	2.758***	2.155***	2.741***
	(4.06)	*(6.80)*	*(4.91)*	*(7.75)*	*(4.23)*	*(7.47)*
External Debt	-0.004*	-0.004*	-0.003*	-0.003	-0.005***	-0.005***
	(-1.79)	*(-1.95)*	*(-1.68)*	*(-1.51)*	*(-2.97)*	*(-2.76)*
External Debt Avg.	-0.004**	-0.004**	-0.006*	-0.007**	-0.010**	-0.011***
	(-2.20)	*(-2.47)*	*(-1.81)*	*(-2.18)*	*(-2.53)*	*(-3.34)*
Current Account	-7.246***	-8.760***	-3.700**	-3.586**	-3.137	
	(-3.67)	*(-4.84)*	*(-2.18)*	*(-2.18)*	*(-1.16)*	
Current Account Avg.	-3.321		0.123		2.955	
	(-0.78)		*(0.03)*		*(0.63)*	
Reserves	1.423**	1.710***	0.064		-0.100	
	(3.63)	*(4.61)*	*(0.19)*		*(-0.23)*	

Table 2 – Random effects estimation (continued).

Reserves Avg.	1.475	1.254	1.909**	1.988**	3.090***	2.987***
	(1.60)	*(1.43)*	*(2.06)*	*(2.28)*	*(3.59)*	*(3.78)*
Def 1	-1.998***	-2.075***	-1.307***	-1.337***	-1.523***	-1.331***
	(-6.87)	*(-8.11)*	*(-5.23)*	*(-6.74)*	*(-4.13)*	*(-4.60)*
Def 2	-0.015		-0.018		0.075	
	(-0.32)		*(-0.33)*		*(1.15)*	
EU (2)	1.598***	1.650***	0.415**	0.418**	0.507**	0.554**
	(6.63)	*(6.69)*	*(2.41)*	*(2.48)*	*(2.03)*	*(2.40)*
IND	2.289***	3.157***	2.831***	3.438***	2.781***	2.634***
	(2.89)	*(4.61)*	*(3.03)*	*(4.69)*	*(2.61)*	*(3.55)*
LAC	-0.903*		-0.459		-0.718	
	(-1.93)		*(-0.94)*		*(-1.29)*	
R^2	0.945	0.940	0.948	0.946	0.947	0.944
Countries	66	66	65	65	58	58
Observations	551	557	564	565	480	481
Hausman Test $	21.93 (0.06)	14.30 (0.160)	16.77 (0.210)	10.73 (0.467)	12.68 (0.473)	3.68 (0.816)

Notes: White diagonal standard errors & covariance (d.f. corrected). The t statistics are in parentheses. *, **, *** - statistically significant at the 10, 5, and 1 per cent $ The null is that RE estimation is consistent and therefore preferable to fixed effects. The test statistic is to be compared to a χ^2 with 13 and 11 degrees of freedom respectively (the number of time-varying regressors). The p-value is in brackets.

We report the results of two models for each of the rating agencies, the unrestricted and the restricted model. While the unrestricted model incorporates all variables discussed above, the restricted model contains only the variables which were found to have a statistically significant impact, at a 10% significance level. As can be seen from the statistics reported at the end of each table, the explanatory power of the models is very high with R-square values around 95 per cent and it remains almost constant moving from the unrestricted to the restricted versions, while the number of observations increases marginally. In addition, the variables found to be significant in the unrestricted model generally remain significant with the same sign in the restricted version.

The restricted models reveal a homogenous set of explanatory variables across agencies. On the real side, GDP per capita and GDP growth rates turn out significant for all three companies. In the fiscal area, this applies to the government debt ratio as a difference from the average and to the government effectiveness indicator. On the external side, the average external debt ratio and the average level of reserves are found to be significant across agencies. Default, EU and industrial country dummies are also significant for all agencies. Moreover, the size of the coefficients is of the same order of magnitude of the unrestricted models and they have the expected signs. In particular, the level and growth rate of real income drive up the rating, government and external debt have a negative impact and government effectiveness and higher external reserves have a positive impact.

Beyond this set of core variables, the agencies appear to employ a limited number of additional variables. For Fitch the analysis finds the smallest set of additional variables, comprising government effectiveness as a deviation from the average and foreign currency reserves also as the short-run deviation. By contrast, the analysis finds more significant explanatory variables for Moody's and Standard and Poor's, with a large degree of homogeneity between these two agencies. In particular, on the real side inflation is found to have a significantly negative impact. In the fiscal area, the average debt level exerts an additional negative impact on the ratings level, whereas the fiscal balance has a strong positive impact. With regard to the external sector, the current account balance has a negative impact. A current account deficit could in fact serve as an indicator for the willingness of foreigners to cover the current account gap through loans and foreign investment. In this situation, a higher current account deficit would be associated with either higher credit-worthiness or good economic prospects of the economy and consequently a higher sovereign rating.

Finally, the impact of the unemployment on the rating ilustrates the importance of distinguishing short and long run impacts. While the average (stuctural) level of unemployment is found to have a significant negative impact on the rating by Moody's, the short-run deviation from the average enters positively and significantly in the S&P model. Unemployment in the short run imply re-adjustments of economic activity that might improve economic performance in the future. Also, structural reforms that raise unemployment in the short run but improve fiscal sustainability in the long run could provide an explanation for this latter finding.

One can also assess how successful and important our specification is. First, most of the time averages of the explanatory variables are significant, which proves that if we did not include them we would be mispecifying the model.[4] Second, the models pass the Hausman test, which sugested that the problem was entirely corrected.[5]

Differentiation across sub-periods and ratings levels

The separation of the overall sample into different sub-samples allows to assess broadly the robustness of the empirical models. [6] In particular, the results for the sub-periods 1996-2000 and 2001-2005 are generally in line with those for the full estimation period, although the significance levels of the individual coefficients are reduced. The lower significance levels reflect the reduction in the respective sample sizes in half, which makes the coefficient estimates less certain. Taking this into account, signs and orders of magnitude of the coefficient estimates from the full-period models are mostly confirmed for the sub-periods. In particular, the core variables identified above enter the models for the sub-periods with the correct sign and generally significantly with a comparable order of magnitude.

As a further test of the robustness of the results, the sample was split into two groups according to the ratings level: regressions were run separately for high-rated countries with grades BBB+ and below and those above this grade. The choice of the threshold reflects practical considerations. While market participants generally divide bond issuers into investment-grade and non-investment grade at the threshold of BBB-, this threshold would result in a relatively small number of observations for low ratings making inference problematic. From the estimation of the ratings above BBB+, we removed the variable external debt because there were too few observations of non-industrial countries.

The results for the separate regressions according to ratings levels again confirm the overall results from the full sample. Looking at the random effects estimation for each agency, the variables that were found to be significant across agencies in the full sample also show up consistently with the correct sign in the individual regression models for high and low ratings. Most of the coefficients are statistically significant. Notably, the importance of average external reserves appears to rise for

---

[4] This is in fact the cause why without including time-averages the models would not pass the Hausman test.

[5] We also estimated the model with the average rating of the three agencies, and also pooling the data for the three agencies, but the results where quite similar.

[6] Results not reported for space sake, but available in Afonso et al. (2007).

low ratings in the models for Fitch and S&P. In the cases of statistical significance external reserves always have a positive impact on the ratings.

4.4. Ordered probit results

In view of the discussion of econometric issues above, ordered probit models should give additional insight into the determinants of sovereign ratings. In particular, this method allows to relax the rigid assumption on the shape of the ratings schedule. Instead it generates estimates of the threshold values between rating notches allowing an assessment of the shape of the ratings curve. Given the data requirements, the method was only applied to the full sample, which appears appropriate in view of the overall robustness of the empirical results to the use of sub-samples.

The results from the ordered probit estimation validate the findings highlighted above (see Table 3 for the random effects ordered probit). The core variables identified in the linear regressions also show up with the correct sign in the ordered probit approach. In addition, the ordered probit models suggest the significance of somewhat more explanatory variables, namely inflation and the current account, which were significant only in some specifications in the linear approach. At the same time, in the area of external variables, reserves do not show up significantly for S&P and Fitch in the restricted specifications. Finally, for the current account variable, the restricted specification for Moody's shows a negative sign for deviations from the long-term average, but a positive sign for the average, and similar sign switches appear also in some instances for the other agencies. This result goes some way in reconciling the counter intuitive result of the negative effect of current account on sovereign ratings, with the conventional wisdom.

Table 3 – Random effects ordered probit

	Moody's		S&P		Fitch	
	(1)	(2)	(3)	(4)	(5)	(6)
GDP per capita	3.422***	3.349***	3.246***	2.686***	4.087***	4.160***
	(9.40)	*(9.14)*	*(9.02)*	*(8.12)*	*(12.15)*	*(13.12)*
GDP per capita Avg.	0.478***	0.562***	1.117***	0.614***	1.132***	0.913***
	(2.75)	*(3.84)*	*(6.03)*	*(3.94)*	*(7.81)*	*(5.45)*
GDP growth	6.464**	7.852**	5.979*	7.729***	-5.119*	
	(2.06)	*(2.30)*	*(1.93)*	*(2.60)*	*(-1.73)*	
GDP growth Avg.	-9.387**		-8.43*		-6.083	
	(-2.04)		*(-1.79)*		*(-1.31)*	
Unemployment	0.016		0.152***	0.135***	0.012	
	(0.50)		*(4.57)*	*(3.01)*	*(0.36)*	
Unemployment Avg.	-0.078***	-0.085***	0.002		-0.073***	-0.033**
	(-4.40)	*(-5.18)*	*(0.10)*		*(-4.40)*	*(-2.09)*
Inflation	-0.199	-0.214	-0.353**	-0.418***	-0.273**	-0.245*
	(-1.41)	*(-1.51)*	*(-2.53)*	*(-2.93)*	*(-1.96)*	*(-1.79)*
Inflation Avg.	-0.623***	-0.939***	-0.532***	-0.949***	-0.713***	-0.272*
	(-4.01)	*(-6.11)*	*(-3.41)*	*(-6.08)*	*(-4.62)*	*(-1.84)*
Gov Debt	-0.03***	-0.032***	-0.085***	-0.088***	-0.043***	-0.051***
	(-4.61)	*(-4.94)*	*(-11.90)*	*(-12.41)*	*(-7.24)*	*(-9.07)*
Gov Debt Avg.	-0.026***	-0.028***	-0.027***	-0.031***	0.001	
	(-6.99)	*(-8.80)*	*(-8.77)*	*(-10.47)*	*(0.26)*	
Gov Balance	13.898***	10.937***	10.187***	11.559***	9.487***	
	(3.74)	*(2.77)*	*(3.07)*	*(3.32)*	*(3.00)*	
Gov Balance Avg.	6.757*		8.873**		22.304***	21.812***
	(1.84)		*(2.40)*		*(6.18)*	*(5.83)*
Gov Effectiveness	0.223		0.707**	0.794**	1.761***	1.838***
	(0.64)		*(2.08)*	*(2.42)*	*(4.86)*	*(5.17)*
Gov Effectiveness Avg.	3.679***	3.547***	4.606***	3.752***	2.722***	3.104***
	(13.46)	*(15.44)*	*(16.30)*	*(15.62)*	*(11.37)*	*(12.28)*
External Debt	-0.004**	-0.002**	-0.002			
	(-2.29)	*(-2.21)*	*(-0.79)*			
External Debt Avg.	-0.004***		-0.008***	-0.014***		
	(-3.11)		*(-6.40)*	*(-10.39)*		
Current Account	-8.57***	-12.863***	-4.899**		2.772	
	(-3.62)	*(-5.94)*	*(-2.04)*		*(1.23)*	
Current Account Avg.	5.24**	3.723*	18.39***	5.769**	18.993***	26.980***
	(2.21)	*(1.73)*	*(7.21)*	*(2.54)*	*(7.89)*	*(11.27)*
Reserves	2.246***	2.952***	0.205		-0.549	
	(4.37)	*(5.82)*	*(0.42)*		*(-1.14)*	
Reserves Avg.	0.416		3.365***	2.520***	0.876*	
	(0.88)		*(6.94)*	*(5.57)*	*(1.83)*	
Def 1	-3.101***	-2.936***	-1.789***	-2.077***	-2.176***	-1.266***
	(-12.18)	*(-11.95)*	*(-8.05)*	*(-9.25)*	*(-9.33)*	*(-6.03)*
EU	2.197***	2.237***	0.324		0.336	
	(9.04)	*(8.90)*	*(1.55)*		*(1.57)*	
IND	3.554***	3.626***	3.923***	5.848***	4.982***	6.163***
	(7.71)	*(9.08)*	*(8.18)*	*(11.38)*	*(13.24)*	*(15.54)*
LAC	-1.766***	-1.711***	-1.485***	-0.901***	-2.570***	-3.165***
	(-7.08)	*(-8.86)*	*(-6.38)*	*(-4.34)*	*(-11.08)*	*(-13.78)*

Table 3 – Random effects ordered probit (cont.)

	Moody's		S&P		Fitch	
	(1)	(2)	(3)	(4)	(5)	(6)
Constant	8.13	7.00	3.22	7.63	2.46	3.71
Cut1	1.00	1.00	1.00	1.00	1.00	1.00
Cut2	2.00	2.06	2.19	2.16	2.35	2.38
Cut3	3.40	3.36	4.12	4.07	3.33	3.43
Cut4	4.94	5.01	5.34	5.34	4.64	4.82
Cut5	5.94	6.14	7.11	7.19	5.77	5.93
Cut6	7.09	7.35	9.15	9.32	7.51	7.54
Cut7	8.65	8.92	10.75	10.80	9.13	9.02
Cut8	10.72	10.75	13.11	12.92	10.80	10.81
Cut9	11.76	11.82	14.59	14.30	11.82	12.02
Cut10	12.97	13.13	15.46	14.99	12.92	13.10
Cut11	14.25	14.49	17.49	16.59	15.30	15.42
Cut12	15.50	15.72	18.96	18.00	16.99	17.52
Cut13	17.62	17.50	21.51	19.99	17.63	18.42
Cut14	19.11	18.86	22.72	21.07	19.85	20.87
Cut15	20.60	20.26	24.54	23.00	22.11	23.07
Cut16	21.64	21.26	27.07	25.69	24.06	25.04
LogLik	-566.33	-578.24	-514.45	-531.22	-537.09	-533.09
Observations	551	557	564	565	553	564
Equal differences $	29.26 (0.009)	19.91 (0.133)	52.21 (0.000)	59.68 (0.000)	68.57 (0.000)	70.23 (0.000)
Jump&	[7-8]	[7-8]		[9-10]	[12-13]	
Different Slopes#			[2-3 ,5-6, 7-8, 10-11,12-13, 14-15, 15-16]	[2-3, 5-6, 7-8, 12-13, 14-15, 15-16]	[10-11, 13-14, 14-15,15-16]	[10-11, 11-12, 13-14,14-15, 15-16]
Test*	18.22 (0.149)	12.22 (0.510)	19.23 (0.116)	14.02 (0.300)	22.03 (0.037)	16.69 (0.214)

Notes: The t statistics are in parentheses. *, **, *** statistically significant at the 10, 5, and 1 per cent $ The null is that the differences between categories is equal for all categories. The test statistic is to be compared to a χ^2 with 14 degrees of freedom. & Identifies two cut points that have a irregular difference. # Identifies a cluster of categories that seem to have a higher slope (increase difficulty in transition between adjacent notches). *The null is that, excluding the jump point, within the two identified clusters the slopes are equal. The test statistic is to be compared to a Qui-Square with either 13 degrees of freedom (if only a jump or different slopes was identified) or 12 degrees of freedom (if both where identified). The p-value is in brackets.

The correspondence between the ratings and the cut-off points is specified in (6).

The estimated threshold coefficients reported in the second part of Table 3 suggest that the linear specification assumed for the panel regression above is appropriate. For instance, the results show that for all three agencies the thresholds between rating notches are broadly equally distributed across the ratings range. In other words, the distance for a country to move e.g. from B– to B is roughly equal to that for moving from AA to AA+. Nevertheless, the econometric tests at the bottom of the tables reveal additional insights. For the restricted model of Moody's, the test does not reject the null hypothesis of equal distances between thresholds, but the significance level is close to 10 per cent. Indeed the estimated thresholds point to a relatively large jump between the ratings for BBB– and BBB. This suggests that countries close to the non-investment grade rating are given a wider range before they actually cross that threshold. For Fitch, the hypothesis of equal distances is strongly rejected as the thresholds for higher ratings are further apart than those of the lower ratings. In this case the kink lies at the A rating. For S&P, different distances are found throughout the ratings scale and it appears that for lower ratings the relative distance between thresholds of S&P coincides with that of Moody's. However, above the investment grade limit, the distances between thresholds at first decline and then increase, resulting in a slightly curved ratings schedule that makes the transition to the highest grades most difficult.

4.5. Prediction analysis

Our prediction analysis will focus on two elements: the prediction for the rating of each individual observation in the sample, as well as the prediction of movements in the ratings through time. Prediction with the pooled OLS model was done by rounding the fitted value (which is continuous) to the closest integer between 1 and 17. For the random effects estimations we can have two predictions, with or without the country specific effect, ε_i, and we can write the corresponding estimated versions of (4) as:

$$\hat{R}_{it} = \hat{\beta}(X_{it} - \overline{X}_i) + \hat{\delta}\overline{X}_i + \hat{\lambda}Z_i + \hat{\varepsilon}_i, \quad (7a)$$

$$\tilde{R}_{it} = \hat{\beta}(X_{it} - \overline{X}_i) + \hat{\delta}\overline{X}_i + \hat{\lambda}Z_i. \quad (7b)$$

We can then estimate each country specific effect by taking the time average of the estimated residual for each country. As a result we can include or exclude this additional information that comes out of the estimation. In other words, we generate in-sample and out-of-sample prediction. After the fitted value is computed it is then also rounded to the closest integer between 1 and 17. The prediction with both ordered probit and the random effects ordered probit was done by fitting the value of the latent variable, setting the error term to zero, and then match it up to the cut-off points do determine the predicted rating. Table 4 presents an overall summary of the prediction errors, for the three agencies and for the several methods using the respective restricted specifications.

Table 4 – Summary of prediction errors

	Estimation Procedure	Obs.	Prediction error (notches) 5	4	3	2	1	0	-1	-2	-3	-4	-5	% Correctly predicted	% Within 1 notch *	% Within 2 notches **
Moody's	OLS	557	0	5	12	42	**88**	**209**	**141**	58	2	0	0	37.5	78.6	96.6
	RE with ε_i	557	0	0	1	17	**78**	**361**	**91**	8	1	0	0	64.8	95.2	99.6
	RE without ε_i	557	0	6	15	49	**92**	**188**	**141**	53	12	1	0	33.8	75.6	93.9
	Ordered Probit	557	4	4	14	35	**99**	**259**	**86**	46	10	0	0	46.5	79.7	94.3
	RE Ordered Probit	557	0	8	23	59	**106**	**244**	**71**	34	11	1	0	43.8	75.6	92.3
S&P	OLS	568	0	3	15	34	**104**	**218**	**147**	41	6	0	0	38.4	82.6	95.8
	RE with ε_i	565	0	0	1	6	**80**	**392**	**83**	2	1	0	0	69.4	98.2	99.6
	RE without ε_i	565	0	5	12	39	**98**	**216**	**133**	52	10	0	0	38.2	79.1	95.2
	Ordered Probit	565	0	10	14	28	**99**	**262**	**118**	23	10	1	0	46.4	84.8	93.8
	RE Ordered Probit	565	1	12	13	41	**115**	**218**	**130**	29	6	0	0	38.6	81.9	94.3
Fitch	OLS	481	1	3	6	32	**87**	**196**	**113**	43	0	0	0	40.7	82.3	97.9
	RE with ε_i	481	0	1	2	4	**63**	**339**	**71**	1	0	0	0	70.5	98.3	99.4
	RE without ε_i	481	1	3	7	39	**93**	**174**	**106**	57	1	0	0	36.2	77.5	97.5
	Ordered Probit	481	1	0	16	32	**91**	**209**	**95**	31	6	0	0	43.5	82.1	95.2
	RE Ordered Probit	553	1	3	25	53	**115**	**191**	**121**	36	8	0	0	34.5	77.2	93.3

Notes: * prediction error within +/- 1 notch. ** prediction error within +/- 2 notches.

The first conclusion is that the random effects model including the estimated country effect is the method with the best fit. On average for the three agencies, it correctly predicts about 70 per cent of all observations and more than 95 per cent of the predicted ratings lie within one notch (99 per cent within two notches). This is not surprising, the country errors capture factors like political risk, geopolitical uncertainty and social tensions that are likely to systematically affect the ratings, therefore, such term acts like a correction for these factors.

This additional information cropping up from the random effects estimation with the country specific effect can be very useful if we want to work with countries that belong to our sample. However, if we want to make out of sample predictions we will not have this information. In that case, only the random effects estimation excluding the country error is comparable to the OLS specification, to the ordered probit and to the random effects ordered probit. We can see that in general both ordered probit and random effects ordered probit have a better fit than the pooled OLS and random effects for all three agencies, though not as clearly for Fitch. Overall, the simple ordered probit seems the best method as far as prediction in levels is concerned as it predicts correctly around 45 per cent of all observations and more then 80 per cent within one notch.

Let us now turn to how the models perform in predicting changes in ratings. Table 5 presents the total number of sample upgrades (downgrades), the predicted number of upgrades (downgrades) and the number of upgrades (downgrades) that where correctly predicted by the several models.

Table 5 – Upgrades and downgrades prediction

		Sample Upgrades	Predicted Upgrades	Upgrades correctly predicted at time		Sample Downgrades	Predicted Downgrades	Downgrades correctly predicted at time	
				t	t+1			t	t+1
Moody's	OLS	60	95	23	20	34	55	20	10
	RE with ε_i	60	87	28	17	34	51	16	12
	RE without ε_i	60	89	23	16	34	51	17	8
	Ordered Probit	60	127	31	25	34	72	20	8
	RE Ordered Probit	60	101	23	23	34	65	18	8
S&P	OLS	79	79	32	17	41	50	16	15
	RE with ε_i	79	79	31	14	41	52	18	12
	RE without ε_i	79	90	34	15	41	61	19	14
	Ordered Probit	79	102	38	14	41	64	20	13
	RE Ordered Probit	79	90	31	15	41	68	20	12
Fitch	OLS	68	74	28	19	25	35	13	3
	RE with ε_i	68	67	25	19	25	34	15	7
	RE without ε_i	68	89	24	20	25	53	15	5
	Ordered Probit	69	115	30	24	25	71	15	5
	RE Ordered Probit	89	154	43	29	26	77	13	7

Note: ε_i - estimated country specific effect.

Roughly the models correctly predict between one third and one half of both upgrades and downgrades. In our opinion this is quite satisfactory given that the empirical approach used here necessarily neglects two sources of information that are known to enter the decision of the rating agencies. First, in contrast to the backward-looking models presented above, rating agencies base their decision to a considerable extent on projected economic developments. Thus, a full empirical model of the agencies' approach would need to incorporate the agencies' expectations regarding the relevant explanatory variables. However, as the agencies generally do not publish their projections, any such modelling attempt would remain highly tentative. Still, the observation that many of the actual rating changes are predicted by the models with a lag of one or two years appears to support the relevance of this point. Second, ratings agencies also generally make a clear point that they cover qualitative variables in addition to quantitative data in the ratings process. While the relative importance of the qualitative and quantitative factors that enter the ratings decision is uncertain (and might well vary across countries), rating agencies' public statements indicate that such factors can play an important role.[7]

The most noticeable difference between the models is not the number of corrected predicted changes but the total number of predicted changes. In fact, the ordered probit and random effects ordered probit predict significantly more changes than the OLS and random effects counterparts. For instance, for S&P, while both OLS and random effects predict around 79 upgrades and 50 downgrades, the ordered probit model predicts 102 upgrades and 64 downgrades.

4.6. Examples of specific country analysis

In Table 6 we show, as an example, the rating for some European countries and some emerging markets both in 1998 and 2005. Then, we use the estimated short-run coefficients of the random effects ordered probit together with the values for the relevant variables. Afterwards, we divide the overall prediction change in the rating for each agency into the contributions of the different blocks of explanatory variables: macroeconomic performance, government and fiscal performance, external elements and European Union.[8] The upper and lower bound presented are computed by adding and subtracting one standard deviation to point estimate of the coefficients.

Let us compare, for instance, Portugal and Spain (Table 6a). In 1998 they both had an AA (Aa2) rating but in 2005 while Spain had been upgraded to AAA (Aaa) by all agencies, Portugal had been downgraded by S&P. If we analyse the contributions of the main key variables we see that, for Portugal the positive contribution of the macroeconomic performance was overshadowed by the negative government developments. For such government performance contributed the worsening of the budget deficit since 2000, the upward trend in government debt and the worsening in the World Bank governance effectiveness indicator. As for Spain, the good macroeconomic performance was the main cause of the upgrade, specially the reduction of structural unemployment since the mid nineties and the increase of GDP per capita due to the persistent high growth.

---

[7] For example, see Rother (2005) for an analysis of the impact of EMU convergence on country ratings in eastern Europe.

[8] As an exception, we used the long-run coefficient of unemployment instead of the short-run coefficient. We are implicitly assuming that all the changes in unemployment between these two years were structural.

As a final example for the emerging economies, we report the results for five countries that have, in general also been upgraded: Brazil, Mexico, Malaysia, Thailand and South Africa (Table 6b). We should briefly highlight that for Brazil the main positive contribution came from the external area specially the reduction of external debt and the increase in foreign reserves. This effect is particular to Fitch. For Malaysia and Thailand the main contribution came from the macro side, while for Mexico and South Africa the contributions are more balanced.

Table 6a – Example of country analysis: variables' contribution to expected rating changes (european countries)

		Portugal			Spain			Greece			Italy			Ireland		
		1998		2005	1998		2005	1998		2005	1998		2005	1998		2005
Rating$	Moody's	Aa2 (15)		Aa2 (15)	Aa2 (15)		Aaa (17)	Baa1 (10)		A1 (13)	Aa3 (14)		Aa2 (15)	Aaa (17)		Aaa (17)
	S&P	AA (15)		AA- (14)	AA (15)		AAA (17)	BBB (9)		A (12)	AA (15)		AA- (14)	AA+ (16)		AAA (17)
	Fitch	AA (15)		AA (15)	AA (15)		AAA (17)	BBB (9)		A (12)	AA- (14)		AA (15)	AAA (17)		AAA (17)
Moody's	Macro contribution	0.53	0.73	0.93	1.69	1.98	2.28	1.33	1.52	1.70	0.91	1.08	1.26	1.46	1.83	2.20
	Gov. contribution	-0.69	-0.46	-0.23	0.27	0.65	1.03	-0.05	-0.01	0.02	-0.03	0.14	0.31	0.20	0.39	0.58
	External contribution	0.09	0.12	0.15	0.22	0.31	0.39	0.18	0.24	0.31	0.17	0.24	0.30	0.15	0.21	0.26
	European Union	0.00	0.00	0.00	0.00	0.00	0.00	0.00	0.00	0.00	0.00	0.00	0.00	0.00	0.00	0.00
	Overall change	**-0.07**	**0.39**	**0.86**	**2.19**	**2.95**	**3.70**	**1.46**	**1.75**	**2.03**	**1.05**	**1.46**	**1.87**	**1.81**	**2.43**	**3.05**
S&P	Macro contribution	0.42	0.57	0.73	0.94	1.07	1.20	0.99	1.13	1.27	0.56	0.67	0.77	0.91	1.15	1.38
	Gov. contribution	-1.06	-0.88	-0.70	0.48	0.77	1.06	-0.13	-0.10	-0.08	0.07	0.21	0.34	0.83	0.98	1.14
	External contribution	0.03	0.05	0.08	0.07	0.14	0.21	0.06	0.11	0.16	0.05	0.11	0.16	0.05	0.09	0.14
	European Union	0.00	0.00	0.00	0.00	0.00	0.00	0.00	0.00	0.00	0.00	0.00	0.00	0.00	0.00	0.00
	Overall change	**-0.61**	**-0.25**	**0.11**	**1.49**	**1.98**	**2.47**	**0.91**	**1.14**	**1.36**	**0.69**	**0.98**	**1.26**	**1.78**	**2.22**	**2.66**
Fitch	Macro contribution	0.90	0.99	1.08	1.78	2.01	2.25	1.43	1.56	1.69	1.06	1.18	1.30	1.92	2.14	2.35
	Gov. contribution	-1.26	-1.05	-0.85	-0.46	-0.13	0.19	-0.11	-0.08	-0.06	-0.45	-0.29	-0.14	0.15	0.31	0.47
	External contribution	-0.06	-0.03	-0.01	-0.16	-0.09	-0.02	-0.13	-0.07	-0.01	-0.12	-0.07	-0.01	-0.11	-0.06	-0.01
	European Union	0.00	0.00	0.00	0.00	0.00	0.00	0.00	0.00	0.00	0.00	0.00	0.00	0.00	0.00	0.00
	Overall change	**-0.42**	**-0.10**	**0.23**	**1.16**	**1.79**	**2.42**	**1.19**	**1.40**	**1.62**	**0.49**	**0.81**	**1.14**	**1.97**	**2.39**	**2.81**

Notes: The block contributions were calculated using the changes in the variables multiplied by the short-run coefficients estimated by random effects ordered probit, and then aggregated. The only exception was unemployment, for which we used the long-run coefficient. The upper and lower bounds where calculated using plus and minus one standard deviation.

$ The quantitative rating scale is in brackets.

Table 6b – Example of country analysis: variables' contribution to expected rating changes (emerging economies)

		Brazil			Malaysia			Mexico			South Africa			Thailand		
		1998		2005	1998		2005	1998		2005	1998		2005	1998		2005
Rating$	Moody's	B2(3)		Ba3 (5)	Baa3 (8)		A3 (11)	Ba2 (7)		Baa1 (10)	Ba1 (7)		Baa1 (10)	Baa3 (8)		Baa1 (10)
	S&P	BB- (5)		BB- (5)	BBB- (8)		A- (11)	BB (6)		BBB (9)	BBB- (8)		BBB+ (10)	BB+ (7)		BBB+ (10)
	Fitch	B+ (4)		BB- (5)	BB (6)		A- (11)	BB (6)		BBB (9)	BB+ (7)		BBB+ (10)	BB (6)		BBB+ (10)
Moody's	Macro contribution	-0.59	-0.49	-0.39	1.00	1.19	1.37	0.95	1.17	1.39	0.79	1.03	1.27	0.91	1.19	1.47
	Gov. contribution	-0.37	-0.16	0.06	-1.06	-0.79	-0.53	0.26	0.45	0.64	0.34	0.61	0.88	-0.31	-0.14	0.04
	External contribution	-0.15	0.18	0.50	-0.70	-0.35	-0.01	0.13	0.26	0.38	0.28	0.38	0.48	-0.36	-0.12	0.12
	Overall change	**-1.11**	**-0.47**	**0.17**	**-0.76**	**0.04**	**0.83**	**1.34**	**1.88**	**2.42**	**1.41**	**2.02**	**2.64**	**0.24**	**0.94**	**1.64**
S&P	Macro contribution	-0.19	-0.16	-0.13	0.77	0.91	1.05	0.71	0.88	1.05	0.86	0.99	1.13	0.70	0.92	1.13
	Gov. contribution	-1.01	-0.84	-0.67	-0.93	-0.73	-0.53	0.25	0.40	0.54	0.75	0.96	1.17	-0.68	-0.54	-0.40
	External contribution	-0.22	0.06	0.34	-0.56	-0.28	0.00	-0.06	0.04	0.15	0.00	0.08	0.17	-0.15	0.06	0.26
	Overall change	**-1.42**	**-0.94**	**-0.45**	**-0.71**	**-0.10**	**0.52**	**0.90**	**1.32**	**1.73**	**1.61**	**2.04**	**2.46**	**-0.13**	**0.43**	**0.99**
Fitch	Macro contribution	-0.56	-0.49	-0.41	1.04	1.14	1.25	1.26	1.39	1.52	0.92	1.09	1.25	0.80	0.89	0.97
	Gov. contribution	-0.46	-0.28	-0.11	-0.61	-0.40	-0.18	-0.08	0.08	0.24	0.91	1.14	1.37	-0.18	-0.03	0.12
	External contribution	0.72	1.36	2.01	0.12	0.52	0.91	0.13	0.35	0.56	-0.06	0.07	0.20	0.43	0.86	1.28
	Overall change	**-0.30**	**0.60**	**1.49**	**0.55**	**1.26**	**1.97**	**1.31**	**1.82**	**2.32**	**1.76**	**2.30**	**2.83**	**1.06**	**1.72**	**2.38**

Notes: The block contributions were calculated using the changes in the variables multiplied by the short-run coefficients estimated by random effects ordered probit, and then aggregated. The only exception was unemployment, for which we used the long-run coefficient. The upper and lower bounds where calculated using plus and minus one standard deviation.

$ The quantitative rating scale is in brackets.

5. Conclusion

In this paper we studied the determinants of global sovereign debt ratings using ratings from the three main international rating agencies, for the period 1995-2005. Overall, our results point to a good performance of the estimated models, across agencies and across the time dimension, as well as a good overall prediction power.

Regarding the methodological approach, we used both a linear framework and an ordered probit estimation. We modelled the country specific error using a random effects approach, which in practical terms implied adding time-averages of the explanatory variables as additional time-invariant regressors. This setting allowed us to distinguish between immediate and long-run effects of a variable on the sovereign rating level. Moreover, we also used a limited dependent variable framework by means of an ordered probit and random effects ordered probit specifications. The latter is the best procedure for panel data as it considers the existence of an additional normally distributed cross-section error term. This approach allowed both to determine the cut-off points throughout the rating scale as well as assessing whether a linear quantitative transformation of the ratings is actually more appropriate than a possible non-linear transformation.

Our main findings in the panel random effects framework allowed us to detect a set of core variables that are relevant for the determination of the ratings: per capita GDP; GDP real growth rate; government debt; government effectiveness; external debt and external reserves; sovereign default indicators. Moreover, the importance of fiscal variables appears stronger than in the previous existing literature.[9]

The ordered probit analysis confirmed the overall estimation results from the linear panel regressions. Interestingly, there is some evidence for different approaches of the agencies with regard to the distance between ratings thresholds. For instance, for Moody's the estimated thresholds point to a relatively large jump between the ratings for BBB– and BBB. This suggests that countries close to the non-investment grade rating are

---

[9] We performed additional analysis from different perspectives. For instance, we used the information on credit rating outlooks but no relevant improvement on the fit of the models occurred. In addition, we also assessed whether different exchange rate regimes added information to the rating determination, but that was not the case.

given a wider range before they actually cross that threshold. For Fitch, the hypothesis of equal distances is strongly rejected as the thresholds for higher ratings are further apart than those of the lower ratings. In this case the kink lies at the A rating. On the other hand, no clear switching pattern emerges for S&P.

The panel sample we used is quite comprehensive, which allowed for a sub-period analysis and for a differentiated high and low rating analysis. While the results are roughly stable across agencies, time periods and ratings levels, some additional interesting results emerge. For instance, for the low rating levels, external debt and external reserves are more relevant. On the other hand, for the early sub-period, 1996-2000, the current account balance was more important, while external reserves were possibly somewhat more important in the later period, 2001-2005 (for Moody’s and S&P).

Finally, regarding the prediction analysis, the random effects model including the estimated country effect turns out to be the method with the best fit. On average for the three agencies, such specification correctly predicted 70 per cent of all observations and more than 95 per cent of the predicted ratings lay within one notch. Moreover, the models also correctly predicted between one third and one half of respectively upgrades and downgrades. This is quite satisfactory for two reasons: first, the rating agencies also have a forward looking behaviour that is absent from our models and second, other qualitative factors not captured in our variables may play an important role.

References

Afonso, A. (2003), Understanding the determinants of sovereign debt ratings: evidence for the two leading agencies. *Journal of Economics and Finance*, 27, 56-74.

Afonso, A.; Gomes, P. and Rother, P. (2007), “What ‘hides’ behind sovereign debt ratings?”, European Central Bank Working Paper 711.

Alexe, S.; Hammer, P.; Kogan, A. and Lejeune, M. (2003), A non-recursive regression model for country risk rating. Rutcor Research Report 9, Rutgers Center for Operational Research, March.

Bissoondoyal-Bheenick, E. (2005), An analysis of the determinants of sovereign ratings. *Global Finance Journal*, 15, 251-280.

Bissoondoyal-Bheenick, E.; Brooks, R. and Yip, A. (2006), Determinants of sovereign ratings: A comparison of case-based reasoning and ordered probit approaches. *Global Finance Journal*, 17, 136-154.

Borio, C. and Packer, F. (2004), Assessing new perspectives on country risk. BIS *Quarterly Review*, BIS, December, 47-65.

Butler, A. and Fauver. L. (2006), Institutional Environment and Sovereign Credit Ratings. *Financial Management*, 35, 53-79.

Cantor R. and Packer, F. (1996), Determinants and impact of sovereign credit ratings. *Economic Policy Review*, 2, 37-53. Federal Reserve Bank of New York.

Eliasson, A. (2002), Sovereign credit ratings. Working Papers 02-1, Deutsche Bank.

Fitch Ratings (2006), Fitch sovereign ratings transition and default study.

Frechette, G. (2001a), sg158: Random-effects ordered probit, *Stata Technical Bulletin* 59, 23-27. Reprinted in *Stata Technical Bulletin Reprints* 10, 261-266.

Frechette, G. (2001b), sg158.1: Update to random-effects ordered probit, *Stata Technical Bulletin* 61, 12. Reprinted in *Stata Technical Bulletin Reprints* 10, 266-267.

Hajivassiliou, V. (2006), A Modified Random Effects Estimator for Panel Data Models with Correlated Regressors, *mimeo*.

Hajivassiliou, V. and Ioannides, Y. (2007), Unemployment and Liquidity Constraints. *Journal of Applied Econometrics*, 22, 479-510.

Hu, Y.-T.; Kiesel, R. and Perraudin, W. (2002), The estimation of transition matrices for sovereign credit ratings. *Journal of Banking & Finance*, 26, 1383-1406.

Jaimovich, D. and Panizza, U. (2006), Public Debt around the World: A New Dataset of Central Government Debt. Working Papers 1019, Inter-American Development Bank, Research Department.

Mellios, C. and Paget-Blanc, E. (2006), "Which factors determine sovereign credit ratings?" *European Journal of Finance*, 12, 361-377.

Monfort, B. and Mulder, C. (2000). Using credit ratings for capital requirements on lending to emerging market economies - possible impact of a new Basel accord. IMF Working Papers 00/69.

Rabe-Hesketh, S.; Pickles, A. and Taylor, C. (2000). sg120: Generalized linear latent and mixed models. *Stata Technical Bulletin* 53, 47-57. Reprinted in *Stata Technical Bulletin Reprints* 9, 293-307.

Reisen, H. and Maltzan, J. (1999). Boom and Burst and Sovereign Ratings. *International Finance,* 2, 273-293.

Rother, P. C. (2005). The EU Premium: Ratings Strengthened for Countries Moving Toward EMU Convergence, Moody's Special Comment, Moody's Investors Service, August.

Wooldridge, J. (2002), *Econometric Analysis of Cross Section and Panel Data*. MIT Press.

Acknowledgements

We are grateful to Fitch Ratings, Moody's, and Standard & Poor's for providing us historical sovereign rating data, to Renate Dreiskena for help with the data, to Vassilis Hajivassiliou and Philip Vermeulen for helpful clarifications, to Moritz Kraemer, Guido Wolswijk, and to participants at European Central Bank and at ISEG/UTLisbon - Technical University of Lisbon seminars, at the 2007 North American Summer Meeting of the Econometric Society, at the Money, Macro and Finance Research Group 39th Annual Conference, and at the XLI Euro Working Group on Financial Modelling conference for useful comments on different and previous versions of the text. The opinions expressed herein are those of the authors and do not necessarily reflect those of the ECB or the Eurosystem. UECE – Research Unit on Complexity and Economics is supported by FCT (Fundação para a Ciência e a Tecnologia, Portugal). Pedro Gomes would like to thank the Fiscal Policies Division of the ECB for its hospitality and acknowledge financial support of FCT.

CHAPTER FOURTEEN

A MODIFIED TEMPERED STABLE DISTRIBUTION WITH VOLATILITY CLUSTERING

YOUNG SHIN KIM, SVETLOZAR T. RACHEV, DONG MYUNG CHUNG AND MICHELE LEONARDO BIANCHI

Abstract

We introduce a new variant of the tempered stable distribution, named the modified tempered stable (MTS) distribution and we develop a GARCH option pricing model with MTS innovations. This model allows one to describe some stylized phenomena observed in financial markets such as volatility clustering, skewness, and heavy tails of the return distribution.

Keywords: Option pricing, GARCH process, Tempered stable distribution, Volatility clustering

1. Introduction

Since Black and Scholes (1973) introduced the pricing and hedging theory for the option market, their model has been the most popular model for option pricing. However, the model which assumes homoskedasticity and lognormality, cannot explain stylized phenomena such as skewness, heavy tails, and volatility clustering of the stock returns, which are observed in stock prices.

To explain the stylized phenomena, Mandelbrot (1963a, 1963b) was the first to use a non-normal Lévy process as asset price process. Hurst,

Platen and Rachev (1999) used a model based on stable processes to price options. However, stable distributions have infinite moments of the second or higher order because of the heavy distributional tails. To have more adaptability, a new class of Lévy processes called the tempered stable (TS) process has been introduced under different names including: "truncated Lévy flight" (Koponen (1995)), "KoBoL" process (Boyarchenko and Levendorskiĭ (2000)), and "CGMY" process (Carr et al. (2002)). Subsequently, the Normal Tempered Stable (NTS) distribution has been introduced and applied in finance (Barndorff-Nielsen and Levendorskiĭ (2001), and Barndorff-Nielsen and Shephard (2001)). The NTS distribution is obtained by a time changed Brownian motion with a tempered stable subordinator. In order to obtain a closed form solution of the European option price, the FFT option price method (Carr and Madan (1999) and Lewis (2001)) is used under the assumption of the Markov property. However, the Markov property is often rejected by the empirical evidence as in the case of volatility clustering.

Autoregressive conditional heteroskedastic (ARCH) models introduced by Engle (1982) and generalized ARCH (GARCH) models by Bollerslev (1986) have become standard tools in empirical finance. The GARCH option pricing models have been developed to price options under the assumption of volatility clustering. GARCH models of Duan (1995) and Heston and Nandi (2000) are remarkable works on the non-Markovian structure of asset returns even though they did not take into account conditional leptokurtosis and skewness. Duan et al. (2004) modified the classical GARCH model by adding jumps to the innovation processes. Furthermore, Menn and Rachev (2005a,2005b) introduced an enhanced GARCH model with innovations which follow the smoothly truncated stable (STS) distribution, which has a finite variance and at the same time allows for conditional leptokurtosis and skewness.

In this paper, we introduce a variant of the tempered stable distributions, called a modified tempered stable (MTS) distribution, and we apply it to the GARCH option pricing model.

The MTS distribution is obtained by taking an α-stable law and multiplying the Lévy measure by a modified Bessel function of the second kind onto each half of the real axis. It is infinitely divisible, has a closed form characteristic function, finite moments of all orders, and its Lévy measure behaves asymptotically like the α-stable distribution near zero and like the $\alpha/2$-TS distribution on the tails.

The GARCH option pricing model presented in this paper follows the method introduced by Menn and Rachev (2005a,2005b). However, instead of STS innovations, we assume that the innovations of the classical GARCH model follow the MTS distribution with zero mean and unit variance, and we are able to describe both leptokurtosis and skewness. In contrast to the STS distribution, the Laplace transform of a MTS distribution is analytic, therefore it is more tractable. Moreover, it is infinitely divisible and its characteristic function provides a concrete method to find an equivalent martingale measure by applying a general result on density transformations for Levy processes, presented by Sato (1999).

The remainder of this paper is organized as follows: In Section 2 we summarize some features of the TS distributions. Section 3 introduces the MTS distribution. The properties of the MTS distribution, the relation to the NTS distribution, and measure changes of the MTS distributions will be discussed in this section. The GARCH model with MTS innovations is reported in the forth section. Section 5 is a summary of our conclusions.

2. Preliminary

Before introducing the MTS distribution and the MTS-GARCH model, let us review the tempered stable distribution. It is well known that α-stable distributions have infinite p-th moments for all $p \geq \alpha$. This is due to the fact that its Lévy density decays polynomially. Tempering of the tails with the exponential rate is one choice to ensure finite moments. The Tempered Stable (TS) distribution is obtained by taking a symmetric α-stable distribution and multiplying the Lévy measure with exponential functions on each half of the real axis. Indeed, it is defined in the following:

Definition 1. An infinitely divisible distribution is called a *tempered stable* (*TS*) *distribution* with parameter $(C_1, C_2, \lambda_+, \lambda_-, \alpha)$, or *$\alpha$-tempered stable* (*$\alpha$-TS*), if its Lévy triplet (σ^2, ν, γ) is given by $\sigma = 0$, $\gamma \in R$ and

$$\nu(dx) = \left(\frac{C_1 e^{-\lambda_+ x}}{x^{1+\alpha}} 1_{x>0} + \frac{C_2 e^{-\lambda_- |x|}}{|x|^{1+\alpha}} 1_{x<0} \right) dx, \tag{1}$$

where $C_1, C_2, \lambda_+, \lambda_- > 0$ and $\alpha < 2$.

This process was first constructed by Koponen (1995) which he named truncated Lévy flights. In particular, if $C_1 = C_2 = C > 0$, then this distribution is called the CGMY distribution which has been used in Carr et al. (2002) for financial modeling.

In the above definition, λ_+ and λ_- give the tail decay rates, α describes the jumps near zero, and C_1 and C_2 determine the arrival rate of jumps for a given size.

The characteristic function $\phi_{TS}(u)$ for a tempered stable distribution is given by

$$\phi_{TS}(u) = \exp(iu\mu + C_1\Gamma(-\alpha)((\lambda_+ - iu)^\alpha - \lambda_+^\alpha) \quad (2)$$

$$+C_2\Gamma(-\alpha)((\lambda_- + iu)^\alpha - \lambda_-^\alpha)),$$

for some $\mu \in R$. Moreover, ϕ_{TS} can be extended to the region $\{z \in C : Im(z) \in (-\lambda_-, \lambda_+)\}$. The proof can be found in Carr et al. (2002), Cont and Tankov (2004), and Kim (2005). Using the characteristic function, we obtain cumulants

$$c_m(X) = \frac{d^m}{du^m} \log \phi_{TS}(u)|_{u=0}$$

of all orders.

Proposition 2. Let X be a tempered stable distributed random variable whose characteristic function is given by (2). The cumulant $c_n(X)$ of X is given by
$c_n(X) = \Gamma(n-\alpha)C_1\lambda_+^{\alpha-n} + (-1)^n\Gamma(n-\alpha)C_2\lambda_-^{\alpha-n}$, for $n \in N$, $n \geq 2$,
and $c_1(X) = \mu + \Gamma(1-\alpha)C_1\lambda_+^{\alpha-1} - \Gamma(1-\alpha)C_2\lambda_-^{\alpha-1}$.

The infinitely divisibility of this distribution allows one to construct the corresponding Lévy process.

Definition 3. The Lévy process $X = (X_t)_{t \geq 0}$ is said to be a *tempered stable process* if X_1 follows a tempered stable distribution.

The properties of infinite activity and infinite variation are determined by the value of α.

Proposition 4. The tempered stable process is

1. of finite activity if $\alpha < 0$ and of infinite activity if $0 < \alpha < 2$.

2. of finite variation if $0 < \alpha < 1$ and of infinite variation if $1 < \alpha < 2$.

As a generalization of the tempered stable process, the Regular Lévy Process of Exponential type (RLPE) presented in Boyarchenko and Levendorskiĭ (2000).

Definition 5. A Lévy process X with Lévy measure ν is called a *Lévy process of exponential type* $[-\lambda_-, \lambda_+]$ if $\lambda_+, \lambda_- > 0$ and ν satisfies

$$\int_{-\infty}^{-1} e^{\lambda_-|x|} \nu(dx) < \infty \quad \text{and} \quad \int_{1}^{\infty} e^{\lambda_+ x} \nu(dx) < \infty. \tag{3}$$

The Lévy process with Lévy triplet $(0, \nu, \gamma)$ is called a *pure jump* Lévy process.

Definition 6. Let $\lambda_+, \lambda_- > 0$ and $\beta \in (0,2)$. A pure jump Lévy process X with Lévy triplet $(0, \nu, \gamma)$ is called a *RLPE* of type $[-\lambda_-, \lambda_+]$ and order β if its Lévy measure ν satisfies the following two conditions:

1. X is a Lévy process of exponential type $[-\lambda_-, \lambda_+]$.

2. In a neighbourhood of zero, a representation $\nu(dx) = f(x)dx$ where f satisfies the condition: there exist $\beta' < \beta$, k and K such that

$$|f(x)-k|x|^{-\beta-1}| \leq K|x|^{-\beta'-1}, \quad \forall |x| \leq 1.$$

Example 7. From (1) we can show that a tempered stable process is the RLPE of type $[-\lambda_2, \lambda_1]$ and order α.

3. The Model

3.1 The Modified Tempered Stable Distributions

In this section, we introduce a variant of the tempered stable distribution named modified tempered stable (MTS) distribution. The proofs can be found in Kim (2005). The MTS distribution is defined as follows:

Definition 1. An infinitely divisible distribution is said to be an *α-modified tempered stable (α-MTS) or modified tempered stable (MTS) distribution* if its Lévy triplet is given by

$$\sigma^2 = 0$$

$$\nu(dx) = C\left(\frac{\lambda_+^{\frac{\alpha+1}{2}} K_{\frac{\alpha+1}{2}}(\lambda_+ x)}{x^{\frac{\alpha+1}{2}}} 1_{x>0} + \frac{\lambda_-^{\frac{\alpha+1}{2}} K_{\frac{\alpha+1}{2}}(\lambda_- |x|)}{|x|^{\frac{\alpha+1}{2}}} 1_{x<0}\right) dx$$

$$\gamma = \mu + \frac{C\Gamma\left(\frac{1-\alpha}{2}\right)}{2^{\frac{\alpha+1}{2}}}\left(\lambda_+^{\alpha-1} - \lambda_-^{\alpha-1}\right)$$
$$-C\lambda_+^{\frac{\alpha-1}{2}} K_{\frac{\alpha-1}{2}}(\lambda_+) + C\lambda_-^{\frac{\alpha-1}{2}} K_{\frac{\alpha-1}{2}}(\lambda_-),$$

where $C > 0$, $\lambda_+, \lambda_- > 0$, $\mu \in R$, $\alpha \in (-\infty, 2)$, {1} and $K_p(x)$ is the modified Bessel function of the second kind. We denote an MTS distributed random variable X by $X \sim MTS(\alpha, C, \lambda_+, \lambda_-, \mu)$. The Lévy measure $\nu(dx)$ is called the *MTS Lévy measure with parameter* $(\alpha, C, \lambda_+, \lambda_-)$.

The definition and properties for the modified Bessel function of the second kind $K_p(x)$ can be found in Andrews (1998). The MTS distribution is obtained by taking a symmetric α-stable distribution with $\alpha \in (0,2)$ and multiplying the Lévy measure with $(\lambda|x|)^{\frac{\alpha+1}{2}} K_{\frac{\alpha+1}{2}}(\lambda|x|)$ on each half of the real axis. The measure can be extended to the case of $\alpha \leq 0$. If $\alpha = 1$, then γ may not defined. Hence, we remove it. The following result shows that $\nu(dx)$ is a Lévy measure.

Proposition 2. Let ν be a Borel measure on R such that $\nu(0) = 0$ and

$$\nu(dx) = C\left(\frac{\lambda_+^{\frac{\alpha+1}{2}} K_{\frac{\alpha+1}{2}}(\lambda_+ x)}{x^{\frac{\alpha+1}{2}}} 1_{x>0} + \frac{\lambda_-^{\frac{\alpha+1}{2}} K_{\frac{\alpha+1}{2}}(\lambda_- |x|)}{|x|^{\frac{\alpha+1}{2}}} 1_{x<0}\right) dx, \quad (4)$$

where $C > 0$, $\lambda_+, \lambda_- > 0$, and $\alpha < 2$. Then the measure ν is a Lévy measure on R.

The following result obtained from the asymptotic behavior of the modified Bessel function of the second kind.

Proposition 3. Let

$$f(x) = C\left(\frac{\lambda_+^{\frac{\alpha+1}{2}} K_{\frac{\alpha+1}{2}}(\lambda_+ x)}{x^{\frac{\alpha+1}{2}}} 1_{x>0} + \frac{\lambda_-^{\frac{\alpha+1}{2}} K_{\frac{\alpha+1}{2}}(\lambda_- |x|)}{|x|^{\frac{\alpha+1}{2}}} 1_{x<0}\right),$$

where $C > 0$, $\lambda_+, \lambda_- > 0$ and $\alpha \in (0,2) \setminus \{1\}$. Then

$$f(x) \sim 2^{\frac{\alpha-1}{2}} C\Gamma\left(\frac{\alpha+1}{2}\right)\frac{1}{x^{\alpha+1}}, \quad \text{as } x \to 0 \tag{5}$$

$$f(x) \sim \sqrt{\frac{\pi}{2}}\lambda_+^{\frac{\alpha}{2}} C \frac{e^{-\lambda_+ x}}{x^{\frac{\alpha}{2}+1}}, \quad \text{as } x \to \infty \tag{6}$$

$$f(x) \sim \sqrt{\frac{\pi}{2}}\lambda_-^{\frac{\alpha}{2}} C \frac{e^{-\lambda_- x}}{x^{\frac{\alpha}{2}+1}}, \quad \text{as } x \to \infty \tag{7}$$

Remark 4. If $\alpha \in (0,2) \setminus \{1\}$, the Lévy measures of the α -stable, the α -TS and the α -MTS distribution have the same asymptotic behavior at the zero neighborhood. However, the tails of the Lévy measures for the α -MTS distribution are thinner than those of the α -stable and fatter than those of the α -TS distribution.

The characteristic function of the MTS distribution is given in the following result.

Theorem 5. Let $X \sim MTS(\alpha, C, \lambda_+, \lambda_-, \mu)$. Then the characteristic function of X is given by

$$\begin{aligned}&\phi_X(u;\alpha,C,\lambda_+,\lambda_-,\mu)\\&= \exp(iu\mu + G_R(u;\alpha,C,\lambda_+,\lambda_-) \mid G_I(u;\alpha,C,\lambda_+,\lambda_-)),\end{aligned}$$

where for $u \in R$,

$$\begin{aligned}&G_R(u;\alpha,C,\lambda_+,\lambda_-)\\&= \sqrt{\pi}\, 2^{-\frac{\alpha}{2}-\frac{3}{2}} C\Gamma\left(-\frac{\alpha}{2}\right)\left((\lambda_+^2+u^2)^{\frac{\alpha}{2}} - \lambda_+^\alpha + (\lambda_-^2+u^2)^{\frac{\alpha}{2}} - \lambda_-^\alpha\right)\end{aligned}$$

and

$$G_I(u;\alpha,C,\lambda_+,\lambda_-)$$

$$=\frac{iuC\Gamma\left(\frac{1-\alpha}{2}\right)}{2^{\frac{\alpha+1}{2}}}\left[\lambda_+^{\alpha-1}F\left(1,\frac{1-\alpha}{2};\frac{3}{2};-\frac{u^2}{\lambda_+^2}\right)-\lambda_-^{\alpha-1}F\left(1,\frac{1-\alpha}{2};\frac{3}{2};-\frac{u^2}{\lambda_-^2}\right)\right],$$

where F is the hypergeometric function (See Andrews (1998)). Moreover, ϕ_X can be extended to the region $\{z\in C:|Im(z)|<\lambda_+\wedge\lambda_-\}$.

Corollary 6. Let $X\sim MTS(\alpha,C,\lambda_+,\lambda_-,\mu)$. Then the Laplace transform of X is given by

$$E[\exp(uX)]=\exp\left(u\mu+G_R(-iu;\alpha,C,\lambda_+,\lambda_-)+G_I(-iu;\alpha,C,\lambda_+,\lambda_-)\right) \quad (8)$$

for $u\in C$ with $|Re(u)|<\lambda_+\wedge\lambda_-$.

Using the characteristic function, we obtain the cumulants of all orders.

Proposition 7. Let $X\sim MTS(\alpha,C,\lambda_+,\lambda_-,\mu)$. The cumulants $c_m(X)$ of X are given as follows :

$$c_m(X)=\begin{cases}\mu+2^{-\frac{\alpha+1}{2}}C\Gamma\left(\frac{1-\alpha}{2}\right)(\lambda_+^{\alpha-1}-\lambda_-^{\alpha-1}) & \text{if } m=1\\ 2^{m-\frac{\alpha+3}{2}}\left(\frac{m-1}{2}\right)!C\Gamma\left(\frac{m-\alpha}{2}\right)(\lambda_+^{\alpha-m}-\lambda_-^{\alpha-m}) & \text{if } m=3,5,\cdots\\ 2^{-\frac{\alpha+3}{2}}\sqrt{\pi}\frac{m!}{(m/2)!}C\Gamma\left(\frac{m-\alpha}{2}\right)(\lambda_+^{\alpha-m}+\lambda_-^{\alpha-m}) & \text{if } m=3,5,\cdots\end{cases} \quad (9)$$

Remark 8. Let $X\sim MTS(\alpha,C,\lambda_+,\lambda_-,\mu)$.

1. By Proposition 7, we obtain the mean, variance, skewness and excess

kurtosis of X which are given as follows :

$$E[X]=c_1(X)=\mu+2^{-\frac{\alpha+1}{2}}C\Gamma\left(\frac{1-\alpha}{2}\right)\left(\lambda_+^{\alpha-1}-\lambda_-^{\alpha-1}\right)$$

$$Var(X)=c_2(X)=2^{-\frac{\alpha+1}{2}}\sqrt{\pi}C\Gamma\left(1-\frac{\alpha}{2}\right)\left(\lambda_+^{\alpha-2}+\lambda_-^{\alpha-2}\right)$$

$$s(X)=\frac{c_3(X)}{c_2(X)^{\frac{3}{2}}}=\frac{2^{\frac{\alpha+9}{4}}\Gamma\left(\frac{3-\alpha}{2}\right)\left(\lambda_+^{\alpha-3}-\lambda_-^{\alpha-3}\right)}{\pi^{\frac{3}{4}}C^{\frac{1}{2}}\left(\Gamma\left(1-\frac{\alpha}{2}\right)\left(\lambda_+^{\alpha-2}+\lambda_-^{\alpha-2}\right)\right)^{\frac{3}{2}}}$$

$$k(X)=\frac{c_4(X)}{c_2(X)^2}=\frac{3\cdot 2^{\frac{\alpha+3}{2}}\Gamma\left(2-\frac{\alpha}{2}\right)\left(\lambda_+^{\alpha-4}+\lambda_-^{\alpha-4}\right)}{\sqrt{\pi}C\left(\Gamma\left(1-\frac{\alpha}{2}\right)\left(\lambda_+^{\alpha-2}+\lambda_-^{\alpha-2}\right)\right)^2}.$$

2. Figure 1 illustrates the dependence of skewness $s(X)$ and excess kurtosis $k(X)$ on λ_+ and λ_- when α and C are fixed.

3. λ_+ and λ_- control the rate of decay on the positive and negative part, respectively. If $\lambda_+ > \lambda_-$ ($\lambda_+ < \lambda_-$), then the distribution is skewed to the left (right). Moreover, if $\lambda_+ = \lambda_-$, then it is symmetric. Figure 2 illustrates this fact.

4. C controls the kurtosis of the distribution. If C increases, then the peakness of the distribution decreases. Figure 3 shows the effect of C.

5. Figure 4 shows that as α decreases, the distribution has fatter tails and increased peakness.

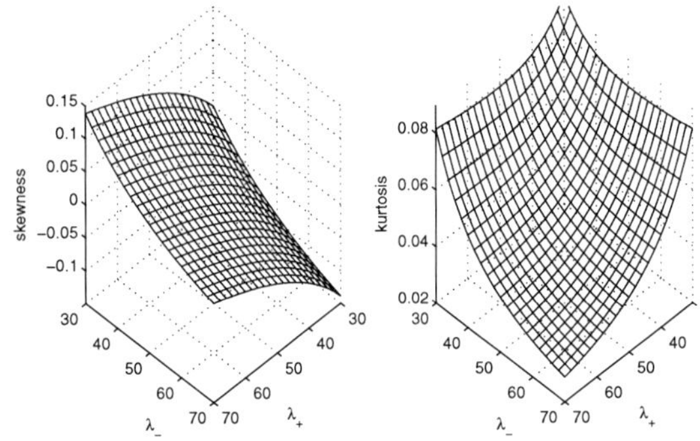

Figure 1 Skewness and Excess Kurtosis of MTS distributions : dependence on λ_+ and λ_-. Parameters : $\alpha = 1.4$, $C = 0.02$, $\mu = 0$.

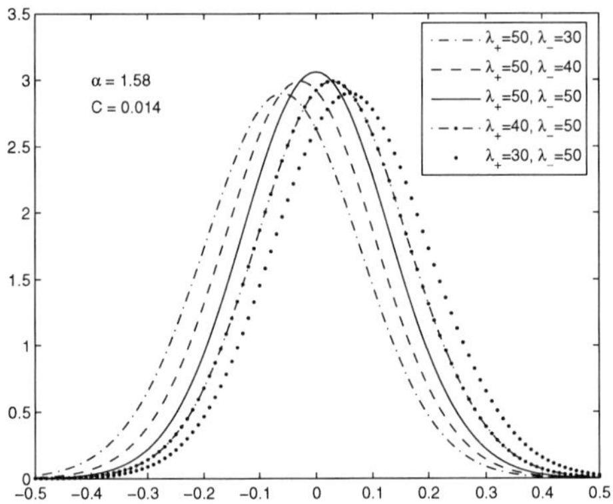

Figure 2 Probability density of the MTS distributions: dependence on λ_+ and λ_- . Parameters : $\lambda_+ = 50$, $\lambda_- \in \{30, 40, 50, 60, 70\}$, $\alpha = 1.58$, $C = 0.02$, $\mu = 0$.

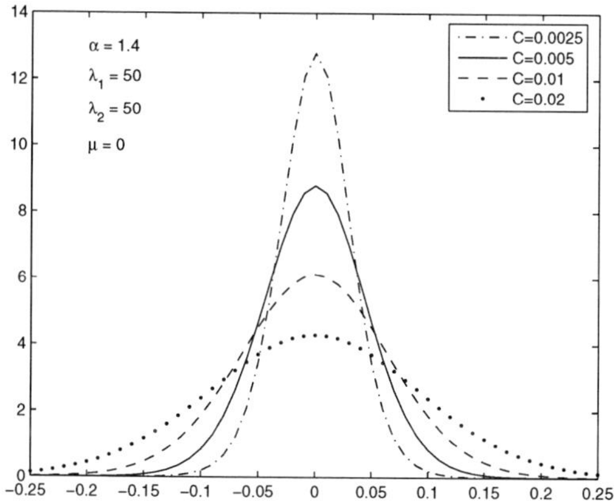

Figure 3 Probability density of the MTS distributions: dependence on C. Parameters : $C \in \{0.0025, 0.005, 0.01, 0.02\}$, α = 1.4, λ_+ = 50, λ_- = 50, $\mu = 0$.

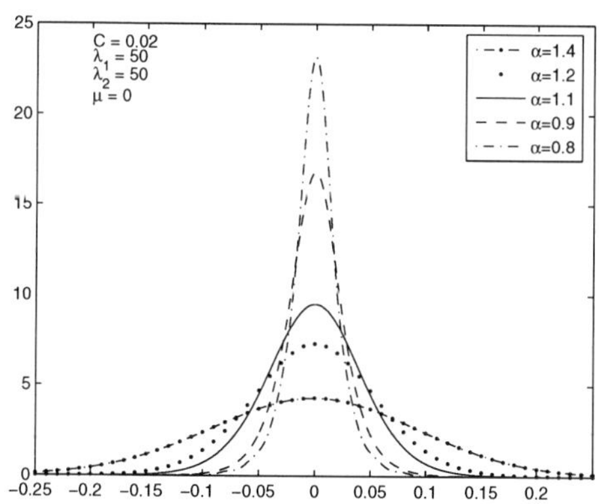

Figure 4 Fat Tail Probability density of the MTS distributions: dependence on α. Parameters : $\alpha \in \{0.8, 0.9, 1.1, 1.2, 1.4\}$, $C = 0.02$, λ_+ = 50, λ_- = 50, $\mu = 0$.

If we put

$$C = 2^{\frac{\alpha+1}{2}}\left(\sqrt{\pi}\Gamma\left(1-\frac{\alpha}{2}\right)\left(\lambda_+^{\alpha-2}+\lambda_-^{\alpha-2}\right)\right)^{-1}$$

and

$$\mu = -2^{-\frac{\alpha+1}{2}}C\Gamma\left(\frac{1-\alpha}{2}\right)\left(\lambda_+^{\alpha-1}-\lambda_-^{\alpha-1}\right),$$

then $X \sim MTS(\alpha, C, \lambda_+, \lambda_-, \mu)$ has zero mean and unit variance. In this case, we say that the random variable X has the *standard MTS distribution*, and denote $X \sim stdMTS(\alpha, \lambda_+, \lambda_-)$.

Since the MTS distribution is infinitely divisible, we can generate a Lévy process called the MTS process.

Definition 9. A Lévy process $X = (X_t)_{t\geq 0}$ is said to be a *modified tempered stable(MTS) Lévy process* with parameter $(\alpha, C, \lambda_+, \lambda_-, \mu)$ if $X_1 \sim MTS(\alpha, C, \lambda_+, \lambda_-, \mu)$.

Proposition 10. An MTS Lévy process $X = (X_t)_{t\geq 0}$ with parameter $(\alpha, C, \lambda_+, \lambda_-, \mu)$ is an RLPE of type $[-\lambda_-, \lambda_+]$ and order α.

The path behavior of the MTS process is determined by the parameter α.

Proposition 11. The MTS Lévy process is

1. of finite activity if $\alpha \in (-\infty, 0)$, and of infinite activity if $\alpha \in (0, 2)$.

2. of finite variation if $\alpha \in (0,1)$, and of infinite variation if $\alpha \in (1,2)$.

3.2 The Exponential Tilting and the Normal Tempered Stable Distribution

Let ν be a Lévy measure. If there exist $\theta \in R$ such that

$$\int_{|x|\geq 1} e^{\theta x}\nu(dx) < \infty$$

then the measure $\tilde{\nu}$ defined by $\tilde{\nu}(dx) = e^{\theta x}\nu(dx)$ is also a Lévy measure. This transform is called *exponential tilting* of the Lévy measure. The procedure of tilting is also related to the *Esscher transform* (Gerber and Shiu (1994, 1996)) where it can be viewed as tilting but on the level of stochastic processes. Let $\phi(u)$ and $\tilde{\phi}(u)$ be the characteristic functions for the infinitely divisible distributions with Lévy triplets $(0,\nu,\gamma)$ and $(0,\tilde{\nu},\tilde{\gamma})$ respectively, then we can show that

$$\log\tilde{\phi}(u) = \log\phi(u-i\theta) - \log\phi(-i\theta) + iu\left(\tilde{\gamma} - \gamma - \int_{-1}^{1} x(e^{\theta x}-1)\nu(dx)\right). \quad (10)$$

If we set $\lambda = \lambda_+ = \lambda_-$ then we obtain a symmetric MTS distribution. The value of G_I for the symmetric MTS process is always zero, and hence we obtain the characteristic function as

$$\phi(u) = \exp\left(i\mu u + \frac{\sqrt{\pi}C\Gamma\left(-\frac{\alpha}{2}\right)}{2^{\frac{\alpha+1}{2}}}\left((\lambda^2+u^2)^{\alpha/2} - \lambda^\alpha\right)\right). \quad (11)$$

If $\beta \in R$ satisfied $-\lambda < \beta < \lambda$, then $\int_{|x|\geq 1} e^{\beta x}\nu(dx) < \infty$, and hence we can apply exponential tilting to the symmetric MTS distribution. Indeed, the measure

$$\tilde{\nu}(dx) = e^{\beta x}\nu(dx) = Ce^{\beta x}\frac{(\lambda|x|)^{\frac{\alpha+1}{2}}K_{\frac{\alpha+1}{2}}(\lambda|x|)}{|x|^{\alpha+1}}dx, \quad -\lambda < \beta < \lambda$$

is a Lévy measure. By (10) and (11), we obtain the characteristic function $\tilde{\phi}(u)$ of the infinitely divisible distribution with Lévy triplet $(0, \tilde{\nu}, \tilde{\gamma})$ as

$$\tilde{\phi}(u) = \exp\left(i\tilde{\mu}u + \frac{C\sqrt{\pi}\Gamma\left(-\frac{\alpha}{2}\right)}{2^{\frac{\alpha+1}{2}}}\left((\lambda^2 - (\beta + iu)^2)^{\alpha/2} - (\lambda^2 - \beta^2)^{\alpha/2}\right)\right),$$

which is the Normal Tempered Stable (NTS) distribution introduced by Barndoroff-Nielsen and Levendorskii (2001), where $\tilde{\mu}$ is a real number.

3.3 Measure Change On Modified Tempered Stable Distributions

To apply the MTS distributions to no-arbitrage option pricing, we would need to determine an equivalent martingale measure (EMM). In this section, we review a general result of equivalence of measures presented by Sato (1999) and apply it to the MTS distribution.

The following Theorem is a particular case of Theorem 33.1 in Sato (1999).

Theorem 12. Let $(X, \mathbf{P})$ and $(X, \mathbf{Q})$ be two infinitely divisible random variables on R with Lévy triplet (σ^2, ν, γ) and $(\tilde{\sigma}^2, \tilde{\nu}, \tilde{\gamma})$ respectively. Then $\mathbf{P}$ and $\mathbf{Q}$ are equivalent if and only if the Lévy triplet satisfies

$$\sigma^2 = \tilde{\sigma}^2, \tag{12}$$

$$\int_{-\infty}^{\infty} (e^{\psi(x)/2} - 1)^2 \nu(dx) < \infty, \tag{13}$$

where $\psi(x) = \log\left(\frac{\tilde{\nu}(dx)}{\nu(dx)}\right)$. If $\sigma^2 = 0$ then

$$\tilde{\gamma} - \gamma = \int_{|x|\le 1} x(\tilde{\nu} - \nu)(dx). \tag{14}$$

When $\mathbf{P}$ and are equivalent, the Radon-Nikodym derivative is

$$\frac{d\mathbf{Q}}{d\mathbf{P}} = e^U \tag{15}$$

where $(U, \mathbf{P})$ is an infinitely divisible random variable with Lévy triplet $(\sigma_U^2, \nu_U, \gamma_U)$ given by

$$\begin{cases} \sigma_U^2 = \sigma^2 \eta^2 (16) \\ \nu_U = \nu \circ \psi^{-1} (17) \\ \gamma_U = -\dfrac{\sigma^2 \eta^2}{2} - \int_{-\infty}^{\infty} (e^y - 1 - y 1_{|y| \le 1}) \nu_U (dy) \end{cases} . \tag{18}$$

Here η is such that

$$\tilde{\gamma} - \gamma - \int_{|x| \le 1} x(\tilde{\nu} - \nu)(dx) = \sigma^2 \eta$$

if $\sigma > 0$ and zero if $\sigma = 0$.

Since MTS distributions are infinitely divisible, we can apply Theorem 12 to obtain the change of measure.

Proposition 13. Let $(X, \mathbf{P})$ and $(X, \mathbf{Q})$ be two MTS distributed random variables on R with parameters $(\alpha, C, \lambda_+, \lambda_-, \mu)$ and $(\tilde{\alpha}, \tilde{C}, \tilde{\lambda}_+, \tilde{\lambda}_-, \tilde{\mu})$, respectively. Then $\mathbf{P}$ and $\mathbf{Q}$ are equivalent if and only if $C = \tilde{C}$, $\alpha = \tilde{\alpha}$ and $\tilde{\mu} = \mu$. When $\mathbf{P}$ and $\mathbf{Q}$ are equivalent, the Radon-Nikodym derivative is

$$\frac{d\mathbf{Q}}{d\mathbf{P}} = e^U \tag{19}$$

where $(U, \mathbf{P})$ is an infinitely divisible random variable with Lévy triplet $(0, \nu_U, \gamma_U)$ given by

$$\begin{cases} \nu_U = \nu \circ \psi^{-1}(20) \\ \gamma_U = -\int_{-\infty}^{\infty} (e^y - 1 - y 1_{|y|\le 1})(\nu \circ \psi^{-1})(dy) \end{cases}, \quad (21)$$

where

$$\psi(x) = \log\left(\frac{\tilde{\lambda}_+^{\alpha+\frac{1}{2}} K_{\alpha+\frac{1}{2}}(\tilde{\lambda}_+ x)}{\lambda_+^{\alpha+\frac{1}{2}} K_{\alpha+\frac{1}{2}}(\lambda_+ x)} \right) 1_{x>0} - \log\left(\frac{\tilde{\lambda}_-^{\alpha+\frac{1}{2}} K_{\alpha+\frac{1}{2}}(\tilde{\lambda}_- x)}{\lambda_-^{\alpha+\frac{1}{2}} K_{\alpha+\frac{1}{2}}(\lambda_- x)} \right) 1_{x<0}.$$

4. The MTS-GARCH Model

The MTS-GARCH stock price model is defined over a filtered probability space $(\Omega, F, (F_t)_{t\in N}, P)$ which is constructed as follows: Consider a sequence $(\varepsilon_t)_{t\in N}$ of iid real random variables on a sequence of probability spaces $(\Omega_t, \mathbf{P}_t)_{t\in N}$, such that $\varepsilon_t \sim stdMTS(\alpha, \lambda_+, \lambda_-)$ on the space $(\Omega_t, \mathbf{P}_t)$. Next, we define $\Omega := \prod_{t\in N} \Omega_t$, $F_t := \otimes_{k=1}^{t} \sigma(\varepsilon_k) \otimes F_0 \otimes F_0 \cdots$, $F := \sigma\left(\cup_{t\in N} F_t\right)$, and $P := \otimes_{t\in N} \mathbf{P}_t$, where $F_0 = \{\varnothing, \Omega\}$ and $\sigma(\varepsilon_k)$ means the σ-algebra generated by ε_k on Ω_k.

We propose the following model for the stock price dynamics:

$$\log \frac{S_t}{S_{t-1}} = r_t - d_t + \lambda_t \sigma_t - g(\sigma_t; \alpha, \lambda_+, \lambda_-) + \sigma_t \varepsilon_t, \; t \in N, \quad (22)$$

where S_t denotes the price of the underlying asset at time t, r_t and d_t denote the risk free rate and dividend rate for the period $[t-1, t]$, and λ_t is a F_{t-1} measurable random variable. S_0 is the present observed price. The function $g(x; \alpha, \lambda_+, \lambda_-)$ is the characteristic exponent of the Laplace transform for the distribution $stdMTS(\alpha, \lambda_+, \lambda_-)$, i.e. $g(x; \alpha, \lambda_+, \lambda_-) = \log(E_{\mathbf{P}_t}[\exp(x\varepsilon_t)])$. The function $g(x; \alpha, \lambda_+, \lambda_-)$ is defined if $x \in (-\lambda_-, \lambda_+)$ and its value can be obtained from (5) if $|x| < \lambda_+ \wedge \lambda_-$, and by numerical calculation if $x \in \{x \in (-\lambda_-, \lambda_+) \,|\, |x| \geq \lambda_+ \wedge \lambda_-\}$. The one period ahead conditional variance σ_t^2 follows a GARCH(1,1) process with a restriction $0 < \sigma_t < \lambda_+$, i.e.

$$\sigma_t^2 = (\alpha_0 + \alpha_1 \sigma_{t-1}^2 \varepsilon_{t-1}^2 + \beta_1 \sigma_{t-1}^2) \wedge \rho, \ t \in N, \ \varepsilon_0 = 0, \tag{23}$$

where the coefficients α_0, α_1, and β_1 are non-negative, $\alpha_1 + \beta_1 < 1$, $\alpha_0 > 0$, and $0 < \rho < \lambda_+^2$. Clearly σ_t is F_{t-1}-measurable and hence the process $(\sigma_t)_{t \in N}$ is predictable. Moreover, the conditional expectation $E[\hat{S}_t / \hat{S}_{t-1} \,|\, F_{t-1}]$ equals $\exp(r_t + \lambda_t \sigma_t)$ where $\hat{S}_t = S_t \exp(\sum_{k=1}^{t} d_k)$ is the stock price considering re-investment of the dividends, thus λ_t can be interpreted as the market price of risk.

Remark 1. If ε_t equals the standard normal distributed random variable for all $t \in N$, g is to be the Laplace transform of ε_t and we ignore the restriction $\sigma_t < \lambda_+$, then the model becomes 'the normal GARCH model' introduced by Duan (1995).

Proposition 2. Let $t \in N$ be fixed and $\varepsilon_t \sim stdMTS(\alpha, \lambda_+, \lambda_-)$ under $\mathbf{P}_t$. Suppose positive real numbers $\tilde{\lambda}_+$ and $\tilde{\lambda}_-$ satisfy the equation

$$\lambda_+^{\alpha-2} + \lambda_-^{\alpha-2} = \tilde{\lambda}_+^{\alpha-2} + \tilde{\lambda}_-^{\alpha-2}. \tag{24}$$

Let

$$k = 2^{-\frac{\alpha+1}{2}} C\Gamma\left(\frac{1-\alpha}{2}\right)\left(\lambda_+^{\alpha-1} - \lambda_-^{\alpha-1} - \tilde{\lambda}_+^{\alpha-1} + \tilde{\lambda}_-^{\alpha-1}\right), \tag{25}$$

where

$$C = 2^{\frac{\alpha+1}{2}}\left(\sqrt{\pi}\Gamma\left(1-\frac{\alpha}{2}\right)(\lambda_+^{\alpha-2}+\lambda_-^{\alpha-2})\right)^{-1}.$$

Then, there is a probability measure $\mathbf{Q}_t$ equivalent to $\mathbf{P}_t$, such that $(\varepsilon_t + k) \sim stdMTS(\alpha, \tilde{\lambda}_+, \tilde{\lambda}_-)$.

Assumption (A) (i) There exist $\tilde{\lambda}_+$ and $\tilde{\lambda}_-$ satisfying equations (24) and $\tilde{\lambda}_+ \geq \lambda_+$. (ii) The market price of risk λ_t is given by $\lambda_t = k - (g(\sigma_t;\alpha,\tilde{\lambda}_+,\tilde{\lambda}_-) - g(\sigma_t;\alpha,\lambda_+,\lambda_-))/\sigma_t$, for each $0 \leq t \leq T$, where k is defined as (25).

Under Assumption (A), let $\mathbf{Q}_t$ be the measure described in Proposition 2.

Definition 3. Let $T \in N$ be the time horizon. Define a new measure Q on F_T equivalent to measure P, with Radon-Nikodym derivative $\frac{dQ}{dP} = Z_T$ where the density process $(Z_t)_{0\leq t\leq T}$ is defined according to

$$Z_0 \equiv 1,$$
$$Z_t := \frac{d(\mathbf{P}_1 \otimes \cdots \otimes \mathbf{P}_{t-1} \otimes \mathbf{Q}_t \otimes \mathbf{P}_{t+1} \otimes \cdots \otimes \mathbf{P}_T)}{dP} Z_{t-1},$$

where $t = 1, 2, \cdots, T$.

Lemma 4. The measure Q satisfies the following requirements:

(a) The discount asset price process $(e^{-r_t}\hat{S}_t)_{1\leq t\leq T}$ is a Q-martingale w.r.t. the filtration $(F_t)_{1\leq t\leq T}$.

(b) We have

$$Var_Q\left(\log\frac{S_t}{S_{t-1}} \mid F_{t-1}\right) \overset{a.s.}{=} Var_P\left(\log\frac{S_t}{S_{t-1}} \mid F_{t-1}\right),\ 1 \le t \le T$$

(c) The stock price dynamics under Q can be written as

$$\log\frac{S_t}{S_{t-1}} = r_t - d_t - g(\sigma_t;\alpha,\tilde{\lambda}_+,\tilde{\lambda}_-) + \sigma_t\xi_t,\ 1 \le t \le T$$

where $(\xi_t)_{1\le t\le T}$ is a sequence of real random variables on Ω_t satisfying $\xi_t \sim stdMTS(\alpha,\tilde{\lambda}_+,\tilde{\lambda}_-)$ under $\mathbf{Q}_t$ for $1 \le t \le T$. The variance process under Q has the form

$$\sigma_t^2 = (\alpha_0 + \alpha_1\sigma_{t-1}^2(\xi_{t-1} - k)^2 + \beta_1\sigma_{t-1}^2) \wedge (\lambda_+^2(1-\varepsilon)), t \in N, \xi_0 = 0.$$

The stock price dynamics under Q which is stated in Lemma 4 (c) is called *the MTS-GARCH risk neutral price process*. The arbitrage free price of a call option with strike price K and maturity T is given by

$$C_t = \exp\left(-\sum_{k=t+1}^{T} r_k\right) E_Q[(S_T - K)^+ \mid F_t] \tag{26}$$

where the stock price S_T at time T is given by

$$S_T = S_t \exp\left(\sum_{k=t+1}^{T} \left((r_k - d_k) - g(\sigma_t;\alpha,\tilde{\lambda}_+,\tilde{\lambda}_-) + \sigma_k\xi_k\right)\right).$$

5. Conclusion

This paper introduces an alternative class of tempered stable distributions which we call the Modified Tempered Stable distribution. It is sufficiently flexible in describing the skewness and kurtosis of asset returns and has all moments finite. The Lévy process derived from the MTS distribution is included in the class of RLPE. Furthermore, we obtain the NTS distribution applying the exponential tilting to the symmetric MTS distribution. Next, we introduced an enhanced GARCH-model, namely the MTS-GARCH model, by applying MTS innovations to the classical GARCH model. As a result, the MTS-GARCH time series model for stock returns explains the volatility clustering phenomenon, the leverage effect, and both conditional skewness and leptokurtosis. The risk neutral measure is obtained by applying a change of measure to the MTS distribution. The MTS-GARCH model can be a more realistic model than the normal-GARCH model.

References

Andrews, L. D. (1998), *Special Functions of Mathematics for Engineers*, 2nd ed., Oxford University Press.

Barndorff-Nielsen, O. E. and S. Z. Levendorskiĭ (2001), Feller processes of normal inverse Gaussian type, *Quantitative Finance*, 1, 318-331.

Barndorff-Nielsen, O. E. and N. Shephard (2001), Normal modified stable process, *Theory of Probability and Mathematical Statistics*, 65, 1-19.

Black, F. and M. Scholes (1973), The pricing of options and corporate liabilities, *The Journal of Political Economy*, 81, pp. 637–654.

Bollerslev, T. (1986), Generalized autoregressive conditional heteroskedasticity, *Journal of Econometrics*, 52, 115–127.

Boyarchenko, S. I. and S. Z. Levendorskiĭ (2000), Option pricing for truncated Lévy processes, *International Journal of Theoretical and Applied Finance*, 3, 549–552.

Carr, P., Geman, H., Madan, D. and M. Yor (2002), The Fine Structure of Asset Returns: An Empirical Investigation, *Journal of Business*, 75, 305–332.

Cont, R. and P. Tankov (2004), Financial Modelling with Jump Processes, Chapman & Hall / CRC.

Duan, J.-C. (1995), The GARCH option pricing model, *Mathematical Finance*, 5, 13–32.

Duan, J.-C., Ritchken, P. and Z. Sun (2004), Jump Starting GARCH: Pricing and Hedging Options with Jumps in Returns and Volatilities, *working paper, University of Toronto and Case Western Reserve University*.

Engle, R. (1982) Autoregressive conditional heteroskedasticity with estimates of the variance of united kingdom inflation, *Econometrica*, 50, 987–1007.

Gerber, H. U. and E. S. W. Shiu (1994), Option pricing by Esscher transforms (with disscusions), *Transactions of the Society of Actuaries*, 46, 99–191.

Gerber, H.U. and E. S. W. Shiu (1996), Actuarial bridges to dynamic hedging and option pricing, *Insurance: Mathematics and Economics*,

18, 183–218.

Heston, S. L. and S. Nandi (2000), A Closed-Form GARCH Option Valuation Model, *The Review of Financial Studies*, 13, 585–625.

Hurst, S. R., Platen, E. and S. T. Rachev (1999), Option pricing for a logstable asset price model, *Mathematical and Computer Modelling*, 29, 105–119.

Kim, Y. S. (2005), The Modified Tempered Stable Processes with Application to Finance, *Doctoral Thesis, Sogang University*.

Koponen, I. (1995), Analytic approach to the problem of convergence of truncated Lévy flights towards the Gaussian stochastic process, *Physical Review E*, 52, 1197–1199.

Mandelbrot, B. B. (1963a), New methods in statistical economics, *Journal of Political Economy*, 71, 421–440.

Mandelbrot, B. B. (1963b), The Variation of Certain Speculatives Prices, *Journal of Business*, 36, 394–419.

Menn, C. and S. T. Rachev (2005a), A GARCH option pricing model with α -stable innovations, *European Journal of Operational Research*, 163, 201–209.

Menn, C. and S. T. Rachev (2005b), Smoothly Truncated Stable Distributions, GARCH-Models, and Option Pricing, Technical Report, (http://www.statistik.uni-karlsruhe.de/technical_reports/sts-option.pdf).

Sato, K. (1999), Lévy Processes and Infinitely Divisible Distributions, Cambridge University Press.

Acknowledgments

Svetlozar Rachev's research was supported by grants from Division of Mathematical, Life and Physical Sciences, College of Letters and Science, University of California, Santa Barbara, and the Deutschen Forschungsgemeinschaft. Michele Leonardo Bianchi's research was supported by a Ph.D. scholarship of the University of Bergamo.

CONTRIBUTORS

Andrzej M.J. Skulimowski
AGH University of Science and Technology, Department of Decision Sciences
and
International Centre for Decision Sciences and Forecasting, Progress and Business Foundation
Al. Mickiewicza 30, 30-059 Kraków, Poland
E-mail: ams@agh.edu.pl
Professor at the Chair of Automatic Control, AGH University of Science and Technology. Main field of expertise is multicriteria decision analysis, decision support systems, AI methods in forecasting, risk management, and foresight. From 1987 to 1988 Fellow of the Swiss Confederation at the ETH Zurich, 1988-90 Research Associate at the Institute of Communication Technology at the ETH, and from 1990 to 1995 Visiting Professor at the Institute of Information Management at the University of St. Gallen. Since 1995 provided consulting support to the European Commission, national governments and private companies. Author of over 130 scholarly papers and four monographs.

António Afonso
Instituto Superior de Economia e Gestão – Technical University of Lisbon, Department of Economics, UECE – Research Unit on Complexity and Economics
R. Miguel Lupi 20, 1249-078 Lisbon, Portugal
and
European Central Bank, Directorate General Economics.
Kaiserstraße 29, D-60311 Frankfurt am Main, Germany.
E-mail: aafonso@iseg.utl.pt; antonio.afonso@ecb.europa.eu
Dr. Afonso is Assistant Professor with Habilitation at I.S.E.G. – Technical University of Lisbon, and Principal Economist at the European Central Bank. Previously, he worked in the banking sector, was a Consultant and Adviser at the Portuguese Ministry of Finance and has published notably in *Applied Economics*, *Economic Modelling, Public Choice*, *Journal of International Money and Finance*, *Journal of International Financial Markets, Institutions & Money*, *FinanzArchiv*, and *Regional Economics*.

Diana Bonfim
Banco de Portugal
Banco de Portugal, Av. Almirante Reis, 71 1150 Lisbon, Portugal
E-mail: dbonfim@bportugal.pt
Works in the Financial Stability Division of the Economic Research Department of Banco de Portugal and has completed the Research Master in Economics at Universidade Nova de Lisboa. Her research interests are empirical banking and applied microeconometrics.

Dimitrios Askounis
Electrical and Computer Engineering Department, National Technical University of Athens
9, Iroon Polytechniou Str., 15773, Athens, Greece
E-mail: askous@epu.ntua.gr
Assistant Professor at the Electrical and Computer Engineering Department of the National Technical University of Athens (N.T.U.A.). Main research, professional and teaching interests focus on the areas of Production Management and Information Systems. Dr. Askounis has also extensive consulting experience.

Dong Myung Chung
Department of Mathematics, The Catholic University of Korea
Yeokgok 2-dong 43-1, Wonmi-gu, Bucheon-si,
Gyeonggi-do 420-743, Korea
E-mail: dmchung@catholic.ac.kr
Ph.D Degree from the University of Tennessee in Knoxville, U.S.A. He is currently a professor in the department of Mathematics at The Catholic University of Korea, and Professor Emeritus at Sogang University, Seoul Korea. Professor Chung has published over 60 research articles, was president of the Korean Mathematical Society and has been a member of the Korean Academy of Science and Technology.

Dorra Mezzez Hmaied
Laboratoire d'Economie et de Finance Appliquées, Institut des Hautes Etudes Commerciales
2016 Carthage, Tunisia
E-mail: dorrahmaied@yahoo.fr
Professor of Finance and Head of the Finance Department at the HEC Carthage. Research interests in market microstructure and mergers & acquisitions. She has several publications in these areas.

Emanuel Kopp
Institute of Investment Banking and Catallactics, Department of Finance and Accounting, Vienna University of Economics and Business Administration.
Althanstrasse 39-45 (UZA-3), A-1090 Vienna (Austria)
E-mail: emanuel.albin.kopp@wu-wien.ac.at
Research fellow at the Institute of Investment Banking and Catallactics.

Filipa Lima
Banco de Portugal
Av. Almirante Reis, 71, 3.º, 1150-012 Lisboa, Portugal
E-mail: slima@bportugal.pt
Head of the Methodological Developments Unit of the Statistics Department of Banco de Portugal. Previously worked at the European Central Bank and at the Bank for International Settlements. She is also a Ph.D. student at Universidade Nova de Lisboa.

Francesco Franco
Universidade Nova de Lisboa
Universidade Nova de Lisboa, Faculdade de Economia, Campus de Campolide, 1099-032 Lisbon, Portugal
E-mail: francesco_franco@fe.unl.pt
PhD in Economics from MIT in 2004. His main area of interests is Macroeconomics and Imperfections together with financial economics.

Ghassan Chammas
Central Bank of Lebanon, Islamic Financial Affairs
E-mail: nghassan@yahoo.com
Advisor to the Governor of the Central Bank of Lebanon, Islamic financial affairs.

Jaap Spronk
Department of Finance, Erasmus University Rotterdam
P.O. Box 1738, 3000 DR Rotterdam, The Netherlands
E-mail: spronk@few.eur.nl
Vice-Dean International New Business Development & Professor of Finance and Investment in the Department of Finance and Investment at Erasmus University Rotterdam. His editorial work includes being the Managing Editor of the Springer series in Financial Modelling, Associate Editor of the Revue Belge de Statistique, d'Informatique et de Recherche Operationnelle, Associate Editor of the Journal of Multiple Criteria

Decision Analysis, and Associate Editor of Operations Research. His publications encompass many fields, such as Capital Market Theory, Decision Models for Managerial Finance, Performance Evaluation, Financial Risk Management, and Multiple Objective Decision Making.

Jasper Blom
M&A Advisory, ABN AMRO Bank / RBS
Gustav Mahlerlaan 10, 1082 PP Amsterdam
E-mail: jasper.blom@nl.abnamro.com
Assistant Director within the M&A Advisory group at ABN AMRO Bank N.V. / RBS.

Johannes Prix
Institute of Investment Banking and Catallactics, Department of Finance and Accounting, Vienna University of Economics and Business Administration.
Althanstrasse 39-45 (UZA-3), A-1090 Vienna (Austria)
E-mail: Johannes.prix@wu-wien.ac.at
Studied at the Karl Franzens University of Graz (Austria), and at the Vienna University of Economics and Business Administration (Austria). Worked as research fellow at the Institute of Investment Banking and Catallactics. Now works for DWS Frankfurt (Germany).

John Psarras
National Technical University of Athens
9, Iroon Polytechniou Str., 15773, Athens, Greece
E-mail: john@epu.ntua.gr
Professor of Operational Research & Management Science at the Electrical and Computer Engineering Department of the National Technical University of Athens (N.T.U.A.). Director of the Management & Decision Support Systems Laboratory of the N.T.U.A. Main research, professional and teaching interests focus on the areas of Operational Research and Management Science. Extensive consulting experience, having assisted numerous private firms and government organisations to develop innovative and successful business strategies.

Lars Nordén
Stockholm University School of Business, SE 10691 Stockholm, Sweden.
E-mail: ln@fek.su.se
Associate Professor of Finance at Stockholm University School of Business. Research interests include options and futures markets, market

microstructure, individuals' investment decisions, and corporate governance.

Marc B.J. Schauten
Finance Group, Erasmus School of Economics, Erasmus University Rotterdam
Burgemeester Oudlaan 50
3000DR Rotterdam
E-mail: schauten@few.eur.nl
Assistant professor in Finance at the School of Economics of the Erasmus University Rotterdam and lecturer at the Mondriaan Onderwijsgroep in Delft (former Tinbergen Economie). Previously fulfilled several positions in education and business. Director of the Erasmus Center for Financial Training (www.ECFT.nl) from 1998-2004, and business analyst for De Nationale Investeringsbank N.V. in The Hague.

Maria Blangiewicz
Department of Econometrics, University of Gdańsk
ul. Armii Krajowej 101, 81-824 Sopot, Poland
E-mail: zrmaria@panda.bg.univ.gda.pl
Research assistant at the Department of Econometrics, University of Gdańsk, Poland. Main fields of interest are linear and nonlinear modelling of time series, and econometric software.

Michael Huetl
Institute of Investment Banking and Catallactics, Department of Finance and Accounting, Vienna University of Economics and Business Administration
Althanstrasse 39-45 (UZA-3), A-1090 Vienna (Austria)
E-mail: michael.huetl@wu-wien.ac.at
Research fellow at the Institute of Investment Banking and Catallactics.

Michele Leonardo Bianchi
Department of Mathematics, Statistics, Computer Science and Applications, University of Bergamo
Via dei Caniana 2, I-24127, Bergamo, Italy
E-mail: michele-leonardo.bianchi@unibg.it
Ph.D. student in Computational Methods for Economic and Financial Decisions and Forecasting at the Department of Mathematics, Statistics, Computer Science and Applications of the University of Bergamo. He

holds a degree in Mathematics from the University of Pisa. His research interests are in the areas of mathematical finance and optimization.

Otto Loistl
Institute of Investment Banking and Catallactics, Department of Finance and Accounting, Vienna University of Economics and Business Administration.
Althanstrasse 39-45 (UZA-3), A-1090 Vienna (Austria)
E-mail: otto.loistl@wu-wien.ac.at
Since 1991 Full Professor at the University of Economics and Business Administration, Vienna. Chair of the Institute of Investment Banking and Catallactics. Main Research Area: Realistic Modelling of Individual Actions and Interactions Leading to the Emergence of Markets Beyond Equilibrium but with Arbitrage Opportunities.

Panagiotis Xidonas
National Technical University of Athens
9, Iroon Polytechniou Str., 15773, Athens, Greece
E-mail: pxid@epu.ntua.gr
Ph.D. Candidate in the Electrical & Computer Engineering Department of the National Technical University of Athens (N.T.U.A.). Holds an M.Sc. degree in Applied Mathematics with specialization in Financial Engineering from the Department of Applied Mathematics & Physical Sciences of the N.T.U.A., as well as a B.Sc. degree in Mathematical Physics from the National Kapodistrian University of Athens.

Paweł Miłobędzki
Department of Econometrics, University of Gdańsk
ul. Armii Krajowej 101, 81-824 Sopot, Poland
E-mail: milobedp@wzr.pl
Professor at the Department of Econometrics, University of Gdańsk, Poland. Works on dynamics of financial markets, asset pricing and international equity market integration.

Pedro Gomes
London School of Economics, Economics Department; STICERD-Suntory and Toyota International Centres for Economics and Related Disciplines.
Houghton Street, London WC2A 2AE, United Kingdom.
E-mail: p.gomes@lse.ac.uk

1st degree in Economics from ISEG/UTL – Technical University of Lisbon. MSc. in Economics from the London School of Economics. Currently PhD. candidate at the London School of Economics.

Philipp C. Rother
European Central Bank
60311 Frankfurt, Germany
E-mail: philipp.rother@ecb.europa.eu
PhD in macroeconomics from the University of Mannheim. Worked several years at the IMF with a focus on developing and transition countries. At the ECB, he co-ordinates work on fiscal surveillance of euro area and EU countries and works on a range of current fiscal policy issues.

Qinglei Dai
Universidade Nova de Lisboa
Universidade Nova de Lisboa, Faculdade de Economia, Rua Marques de Fronteira 20, 1099-038 Lisbon, Portugal
E-mail: qinglei.dai@fe.unl.pt
Assistant professor in finance at Faculdade de Economia, Universidade Nova de Lisboa. She received her PhD degree from Norwegian School of Management. Her major research interests are corporate finance and banking.

Serkan Aran

Is Bank
Is Kuleleri, Kule 2, Kat 13 - 4. Levent 34330 Istanbul / Turkey
E-mail: saran@isyatirim.com.tr
Head of Equity and Future Trading Is Bank, Istanbul, Turkey. Experience in emerging markets trading, cash market and derivatives market. Dr Aran has written various articles on Market Micro Structure for Turkish Capital Markets.

Svetlozar T. Rachev
Kollegium am Schloss, Bau II, 20.12, R210,
Postfach 6980, D-76128, Karlsruhe, Germany
E-mail: rachev@statistik.uni-karlsruhe.de
Professor Rachev holds a PhD Degree from Moscow State (Lomonosov) University, and a Doctor of Science Degree from Steklov Mathematical Institute in Moscow. He is Chair-Professor in Statistics, Econometrics and Mathematical Finance at the University of Karlsruhe and the Karlsruhe

Institute of Technology, in the school of Economics and Business Engineering. He is also Professor Emeritus at the University of California, Santa Barbara, in the Department of Statistics and Applied Probability. He has published seven monographs, eight handbooks and special-edited volumes, and over 250 research articles. Professor Rachev is cofounder of Bravo Risk Management Group specializing in financial risk-management software. Bravo Group was recently acquired by FinAnalytica for which he currently serves as Chief-Scientist.

Therese Strand
Department of International Economics and Management, Copenhagen Business School, DK-2000 Frederiksberg, Denmark
E-mail: ts.int@cbs.dk
Researcher at the Center for Corporate Governance, Dept. of International Economics and Management, Copenhagen Business School, Denmark; and external researcher to the Center for Business and Policy Studies (SNS), Stockholm, Sweden. Research interests include shareholder activism, institutional investors, agency problems and agency costs, annual general meetings, shareholder democracy, and codes of conduct.

Theodoros G. Stamatiou
University of Piraeus, Department of Banikng and Financial Management, Office 328, Karaoli & Dimitriou 80, 185 34, Piraeus, Greece.
E-mail: theostam@unipi.gr
Dr Stamatiou wrote a PhD Thesis on Market Microstructure, and holds a MSc in Economic Analysis and another in Banking and Finance. His BA is in Economics. Among his research interests are market microstructure, financial economics, game theory and real estate.

Young Shin Kim
Department of Statistics, Econometrics and Mathematical Finance,
School of Economics and Business Engineering, University of
Karlsruhe and the Karlsruhe Institute of Technology
Kollegium am Schloss, Bau II, 20.12, R210,
Postfach 6980, D-76128, Karlsruhe, Germany
E-mail: kim@statistik.uni-karlsruhe.de
Dr. Kim studied at the Department of Mathematics, Sogang University, in Seoul, Korea, where he received his doctorate degree in 2005. Currently, he is a scientific assistant in Department of Statistics, Econometrics and Mathematical Finance, at the School of Economics and Business Engineering, University of Karlsruhe and the Karlsruhe Institute of

Technology. His current professional and research interests are in the area of Lévy processes including tempered stable processes, time varying volatility models, and its application to finance.

INDEX